MUSIC IN THE AIR:

America's Changing Tastes in Popular Music,

1920 – 1980

by

Philip K. Eberly

Communication Arts Books

HASTINGS HOUSE, PUBLISHERS

New York 10016

For Lois
The Song Is You

Library of Congress Cataloging in Publication Data

Eberly, Philip K.
   Music in the air.
   (Communication arts books)
   Bibliography: p. 354
   Discography: p. 394
   Includes index.
   1. Radio and music. 2. Radio audiences.
3. Music, Popular (Songs, etc.)—United States—
History and criticism. I. Title. II. Series.
ML68.E23 1982   780'.973   82-6252
ISBN 0-8038-4743-2 (pbk.)   AACR2

Published simultaneously in Canada by
Saunders of Toronto Ltd., Markham, Ontario

Designed by Al Lichtenberg
Printed in the United States of America

Acknowledgements

ONE DOES NOT have to write a book to discover there are many generous people who will extend a helping hand just for the asking. Still, getting a project such as this off the ground drives the point home with enormous impact. To those persons who made available graphics, photographs, recordings, fragments of information, and other miscellaneous items, and to those who submitted to interviews and responded cheerfully and openly—my unbounded gratitude. In addition, I should like to single out the following for special acknowledgement:

To my compleat wife—for being supportive beyond normal bounds: in mustering the patience to cope with adjustment through countless evenings and weekends; in assisting with the research; and in offering constructive suggestions. And to my sons, Michael and David—for their forbearance in enduring the author's idiosyncrasies, heightened while this work was in preparation.

To Louis J. Appell, Jr., president, Susquehanna Broadcasting Company, my employer—for his enlightened leadership distinguished by setting impeccable standards and creating the proper climate where dedicated professionals can grow and thrive.

To colleague Bob Shipley—for shaking his memory bank to release recollections of the Top 40 milieu.

To Diane Peters who waded through endless pages of longhand-written yellow sheets—for her patience and efficiency in typing the manuscript (with an assist from Brenda Fauth).

To Helen M. Gotwalt—for her valuable counsel so generously given.

To Eastman Radio's Frank Boyle, U.S. Broadcasting's Renaissance Man—for filling in several important gaps of radio history of the 1960s and 1970s.

To Ken Costa (Radio Advertising Bureau); Phyllis Doutrich (Martin Memorial Library); Ron Hanna (Periodicals Division, Ganser Library, Millersville State College); Catherine Heinz (Broadcast Pioneers Library); Susan Hill (National Association of Broadcasters); and Robert Saudek and staff (Museum of Broadcasting)—for their kindnesses that helped smooth out some bumps in the research road.

To the following individuals, publications and organizations—for their kind permission to reprint copyrighted material: Arbitron; Toby Arnold; N. W. Ayer; Ted Bates Co.; *Billboard; Broadcasting* Publications; Century 21; Chappell Music; Drake-Chenault; Electronic Industries Association; The *Gavin Report;* Al Ham; *Inside Radio;* The Kellogg Co.; KHJ; Katz Radio; McGavern-Guild; Bill O'Shaughnessy; Radio Advertising Bureau; Radio Marketing Research; *Radio and Records;* Recording Industry Association of America; Simmons Market Research Bureau; Standard Rates and Data Service; Statistical Research; *Variety;* Joel Whitburn's *Record Research;* WLS; WARM; WSBA.

Contents

*I have in mind a plan of development
which would make radio a "household
utility" in the same sense as the
piano or phonograph. The idea is to
bring music into the house by wireless . . .
the receiver can be designed in the form
of a simple "Radio Music Box" arranged
for several different wave lengths, which
should be changeable with the throwing
of a single switch or pressing of a
single button . . . the box can be placed on
a table in the parlor or living room,
the switch set accordingly and the
transmitted music received.*

—DAVID SARNOFF, in a letter
to Edward J. Nally, General
Manager, Marconi Co., 1916.

Introduction

IN SEARCH OF AN AMERICAN POP

"When I use a word," Humpty Dumpty
*said, in a rather scornful tone, "it
means just what I choose it to mean—
neither more, nor less."*

> —LEWIS CARROL,
> *Through the Looking
> Glass*

Introduction:
In search of an
American pop

ONCE DURING a discussion of American popular music, Louis Armstrong, supposedly offered a definition of elegant simplicity: "It's all folk music, man. Whoever heard of horse music?"

The very term, *popular music*, implies there is one universal body of music for the masses, as differentiated from a more arty form called *serious*, or *classical*, music. This, of course, was never the case. Different types and styles of popular songs have been identified with various periods of American history. Between the nation's first popular tune, "Yankee Doodle," and the latest Top 40 hit, there have been marches, Stephen Foster compositions, minstrel show pieces, rags, fox trots, romantic ballads, novelties, patriotic airs, hymns, blues, movie and TV mood music, Broadway show tunes, and even jazz—all of which, at one time or another, have been called "popular."

Not that we don't find some common characteristics indigenous to the popular music of any given era. Love (fulfilled or unrequited) is the most frequent one. There is, too, a strain of nonsense—it might even be called absurdity—running through American popular music. Flapdoodle phrases, or lines, are continually leaping from pop songs and swirling around in our brains. We haven't resisted compulsive urges to repeat such onomatopoeia as *hey-nonny-nonny, ta-ra-ra-boom-der-e', vo-deo-do, bom-bom-Beedle-um-bo, Hey-bop-a-re-bop,* the *Flat-Foot-Floogie-with-a-floy-floy, ting-tang-walla-walla-bing-bang, rama-lama-ding-dong, do-lang-do-lang, do-doo-ron-ron.*

3

Diversity, then, has been the distinguishing attribute of that branch of entertainment we call popular music, and it got that way because of two uniquely American phenomena: our vibrant, pluralistic society, and our entrepreneurial spirit. The second developed from the first. The business of American "show biz," of course, is business, and popular music is first and foremost a business. Just as Coca Cola, U.S. Steel and Saks Fifth Avenue are functions of the marketplace, so most assuredly is that liveliest of the lively arts, the popular song. If there is to be a motto for American popular music let it be this: *Ars Gratia Pecuniae.*

Cultural pluralism and the profit motive may have provided the sparks, but technology and media have helped keep the pop music fires burning. Thomas Edison's phonograph and Emile Berliner's flat disc recording inventions, and the introduction of the home radio receiver transfigured American popular music. Each year, as these two in-home entertainment contraptions were improved technically, and as more Americans partook of auditory delights, their appetites for information *about* the music increased. Newspapers and magazines, the only major mass media on the scene when records and radio arrived, were happy to oblige. Beginning in the early 1920s, the expression, "popular music," took on a more authentic ring. It achieved a basis of credibility. For now Americans in every corner of the nation virtually simultaneously could identify with a performance. Popular music rode the crest of the media wave that swept over America in the 1920s. As somebody's law states, "A term accrues a definition simply by being used in the media."

The American appetite for popular songs, created by the phonograph and by radio, meant that much of the music would be gobbled up like popcorn, providing a measure of instant gratification, tempting the eater to come back for more. As the appetite for pop music increased, so did the thirst to read anything relating to it. Thus, the aura created by the media has often upstaged the music itself.

The counterpoint strains of hype, nostalgia and re-cycling continually weave in and out of the annals of American popular music. Any one of these—or a combination of all three—often dictate the image, rather than reality, will be what we remember.

The so-called Jazz Age is a prime example. Conventional folklore holds that the 1920s were when the nation made jazz *the* popular music of the decade, and "Jazz Age" could define the entire social milieu of that period. We all know about the 1920s: hip flasks, raccoon coats, rumble seats, sheiks, flappers, the Fitzgeralds. Scott and Zelda were said to be the stylesetters of the then chic. John Held was the decade's graphic designer. Sixty years of media conditioning have kept the "Jazz Age" legend alive.

When we think of those "Roaring Twenties" we think of good times, of having a good time, of youth rebellion against Puritan behavior codes. We know pop music played an important part in shaping the *mores* of that post-World War I era of prosperity. For this was, after all, the first time in our history that we developed a national consciousness about a popular music. It was listenable (radio and records), and it was danceable (the Charleston and fox trots). As the 1920s wore on and this razz-ma-tazz music, with its insinuating rhythm, seeped into all sections of the nation, more and more it was referred to as "jazz." Most of it was not. It was white America's music and bore only superficial resemblances to the new black music bearing the same name.

White dance orchestras of the period often imitated black models, and in some cases the copies were excellent. Playing jazz, however, was not the same thing as playing *jazz-y*. A jazz-y performance could mean anything from tearing off an undisciplined chorus of group improvisation to laying down a banjo break; it could mean the studied jazz mannerism of a moaning saxophone riff or a self-conscious impersonation of Louis Armstrong.

Jazz. The term itself carried a naughty connotation. What better code word to convey the manners, morals and music of the 1920s? What better designation to impart a mystique of roguishness?

The mass media went right along. Vachel Lindsay was commissioned by *Liberty* magazine to write a poem celebrating the decade. He called it—what else?—"The Jazz Age." Lindsay instructed his readers, that for maximum enjoyment, his work "be read and chanted, quite aloud, by an open-hearth fire, with the radio turned down." No less a sometime-music critic than H.L. Mencken, responding to conventional wisdom of the day that jazz was responsible for the increasing promiscuity, observed: "If jazz is an aphrodisiac, then the sound of riveting is also aphrodisiac. What fetches the flappers to grief in jazz parlors is not the music, but the alcohol."

What Lindsay and Mencken and the mass media were writing about was not jazz at all. It is true that elements of jazz turned up in many dance band arrangements. Jazz flavorings were even sprinkled through some of Gershwin's and Milhaud's works. Newspaper and magazine articles, however, didn't bother to sort out the details. Few readers would have cared or known the difference.

Names made much better copy. Names like Paul Whiteman. The large, rotund Whiteman was the quintessential showman of the 1920s, and popular music was his medium. He fronted an aggregation that functioned comfortably on several levels, and therefore appealed to different audiences. Whiteman shrewdly took advantage of the dancing craze and led one of the decade's premier dance orchestras. Paul Whiteman's 28-piece unit with its symphonic jazz repertory broke new ground for the concert stage as well. (It was Whiteman who introduced George Gershwin's "Rhapsody in Blue" at New York's Aeolian Hall in 1924.) Paul Whiteman paid well and offered steady work. He was thus able to attract the cream of the musician crop. A month scarcely went by in the 1920s without some reference in a major newspaper or magazine to some portion of the Whiteman entertainment colossus.

In a triumph of 1920s hype, Paul Whiteman made a movie, *The King of Jazz*. The cast was all white. Whiteman's orchestra did feature a "jazz wing" which served as an incubator for a number of important white jazz artists. But "King of Jazz"? Hardly. Paul Whitemen was no more the royal figure of jazz than the 1920s were the Jazz Age. It was possible to go through the popular press of that decade without encountering Louis Armstrong or Fletcher Henderson, either one of whom could rightly have worn the crown.

If echoes of the Jazz Age come to us accompanied by the drums of media hype, the "Swing Era" picked up the beat. Swing, the music that lent its name to describe the last half of the 1930s, was scarcely the predominant pop music of the period. A few white swing band leaders developed significant followings, and one, Benny Goodman, even became a millionaire. Swing provided grist for the media mills, down to such fine points as jitterbugs and hepcats replacing the flappers and sheiks. Popular taste in music followed the pattern set in the 1920s: white middle America overwhelmingly favored the "sweet" bands. They got the airplay, sold the most records and drew the biggest crowds. Ballroom popularity was a good gauge. Attendance record-holders in the 1930s at the Valencia Ballroom, York, Pa., (an important stop on the dance band circuit) were typical of many spots in the country. Sweet, not swing, was boffo at the Valencia box office as this list of top drawing cards for each year attests:

YEAR	BAND
1930	Casa Loma
1931	Freddy Bergen
1932	Guy Lombardo
1933	Hal Kemp
1934	Guy Lombardo
1935	Ozzie Nelson
1936	Horace Heidt
1937	Hal Kemp
1938	Kay Kyser
1939	Kay Kyser

—Source: *Valencia Ballroom Souvenir Yearbook*, 1939

A number of black swing bands, of course, did find a space in the 1930s music spectrum. Back then, though, when the media celebrated swing, White was dominant over Black. Thanks to our contemporary entertainment re-cycling machinery (Broadway, television, recording re-issues, nostalgia factories) the Ellingtons, Luncefords and Basies are now regarded as *jazz*, not swing, figures.

If image rather than reality shaped our earliest important perceptions of pop, the two blended into one with the tumultuous arrival of rock and roll. Never before had a popular music so pervaded the culture. The controversies of the 1920s and 1930s were grace notes compared to the uproar of the rock ruckus. Radio, the launching pad for what went before in pop, became "mission control" for rock and roll. In turn, rock contributed to the resurgence of radio in a television age.

In the wonderful world of show biz, rock and roll was a press agent's dream come true. Print media, enjoying an explosion of their own in the 1950s and 1960s, found in rock a great circulation builder. It was new. It was trendy. It was performed by unique, often bizarre, characters whose celebrity was on a par with other show biz figures. Editors went berserk. ("Did Elvis really give Cadillacs to poor widows?" "Were Mick and Bianca finally going to call it quits?")

Entire publications devoted to rock and roll sprang up. (Many kept right on flourishing.) Social scientists found rock the ideal subject for papers to read at their conventions. (Pop music has always been good for an occasional go-round in scholarly circles.) But ultimately it was the daily and weekly press that shrewdly endowed rock and roll with its mantle of respectability, making its safe for middle American consumption. The "paper of record" now employs several reviewers to cover the rock beat. The same *New York Times,* from time to time, even carries a weekly chart of the Top 10 pop records and albums. The *Times* stepped up its coverage of popular music beginning in the 1960s. John Rockwell, who served as the paper's first-string rock critic through the 1970s, also sporadically covered classical music events; he reviewed the former with the same perspicacity as the latter. When Rockwell and his fellow *Times*men reported from rockland, they wrote "seriously" but shunned cosmic profundity. Mercifully, they stuck to criticism and skipped the "lifestyle" nonsense and other pop sociological claptrap.

Meanwhile, back in radioland, where the stakes are high and the music game is played in deadly earnest, rock-and-roll turned out to be the fount from which profits flowed. Few music stations by the late 1970s were not playing some derivative of rock. The 1950s schism that split broadcasters into rockers and non-rockers had all but disappeared. The early bitterness of the non-rockers ("We'll never play that crap") has long since dissolved. Some of Elvis and the Beatles have slipped comfortably into a niche called, of all things, "middle of the road." Many of rock and roll's original programming foes now fall all over themselves to "break" a new recording by Eric Clapton or the Rolling Stones. In broadcasting, enlightened self-interest does not always begin in the ear of the beholder.

Just as an uproar greeted rock in its early days, so controversy swirled around disco when it thumped onto the pop music stage in the mid-1970s. It was too Black, Hispanic and homosexual, went the whispering campaigns. ("Wouldn't touch it with a ten-foot tone arm!".) But toward the end of the decade, accommodations were being made. Studio 54, a trendy New York discotheque, was home to the "beautiful people." Disco dancing spots cropped up everywhere. Disco recordings climbed the Top 40 charts. Disco-formatted stations began piling up significant ratings. WKTU, an all-disco station, quickly became number-one in New York. Disco, in a word, was the pop music phenomenon of 1979. A *New York Times Magazine* article made it official. Disco's $4 billion bottom line was bigger than network television, according to the *Times*.

But before 1980 was over, the disco dynamo had sputtered to a virtual standstill. Disco clubs went dark. Designers who had cut their fashions to fit the disco fad dropped the theme without missing a beat. Radio stations scrapped the format as fast as they had adopted it. The thump-thump-thump monotony of the rhythm, probably more than any other factor, was responsible for disco petering out before it could make it to the popular music mainstream.

Irrespective of what non-musical forces interplay to make a given body of music "popular," radio in all likelihood will be the ultimate testing ground. Radio will decree what tunes and artists will succeed and how long they will last. The wide range of music available up and down the dials of our radio music boxes is proof there is no single American popular music. *There are dozens and dozens.* Like Humpty Dumpty, we can, when we say "pop," make it mean just what you and I choose—neither more nor less. Most Americans, however, *can* agree there's one place above all where they can find the greatest variety. On the radio.

Part One
(1920—1929)

TUNING IN AND
TURNING ON

The isle is full of noises
Sounds and sweet airs
That give delight, and hurt not.

—*The Tempest*
Act III, Scene 2

.

First Notes from Space: The Music Box Terrestrial

LONG BEFORE DAVID SARNOFF wrote his prophetic "music box" memo, there were fantasies of a device capable of reproducing and transmitting sounds mechanically. Savinien Cyrano de Bergerac wrote in 1694 of an imaginary trip to the moon where he discovered "a box somewhat of metal. It was a book, indeed, but a strange and wonderful book, made wholly for the ears and not the eyes. So that when anybody has a mind to read in it, he winds up the machine with a great many little springs, and straight, as from the mouth of a man, or a musical instrument, proceed all the distinct and different sounds."

Although the phonograph rather than the radio may more accurately fit the French poet's fanciful notion, there is an interesting similarity in the development of both. Labels on early recordings did not feature artists' names, only generic classifications such as "Sentimental," "Comic," or "Irish." A similar anonymity often prevailed in radio during the early 1920s. Newspaper logs that appeared soon after stations adopted some semblance of program schedules frequently indicated merely general categories. Such information supplied by the station gave the reader no idea who the performer was, and at times no indication of the kind of music. A listener interested in turning on the radio for some popular music in late 1923 was not able to tell from his *New York Times* newspaper log exactly what he was getting:

11

WHN, New York

2:15 p.m.—Popular songs; piano select-
tions

3:45 p.m.—Popular songs

WJAR, Providence

1:05p.m.—Orchestra; weather report

WOO, Philadelphia

12 Midnight—Tearoom orchestra

WIP, Philadelphia

3:00 p.m.—Vocal solos

WGR, Buffalo

4:00 p.m.—Tea-time music

KDKA, Pittsburgh

10:00 a.m.—Music

WRC, Washington

8:00 p.m.—Songs; instrumental solos

WWJ, Detroit

8:30 p.m.—Orchestra

WDAP, Chicago

11:00 p.m.—Dance music

WBAP, Fort Worth

10:30 p.m.—Dance orchestra [1]

Despite the slivers of early musical radio history that bore blank name tags, popular music was being served up by many stations. By the start of 1923, over 500 of them were exploding signals into the airwaves. Any hobbyist who could figure a way to hook up coils and tubes in a five-watt transmitter was a broadcaster, and when he got his license from the Bureau of Navigation, that made it official. Robert J. Landry, one of *Variety's* first radio reviewers, recalled that the pioneer licensees were often

> . . . automobile salesmen, music store proprietors, commercial printers, and high-voltage evangelists apart from youthful "hams" . . . They did not have the flavor, the tone, the memories, or nostalgia of show biz.[2]

Benedict Gimbel, Jr., scion of the Philadelphia department store family, described how it was done: "I remember going for a license. You just went to Washington and asked for one. You got the license the same day; the next day you picked your call letters out of a hat."[3] Gimbel drew WIP.

Few items of American folklore have been repeated more often than that early 1920s scene featuring a listener, headphones in place, seated at a crystal set, trying to fish out some distant station. Red Barber, the sportscaster, considers his first encounter with radio in central Florida in 1924, one of his "strongest, earliest memories." Barber recalls the difficulty in listening to stations

> . . . through the squealing, the twisting and turning of dials and knobs . . . You didn't have much footroom because you had so many batteries on the floor. All radio was run off batteries in those days. You had rechargers for batteries, and you had red lights on the re-chargers. We used to bring in KDKA. And then we'd bring in WSB in Atlanta. And, my gracious, what a triumph if we could hear Kansas City . . . I think young

---

[1] Numbered footnotes are at the end of each Chapter in this book.

people today who just pick up a transistor radio . . . have no idea of the excitement that hit this country when radio was young.[4]

A primitive set consisted of a "cat tail" crystal rubbing against a cylinder of wound copper wire. This device was supposed to capture and tune a signal, and serve as the receiver's power source. Earphones made of hard, black bakelite were strictly "low-fi." For Red Barber and his contemporaries who could successfully rig up the right contraption, there was a mysterious fascination in catching random signals, often occupying the same wave length. Those who had sets went radio-crazy. Shattered domestic tranquility in Minneapolis because of radio was deemed newsworthy enough to make page two of the *New York Times* in 1923. The story told of a Mrs. Cora May White who filed for divorce, alleging her husband "paid more attention to his radio apparatus than to her or their home, and that 'radio mania' has alienated his affections."[5]

Zealous hobbyists and experimenters sought out scattered broadcasts while local stations shut down during specified hours so out-of-town stations could be heard. Boasts were exchanged on who could pull in the most distant stations, as "d-xing" became an obsessive conversation topic. Crystal set freaks were not interested in specific programs at first, and they paid even less heed to the pitches for marginal nostrums, elixirs, and health foods. D-xing was entertaining in and of itself; that is, if you could call "entertaining" the cacophony that Robert Landry dubbed "soupy sounds, disembodied cosmic yowls, coughings, sputterings and perverse silences."[6]

Until the emergence of radio in the early 1920s, music popularity was measured by sheet music and phonograph sales. Using those guidelines, pioneer broadcasters offered listeners a static-encased hodgepodge of leftovers from the previous decade—songs from operettas, Broadway musicals and revues, novelty and nonsense ditties, and, surprisingly, classical music. Performances emanating from primitive studios depended on the versatility and repertory of the artist, and this included the announcer who was often chosen for his musical talent rather than his speaking voice. Live music was the standard. Phonograph records bore the onus of second-rate programming and were to be used only in emergencies or for testing purposes. Managements varied in their attention to broadcast content. If a department store owned the station, the value of the outlet for commercial *quid pro quo* was carried over into the store's sheet music department, and the music heard on the station reflected that fact. Since owner-operators ranged from hobbyists and tinkerers to colleges and churches to newspapers and automobile dealers, music selection for any given program was unpredictable and usually not covered by station policy. At the receiving end, it must be remembered, listeners were intrigued with radio's novelty and its gradual technological advances. A melange of vocal and instrumental soloists, trios, quartets, dance bands, pluckers, pickers and drummers of every musical persuasion went rising through the ether.

Pioneer stations were established principally in the larger cities. Across the land, radio became the musical expression of America's rich diversity. In Memphis, the Wooten family, founders of KFNG (predecessor of WREC), first used their home as a studio. To accommodate citizens who didn't own sets, the Wootens rigged up outside speakers for appreciative crowds who thronged over the lawn and streets for the free entertainment. When no musicians were available, a stand-by player-piano was pressed into service to pump out "Let Me Call You Sweetheart" and dozens of other piano rolls—"palmed off" as live performances. Recordings were touted as the live "Coldwater Hotel Orchestra," and listeners as far away as Seattle and Kansas City were none the wiser. After moving the station to several intermediate spots, the owners were sold an idea by the president of the Hotel Peabody. He had been impressed on visits to New York by Vincent Lopez's Hotel Taft Grill Room broadcasts. The Wootens liked the idea and WREC re-located in the Hotel Peabody.*

Like those of WREC, the first studios of WMT (originally KWCR), Cedar Rapids, Iowa were in a home. WMT's inaugural broadcast was an hour of dance music by the Manhattan Dance Orchestra, whose song selection for the auspicious occasion included "Don't Bring Me Posies When It's Shoesies That I Need" and "Deedle Deedle Dum." Popular music performed by groups in and around Cedar Rapids was a WMT mainstay in the early 1920s: the Weatherwax Quartet, the Murray Family Orchestra, The Sunshine Six, Bill Boutly's Novelty Orchestra and Guy Clark's Orchestra. WMT started remotes featuring Clark's outfit from Cedar Rapids' Dreamland Ballroom in the summer of 1924.

Broadcasting outside regular studios was becoming popular elsewhere in radioland around 1924. WHAS opened a half dozen remote studios in music stores around Louisville, obviously to be near this source of supply. If musicians failed to show up at WHAS's main studio, a hurried call by the owner-founder, Credo Harris, to one of the six stores meant some much-desired radio exposure for a pick-up group. On one occasion, a four-banjo/string bass combo became the unorthodox stand-by WHAS house band. Exhibiting the ingenuity that distinguished so many pioneer stations, WHAS, in July, 1922, piped music played from its main studio to a mobile unit stationed at a country club, a first in Louisville Terrace Dancing history.

Across the river in Cincinnati, call letters that were to become one of the nation's best known, WLW, began in the home of their originator, Powell S. Crosley, Jr. A pioneer manufacturer of receivers, Crosley recognized a station as a natural adjunct to promote set sales. Some of WLW's first popular music was produced by placing the horn of the phonograph

---

* The hotel-radio connection—that is, the hotel as a station operating site and as an origination point for dance music—was a strong one throughout the 1920s and 1930s. The potential in reciprocity (hotel space for air plugs) was beneficial to both parties. Besides, the hotel was usually the tallest building in town, often no small matter in beaming out a signal.

player against the 8-foot long morning glory horn that served as the microphone. The Crosley studio orchestra and remotes from the now-defunct Sinton Hotel supplied Cincinnatians with their first taste of popular music on radio. WLW's reputation as an originator of major programming outside the leading entertainment centers began in the 1920s. An early policy that encouraged generous allotments of time to up-and-coming talent started a wave of show business beginnings that did not crest until a lengthy roster of ultimately well-known artists had appeared before a WLW microphone: Andy Williams, Doris Day, Jane Froman, Fats Waller, Singin' Sam, Little Jack Little, the McGuire Sisters, Merle Travis, Rosemary and Betty Clooney and Janette Davis.

Throughout the heartland, the story was the same: more music in the air—every day, every month. On South Dakota's first station WNAX, Yankton, the accordianist in one of the area's favorite combos was Lawrence Welk. The collegiate flavor of the 1920s spilled into Flint, Michigan, via WFDF, and made household names of Frank Zeiter and his Varsity Boys. Listeners to WMAQ, Chicago could hear a trio, the "Three Doctors," featuring a flutist named Ransom Sherman, who later served as emcee for a highly-acclaimed network afternoon show of pop music and satire, *Club Matinee*. On WGN, Chicago, a variety program, the *Radio Floor Walker* used liberal helpings of popular music. KSD, St. Louis offered a quartet as its first sponsored program. In 1924, the Hoosier State's WFBM was already doing dance band remotes from the Indianapolis Athletic Club.

The founder of Denver's pioneer KLZ, Dr. W.D. Reynolds, a dentist, knowing the station's need for a piano or organ, arranged to buy one on the installment plan. When he couldn't move it from the freight station, he traded a third interest in KLZ to have it transported. The time salesman with whom he made the deal hustled politicians to buy air time and with the funds moved the organ. Stepping out of a West Coast vocal trio on KHJ, Los Angeles, to become an announcer was Don Wilson. KHJ owner, Don Lee, arranged dance band pick-ups from San Francisco's KFRC. Out of the two-station connection grew the Don Lee Network, one of radio's most successful regional networks. In Albuquerque, KOB had a monthly talent budget of $125.00, enabling each artist to receive fifty cents per performance. Appeals by mail to music publishers helped reduce costs for orchestrations. On KTAR, Phoenix, a favorite western jamboree show was called the *Amalgamated Order of Wild Eyed Apaches*. WOAI, San Antonio, implemented its early policy of paying performers in order to have complete control over their appearances.

A new radio station coming on the air in the early 1920s was a top local news story. In Buffalo, WGR received an accolade from the *Evening News* the day following the pioneer outlet's opening:

WGR is the highest powered broadcasting station between Schenectady and Detroit and is said by radio experts to have the highest percentage of

efficiency in the country. The station has been attractively arranged and
furnished. The broadcasting room is hung with heavy gray drapes. These
are not only pleasing to the eye but necessary to kill off any ring or echo
that might interfere with the broadcasting. They improve the acoustics.
There is an adjoining lounge and waiting room comfortably arranged with
wicker furniture.[7]

At WGR, as at many trailblazer stations, the close ties between the hotel,
a dance orchestra and the broadcast operation were in evidence from the
beginning. The following telegram to the WGR house band leader attests
to the value of 1920s pop music group in making a radio connection:

TORONTO, ONT.

CLIFF KEYSER
CARE OF WGR RADIO ATATION HOTEL STATLER BUFFALO NY
ANNOUNCER SPIGGOTT RECOMMENDED YOUR BAND TO ME
CAN GIVE YOU JOB AT TORONTO FROM APRIL FIFTEENTH TO
MAY TWENTY FOURTH FOR SEVEN OR EIGHT MEN STOP TELE-
PHONE ME TONIGHT AT LOMBARD ONE FIVE FOUR TWO TO-
RONTO
W.E. MACDONALD 4 CROSS ST.[8]

Composer Jimmy van Heusen was a pianist for WSYR, Syracuse. He
served as an accompanist for a father-and-very-young son duet; Gordon
MacRae was the son. WCAU, Philadelphia, alumni whose early work involved announcing popular music shows of one kind or another included
Paul Douglas, Harry Marble, Henry Morgan, Norman Brokenshire, Rex
Marshall and Ezra Stone. Radio's most celebrated musical signature, the
three-note identification chime was first heard on WJAR, Providence.
Originated by a young announcer, R.C. Blanchard, in 1922 and later
adopted by NBC, the chime notes were developed to identify WJAR for
dx fans who missed the call letters through the static.
    In Atlanta, a Georgia Tech student, Arthur Murray, set up one of
radio's first dance remotes from the experimental campus station, 4FT, to
dancers in downtown Atlanta. Dancers glided over the floor wearing earphones. When better receivers became available, Murray promoted tea
dances over WGST and was reported to have earned $15,000 as a student.
Later in the 1920s, tea dances became a national fad and provided radio
with an invaluable source of free programming.
    What passed for popular music in radio's formative years often varied
from city to city. (New York listeners could expect bigger names, more
variety, and a higher level of professionalism.*) North, east, south and

---

* New York Stations, by the same token, could expect more scrutiny. *Variety's* radio columnist often came down hard on what he heard: "Same old stuff—every night alike on the
air." (December 2, 1925, p. 45); "Evenings at home with set commencing to sound alike—
too much advertising, song plugging, among other dullnesses." (December 24, 1924, p 35).
But he could be generous too: "Friday night's radio program should make theaters worry."
(March 24, 1926, p. 41).

west, day and night, radio rhythms were wafting through the American air. This was the only common characteristic in the new entertainment medium where the word, *frequency,* was a double entendre.

It was to the most familiar segment of the established show business structure—vaudeville and musical comedy performers and dance orchestras—to which radio turned for its first program fare. Artists often had to be satisfied with air plugs and midnight buffets as their only payment. While other branches of the entertainment field—the legitimate theater, in particular—looked with contempt on radio, the denizens of the vaudeville theater and the dance hall were the important musical trend-setters and welcomed the opportunity to go on radio. Astute showmen that they were, they quickly recognized the new medium could draw its strength from only two sources: the human voice and music. Radio's first successful popular music skillfully exploited both.

The logic of using dance music to fill air-time was apparent from the start. Vincent Lopez, who led one of the popular orchestras of the day, loved to relate his experience as the first maestro to appear on a live pick-up of dance music. It occurred in WJZ's studio in Newark on November 27, 1921. A month later gear was set up in the Grill of New York's Hotel Pennsylvania to present regular broadcasts by the Lopez aggregation. After the initial Grill remote, Lopez wondered what kind of response to expect. He found out within the hour:

> Telephone calls had soaked up every table reservation for the following evening and the calls kept coming in that night and all next day . . . What's more, the entire hotel was sold out by mid-afternoon . . . The mail response to our next broadcast was simply unbelievable. At the microphone . . . I blurted out an offer of a photograph to anyone who'd write us. The next day's mail filled ten big clothes hampers . . . I couldn't possibly take care of it and apologized on the air, but offered an autographed photo to people who telephoned their requests to Hotel Pennsylvania. The in-coming calls so jammed the hotel switchboard the next two days that people calling for room reservations grew tired of getting a busy signal.[9]

Starting with his earliest broadcasts, Vincent Lopez did his own announcing ("Hello everybody; Lopez speaking"), initiating a practice that was to be emulated by other leaders who recognized in radio a means of exposure no other entertainment form could match.

Orchestra leaders, in the great tradition of show business, have never been bashful in copying successful models. Surprisingly, however, it took a year to top Lopez's radio act. As it turned out, the commotion caused by the Hotel Pennsylvania broadcasts was a "local" marvel, despite taking place in New York. The phenomenon that dwarfed Vincent Lopez's sprang up in the Midwest and became radio's first popular music display with national repercussions. Carlton Coon and Joe Sanders were co-leaders of the house band in Kansas City's Muehlebach Hotel when WDAF

installed a radio wire in late 1922 for post-midnight broadcasts. Because
of the time slot, the orchestra adopted the name, Nighthawks. Introduced
by Sanders ("Howj' do, howja do, howja do—you big ol' raddio pooblic")
the WDAF broadcasts were soon picked up in distant reaches. Coon the
drummer and Sanders the pianist varied the programs by singing occasionally through megaphones aimed at primitive microphones. Their vocal
choruses were done in an easy-going style that was to be perfected by Bing
Crosby. Following an offer to read listeners' names on the air, the program
was inundated with a nightly telegram shower. Finally, in order to handle
the messages, Western Union installed a ticker tape between the piano and
drums so Coon and Sanders could make acknowledgements immediately.
Their chitchat and commentaries between tunes made Coon and Sanders
precursors of the disc jockey. They started one of radio's first fan clubs,
"Knights and Ladies of the Bath."As the Coon-Sanders Nighthawks' radio
popularity increased, so did their in-person appeal. They were, after all, a
dance orchestra and personal appearances went with the territory.

In 1926, Otto Roth, owner of Chicago's Blackhawk Restaurant, was
convinced by his head-waiter to install a dance floor, change from string
ensembles to pop groups, and "go on the radio." The Coon-Sanders Nighthawks were an obvious choice to implement the new music policy. At the
Blackhawk, the Nighthawks continued the formula that had worked so
well at the Muehlebach. Their music was neither sweet nor hot, but a
relaxed and danceable mixture, marked by a healthy respect for rhythm and
time. Nighthawk broadcast favorites became best-sellers on Victor records
("Sluefoot," "Wabash Blues," "Flamin' Mamie" and "What a Girl! What
a Night!"). The band's book included other 1920s workhorses ("Yes Sir!
That's My Baby," "Everything Is Hotsy-Totsy," "I'm Gonna Charleston
Back to Charleston"). Unlike many dance groups of the period, the Nighthawks avoided the frenzy. As one listener observed,

> They exuded youthful abandon and charm, all in doses of clean fun. They
> mildly satirized conventions of society in semi-sentimental ditties like "Lit-
> tle Orphan Annie" or "I Ain't Got Nobody," or goodtime tunes like "Here
> Comes My Ball and Chain" or "Red Hot Mama." The band also served
> up jazz instrumentals like "Brainstorm," "High Fever" and "Hallucina-
> tions" . . . The band was steady with both leaders holding down the
> rhythm section and the lead trumpet and saxophone work was as smoothly
> integrated as in any group of the day . . . It showed how a dance band
> could work as a force in pop music.[10]

With their Blackhawk Restaurant base, Coon and Sanders toured the
Midwest, making one-nighters important events in local dance halls and
Masonic temples. It was the first major use of radio to build up personal
appearances for pop music artists—a practice that foreshadowed the coming big band and record hop eras. Landing a booking at Manhattan's Hotel New Yorker made the band's national reputation secure. But after re-

turning to Chicago in the spring of 1932, the Coon-Sanders Nighthawks' bid for pop music stardom came to an abrupt halt with the death of Carlton Coon. The "Ole' Lefthander," as Sanders billed himself, carried on for a year, but the magic was gone. Efforts by Sanders to capture the spirit of the original Nighthawks in the 1930s and 1940s with ghost bands were met with little success. One measure of radio's early impact on disseminating a body of popular music could be found 50 years later in Pleasant Garden, North Carolina, where is headquartered an active Coon-Sanders Nighthawk Club. "Golden oldies" all, they may hold the all-time record for Membership Seniority in a Fan Club Induced by Musical Radio.

In addition to their American celebrity, Coon-Sanders were among the first radio-developed pop artists to gain a measure of international acclaim. Among the Nighthawks' Canadian followers were four young brothers who dabbled in dance music. They were Guy, Carmen, Victor and Leibert Lombardo. Seeking to further their careers, the Lombardo brothers were aware of two seemingly unrelated events occurring on United States radio at the time: one was the Nighthawks-WDAF broadcasts reaching them in Ontario; the other was the periods of silence they observed on WTAM, a Cleveland powerhouse to which they regularly turned. Why, the Lombardos reasoned, putting the two circumstances together, couldn't *they* organize a dance orchestra and fill the WTAM voids? With little more than youthful bravado and an agent, the newly-minted band set out for Cleveland. It was one of the most fortuitous day-coach migrations in popular music history.

Mike Shea, their agent, came through with a few bookings, but the early Lombardo Cleveland experience was a familiar scenario: rough. Lombardo relates in his autobiography,

> We were about ready to start the rounds of chop suey joints when Mike Shea came through again. He had a date in two weeks for a private party in a hotel. It would pay $250 and that meant we could stay another two weeks. It gave us time to take a crack at our original target—Radio Station WTAM. It didn't turn out to be a problem. The station manager permitted us to play a couple of half-hour segments, advising us there was no salary attached to it. We played for free gladly, and the reward was twenty or thirty complimentary letters from listeners.[11]

Still, the Royal Canadians lacked a permanent nightclub base and the vital radio wire that they regarded as essential to get the band recognition. In 1924, came what looked like the big break—a job in the Claremont Tent, a small Cleveland cabaret. SRO business at the Claremont emboldened Guy Lombardo to make a pitch to the WTAM management for a critical remote line. He found, however, WTAM wanted no part of the idea since the Claremont was formerly a speakeasy raided by the Feds, and hence unsavory for WTAM association. But as Lombardo recalls,

The station was magnanimous about permitting us to play—from the studio and for free. Actually, there were numerous bands in Cleveland that could have availed themselves of the same opportunity. But in none of them were the personnel willing to work without renumeration . . . I don't suppose we ever made a more important investment in time or effort than that gratuitous engagement on radio . . . I knew we were sounding more like a fine orchestra every day. The radio listeners confirmed it. We got batches of mail daily . . .[12]

One-nighters in Ohio proved to the Lombardo brothers that radio had paved the way for their acceptance. Their most important WTAM listener was not a Clevelander, however. He was the operator of a Chicago night spot, recently re-named the Granada, who liked what he heard, and brought the band to the Windy City. Regular broadcasts over Chicago's WBBM enabled Guy Lombardo to add further polish to the band's professional sheen—a sweet, velvety melange produced by a vibrato-abundant saxophone section, muted brass, tuba and a tinkling piano. Regular appearances at the microphone also gave Guy Lombardo, the emcee, a poise that resulted in making him a recognizable air personality. Sticking with the basic instrumentation evolved in Cleveland and Chicago and with his animated movements on the bandstand, Lombardo eventually waved his baton through more network commercial radio shows than any popular music outfit in history. When television arrived, millions of Americans welcomed in over 20 New Years with "The Sweetest Music This Side of Heaven." Rock station program directors who couldn't list a handful of names from the big band era know that Guy Lombardo's "Auld Lang Syne" recording at 11:59 p.m. is mandatory each December 31st.

Those $500-a-couple televised Lombardo New Year's Eve soirees helped further to etch a lingering picture of the celebrated Royal Canadian "business man's bounce." Many of the well-heeled Lombardo followers were the fans he took with him through the years. They were the pop music addicts of the 1920s when dance orchestras were the province of the young. No less a figure than Louis Armstrong made numerous flattering references to the Royal Canadians, and any number of Satchmo's big band recordings bear evidence that his saccharine sax section was often styled along the lines of Lombardo's. With the advent of swing, campus chic required referring derisively to Guy Lombardo's "Mickey Mouse band." But in the late 1920s, the collegiate crowd sought out Lombardo on the dial and in person; he called them "our biggest boosters."

Although Guy Lombardo was not aware of the sociological implications at the time, increasing college enrollments coincided with radio's rapid growth. No previous decade had experienced so keen an awareness of higher education; in addition, the 18–24 demographic group grew faster in the 1920s than at any previous period in history. The following table offers vivid evidence of both phenomena:

YEAR	STUDENTS ENROLLED IN COLLEGE (In Thousands)	PERCENT OF POPULATION 18–24
1918	441	3.6
1920	598	4.7
1922	681	5.1
1924	823	5.9
1926	941	6.6
1928	1,054	7.1
1930	1,101	7.2

—Source: *Historical Statistics, Colonial Times to 1970,* U.S. Department of Commerce, Bureau of Census

The enduring symbols of the 1920s in one way or other lead to youth and college students: raccoon coats, sheiks, flappers, cloche hats, silk stockings, bobbed hair, rumble-seated cars and Prohibition. The automobile itself was emblematic of a new emphasis on mobility—to go places and do things. Car registrations went from 9,340,000 in 1921 to 17,500,000 in 1926. Sampling a new road house or ballroom was now a simple matter. "Flaming youth," romanticized in the novels of F. Scott Fitzgerald, usually meant *college youth.* This was the crowd that had gained a reputation for naughtiness and outright flaunting of conventions. Youth in the 1920s demonstrated its liberation in any number of ways, but the greatest symbols of rebellion were smoking, drinking and dancing.

Especially dancing. Popular music and dancing were inseparable. Spurred by trend-setting collegians, off-campus youth acquired the mania for dancing too. "Everybody's Doing It," the song said. (Movie makers and television documentarians have long known the best way to conjure up a 1920s atmosphere is merely crank up a few bars of the obligatory "Black Bottom" or "Charleston.")

Sensing that the "vo-de-oh-do" of their fellow students could be turned into dough-de-oh-dough right then and there, some undergraduates organized orchestras of their own on campus. George Olsen was one of the first—at the University of Michigan. Olsen carried the collegiate motif with him when he left college: two of the best-selling recordings of the period were his outfit's versions of "Varsity Drag" and "Doin' the Raccoon." Managing to get early radio exposure, he landed jobs on leading commercial shows of the late 1920s, pit band assignments for Broadway musicals and choice hotel bookings. In addition to Olsen, Fred Waring (Penn State), Hal Kemp and Kay Kyser (University of North Carolina), and Ozzie Nelson (Rutgers) began their show business careers leading campus dance orchestras during radio's first decade.

The country was in a dancing mood, and radio played to the dancing gallery. When contemporary critics inveighed against the decline of morals radio, the carrier of "jazz music," was a favorite whipping boy. In the Introduction to this study it was pointed out that most popular dance music of the 1920s was perceived as jazz. George Jean Nathan, the acerbic theater critic who occasionally lapsed into social commentary, aimed a shaft at radio, observing that "nightly the front parlors of the proletariat resound to the strains of alley jazz pounded out by bad hotel orchestras." One irate listener in a letter to *Radio Broadcast* in 1925 summed up the sentiments in the anti-dance-music-on-radio camp:

> If it weren't for the constant stream of jazz flowing from nearly every broadcasting antenna, I would enjoy radio a lot more. These jazz orchestras from every radio station in the country, all practically banging away at the same time, are more than annoying.[13]

In response, the editor of the magazine's sound-off forum at least put the semantics of the musical radio argument in proper perspective:

> The trouble with criticism such as this is that it groups all dance music as *jazz*, which is only true because we have no term which allows us to distinguish between the grades of jazz. We use the same term to describe the soft symphonic effects of Art Hickman, Ben Bernie and Vincent Lopez as we use for the Five Melody Kings of Four Corners, Oklahoma . . .[14]

Semantics aside, the *Radio Broadcast* discussion was an early shot fired in what would become one of radio's liveliest and most abiding controversies, and reach its fiercest crescendo with the advent of Top 40. Simply stated, it is this: does air play make a tune popular, or does radio merely re-inforce popularity? The editor went on:

> They [radio stations] have been too heavily loaded with this orchestra dud that was playing the currently popular tunes. Too much of the program has been devoted to dance orchestras . . . who have nothing in their repertoire but whatever numbers were being sold in the music shops as "the latest thing," or worse, to song "pluggers" in the employ of music publishers. This practice of broadcasters, we firmly believe, has shortened the life of many moderately good popular numbers, which otherwise might have retained popularity for a considerably longer time.[15]

Everywhere the signs were the same by the mid-1920s: radio was moving in on popular music. A Tin Pan Alley veteran, in assessing the effects of radio, could well have been speaking for fellow members of the contemporary pop music establishment when he lamented,

> The gal in Kalamazoo don't buy sheet music any more . . . It's not so much that radio stations don't pay us for broadcasting. It's that the gal

in Kalamazoo don't buy sheet music. The radio can make a song—sure! But let me tell you, it can kill it just as quick. Me—I'm no fan. But I listened in with one of the radio nuts last night. He could get Chicago, Schenectady, and all the local stations. We tune in Chi and hear "Follow the Swallow." At Schenectady we hear it again. An orchestra at a hotel in New York is playin' it too. I was fed up with the song myself before we got through . . .[16]

No doubt about it—dance orchestras were in the driver's seat. And radio paid them their proper due. Any station of consequence had to have a studio orchestra, and every radio studio orchestra, whether made up of three or 23 pieces, had to be a versatile unit. It might be called upon to accompany a classical singer, to glide through a lilting Strauss waltz or to perform a rousing Sousa march. (WJR, Detroit held on to its staff orchestra until well into the 1960s.) But it was dance music that station house bands used most often to augment remote pickups from local bistros.

Radio struck popular music with such force that some dance groups made it part of their names. There were the Radiolites, the Radio Rascals Orchestra, the Radio Dance Orchestra and the Radio All-Star Novelty Orchestra.

The other major group of entertainers who provided early stations in the larger cities with a flow of popular music were vaudeville and musical comedy artists. Their climb up the greasy show biz pole had taught them to try anything for exposure—even that intimidating round contraption called a microphone. They often went from station to station to perform their specialty. Although they were already established names in the older entertainment forms, these artists became bigger stars, thanks to radio:

LITTLE JACK LITTLE: Born in London, he had led a college band at the University of Iowa, but scrapped it in favor of a solo act when radio beckoned. Little played Vincent Lopez-inspired piano, mixed with vocal and patter.

VAUGHN DE LEATH: Billed as the "Original Radio Girl," she appeared on Broadway in 1923 in *Laugh Clown Laugh*. de Leath specialized in singing show tunes. Her popularity extended well into the network era, and at one time, she managed a radio station.

BILLY JONES and ERNIE HARE: The "Harmony Boys," were delighting listeners as early as 1921. They made the transition to network radio, continuing with their basic routine of songs and patter. When they went network, they became "The Happiness Boys," "The Interwoven Pair," etc.

MAY SINGHI BREEN: Like most early performers, Breen had a special handle, the "Ukulele Lady." After marrying composer Peter de Rose ("When Your Hair Has Turned to Silver," "Rain," "Deep Purple") the husband-and-wife song team became the "Sweethearts of the Air."

JOSEPH WHITE: Wearing a silver mask was his *schtick*. His identity
thus concealed, White was known to listeners only as the "Silver
Masked Tenor." His acclaim carried over into network shows. When
he decided to drop the mystery routine and discard the mask, his
popularity went the same way.

No music hall artist, however, could come close to Wendell Hall in
mastering the radio primeval. Hall, a three-a-day vaudevillian billed as the
"Singing Xylophonist," appeared first on KYW, then licensed to Chicago.
Traveling from city to city in classic vaudeville style, he built a radio reputation by filling program gaps which so often marked that era of haphaz-
ard scheduling. In 1923, he wrote lyrics and music to "It Ain't Gonna
Rain No Mo'," * a song Hall soon thereafter adopted as his trademark. It
became the first national hit to be created by radio. National sales of the
Victor recording over the years reportedly soared to 2,000,000 copies; the
sheet music version was even more dramatic, selling 10,000,000 pieces.
Wendall Hall was so popular his marriage ceremony was carried over a
four-station network on the *Eveready Hour*. When the Guy Lombardo
Orchestra made its network debut in 1929, Hall was the featured singer.
Hall's reputation declined in the mid-1930s when his highly-vaudeville-
flavored novelty routines went out of fashion and listeners demanded more
sophisticated air fare.

    Any question that radio was perceived as something other than a mu-
sic box was removed as the 1920s wore on. Nowhere was this more apparent than in the sale of phonograph records. The post-War boom in
phonograph players had just gotten underway when radio started sending
its musical calling cards framed in crackling noises, but unable to be ignored. To the well-entrenched recording industry, the message was clear—
and ominous. The primary American home musical instrument now had a
formidable competitor. The following table indicates the alarming slide
that beset phonograph record sales between 1921 and 1925:

CALENDAR YEAR	LIST PRICE VALUE (Millions of Dollars)
1921	105.6
1922	92.4
1923	79.2
1924	68.2
1925	59.2

—Source: Recording Industry Association of
America

---

* Carl Sandburg is reported to have claimed Hall's hit was really an adaptation of an 1870s
Southern folk song.

It would take until 1945 for the industry to match 1921 levels. (See Appendix, p. 361 for graph charting phonograph record sales between 1921 and 1980.)

Radio was also having a noticeable effect elsewhere on the musical front by mid-decade. Although one large Chicago piano manufacturer, Lyon and Healy, blamed radio because it had to drop upright pianos from its inventory, the overall effect of the increasingly popular home entertainment dispenser was positive in the music world. A survey taken during the silver jubilee convention of the music trades in 1925 concluded,

> Radio . . . is directly responsible for the increased sale of the instruments which compose jazz orchestras. The programs contain, as a rule, a considerable portion of such music, and its delights are brought home to many people, especially in remote places. As a result, countless listeners aspire to be jazz artists . . . The radio is thus credited with stimulating many thousands of people to play musical instruments of some form, to which in the past they have been indifferent.[17]

Radio set sales, meanwhile, had jumped from 550,000 in 1923 to 2,000,000 in 1925. That radio was getting off the ground (so to speak) was revealed in a 1926 farm study conducted by WLS, Chicago. The survey, prompting 44,550 individual responses, covering 18,456 farm homes in 42 states, reported a most revealing finding: *20% of all U.S. farm homes were equipped with radios.* Thirty-eight percent of farm households in Pennsylvania, New York, and the New England States were owners of receivers, while the Corn Belt (Iowa, Missouri, Illinois, Indiana and Ohio) was also listed at 38%. The WLS survey also reported: 25% of farmers preferred music (no indication of what kind); 24% liked daily weather and market reports best; farm women chose homemaker programs over music, 41% to 31%. Ninety-five percent of all respondents felt radio was as important an entertainment device as a utility.[18]

Farm families traditionally have been tough listening juries, and figures such as these were welcomed with special elation in all sectors of broadcasting. Nevertheless, 20% set ownership meant 80% of the nation's rural homes were still *without* radios. More remained to be done if radio was to become a truly national medium. Some experiments along these lines had moved ahead encouragingly since the early 1920s. But the pressure became particularly intense at RCA throughout 1926 to get simultaneous blanket radio coverage of some significance moving faster. RCA and A.T. & T. board members huddled extra hours that summer. All the while, engineers, lawyers and accountants shuffled the papers that would, before the year was over, send the bosses on their way rejoicing.

NOTES

1. "Todays Radio Program." *New York Times,* November 21, 1923, p. 23.
2. Robert J. Landry. "Medicine Show with Chimes," *Variety,* August 13, 1980, p. 83.
3. Quoted in, "1922—Year Radio's Population Soared," *Broadcasting,* May 14, 1962, p. 110.
4. Red Barber, Reminiscences. *The First Fifty Years of Radio,* Six-record Documentary, produced by Westinghouse Broadcasting Company, 1970.
5. ———. "Radio As Divorce Case," *New York Times,* December 2, 1923, p. 2.
6. Robert J. Landry, *op. cit.* p. 2.
7. ———. "WGR Is on the Air," *Buffalo Evening News,* May 22, 1922, p. 2.
8. WGR Archives.
9. Vincent Lopez. "I Pioneered in Radio," *International Musician,* March, 1973, p. 3.
10. William J. Schafer. "Rhythm King," *The Mississippi Rag,* July 1978, p. 7.
11. Guy Lombardo, *Auld Acquaintance,* Doubleday, (New York), 1975, p. 32.
12. *Ibid.* pp. 43–44.
13. Kingsly Welles, ed. "The Listener's Point of View," *Radio Broadcast,* December, 1925, p. 478.
14. *Ibid.*
15. *Ibid.*
16. Quoted in "The Ragtime Queen Has Abdicated," *New York Times Magazine,* May 24, 1925, p. 21.
17. ———. "Music Trades Silver Jubilee to Feature Radio Apparatus," *New York Times,* June 7, 1925, Section X, p. 16.
18. ———. "One-Fifth of Rural Homes Use Radio," *New York Times,* April 11, 1926, Section IX, p. 18.

CHAPTER 2

Coast-to-Coast

THREE PROGRAMMING CONCEPTS in broadcasting have been fundamental in establishing radio as America's prime source of popular music: networks, FM and Top 40. Ironically, each in turn would have to endure dire forecasts of its ability to survive. Of the three, program transmittal by networks was to grow the fastest. Before proceeding with the importance of the networks to the spread of popular music, however, it is necessary to understand their origins.

Experiments using long distance telephone lines to transmit program material were taking place even as the earliest stations were coping with growing pains. The American Telephone and Telegraph Company, owner of WEAF, New York, in the fall of 1922 was already testing a hook-up with WNAC, Boston. One year later, A.T. & T. proved the feasibility of inter-connected telephone lines for simultaneous transmission of program matter. The coast-to-coast 22-station hook-up for President Coolidge's speech to the U.S. Chamber of Commerce on October 23, 1924 was certainly not musical, and it may not have been popular, but it was important. It marked the largest linkage to that date of stations carrying the same program at the same time. Soon there were musical offerings and a scattering of regularly scheduled programs. Based on which source one accepts, A.T. & T.'s pioneer "network" included from 16 to 26 affiliates.

Meanwhile, in another part of the fast-moving communications industry of the post–World War I years, David Sarnoff, the telegrapher of Titanic fame had, by 1921, become general manager of Radio Corporation of America when it absorbed the Marconi Company. Sarnoff was pushing his radio music box idea on two fronts. At the time, RCA was part of a manufacturing colossus that included the General Electric Company and Westinghouse Corporation. The conglomerate's main interest in the mid-1920s was producing and selling receivers to an America that, among its other crazes, was going radio-mad. Not content with being limited to merchandising this incredible new home entertainment instrument, young Sarnoff was virtually a one-man lobby to get RCA more involved with what came out of it. Westinghouse had already seen first-hand the stir created by its three owned stations: KDKA, Pittsburgh; WJZ, Newark; and WBZ, Springfield, Massachusetts. General Electric's WGY in Schenectady, New York, had been on the air since early 1922. Spearheaded by WGY, GE had even formed a modest network of its own. They were no match, however, for A.T. & T.'s growing venture.

David Sarnoff, who by now had earned a vice presidency at RCA, had learned well the machinations of corporate politics. By enlisting the right board members, he found support for the idea of establishing a separate broadcasting subsidiary, wholly owned and operated by RCA. A proposal to acquire station WEAF was made to A.T. & T.* After more than a year of involved negotiations, came a press release on July 21, 1926 announcing the sale of WEAF to RCA. So unexpected was the deal it took even some RCA officials by surprise. An announcement read on WEAF assured its listeners ". . . the same programs will continue to come to you. The voices of the same announcers will continue to introduce these features. The programs will be built and presented by the same people. In short, WEAF remains WEAF with an added interest and endeavor to supply you with those programs which you have received so favorably in the past." [1]

It may have been the fear of possible antitrust problems that prompted A.T. & T. to quit the broadcasting business, foreseeing perhaps the lucrative potential that lay ahead as the monopolistic supplier of long distance lines to network operators. In any event, the A.T. & T. spin-off, now known as the National Broadcasting Company, was immediately shaped as a separate entity by RCA. Preparations through the summer and fall of 1926 pointed to an auspicious debut for NBC Radio. The charter network included these stations:

WBZ, Boston	WWJ, Detroit
WEEI, Boston	WTIC, Hartford
WGR, Buffalo	WHAD, Hartford
KYW, Chicago	WCCO, Minneapolis-St. Paul
WTAM, Cleveland	WDRC, New Haven

---

* Actually, A.T. & T.'s broadcasting assets were limited to ownership of WEAF. Member stations of its network were independently owned. Later, as networks grew, their assets would include a legally-set number of prosperous owned-and-operated outlets, in addition to whatever income they derived from their network operations.

WEAF, New York
WGN, Chicago
WSAI, Cincinnati
WJZ, New York
WLIT, Philadelphia
WCAE, Pittsburgh
KDKA, Pittsburgh
WCSH, Portland, Maine
WJAR, Providence

WGY, Schenectady
WBZA, Springfield
WRC, Washington
WTAG, Worcester
. . . plus these specially-
   added stations:
WDAF, Kansas City
KSD, St. Louis

The gala inaugural of the National Broadcasting Company was the kind of media event for which New York is famous. Amid the elegance of the grand ballroom of New York's old Waldorf-Astoria, on November 15, 1926, 300 invited guests, including the *de rigueur* VIP's, looked and listened in awe. Even by television standards, it was a "Spectacular." Through the American heartland the skywaves burst with the effusive sounds of music and laughter. From 8pm until 12:25am, millions listened to the same program at the same time; radio had wiped out barriers of distance and time. Listeners heard over the pioneer hook-up a show that symbolized the something-for-everyone programming philosophy NBC had charted for its future: comedy (Weber and Fields); political satire (Will Rogers, cut in from Independence, Kansas, to dramatize networking's versatility); marching band music (the Goldman Band); "serious" music (The New York Symphony Orchestra, conducted by Walter Damrosch, Metropolitan Opera baritone Titta Ruffo, and pianist Harold Bauer, who in the best show-must-go-on tradition, had to charter a tug to leave the quarantined ocean liner, Franconia, arriving just in time to go on the air).[2] NBC's four-and-a-half hour opening-night extravaganza offered an extra helping of popular music by presenting four of the top five dance orchestras of the day: Vincent Lopez, George Olsen, B.A. Rolfe and Ben Bernie. Only one bigger name was missing—Paul Whiteman, who did not take radio seriously until 1929.

With opening night hoopla out of the way, the new network got down to the business of building a program schedule. NBC's offerings the first year originated in A.T. & T.'s building on lower Broadway where the former owner had maintained its WEAF facilities. A year later the operation was moved to 711 Fifth Avenue, where specially sound-engineered quarters were surrounded by the voguish art deco of the day, and near the site of the future Radio City at Rockefeller Center.

Torrents of mail, telegrams and telephone calls told NBC officials the network concept was the sound wave of the future. Audience response was so great, it became immediately apparent to David Sarnoff that "a single network service was not enough to satisfy the demands of the radio audience for diversified programs of national interest and importance; that if broadcasting were to be popularized at all, there should be more than one type of program simultaneously available. . . ."[3]

Sarnoff's idea for a two-network NBC was not long in taking shape, because on January 1, 1927 a second service was introduced. The older operation whose flagship station was WEAF with 21 affiliates was designated the Red Network; for the diversification Sarnoff espoused, there was now the Blue Network, keyed by WJZ, with six stations tied to it.* From the beginning, the Red Network carried the bulk of NBC's sponsored shows. Many of network's cultural and "service" programs were relegated to the Blue. In 1942, the FCC broke up the duopoly. RCA retained the Red as NBC and sold the Blue to Edward Noble of Life Savers, after which the spin-off became ABC.

During NBC's opening season a listener could find some form of popular music any night of the week. Depending on one's tastes, a week in early 1927 could include a random sampling from the following:

PROGRAM	PRODUCT	TIME & DAY	TYPE
Cliquot Club Eskimos	Soft Drinks	Thurs.–10–10:30pm	Dance and Novelty Orch.
Goodrich Zippers	Tires	Thurs.–9–10:00pm	Banjo Group
Happiness Boys (Jones & Hare)	Candy	Fri.–8:00–8:30pm	Songs & Patter
Hires Harvestors	Soft Drinks	Mon.–8:00–8:30pm	Variety
Ipana Troubadours	Toothpaste	Wed.–9:00–9:30pm	Dance Music
Jolly Wonder Bakers	Bread	Fri.–9:30–10:00pm	Variety

—Source: *A Thirty Year History of Programs Carried on National Radio Networks, 1926–1956.* Harrison B. Summers, ed., Arno, 1971

If NBC had any hit shows its first few seasons, there were two from that group. Although unsubstantiated by ratings in those pre-research days, the *Cliquot Club Eskimos* and the *Ipana Troubadours* ** qualified as pacesetters by the only available yardsticks: sales of sponsors' products, requests for pictures, personal appearances, and the like. Both were pure 1920s pop.

The *Cliquot Club Eskimos* was actually the radio name for Harry Reser's Orchestra, a popular dance/novelty group. Reser, who had built a reputation as a jazz-banjo virtuoso, tailored his radio arrangements to match the good-time, high-spirited feeling of the day. Harry Reser's NBC program helped establish a standard that successful pop music groups would follow in the years to come—an instantly identifiable sound. He did it by

---

* Names for NBC's two networks are said to have derived from the difficulty engineers had at first in identifying the two operations on circuitry maps. Red and blue colored pencils provided a simple solution.

** The practice of incorporating sponsors' names in program titles began as a device to take advantage of the added advertising value in newspaper listings.

featuring a second banjo instead of a violin. (With few variations, the regulation 1920s dance orchestra called for nine or ten pieces: two saxophones; one or two trumpets; trombone; violin; banjo; tuba; piano; and drums.) Audiences for early network programs were perceived as having (and did have) an insatiable appetite for nonsense tunes and novelty effects. Reser and the *Cliquot Club Eskimos* obliged by including in their book such outrageous titles as "Chick, Chick, Chick, Chick, Chicken!," "Henry's Made A Lady Out of Lizzie" and "Olaf, You Ought to Hear Olaf Laff." In spite of (or because of) such assaults on listeners' ears, the Eskimos made Cliquot Club a leader in the soft drink field.

Network radio with its early established policy of single-sponsorship for programs (as opposed to participating co-sponsors) gained immediate advertiser favor in another important way. Cliquot Club was able to build an entire marketing plan around its highly merchandiseable "Eskimos." Publicity shots featured Reser's band wearing fur parkas, an extension of Cliquot Club's print advertising that showed the company's symbol, a parka-clad Eskimo—the connotation being that such connections elicit images of "cold goodness" for the soft drink. From the show's opening—the howl of Eskimo dogs—through Reser's theme, for a half-hour each week, a wait-and-see advertising community got a good taste of how an astute marketer could promote a product in a way that print could never match.

Network radio's potential to harness product marketability was further enhanced in NBC's first years, Wednesday nights at 10pm, when an above-average 1920s dance orchestra was showcased as the *Ipana Troubadours*. Like Cliquot Club, Ipana chose a gimmick to make their radio attraction instantly recognizable. Wherever the band appeared—in print ads, at personal appearances, in WEAF's studio—it wore uniforms. Their garb actually suggested bull-fighting more than popular music. Outfitted in sombreros that resembled Brooks Brothers' hat forms, knickers with white socks, frilly-embroidered jackets and striped shawls over their shoulders, the Ipana Troubadours were drawn from the NBC house band. (Some of New York's most lucrative jobs for musicians were in the network's permanent orchestral company.) In the case of the *Troubadours* unit, a number of its graduates went on to lead groups of their own—Tommy and Jimmy Dorsey, Red Nichols, Benny Goodman and Jack Teagarden. Sam Lanin, brother of society bandleader, Lester, was the nominal leader.

The *Ipana Troubadours* played conventional 1920s pop ("In Araby With You," "Baby Face," "Side By Side," "Give Me a Ukulele and a Ukulele Baby.") Possibly because of some of its exceptionally talented members, the band also tackled the more sophisticated songs of the contemporary Broadway musical theater. So strong was the Ipana-Troubadour association that when the toothpaste sponsor replaced the dance band format with comedian Fred Allen, the show's orchestra was still referred to as the *Ipana Troubadours*.

As other sponsors signed on with NBC, they soon became aware of the sales potential a weekly show offered. Network radio benefited from the good timing of its arrival, coinciding with the wave of aggressive marketing that swept the nation in the 1920s. A heightened advertising awareness encouraged the country's manufacturers to seek campaigns that appealed to customers' wants. "The business of America is business," said the man in the White House. Now it was not only good business to suggest that better living and social acceptance were the end results of buying new cars, using cosmetics, smoking cigarettes, it was also *patriotic*.

Slogans became part of the language ("A thousand things may happen in the dark"—Eveready; "When better automobiles are built, Buick will build them"; "Ask the man who owns one"—Packard; "Don't burn coal!"—Oliver Oil-Gas Burners). Advertising, that necessary handmaiden to prosperity, was being cranked out to the tune of $1,782,000,000 a year. Now here was radio, a medium that wedded entertainment *and* selling.

By 1927–28, Lord and Thomas, a leading ad agency, was placing half its expenditures on NBC. Much of Lord and Thomas's reliance on network radio had to do with a social phenomenon of the period. Cigarette smoking, declared Lord and Thomas, in behalf of its good client, the American Tobacco Company, was not only enjoyable, it was a mark of sophistication. And what better way to promote such 1920s chic than by sponsoring popular music? Cigarettes ultimately became radio's leading sponsor of popular music, a development we will examine further in Chapter 8. Guided by Lord and Thomas's brilliant president, Albert Lasker, NBC made Saturday nights at 10pm dance time in America, compliments of Lucky Strike Cigarettes. B.A. Rolfe's band became the *Lucky Strike Dance Orchestra*. A former circus cornetist, Rolfe had left Vincent Lopez to form an outfit of his own. George Washington Hill, president of the American Tobacco Company, personally chose the Rolfe aggregation because he wanted a brand of popular music that was easily understood— and loud. Rolfe's brassy arrangements set to swirling tempos fit the bill perfectly. Hill, Lord and Thomas's most colorful client, took an active role in putting Lucky Strike's weekly program of dance music together. Network, agency and American Tobacco personnel, headed by Hill, attended Saturday morning rehearsals. At Hill's insistence, the music was put to the test. Persons in the group were required to dance to it, and the better they danced, the more George Washington Hill liked it. Hill had another acid test for the *Lucky Strike Dance Orchestra:*

> . . . He sometimes brought with him an old aunt who was deaf, and who kept time by beating with a pencil on the back of a chair. For her to hear at all, the music had to be abnormally loud. But if she stopped beating at any moment, Hill would say that the program was no good, and demand a change.[4]

The Hill-inspired aggressive Rolfe dance music proved to be the incubator for *Your Hit Parade* almost a decade later. By then however, Hill

had dropped the original Lucky Strike maestro, a sure sign that his popularity had skidded.* Always aware of the dynamic nature of music, and
the fickleness of its audience, Hill kept current with artists and concepts
that appealed to youth. Although he never ran a network or an ad agency,
although he never sang, played or wrote a note, George Washington Hill
was one of the key figures in the first quarter century of popular music on
radio.

National Broadcasting Company executives and agency people may
well have been grateful there was only one G.W. Hill. Had every sponsor
interposed himself in the network program process like Hill, NBC may
well have opted for less popular music as it attempted to build program
schedules in the early years. Still, there is no telling how much client interference may have been tolerated, considering David Sarnoff's music box
bias. For music—all kinds—dominated NBC's prime time line-up into the
early 1930s. No attempt was made to block off certain time periods or
entire evenings for specific types of music programs. It was not uncommon
for a listener to have been lost in the reverie of a half hour string ensemble
and suddenly be jarred loose, after station identification, by Harry Reser
and the *Cliquot Club Eskimos* as they came strutting into his living room.
An average listener took shows of sharply contrasting music types for
granted. However, this sort of juxtapositioning lent further shrillness to
the anti-pop music bias that had grown with radio. Complaining about
the low-calibre popular music on radio, a critic in 1929 spoke for elitists
everywhere:

> The big [advertising] buyers continue [to] favor jazz, "dinner music," and
> mongrel programs designed to hold the wondering attention of those whose
> only standard of entertainment is the movie or second rate vaudeville
> . . . This senseless disturbance of the ether begins at some stations as
> early as 6:45a.m. and continues until midnight . . . Only a radio fan is
> likely to know who the Gold Spot Pals, The Dynacone Diners, or The
> Emerald Instrumentalists may be . . . Instead of maintaining their rela-
> tions with the public through the medium of second- and third-rate pro-
> grams, our millionaire corporations could, through the practical applica-
> tion of that "ideal of service" of which we hear so much, easily assume a
> role in our present civilization comparable to that of the great aristocratic
> patrons of art in the days of the Renaissance.[5]

Obviously, such either-or-criticism was grossly unfair, since the Red
and Blue networks during the 1928–29 season scheduled almost as many
concert music programs in choice time (17) as they did popular (20).

Americans, meanwhile, continued to buy radios at a staggering pace.

---

* Rolfe was the envy of many bandleaders at the time. The choice of his group for a coast-
to-coast show was supposed to certify it as a top musical aggregation—which it was not.
Yet so popular had the Lucky Strike program made Rolfe that a Virginia couple engaged
his orchestra to play for their wedding, via a WEAF broadcast from New York's Palais
d'Or and relayed through WRC, Washington. (*New York Times,* June 4, 1927, p. 15.)

Between 1927 and 1928, they virtually tripled their expenditure in receivers and related paraphenalia. Crystal sets and headphones by this time were only memories for most listeners. Scores of manufacturers—many of whom sprang up expressly to capitalize on the radio fever that had gripped the country—scrambled to keep pace with fast moving technological advances. Assembly lines hummed as mass production helped bring prices within the range of most pocketbooks. In 1927, a Sears Silvertone table unit was selling for $34.95, and console model for $59.95. "Radio," said the 1927 Sears Catalogue, "is the most marvelous gift of the present age, and no family should be without its untold advantages."[6] One inspired catalogue copywriter for a less well-known mail order house, urging the purchase of the firm's radio receiver "to tap the well-nigh inexhaustible supply of music and entertainment," saw fit to invoke the Deity for those ingrate-holdouts:

> When the forces of the Almighty Creator of the Universe and the skill and genius of Man so combine to bring you untold blessings which may be yours to enjoy without even the asking, we ask you in all seriousness why you should not at once show your gratitude and appreciation and accept that which is so freely offered?[7]

There seemed to be no end to the good news from the Wonderful World of Radio. The installation of push-button sets in all 1600 rooms of New York's Park Central Hotel in late 1927 was newsworthy enough to rate a story in the *New York Times*.[8] In a spring, 1928 *Radio Retailing* survey conducted at the Federal Radio Commission's request, both broadcasting and manufacturing arms found good reasons to be pleased with the state of the industry: Estimated listeners—40,000,000; estimated sets in use—12,000,000.[9]

Rich though the musical lode to be mined from those "most marvelous gifts of the present age," there were other beguiling attractions. News commentaries, homemaker hints, religious features, drama, travel talks (surprisingly popular), public affairs/educational programs offered evidence of radio's infinite variety. Next to music, play-by-play accounts of sporting events proved to be radio's best sales vehicle. On January 1, 1927, America listened to its first Rose Bowl game. World Series coverage had begun in 1922. Radio's first blow-by-blow ringside coverage of prize-fighting came on September 22, 1927 with the celebrated Dempsey-Tunney confrontation. "The Golden Age of Sports" coincided with radio's great boom in the 1920s. Household names of the sporting world—Babe Ruth (baseball), Bobby Jones (golf), Bill Tilden (tennis), Red Grange (football)—had their reputations reinforced on the radio.

In other fields, too, the cult of the personality came into its own. Marian Talley (operatic sensation), Rudolph Valentino, Mary Pickford, Pola Negri, Clara Bow (movie stars), Jimmy Walker (New York's colorful

mayor), The Duke of Windsor (royal playboy)—these and others in entertainment, sports and politics developed their worshipful coteries of admirers. No personality, however, captured the American imagination in the
1920s as did Charles A. Lindbergh. His successful nonstop flight across
the Atlantic in May, 1927 made him an instant folk hero. "Lucky Lindy's"
exploits, duly reported on radio, helped build suspense and increased his
degree of celebrityhood.

If aviation, movies, opera and sports were able to create celebrity-
personalities, could radio be far behind? Sooner or later it had to happen—a personality-figure who would issue forth, full-blown, from the radio music box. The creation began, of all places, in the Ivy League.

Rudy Vallee who had transferred from the University of Maine to
Yale in his sophomore year organized a campus dance orchestra and called
it the *Yale Collegians*. Following graduation in 1927, he went straight to
New York, and after a vaudeville stint and a few turns as a sideman with
Vincent Lopez, Vallee put together an eight-piece outfit. With the help of
another bandleader, Bert Lown, the ex-Yalie was booked into a newly-
opened chichi supper club off Park Avenue called the Heigh-Ho Club. Lown
talked WABC, then a small marginal station looking for program fillers,
into installing a radio wire. When the station pleaded a personnel short-
age, Vallee himself took over the announcing chores. In his autobiography,
Rudy Vallee recalled his first days in radio:

> With the naiveté of the pure amateur I decided to begin my radio saluta-
> tion with the phrase used by the doorman outside the club: "Heigh-ho,
> everybody—this is Rudy Vallee announcing and directing the Yale Col-
> legians from The Heigh-Ho Club at Thirty-five East Fifty-third Street,
> New York City." In those days there was no censorship either of tunes
> or of what was said over the air. Therefore, I programmed any music I
> wished, gave out prices on the menu, weather reports; in short, I talked
> about anything that came to mind . . .[10]

Vallee's WABC broadcasts were so well received they led to the installation of a second remote wire by WOR. By spring, 1928, Vallee had
a sponsor for a Sunday program; in all, he was broadcasting 20 hours a
week. At this point, he changed the name of his orchestra from the *Yale
Collegians* to the *Connecticut Yankees,* a designation inspired by the
Rodgers and Hart hit musical playing on Broadway. Fan mail poured in
from New York, New Jersey and Pennsylvania. Vallee says he had a
"sneaking hunch" why he had enjoyed so much success on his early broadcasts:

> Listeners were jaded [with] the same bands playing the same tunes, the
> same way—the same announcers trying to coat song titles with a frosting
> of alleged wit and eloquence . . . Somehow the name "Rudy Vallee"
> suggest Rudy Valentino, conjuring up for female listeners a tall-dark-and-

handsome performer . . . The voice, although it spoke in the nasal manner of a Calvin Coolidge was simple and direct . . . There was no brass
in *The Collegians* . . . I talked about simple songs and made them interesting by relating anecdotes about their composers or the songs themselves . . . I sang in French, Spanish and Italian . . . Our format never
included the verse of a song, only the chorus . . . We never played more
than two choruses of a tune, and they were never in the same key . . .[11]

He might have added one more that was properly in tune with the 1920s:
the collegiate trappings—a megaphone, Y-lettered sweaters worn by the
band on occasion and, most of all, the look of a perennial college senior.
Some network air time led to bookings into the Palace and Paramount
Theaters, and an engagement at a new night spot, the Versailles. So smitten with Vallee's drawing power was the owner of the prestigious cabaret,
he changed its name to Club Vallee. One of his radio and recording hits,
"I'm Just A Vagabond Lover" led to a movie, *The Vagabond Lover*. Vallee admitted the picture was "artistically a dud, but it made a lot of money
due to our enormous radio following."[12]

On October 29, 1929, two days following "Black Tuesday" on Wall
Street, at 8pm, Rudy Vallee stepped up to the NBC microphone and to
the strains of "My Time Is Your Time," introduced himself as the host of
a new variety show, the *Fleischmann Hour*. Although there was no way
of knowing it at the time, network radio had just christened its first
launching pad for a popular music superstar. By May, 1930, NBC knew
the show was hit-bound. Ratings were still a year away, but NBC could
tell by the mail, the telegrams and the phone calls where most dials were
set on Thursday nights. In a test to see what effect radio would have on a
song, the National Broadcasting Company purchased the rights to "The
Maine Stein Song" and gave it to Rudy Vallee to push. Play on the
Fleischmann Hour and local stations made "The Maine Stein Song" a smash
hit, "promising to earn a small fortune for The National Broadcasting
Company."[13]

With its contents heavily weighted by popular music, the *Fleischmann Hour* had a generous budget allocation for guest stars, many of
whom got their first coast-to-coast exposure on Vallee's program: The Mills
Brothers, Bob Burns, Edgar Bergen, Alice Faye, Frances Langford, Bob
Hope, Red Skelton and Milton Berle. Vallee's show went through several
sponsor and time slot changes and lasted well into the 1940s before it
faded. (Thanks to the recycling of American popular culture, well-underway
in the 1960s, Rudy Vallee surfaced in the Broadway musical, *How to Succeed in Business Without Really Trying*. As late as fall, 1980, he was still
a cabaret attraction.)

Vallee's success in the network radio business hardly came without
trying. But it did his cause no harm that his network had virtually no
competition. NBC was, in the words of a song popular at the time, "riding

on the crest of a wave." A spot check of 62 major sponsored prime-time programs during the 1928–29 season, showed 47 of them were on NBC. Some of the remaining 15 running on an upstart chain, it was rumored, were there because they couldn't find choice availabilities on the Red or the Blue. Nevertheless, in the NBC board room, there were no snide remarks about rich men's sons running competitive networks. So far, the young man who headed the recently-formed Columbia Phonograph Broadcasting System was doing all the right things, and although he hadn't even reached his 30th birthday, he seemed to be a person of considerable substance.

Still, the young man appeared a David going against NBC's Goliath in those closing years of the 1920s. It was the kind of challenge deep in the grain of certain sons of immigrants. William Paley was that kind of son. His father, Sam, had come from Russia and built a successful cigar manufacturing business in Chicago and moved it to Philadelphia. After graduation in 1922 from the University of Pennsylvania's Wharton School, he went to work for the family-owned Congress Cigar Company. One of young Paley's first major decisions, committing the firm to a radio program on WCAU, was made when his father and uncle were out of the country. Following the custom of the day, the show was named after the Congress Cigar Company's top-of-the-line stogie, the *La Palina Hour*. Returning and spotting the $50.00 per-program-cost entry in the books, Paley's uncle ordered the broadcasts cancelled. When listeners protested the move, the *La Palina Hour* returned to WCAU. Meanwhile, Sam Paley had been asked by a friend, prominent Philadelphia contractor, Jerome Louchheim, to buy time on a newly-formed small network, United Independent Broadcasters, in which Louchheim had controlling interest. The elder Paley went along with the proposal and the UIB network added a new program, the *La Palina Smoker* to its schedule.

Under the care and feeding of William Paley, the *La Palina Smoker* developed into a respectable weekly half-hour variety package featuring a comedian, a studio orchestra and a girl singer, dubbed Miss La Palina. During his association with the show—aimed at stopping the skidding sales of cigars in the face of rising cigarette popularity—Paley became familiar with the financial plight of the United Independent Broadcasters chain. UIB founder Arthur Judson, who managed an artists' bureau, agreed to change the network's name to the Columbia Phonograph Broadcasting System, in return for the recording Company's financial backing. To celebrate the network's new ownership, a spectacular premier took place September 18, 1927. Unlike NBC's something-for-everyone gala, Columbia's opener went highbrow with *The King's Henchmen*, a specially-commissioned opera by Deems Taylor and Edna St. Vincent Millay.

Despite its gaudy opening night, losses continued to mount as CPBS tried to do battle with NBC. After losses of $220,000 in its first year as the Columbia Broadcasting System—now minus the "phonograph"—

Louchheim wanted out and approached the elder Paley. Sam Paley said, no—he was more interested in converting America's cigarette smokers to La Palina cigars than rescuing sinking radio networks. His son, William, however, had ideas of his own:

> I became tremendously excited at the prospect, and the network's shaky condition did not deter me. It was the great promise of radio itself that impelled me to act and to act immediately. I did not know what it would cost to buy in control or whether Louchheim would sell it to me. But I had the money to buy it . . . a million dollars of my own and I was willing to risk any or all of it in radio.[14]

Paley subsequently acquired controlling stock and became president of the Columbia Broadcasting System in September, 1928. Sixteen affiliates were on the initial CBS roster. It was hardly a national network, with heavy concentration in the northeast and mid-west and nothing further west than Iowa:

WOR, New York	WJAS, Pittsburgh
WCAU, Philadelphia	WADC, Akron
WNAC, Boston	WAIU, Columbus
WMAQ, Chicago	WFBL, Syracuse
KMOX, St. Louis	WMAK, Buffalo
WKRC, Cincinnati	KOIL, Council Bluffs, Ia.
WCAO, Baltimore	WGPH, Detroit
WOWO, Fort Wayne	WEAN, Providence

The disdain with which the new network was regarded by NBC was revealed to Paley when he sought a meeting with NBC president, Merlin H. Aylesworth, so they could get to know each other and discuss the future of radio. But, as Paley recalls in his autobiography, the word came back,

> He didn't want to meet me, because if he did, that would mean that they were acknowledging us as competition. As a matter of policy, NBC did not recognize CBS, just as any established nation might not recognize a newly formed state. He wanted to keep it that way. Aylesworth said we were too small . . .[15]

Merlin H. Aylesworth soon learned NBC not only had a competitor, but a redoubtable one. Paley surrounded himself with a cadre of bright young men who were as dedicated as he. There is little doubt his youthful staff felt that one of the best ways to overcome NBC's lead was through popular music. (We shall look more closely at this weapon in Paley's quiver in subsequent chapters.) Slowly, more advertisers started coming aboard and word was spreading through the broadcasting establishment that Paley and Company knew what they were doing. By January 1929, three months after William Paley had taken command, Columbia's affiliate family had grown to 49.

Like every successful radio executive involved in programming, he paid attention to everything that went on the air. Paley's penchant for personal involvement in programming became his most identifiable business idiosyncrasy—an obsession he was to carry over to television. No detail was too small to escape the attention of the cigar-man turned radio-man. An episode that occurred at Guy Lombardo's Roosevelt Grill opening in the autumn of 1929 illustrates Paley's innate grasp of what listeners would stand for and what they would not. Paley had a table near the bandstand so he could check microphone placement, cues and the like. During the broadcast, David Ross, a rising young announcer on one of his first important assignments, commented at length between numbers on their composers and their origins—an occupational quirk thought at the time essential to the announcing brotherhood. As soon as the broadcast ended, Paley fired him. Such listener empathy, plus his talent for balancing the demands of hard-nosed advertisers with those of thin-skinned performing artists, would serve him well as he prepared for the bigger battles with NBC that lay ahead in the years to come.[16]

During the late 1920s when William Paley was formulating his early ideas on programming, it should be pointed out, American popular music tastes were shaped by a white Tin Pan Alley establishment: white composers and publishers producing product for white artists performing for white consumers. With only a few exceptions, this was especially true in radio. But they were notable ones, and CBS was involved with two of them.

NOTES

1. Quoted in Gleason Archer. *Big Business and Radio*. American Historical Company, (New York), 1939, p. 276.
2. ———. "New WEAF offers a Gala Program," *The New York Times*, November 16, 1926, p. 22.
3. ———. "The NBC Story," *Sponsor*, May 16, 1966, p. 74.
4. John Gunther. *Taken at the Flood*. Popular Library, (New York), 1961, p. 176.
5. Blanch Bloch. "Music in the Air," *The Nation*, June 5, 1929, pp. 670–671.
6. 1927 *Edition of the Sears Catalogue*. Ed. by Alan Merken. Crown Publishers, (New York), 1970, p. 707.
7. Catalog No. 14, Radio Specialty Co., New York, 1926.
8. ———. "Denies Increasing Broadcasts in East," *The New York Times*, December 15, 1977, p. 26.
9. ———. "Radio Receivers Total 12,000,000", *The New York Times*, Section X, May 13, 1928, p. 13.
10. Rudy Vallee. *My Time Is Your Time*. Ivan Obolensky, (New York), 1962, p. 63.
11. *Ibid.* p. 64.
12. *Ibid.* p. 82.
13. ———. "Listening In," *The New York Times*, Section X, May 18, 1930, p. 8.
14. William Paley. *As It Happened*. Doubleday, (New York), 1979, pp. 34–35.
15. *Ibid.* pp. 41–42.
16. The story of William Paley's hand on the CBS throttle, guiding it to become a conglom-

erate approaching $3 billion by 1980, has become a legend in the American business folio. For further reading of CBS history, see *Look Now, Pay Later: The Rise of Network Broadcasting,* by Laurence Bergreen, (Doubleday, 1980) and *The Powers That Be,* by David Halberstam, (Alfred A. Knopf, 1979). Paley's memoir, *As It Happened,* (Doubleday, 1979), appeared shortly after Halberstam's book. An excerpt of *The Powers That Be* in *Atlantic* magazine two years earlier may have prompted Paley to get his version of events on the record. Paley's very title, *As It Happened,* seems aimed at countering Halberstam's heavy-with-warts work.

CHAPTER 3

Direct from Broadway and Harlem

NEW YORK WAS THE place to be if you were a musician in the late 1920s. Network radio had created a demand for players of every musical inclination. As the Eastern hub of show business, New York was especially appealing to young instrumentalists like the Dorsey brothers, Benny Goodman, Jack Teagarden and Red Nichols. They used their network staff orchestra jobs as bases, while playing in dance orchestras and recording in freelance pop groups. There was only one catch—you had to be white. "Blacks need not apply" was the unwritten rule. Blacks knew radio studio work was out of the question. Nevertheless, there was a way to circumvent radio's initial studio color ban. This special kind of broadcast on which black artists were able to appear provided early evidence that there *was* pluralism to American popular music, and if it was denied expression one way, it would find another. But before we explore the first sounds of black music on the air, it is necessary to turn back briefly to the beginning of the decade.

Negro musicians who came North after World War I were taking serious professional risks. The color code was rigidly enforced, and unless a black musician was part of a segregated traveling vaudeville unit, his opportunities were severely circumscribed. There was never any question that white-only orchestras should play behind the potted palms of restaurants, hotel dining rooms and dancing salons. The Original Dixieland Jazz Band, an all-white quintet, had shaken up New York in 1918 by introducing a sanitized form of black music. It was quasi-New Orleans jazz the

41

ODJB played. Its rhythmic base was an infectious two-beat, and it was fun to dance to. Meanwhile, orchestra leaders Paul Whiteman (who had come up with a curious symphonic-jazz-pop hybrid) and Vincent Lopez (who combined personal showmanship and his tinkling piano) with their fox trot creations, were properly in tune with the emerging dancing craze. New dance emporiums opened up all over town. Speakeasies, those legendary by-products of Prohibition, gained special status by offering music for dancing until the early morning hours—by white groups.

Thus, to open a new club in mid-town New York in 1923 and book a black band had to be foolhardiness of the highest order or *avant-guardism* of the chicest kind. Still, these were the 1920s, and an all-white clientele might find the idea fascinating. Such a spot was the Club Alabam, located in the downstairs portion of the 44th Street Theater Building (current site of expanded *New York Times* offices). The premier bill was called "The Creole Follies," starring Edith Wilson, a black vaudeville star, and "Fletcher Henderson and His Famous Club Alabam Orchestra." How Henderson's band could have become "famous" with previously limited exposure was the handiwork of WHN, one of Gotham's early stations. WHN had pioneered the placing of radio wires into cabarets and dance halls, thus beefing up their program schedule with (free) popular music. WHN's regular broadcasts from Club Alabam, one of radio's first outlets for a Negro band, were hardly grounds to declare Henderson "famous" at that stage of his career. But without the WHN airshots, he may have never become one of the important figures of American popular music.

Born in Georgia in 1898, Fletcher Henderson graduated with degrees in chemistry and mathematics. His father, a high school principal, and his mother, a piano teacher, saw to it that their son's musical training began at age six. Encouraged to continue his scientific training, he came to Columbia University in 1920 to work toward a masters degree. Short of funds, the young graduate student-pianist took a song demonstrator's job with Pace and Handy. Through his employers, W.C. Handy ("Father of the Blues") and Harry Pace (who later formed the first Negro-owned recording firm, Swan Records), Henderson encountered many black entertainers and songsmiths.

Henderson met Ethel Waters in 1922 and was persuaded to organize a small band to accompany the singer on a tour, set up primarily to sell Swan records. An obligatory stop on such tours was New Orleans' Lyric Theater. (The Lyric is the black vaudeville house so admirably depicted in the 1980 revue, *One Mo' Time.*) Waters, Henderson and Company were such a smash hit at the Lyric that the *New Orleans Item* arranged a radio broadcast. Tradition has it this was the first appearance of a Negro on radio. According to the *Item's* front page story,

Every shoulder twitched and every foot beat time Friday evening among the people who crowded the rooms of WVG, the *Item*-Interstate radio broadcasting station, when Ethel Waters, the nationally-known negro singer and her famous Black Swan jazz masters opened upon the radio transmitter. A few unoccupied chairs even edged a little in an attempt to keep time with the music.[1]

WVG's broadcast made news as far away as Savannah, Georgia, where a newspaper claimed,

The concert was heard in five states and in Mexico, and thousands of radio fans listened to a colored girl sing through the air. Miss Waters, who has broken many records on this trip, adds another star to her laurels by being the first colored girl to sing over the radio. She was accompanied by the Black Swan Jazz Masters, under the direction of F.B. Henderson, Jr.[2]

When Henderson returned to New York at the conclusion of the Waters tour, he continued making recordings. In January, 1924, Henderson got the Club Alabam job and the important WHN remotes that went with it.

It is not possible to overstress the significance of WHN as a prime carrier of popular music in the 1920s. The station's remotes also served as unique showcases for bookers to audition orchestral possibilities. Owned by Loew's Theaters, and hence with a show business orientation, WHN featured a steady diet of remotes. *Variety* recognized this soon after it began covering radio. In an early review, the entertainment bible noted, "WHN went through the usual schedule of switching from one cabaret to another to broadcast dance music." *

Sent to announce many WHN remote broadcasts was an employee named Nils T. Granlund (later known as N.T.G., the producer) who doubled as the station's public relations director. He was also an early champion of black bands. Without Granlund's continuing efforts, Fletcher Henderson (and other Negro orchestras) would have received even less on-air exposure. Thanks to the Club Alabam job and the airshots that went with it, the operators of Roseland, a leading New York ballroom, booked Fletcher Henderson and His Orchestra for an engagement during the summer of 1924.

Roseland, an important location in the dance band business, was transplanted from Philadelphia to New York (Broadway at 51st Street). Moving Roseland was the idea of Louis J. Brecker, a University of Pennsylvania student, who made the decision to avoid Pennsylvania's Sunday Blue Laws. Brecker, who opened Roseland New Year's Eve, 1919, was determined to run a tight ship and avoid the reputation many ballrooms

---

* The same review also made reference to a black group, "The Clarence Williams Radio Trio and Blue Three, featuring Eva Taylor in indigo ditties." (*Variety*, December 24, 1924, p. 35).

had as trysting spots. Dating and married couples could enjoy an evening of the 1920s favorite pastime, and for ten cents a dance, stags could glide over the floor with a Roseland "hostess." In this connection, Brecker's no-nonsense policy called for careful screening, and once hired, hostesses were subject to strict supervision. (Ruby Keeler, the story goes, was a hostess when she met Al Jolson at Roseland.)

Newspaper listings often showed WHN broadcasts from the ballroom as "The Roseland Dance Orchestra," which did not mean Fletcher Henderson's Orchestra alone, since Roseland featured alternating bands on stands at the opposite ends of the floor. Sam Lanin's Orchestra (in other incarnations, the *Ipana Troubadours*) appeared frequently on the second bandstand. Both Henderson and Lanin played music strictly for dancing— fox trots, waltzes, tangos. As Henderson's material became increasingly jazz-oriented, Lanin's essentially sweet group veered in the same direction. Lanin alumni (Miff Mole, Red Nichols, Tommy Dorsey, et al.) who played at Roseland and went on to successful careers in popular music and jazz drew their inspiration from the Fletcher Henderson band.

Simply put, Henderson's was an all-star aggregation. Louis Armstrong, whom Henderson had heard in New Orleans during the Waters tour, left King Oliver's Creole Jazz Band to join Henderson at Roseland in late 1924; he remained for over a year. Armstrong's cornet had an energizing effect on Henderson's men. The blues style Armstrong brought from New Orleans rubbed off immediately, and so did his innate ability to inject a "swinging" quality into the playing of the entire orchestra. Henderson's sidemen had never been exposed to New Orleans traditional jazz, and Armstrong's introduction of its improvisational possibilities into the fabric of big band arrangements was an exciting thing indeed. One can only guess at the reaction of listeners, heretofore accustomed to tuning in Roseland broadcasts featuring conventional dance music, now hearing on WHN a joyous, new, stomping kind of music, thanks to Louis Armstrong's New Orleans injections.

In addition to Armstrong, Henderson attracted some of the best black musicians of the 1920s. Coleman Hawkins, Rex Stewart, Buster Bailey, Benny Carter and Jimmy Harrison were men who never became familiar names in popular music but, in different ways, they contributed to various aspects of it. Superior musicians, however, were only part of the story.

Fletcher Henderson's reputation as the "father of big band jazz" also derived from his use of written arrangements for existing pop songs and original compositions, leaving gaps for improvised solos. Until then, dance orchestras relied on "stock" scorings. Henderson himself did not write the arrangements for his band. They were the work of Don Redman, a music conservatory graduate from Ohio. A member of Henderson's saxophone section, Redman scored most of the orchestra's material for $25 an arrangement. So taken by Redman's talents was Paul Whiteman, that he plunked down $100 each for 20 arrangements. Don Redman remained as

Fletcher Henderson's chief arranger until late 1927, when the leader took over the writing, incorporating Redman's formula. (Later we will probe Benny Goodman's popularization of the Henderson/Redman technique that resulted in his crowning as the "King of Swing.")

Don Redman's pen and Louis Armstrong's crackling cornet ignited sparks in Fletcher Henderson's band and made Roseland one of the chief entertainment meccas of the 1920s. Re-inforced by the radio broadcasts, records, and word-of-mouth, it was not only the dancing crowd that came to Roseland, but the inevitable seekers of something "new"—a search that has always marked the first intimations of any change in popular music.

Although functional dance music was the main purpose of Henderson's Roseland engagements,* it was the specially-orchestrated *chefs d'oeuvre* that caused the commotion. Basic characteristics of Redman's arranging style included: call-and-response figures by the brass and reed sections, harmonized section solos and unison "riffs" behind improvising soloists. White musicians who listened on the radio or heard Henderson's orchestra in person absorbed like sponges what they heard. There were even times when Henderson himself became so entranced by what his band was playing, he forgot to play himself. White bands vied for Roseland jobs to play opposite Fletcher Henderson. One sideman who played with a band that had come from the coal regions of Pennsylvania, recalled the striking impression the experience made:

> The Scranton Sirens [including the Dorseys] were engaged as the relief band opposite what I think was the greatest Fletcher Henderson orchestra ever assembled, a real landmark in the history of jazz. It just didn't seem right to make a salary for the opportunity to hear such music![3]

Frank Driggs, the jazz historian, has put his finger on another debt American popular music owes to Henderson. His band, claims Driggs, "provided unwittingly . . . material for up-and-coming song writers who wrote out the inspired riffs or solos played by Fletcher's musicians and copyrighted them in their own names."[4]

Fletcher Henderson's popularity reached its peak between 1926 and 1928. At one point the band was broadcasting three times a week on WHN (5p.m. Sundays, 10:10p.m. Wednesdays, and 8:30p.m. Fridays) and on WOR (Fridays, 11:05p.m. and Saturdays, 3:30p.m.). It should be pointed out that remote broadcasts from such spots as Roseland in the 1920s were not limited to night time. Matinee and tea dances were quite popular and offered stations the always-reliable popular music to complete their schedules.

Variety reviewed Henderson's Roseland broadcasts from time to time

---

* White habitues only were permitted on the dance floor. Negro musicians from other orchestras who had come as patrons to hear the Henderson band were required to watch from the side, out of the view of the white dancing patrons.

as part of its radio coverage, and consistently gave the band high marks. Among the plaudits from *Variety*'s radio columnist during different engagements were these:

> . . . The Henderson band (colored) is one of the best in the field, colored or white, and dishes up a corking brand of dance music. (1924)

> Henderson's torrid syncopators are one of the station's [WHN] best orchestral offerings. (1926)

> . . . If it weren't for commercial broadcasters there would be no broadcasting worthwhile except for occasional important news and sports events. True a good dance band like Fletcher Henderson's crack colored jazzists from Roseland comes along, but the commercial programs are the mainstay. (1927)[5]

Roseland's season generally ran from Labor Day to Memorial Day. In Henderson's case, when the band went on national summer tours, it was picked up from such ballrooms along the way as Castle Farms, Cincinnati (WLW) and The Willows, Pittsburgh (KDKA). American show business is replete with indignities that Negro entertainers endured, and broadcasting was party to some of them. An incident involving the touring Henderson orchestra occurred at the Ritz Ballroom in Oklahoma City where a remote was vetoed in spite of numerous requests. No doubt why, according to a contemporary account in a Negro newspaper: "Race prejudice was the cause. The air in Oklahoma is for whites only."[6]

With his Roseland home base, regular broadcasts, a recording contract and personal appearances, all signs pointed to the arrival of the country's first black superstar pop music group. An aware white cognescenti of college students were booking the band for fraternity and prom dates at a few prestigious Eastern colleges. But at the time the band seemed to have reached the pinnacle, it was already on the way down. Lackadaisical in financial matters and eschewing self-promotion, Henderson had always had a casual attitude toward the disciplines of the business side of leading an orchestra. This trait became more pronounced after he was involved in an accident in 1929.

By the end of 1930, the entertainment world (except radio) was feeling the Depression's tightening pinch. Henderson left Roseland during the year and signed on as the house band at Connie's Inn, the Harlem night spot that was considered the Cotton Club's chief competitor. Network broadcasts from the Cotton Club by another black orchestra (which we shall get to presently), begun in 1929 by the Columbia Broadcasting System, were gaining national attention. Thus, it appeared that a CBS contract to broadcast twice weekly from Connie's Inn over the growing network was all that was needed to expose Fletcher Henderson's Orchestra to an even wider audience. William Paley and his young tigers were relying heavily at the time on popular music in their catch-up game with the two-network NBC. Henderson's initial contract with CBS called for two half-hours weekly, Mondays, 11:30p.m., and Saturdays, 8:30p.m. The radio rhythm Fletcher Henderson provided over CBS gave his reputation a further boost on campuses. College and university dates around this time included Yale, Princeton, Lehigh, Penn State, Michigan, University of Pennsylvania (Ivy Ball), Williams, Washington and Lee and Cornell. But as a commercial entity to sell to ballrooms and theaters when the big band era was on its ascendency, Henderson remained an enigma. The leader broke up and re-organized his outfit several times in the early 1930s. After holding together for a short-run 1934 edition (considered the last of the great Henderson orchestras), he turned to arranging. Ironically, Fletcher Henderson's most important contribution to popular music would come in a behind-the-scenes role for Benny Goodman, a role we shall look at more definitively when we get to Swing.

Elsewhere, as Henderson was trying to make ends meet, one of his contemporaries who gave 1920s radio its other important shot of black music, was already an international celebrity. Edward Kennedy Ellington, who had come from Washington, D.C. to New York, was jobbing around at the same time as Fletcher Henderson in the early 1920s. The newly-arrived Washingtonian described Henderson's outfit as "the greatest dance band, playing some formidable music"; it was Ellington's early model. Their careers had a certain parallel. About the time Henderson was playing his first important engagement at Club Alabam, Duke Ellington's small band was booked into the Kentucky Club, a high class speakeasy, at 49th Street and Broadway. Although only in his early 20s, Duke—so named for his fastidious habits of dress—was already writing original compositions, following both the 32-bar Tin Pan Alley form and the traditional 12-bar blues.

Ellington's small Kentucky Club combo started gaining attention as celebrity types, many of whom had heard the band's post-midnight remotes on WHN, came in increasing numbers. "All kinds of people mixed there," former Ellington drummer, Sonny Greer recalled. "Show people, socialites, debutantes, musicians and racketeers."[7] One of the Kentucky Club regulars was Jimmy McHugh, the song writer. McHugh became so enchanted with the Duke's Kentucky Club band, that he convinced the management of Harlem's renowned Cotton Club to book it.

Ellington's subsequent five-year engagement at the Cotton Club, with its network radio wire, not only launched the career of one of America's leading musical originals, it also made possible the first important national propagation of popular music by a black group. (WHN, that remote pioneer, had already been broadcasting pick-ups of Andy Preer's Cotton Club Syncopators in 1925.) However, it was the CBS broadcasts more than any other factor that put the Cotton Club and Duke Ellington into the big time. Tunes for Ellington's airshots came directly from the Cotton Club floor shows, those extravagantly mounted productions that constituted a vital part of the colorful New York entertainment scene of the late 1920s. Jimmy McHugh and Dorothy Fields (daughter of comedian Lew Fields) wrote the Cotton Club shows during Duke's first few years, beginning with his opening, December 4, 1927. Later Harold Arlen and Ted Koehler* took over the writing chores. A chorus line (no darker than light olive), tap dancers and an emcee made up the all-Negro casts, with emphasis always on the music. Marshall Stearns, the jazz and dance historian, who as a student went to the Club, described the floor shows as "an incredible mishmash of talent and nonsense which might well fascinate both sociologists and psychiatrists." He recalled one where,

> A light-skinned and magnificently muscled negro burst through a papier-maché jungle on to the dance floor, clad in an aviator's helmet, goggles, and shorts. He had obviously, been "forced down in darkest Africa," and in the center of the floor, he came upon a "white" goddess . . . being worshipped by a circle of cringing blacks . . . the aviator rescued the blonde, and they did an erotic dance. In the background . . . members of the Ellington band growled, wheezed, and snorted obscenely.[8]

The shows on more than one occasion sought to create jungle atmospheres; hence, the motif that runs through many of Ellington's compositions from that period—"Jungle Jamboree," "Echoes of the Jungle," "Jungle Blues."

It was at the Cotton Club that the "Ellington sound" was created. Whether on a fragment of ephemera, or on one of his own compositions, Ellington's arrangements were scored to take advantage of his versatile sidemen (Johnny Hodges, Harry Carney, "Tricky Sam" Nanton, Bubber Miley, et al.). His instrument, it has been said, was his orchestra. An Ellington cult was not long in starting. On one occasion,

> . . . the entire brass section of the band rose and played such an intricate and beautiful chorus that the usually poised and dignified Eddie Duchin actually rolled under the table in ecstasy.[9]

Marshall Stearns has claimed that only gangsters, whites, and Negro celebrities were admitted to the Cotton Club. It was 1920s chic at its rarest. One *New York Daily News* account noted,

> One can call the roll of guests from the Blue Book of Broadway and the Social Register. Emily Vanderbilt has enjoyed the show . . . Paul Whiteman has steered his dinner-coated tonnage there many a time. Hosts of other celebrities and near celebrities have killed the hours that lie between

---

* Cab Calloway claims in his autobiography, "Dorothy Fields wasn't really funky enough to write the kind of songs that would carry a Negro revue. The real down-to-earth Cotton Club shows, with the double-entendre nasty songs and the hurly-burly and bump-and-grind mixed with high-class swinging jazz, were produced by Harold Arlen and Ted Koehler."

the last act on Broadway and poached eggs in the a.m. inside the Cotton Club's riotous precincts.[10]

Duke Ellington called the Cotton Club,

A classy spot. Impeccable behavior was demanded in the room while the show was on. If someone was talking loud while Leitha Hill, for example, was singing, the waiter would come and touch him on the shoulder. If that didn't do it, the captain would come over and admonish him politely. The headwaiter would remind him that he had been cautioned. After that, if the loud talker still continued, somebody would come and throw him out.[11]

The regular CBS early evening broadcasts of 1929 and 1930 that spurred the crowds on to the Cotton Club were the first encounters most white Americans had with black music. Announcer Ted Husing (and occasionally Norman Brokenshire and David Ross) helped transmit the night spot's ambiance through the ether. But it was the McHugh-Fields/Arlen-Koehler/Ellington music, conjuring up images of sophistication and glamor, that made the Cotton Club a premier entertainment attraction. Unlike most of the era's popular music broadcasts, accompanied by stiff and pretentious continuity, Ellington's Cotton Club remotes were put together in a casual way. Duke Ellington describes in his autobiography the kind of informality that prevailed and the sort of response the CBS (and later NBC) broadcasts evoked:

We recorded ["Mood Indigo"], and that night at the Cotton Club, when it was almost time for our broadcast, Ted Husing the announcer, asked, "Duke, what are we going to play tonight?" I told him about the new number, and we played it on the air, six pieces out of the eleven-piece band. The next day wads of mail came in, raving about the new tune, so Irving Mills [Ellington's manager] put a lyric on it and royalties are still coming in . . . more than forty years later.[12]

When Duke Ellington left the Cotton Club he was succeeded by Cab Calloway who recognized the importance of radio to his predecessor's career ("People all over the country used to tune in almost nightly to this hip, swinging band from New York City.") and to his own ("We were on the radio almost every night when we were in the club, and Ted Husing, the announcer, always gave us a big build-up.").[13]

Both CBS and NBC continued to carry Cotton Club remotes until the Harlem site (second floor, northeast corner, of Lenox Avenue and 142nd Street) closed in 1936. On-location broadcasts resumed at the club's new address, Broadway and 48th Street. But by that time, listeners were taking dance band remotes for granted. Those from the new Cotton Club sounded no different from the thousands that were being cranked out over four national networks. For The Bandstand had now become the shrine of popular music worshippers. And radio made it easy getting there.

NOTES

1. Quoted in Walter C. Allen. *Hendersonia*, Jazz Monographs No. 4 (Highland Park, N.J.), 1973, p. 29.
2. *Ibid.* p. 29.
3. Quoted in Howard J. Waters. *Jack Teagarden's Music,* Walter C. Allen, (Stanhope, N.J.), 1960, p. 15.
4. Frank Driggs. Brochure accompanying *The Fletcher Henderson Story: A Study in Frustration,* Columbia Thesaurus of Classic Jazz, C4L19.
5. *Variety,* July 30, 1924, p. 36/November 17, 1926, p. 44/November 23, 1927, p. 55.
6. Walter C. Allen, *op. cit.* p. 222.
7. Quoted in brochure accompanying *The Ellington Era, Vol.* 2, Columbia Records, C3L39.
8. Marshall Stearns. *The Story of Jazz,* New American Library, (New York), 1958, p. 133.
9. Jim Haskins. *The Cotton Club.* Random House, (New York), 1977, p. 53.
10. Quoted in Allen Schoener Allen, (ed.). *Harlem on My Mind,* Random House, (New York), 1968, pp. 83–84.
11. Duke Ellington. *Music Is My Mistress,* Doubleday (New York), 1973, p. 80.
12. *Ibid.* p. 79.
13. Cab Calloway and Bryant Robbins. *Of Minnie the Moocher and Me,* Crowell, (New York), 1976, pp. 93 & 110.

TWO 1920S EDITIONS OF THE 'RADIO MUSIC BOX'

A 1923 Radiola III

(Courtesy RCA)

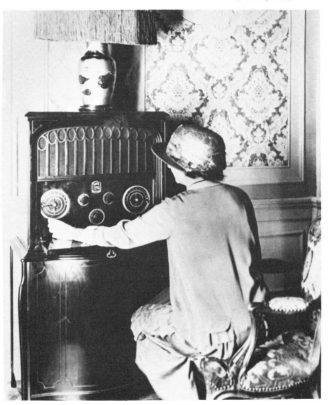

A 1927 Radiola VII

(Courtesy RCA)

KWCR (later WMT) Cedar Rapids, Iowa broadcasting equipment, c. 1922.

Corner of Smaller Studio Both KWCR studio have double glass windows opening on a wide corridor and reception room alcove where the public may watch the performers and announcers ~

(Courtesy WMT)

Live performances made up the majority of local radio programs in the 1920s.

53

(Courtesy WISN)

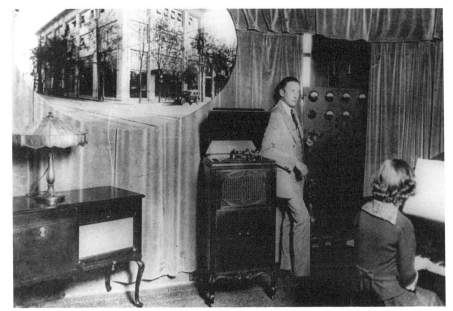

Although "live" music predominated in musical radio of the 1920s, many stations maintained phonographs for emergencies. In early broadcasting, when recordings were played, the microphone was held up against the phonograph speaker. Studios shown belonged to KFI, Los Angeles in above photo and KWCR (later WMT), Cedar Rapids below.

Pop music of the 1920s was sometimes called "potted palm" music because points of origin such as radio studios and hotel bandstands were decorated with potted palms.

RADIO DANCE ORCHESTRA PIONEERS OF THE 1920S

Vincent Lopez
is generally credited as the first dance orchestra leader to do a "remote" broadcast. It took place in November, 1921 over WJZ, New York.

George Olsen
a big favorite in radio's first decade, was one of several leaders who organized a band as a student. When Olsen left the University of Michigan, he kept his band intact.

Guy Lombardo
Inspired by the Coon-Sanders broadcasts, Canadian Guy Lombardo came to Cleveland to begin his radio career in the mid-1920s. He went on to become network radio's most enduring popular music figure.

Bert Lown
Behind many a pop music star stood a benefactor-cheerleader. Rudy Vallee's was Bert Lown. Lown in his own right led off the more popular bands on the air in the late 1920s and early 1930s.

Duke Ellington
Remotes from the legendary Cotton Club over CBS in the late 1920s gave Duke Ellington's career its first big boost.

Eddie Duchin
"Society" orchestra leader Eddie Duchin often joined other white celebrities at the Cotton Club to hear Ellington's "Jungle Music."

(All Photos this page courtesy Steve Tassia)

The Coon-Sanders Nighthawks' late night live broadcasts originating from Kansas City's Hotel Muehlebach were heard in many states as early as 1924, thanks to WDAF's strong signal. By the end of the decade, the Nighthawks were among the most popular radio entertainers.

Across the country, dozens of stations were capitalizing on the dancing craze of the 1920s. WMT's first remote broadcast August 30, 1924 featured Guy Clark's Orchestra from Cedar Rapids' Dreamland Ballroom.

EARLY NBC NETWORK FAVORITES WERE POPULAR MUSIC STARS

(Author's collection)

The "Cliquot Club Eskimos," one of NBC's original shows, was a pop-novelty group led by Harry Reser, (c.)

(author's collection)

(author's collection)

Radio's pioneer song-and-patter men, Billy Jones (l.) and Ernie Hare (r.) were on NBC's first schedule. They billed themselves as the "Happiness Boys" and later the "Interwoven Pair."

Rudy Vallee was one of the first popular music artists to become a radio "personality." His *Fleischmann Hour* began in 1929 on NBC.

Part Two
(1930—1947)

IDOLS OF THE AIRLANES

"The most active unit of radio is the dance band. Day and night it is on the air to lull the country into contentment or rouse it from its lethargy, with the persistent drum beat or whoops of saxophones . . . Most of the band leaders owe their success to broadcasting. Until the advent of radio their popularity was confined to the areas of the honky-tonk dance hall. Today they have become household gods from one end of the land to the other, slowing up or quickening their tempo to satisfy an admiring public."

—ROBERT WEST. *The Rape of Radio.* Rodin Publishing Co., 1941.

CHAPTER 4

Bandstand USA

WHEN THE NEW YEAR'S EVE dance orchestra broadcasts that welcomed in 1930 moved westward across the time zones, 4,428,000 more radio sets were in American homes than were there a year earlier. Sales of units in 1929 set a record that would not be equalled until 1935. "Radio is now a musical instrument," Orrin E. Dunlap, Jr., the *New York Times* first radio editor, wrote in previewing the 1930–31 model year. "Long distance tuning is no longer the most desired factor in a radio set's performance. Tone is what the listeners want and that is what the set builders are planning to give the new 1930–31 instruments. Tone will be the key-note of the 1930 radio campaign." [1]

Such tonal improvements could only help the popular music cause. By the time Mr. Dunlap made his discovery, most of his fellow countrymen, who comprised an audience that had grown from an estimated 16,000,000 in 1925 to 60,000,000 in 1930, had already recognized radio as a *musical instrument*. Radio's pre-eminence in this regard had much to do with the medium's 89% increase in advertising revenues between 1929 and 1931, while the older media slipped badly—newspaper advertising by a whopping 21%.

Local stations and the national networks, without the benefit of ratings, correctly divined public taste and continued to pour out a steady stream of popular music. Testifying before a Senate committee in early 1930, William Paley, president of the new Columbia Broadcasting System, produced a chart* to show his rising network's allocation of time for major program types:

Dramatic - 3%
Civic - 2%
Religious - 4%
Instructive -14%
Symphony/Opera/Chamber Music -26%
Popular Music -29% [2]

Paley described CBS as "a child of the public." He attributed the network's growth to "giving the people a service which they sincerely want and genuinely appreciate."

Whatever reasoning Paley used to make popular music the leading program type on the infant CBS network was no less apparent in the heartland. Almost a continent away in Butte, Montana, KGIR's program schedule was typical of stations without network affiliations. Left to its own devices, KGIR, like outlets in cities large and small, relied heavily on popular music. On an average day in 1930, popular music filled 30% of the broadcast schedule:

"K G I R"
Thursday Program Set-Up

7:00 A.M.   Popular Music
            Road Conditions
            Newscasting
            Time Service

8:00 A.M.   MARKET HOUR (old time Music)
            Miner's Diary
            New Method Laundry
            Gallagher's
            Grains of Gold
            Home Baking

9:00 A.M.   W.P. Fuller & Company (Popular Music)

9:30 A.M.   BLOCK WASHER COMPANY (Hawaiian Music)

10:00 A.M. MONTANA POWER COMPANY (Concert trio)

10:30 A.M. GAMER SHOE COMPANY (Popular Music)

---

* This was the first of many charts the Columbia Broadcasting System would bring to Washington to testify before Congressional committees in the next half-century. Not only did CBS dazzle Madison Avenue with its slick sales presentations, Paley's bright young men prepared eye-catching pitches for House and Senate groups. Politicians early in the game were aware that hearings "looking into" broadcasting matters were always good for some extra newspaper attention. Things hadn't changed much fifty years later.

11:00 A.M.   ELLIS PAINT COMPANY (Organ)

11:30 A.M.   LUBIN'S SAMPLE STORE (Popular Music)

12 NOON   CHILDREN'S LUNCHEON CLUB PROGRAM
             Conducted by Uncle Nibs.

12:30 P.M.   FARM   FLASHES—MONTANA   PRESS   RELEASE—
             WEATHER

12:45 P.M.   KGIR NEWS 'ON THE AIR TODAY'

1:00 P.M.   CLOROX COMPANY (Popular)

1:15 P.M.   MONTANA CEREAL COMPANY "

1:30 P.M.   HOUSEKEEPER'S CHATS Dept. Agriculture
             Recipe Exchange by lady-listeners.

2:00 P.M.   ANNOUNCEMENT & AFTERNOON DANCE PERIOD
             Food Emporium   Mirror Hosiery
             Shirley's   Paxon-Rockefeller
             Reisch   Better Service Station
             Heath Baking   Beaty Bug House

3:00 P.M.   KNOW THE WORLD HOUR
             A Story of a different city everyday
             (Organ background)

3:30 P.M.   BAND CONCERT

4:00 P.M.   DEER LODGE HOUR (Popular Music)
             Keystone Drug
             LaRose Beauty Shop

4:30 P.M.   ANACONDA HOUR (Semi Classical)
             McConnel Electric
             Unique Cleaners

5:00 P.M.   SERVICE HOUR (Popular Music)
             No. American Pub. Corp.
             Standard Motor (Ford)
             David E. Anderson (Firestone)
             Mary McDonald (A & W Rootbeer)
             Largey Lumber
             World Bookman
             News
             Road Conditions

6:00 P.M.   YOUNG FOLKS HAPPY HOUR Conducted by Cousin
             Carl & Air Castle' Electrical transcription.

6:30 P.M.   DENVER BETTER BUSINESS BUREAU

6:45 P.M.   GAMER SHOE NUNN-BUSH PROGRAM

7:00 P.M.   DINNER HOUR Studio Orchestra
             CECIL & SALLY (Electrical Transcription)

Al's Photo Shop	Spillman & Warwick
Snell Spring Service	Texaco Oil Company
Crystal Creamery	N.P. Railway Co.
Montana Auto & Garage	Strain Bros. Dept. Store
The Hat Box	News, Weather & Time

8:00 P.M.	SARGON Electrically transcribed
8:30 P.M.	OLD-TIME " "
9:00 P.M.	TOM & WASH " "
	Gallagher Whix-Way Food Store
9:15 P.M.	RADIO BAFFLERS (Mystery Play)
9:45 P.M.	GOOD NEWS MAGAZINE
10:00 P.M.	U.S. BUILDING & LOAN REQUEST HOUR
11:00 P.M.	THE GOOFS CLUB.[3]

Butte, Montana's popular music tastes were in tune with the rest of the country and KGIR was in step with programming strategy across the dial where dance music dominated. In pre-*Hit Parade* and pre-Top 40 days, the most reliable barometer of popularity were record sales—and to a lesser degree, sheet music sales. In *Variety's* regular charting of recording sales, dance orchestras dominated. Overwhelmingly. It was the same story after *Your Hit Parade* hit the airwaves and *Variety* logged network airplay: public preference for songs between 1930 and 1945 leaned heavily toward those the bands played.

The term, *dance orchestra,* was uniquely 1920s nomenclature, and by the early 1930s, had faded from use, to be replaced by *big bands,* or *name bands.* But the big band was still a *dance* band and popular music remained primarily a function of dancing. "Big" band was not merely a case of terminology; dance units were getting bigger. Orchestras at this time were adding an extra instrument or two to their brass and reed sections. Basic changes were also taking place in the *sound* of the bands: the string bass was gradually replacing the tuba; and the banjo was being phased out in favor of the accoustical guitar. These substitutions in the rhythm section helped fashion an entirely different texture to the music, as 1920s vo-de-oh-do and razz-ma-tazz gave way to a more polished and softened surface.

When it came to the leader, the French proverb was never truer: *Plus ca change, plus c'est la même chose.* He was still the big man in music and getting more powerful all the time. Radio's growing audience, although more discriminating than earlier d-x fanatics but obviously approving trends set in the 1920s, helped increase the prestige of the dance orchestras. Established bandleaders, aware of the medium's power and their own ability to influence music tastes, knew the road map indicated only one route to continued fame and fortune, and it read R-A-D-I-O. To novices, the musical vistas looked bleak: breaking into the popular music business (a not very promising project as the widening Depression touched all phases of American life in the early 1930s) required being heard on the radio. And that usually meant having something to do with a dance band. A musical tale of two cities best illustrates the point.

First, the big city version. In 1930, a Rutgers law student named Oswald Nelson was still leading the band that helped him pay his undergraduate bills. After listening one night to a regularly scheduled dance band program, *Roemer's Homers Radio Hour,* Nelson decided his eight-piece unit sounded every bit as good as the one on WMCA. He went into action. Evidently having benefited from his education in the finer points of advocacy, Nelson talked the WMCA manager into giving him an audition. Station and sponsor liked Nelson's octet and so began Milton Roemer's quest of better furniture sales—and Ozzie Nelson's quest for greater show biz glory. After the show had been on the air a while, the *New York Daily Mirror* started a dance band popularity contest. (Newspapers at the time often ran such contests to increase circulation.) Nelson quickly discovered that Milton Roemer understood what impact popular music (and some imaginative hype) could have in the marketplace. The sponsor, who was involved in every detail of his show, learned from a dealer in Newark that newspaper vendors were given credit for unsold copies if they returned first pages. Whereupon Mr. Roemer acquired thousands of the unsold tabloids, hired a crew to clip the ballots, filled in Ozzie Nelson's name, and sent them to the newspaper.

Roemer's ballot-box stuffing in the *New York Daily Mirror's* Most Popular Bandleader contest was the nudge that Nelson needed. Taking the contest results with him, the resourceful furniture dealer appeared before the Westchester County Park Commission to plead the signing of Ozzie Nelson and His Orchestra as the opening attraction for the new Glen Island Casino. The Board concluded that a band which finished ahead of Rudy Vallee's and all the other big network favorites had to be the one. And so it came to pass, as Nelson recounts in his autobiography,

> I became the first name bandleader to play at the famous Glen Island Casino—the cradle of more name bands than any other dance spot in the world . . . Our opening night was a dream come true. It seemed as if everyone in town was there: Paul Whiteman, Vincent Lopez, Fred Waring, Will Osborne, Ted Lewis, Morton Downey—yes, and even Rudy Vallee himself . . . We were [now] broadcasting coast to coast over the CBS network. Before the evening was over, recording executive Jack Kapp had offered us a contract to record on the Brunswick label.[4]

In dozens of smaller cities such as York, Pennsylvania, dance units played out another kind of radio story in the early 1930s. Local musical groups vied for exposure whenever a new outlet came on the air and one was generally chosen to be that station's house band. Regular broadcasts several times a day made these units the town's first radio celebrities along with the announcers. Thus did Bernard Hochberger and His Orchestra become the staff band at York's first radio station, WORK. Guitar, saxophone, drums, two trumpets and Hochberger's violin made up the band's instrumentation. Harold Miller* who was a staff announcer when WORK went on the air in early 1932 remembered having the Hochberger orchestra at the station's beginning. Every day, six days a week, until the middle 1940s, Hochberger's boys ground out half-hour dance music programs at noon and at 5 p.m. In the middle of the afternoon, they became Bernard Hochberger's Ensemble, playing classical selections. Miller's chief recollection of the band was the repetition factor:

> By having our studio orchestra on the air every day, at the same times, with the same music, by the same musicians, they sounded alike in everything they did. After a while, to get some variety on the station, we developed quarter hours of trios, duets, and the like. We also built a daily program of popular music, featuring the band's regular pianist and myself. We called these shows, *Four Hands Open,* the significance of the title being we were open to requests.[5]

Radio's dependence on bands as the primary source of popular music was heavy throughout the 1930s. In cities of all sizes, this meant a listener could tune in virtually any hour, day or night, and hear one. Abel Green, *Variety's* leading band reviewer and one of the popular music's most astute critics right through the 1950s, observed,

> Say what you will, the average radio fan prefers a straight dance combo to anything else. The practical side for this figures. Average household turns on and either devotes its time to dinner, or reading a paper, or having a cocktail, or just a chinfest, none of which elements favor attention to any lyrics or dialog.[6]

It was not uncommon to find dance music standard daytime network fare. An analysis of the CBS schedule for March 8, 1932 lists only three quarterhours of sponsored programs between 12 noon and 6:30 p.m. Of the remaining time periods Columbia devoted no less than three hours in part or totally to dance music:

12N–12:30—Charles Boulanger with Young's
                    Restaurant Orchestra

---

* Miller actually joined the staff as a pianist. He had just graduated from Cincinnati Conservatory of Music, and without those credentials, he says, he could never have gotten the job. Shortly afterward, boasting "There was nothing to announcing," he got his chance, won the job, went on to become program director, and then station manager.

12:30–1:00—Columbia Revue with Vincent
                 Sorey's Orchestra
1:00–1:30—George Hall's Hotel Taft Orchestra
4:00–4:15—Rhythm Kings
4:30–5:00—George Hall's Orchestra
5:00–5:15—Fred Berren's Orchestra
6:00–6:15—Freddie Rich's Orchestra
6:15–6:30—Fred Berren's Orchestra[7]

Whatever other strengths they may have added to program schedules in the early 1930s, the bands served as welcome antidotes to one of the darkest periods in the nation's history. One needed only a few indicators to grasp America's social and economic plight:

INDICATOR	1930	1931	1932
Unemployment	4,340,000	8,020,000	12,060,000
Business Failures	26,355	28,285	31,822
Farm Income	$4.1 Billion	$3.2 Billion	$1.9 Billion

—Source: *Statistical Abstract of the United States,* 1935, Government Printing Office.

In popular music there were tunes making social statements of one sort or another:

MELANCHOLY
"Brother, Can You Spare a Dime"—1932
"Stormy Weather"—1933

PHILOSOPHICAL RESIGNATION
"Life Is Just a Bowl of Cherries"—1931
"Let's Put Out The Lights (And Go to Sleep)"—1932
"Who's Afraid of the Big Bad Wolf?"—1933
"It's Only a Shanty"—1932

HOPE
"Headin' for Better Times"—1931
"There's a New Day Comin' "—1933
"When My Ship Comes In"—1934

A *Variety* headline spelled out one of the few bits of good news during the early years of the Great Depression: RADIO ONLY SHOW BIZ TO MAKE MONEY FOR '32.

For the networks and their advertisers, big bands were an excellent means of reaching a listening public whose spending power had been lowered with devastating impact. Bandleaders' names were familiar names and their music afforded a congenial environment for commercial messages.

Name bands in choice time slots held up well throughout the 1930s as the Appendix on page 362 indicates. Sponsored prime-time big band programs ranged from those festooned with elaborate production to the kind that had the leader giving simple introductions. The *Paul Whiteman Show*, sponsored by Kraft Cheese on NBC during the 1933–34 season typified the former. Whiteman, who never thought small, found kindred spirits in his sponsor and its advertising agency, J. Walter Thompson. No costs were spared, with Whiteman alone reported to have been pulling down $4500 a week. A live theater audience, whistling and whooping, helped generate the requisite excitement for the folks listening at home. By now, it was recognized that a few hundred appreciative studio fans could be made, with correct microphone emplacement, to sound like a few thousand. With the *Paul Whiteman Show*, Thursday, 10–11 p.m., on NBC, as a prime example, *Variety* called attention to the studio aspects of a big-time radio show:

> [The audience] is great stuff through the mike. They're all cheerleaders who applaud as no paid extras could . . . And as the curtain rises when-ever audience reaction is deserved, how the boys and girls respond . . . A new show business this here Raaadio situation. Looks (or rather, sounds) a great business that hasn't yet begun to get hot.[8]

For the millions of Americans who gathered around their living room consoles, Whiteman's program represented the ultimate in popular music packaging for its day: the latest songs; two boy vocalists; two girl vocal-ists; a male quartet, top-notch instrumentalists; Deems Taylor, as Master of Ceremonies; and the ample maestro himself. For a time during the show's run, Al Jolson was part of the all-star cast. Scripts were deliberately writ-ten with a thin veneer of sophistication, but occasionally got cutesy. Deems Taylor, the high-brow critic, who came down from his lofty music perch, bounded through his lines in a sort of I-enjoy-slumming-with-middle America *joie de vivre*. On a *Paul Whiteman Show* in December, 1933, Taylor brought on Whiteman's male quartet in the mock-serious manner that characterized many of the introductions:

> TAYLOR: And now we're going to hear from the Rondoleers. They're a very expensive quartet Mr. Whiteman acquired three or four weeks ago. I wondered how he could afford them until I discovered he won them playing bridge . . .

Bob Laurence, a male singer, received this build-up:

> TAYLOR: I've been asked by several people who admire Bob Laurence's singing to describe the training and course of study that made him sing so well. So for the benefit of music students, I'm going to outline the Laurence musical education. He grew up in New Orleans which

is very good for singing. He then took a course at Rutgers College in petroleum technology for the sake of his middle voice. Then to upper himself he worked five years in Oklahoma building oil refineries. Feeling he was about ready he made his debut over WTIC, in Hartford, Connecticut. Then he joined the Whiteman organization. And that's how he learned to sing.

Whiteman usually included a few songs from the newest film and stage offerings, a gesture that made listeners feel they were among the first to hear the latest in pop music:

> TAYLOR: Lew Leslie has opened his all-colored revue *Blackbirds of 1934* in New York, and Mr. Whiteman is going to play a medley tonight of the outstanding numbers of the score. The orchestra and the Rondoleers will start off with "Tappin The Bottle." Then we'll hear "I Just Couldn't Take It, Baby," with Peggy Healy, not taking it. Then "I'm Walking the Chalk Line" with Ramona. Then Jack Fulton will elaborate on "One Hundred Years from Today." And we should wind up with "Mother's Son-in-Law," with Ramona in the title role. Mr. Whiteman and the orchestra begin.[9]

Paul Whiteman's rather ostentatious approach to popular music worked; he was able to mount a major radio show during most of the big band era. Only one other aggregation did better. Guy Lombardo's was the sole name band to fill a prime time network slot *with a sponsor,* every season except one, between 1930 and 1945. For two years he was heard on both NBC and CBS every week. That the Royal Canadians' music had universal appeal can be read in a partial list of sponsors who subsidized their programs: Robert Burns, White Owl, Plough, Esso, Bond Bread, Lady Esther, Colgate and Chelsea Cigarettes. Lombardo shows were as simple as Whiteman's were frilly. An Esso braodcast from 1935 illustrates Lombardo's straight-forward, say-it-with music manner:

> LOMBARDO: Each week we play the favorite song of a famous star. Tonight the famous star is lovely Joan Crawford. And her favorite song—"Easter Parade." So with the compliments of Esso Marketers, we play for Joan Crawford, "Easter Parade."[10]

Not so fortunate were some other name band programs. Advertising agencies often diluted shows billed as popular music vehicles with guests, skits, special reports, and the like. Critics in the trade press and listeners complained about such watering down. But because ad agencies packaged commercial radio shows, they controlled them down to the minutest details, and the practice continued. Not untypical was *Jan Garber's Supper Club.* By the title, one would deduce this to be 30-minutes of mostly music by one of the country's most popular dance bands in 1934. But the "memo merchants," as Fred Allen loved to call admen, deemed otherwise. *Variety*, in one of the strongest blasts of the year, let the agency have it:

> The wonder is why any sponsor should spend hard-earned cash for a band as good as Jan Garber (one of the top 20 in the country) and then shove that band into the background where it means little. Garber plays great music, and it's hardly good showmanship to spot him between some phony dialog between a columnist and a hat check girl.[11]

An irate listener wrote to *Radio Guide*, beefing about the same thing:

> Jan Garber has a great orchestra and should be given more time . . . I wish a lot of other people would rather hear more of Jan Garber's music and Lee Bennett's singing and less drama . . .[12]

Advertisers who wished to reach women were partial to bands such as Jan Garber's, noted for their emphasis on romantic ballads. In the larger cities, it was not uncommon for name bands to be showcased live during the daytime. In the mid-1930s, Macy's, along with department stores in 11 major cities, led the way in co-sponsoring dance bands in the morning. Even *Variety's* reviewer, in critiquing the series' opener (Henry King and His Orchestra, WOR, Thursdays, 9–9:45 a.m.) found it "a little startling to hear smart dance rhythms so early in the day."[13]

In spite of their many successes as commercial entities, name bands also conjure up another image. Popular culture historians and misty-eyed nostalgics alike, when they consider this era of popular music, think of the late night remote broadcasts. Indeed, many Americans who grew up in the 1930s and 1940s gained their first perceptions of popular music from these programs. Starting at 11 p.m. and running until well after midnight, the bands played on. Enticed by announcers' alluring word pictures of glamorous locations, listeners frequently got hooked and stayed with the bands until 2 a.m.—in much the same way television talk shows entrap viewers. It was a time, as John S. Wilson put it, "when the first instantly recognizable notes of a theme song surging out of a radio could excite anticipation of incredible pleasures to come." Often playing to empty tables, the bands and their announcers created settings, glamorized in the minds of the listeners. Bands fought for locations, and locations fought for the bands. To make it a unique tripartite back-scratching game, add the networks. *They* held the trump card, because *they* decided where the remote lines should go. The networks had their pick of originations from an endless string of hotels, ballrooms, casinos and pavilions.

Bookings into select spots guaranteed bands those coveted radio wires—sometimes by competing networks in the same evening. (For a listing of some of the major ballrooms, hotel rooms, restaurants, and night spots famous for their big band remote broadcasts, see Appendix on page 363.) In addition to their trademark theme songs, one sure-fire way for leaders to add an extra touch to the packaging of their bands was the adoption of slogans, special catchwords at the beginning of broadcasts, sobriquets and titles. Noteworthy among them were these:

Louis Armstrong—*Satchmo*
Blue Barron—"Music of Yesterday and Today"
Ben Bernie—*The Old Maestro*
Les Brown—. . . "And His Band of Renown"
Cab Calloway—"Heigh-de-Ho!"
Larry Clinton—*The Old Dipsy Doodler*
Jimmy Dorsey—. . . "And His Contrasting Music"
Tommy Dorsey—*That Sentimental Gentleman*
Eddie Duchin—*The Ten Magic Fingers of Radio*
Shep Fields—. . ." And His Rippling Rhythm"
Jan Garber—*The Idol of the Airlanes*
Benny Goodman—*The King of Swing*
Gray Gordon—. . . "And His Tick-Tock Rhythm"
Horace Heidt—. . . "And His Musical Knights"
Fletcher Henderson—*The Colored King of Swing*
Dick Jurgens—"Here's that band again!"
Wayne King—*The Waltz King*
John Kirby—*The Biggest Little Band in The Land*
Red Norvo/Mildred Bailey—*Mr. and Mrs. Swing*
Artie Shaw—*King of the Clarinet*
Anson Weeks—"Let's Go Dancin' with Anson!"

There was no other way to make it in the big time dance band business except through network exposure. Sometimes unknowns went to extremes to crash the network gates. One of the more imaginative contrivances was concocted by Richard Himber, a bush-league leader, and NBC. Himber got the right ear at NBC and somehow sold the network a non-existant band to broadcast from New York's fashionable Essex House. With the Depression on his side, Himber convinced 12 hungry sidemen to join him. What made Himber's sale the more fascinating was the Essex House room from which the broadcasts originated. Joey Nash, Himber's vocalist, reflecting on his Richard Himber days, compared the spot used for broadcasts to

an unoccupied, unkempt, sub-terranean cavern that had the ambiance of a livery stable. In truth it was a junkyard, the last resting place for mounds and mounds of hotel furnishings. Roped cartons of linens, silverware and glassware, scores of one-legged hatracks, dozens of big soup tureens, moth-eaten, ripped divans, swimming-pool size punch bowls, hundreds of broken chairs and tables were strewn anywhere and everywhere . . .[14]

How listeners heard the room described by NBC announcers purring "mellifluous hokum," Nash recalls,

> . . . never failed to break up the band: "There is a sea of happy faces dining and dancing here in this beautiful dining room overlooking lovely Central Park here in New York, listening to the lilting strains of Richard Himber's orchestra and the romantic songs of Joey Nash."[15]

Himber had the last laugh, however, because the Essex House hokum supplied the impetus for him to move on to a successful career that found his orchestra featured on a number of network commercial packages and many remotes.

Flights of fanciful verbal adornment were the order of the day on legitimate remotes too in the early 1930s. Around the time Joey Nash and The Himberians conspired with NBC, Anson Weeks was fronting a West Coast band that had already gained national fame, largely due to its late night remotes from San Francisco's Hotel Mark Hopkins. The broadcasts couldn't have done the hotel any harm either, as this fragment from a 1932 Mark Hopkins air-shot attests:

> ANNOUNCER: Is it the music, or isn't it? There's something in the atmosphere here in the Peacock Court that makes it the rendezvous of smart, pleasure-loving people from all parts of the world? They come to dance the night away, and stay for days, weeks and sometimes months, captivated by the spirit of camaraderie and the haunting melodies of this rare music at the Hotel Mark Hopkins. Now Anson, prove our statement by playing that medley you were talking about.[16]

To a nation gripped by bleak poverty, with many of its citizens more concerned about finding places in bread lines than in dancing the night away in Peacock Court, the incongruity of radio dishing out such fantasies may at first seem incomprehensible. Yet, it was the very escape radio's big bands offered that helped make them so popular duing the Depression. Remote locations had to be "smart and spacious, elegant, glamorous, luxurious."* As times got better and additional discretionary dollars became available for entertainment, night spot and hotel operators cashed in the build-up they got on radio. Those listeners who had been enthralled by announcers' word pictures went in increasing numbers to the places they had heard about over the air. Business generated by remote broadcasts literally "made" some locations and saved some others. It may be one of the most beneficial reciprocities in show business history.

The *quid pro quo* as far as bandleaders were concerned also worked in a much subtler manner. They were forever promoting their next

---

* It is more than a co-incidence that the first disc jockey of consequence, Martin Block, invented a mythical ballroom and described his setting that was on par with the real ones.

personal appearance, their latest recording, their newest composition. Such drop-ins were made to appear ever so casual and unrehearsed. But they were planned with the same adroitness that script writers, say, of the *Bob Hope Pepsodent Show* might have used to slip in a mention of a golf bag manufacturer. Years later *Variety* coined the word "plugola"; if bandleaders didn't invent the practice, they certainly perfected it. Citing two random examples, it is not difficult to grasp why bandleaders found in remotes a sure-fire technique to obtain a nationwide hearing for any side-line ventures they had going. On a Glenn Miller remote from the Cafe Rouge or Hotel Pennsylvania, it was the announcer who made the nicely-packaged pitch:

> ANNOUNCER: It was last summer, I believe, a new tune popped up on one of the Glenn Miller shows, and at that time Glenn Miller predicted a great deal of popularity for it. Well, he's seen that prediction come true. And he's also seen his recording of it become the most popular coast to coast. Ray Eberle singing "Starlit Hour." [17]

When the leader himself did the honors, as in the following instance on a late-night Bob Crosby airshot from Hotel New Yorker's Terrace Room, the intent was the same:

> ANNOUNCER: Words now from the boss man, Bob Crosby
>
> CROSBY: Well, in a rash moment a few years ago, ladies and gentlemen, Roc Hilman, the guitar player in Jimmy Dorsey's band, a druggist in Baltimore, Maryland, and myself got together and wrote a song. Just recently the editors of *Radio Mirror* saw fit to publish the song. So I guess maybe we ought to play it for you and see if you like it. So we made an arrangement and here's the song. Words and music by myself. It's called "It's a Small World." I hope you like it. "It's a Small World." All set fellows? And I hope you like it. [18]

When big bands rode the radio networks, America's social life was still a function of downtown areas. Center city hotels, ballrooms and night clubs were often located near the originating station's facilities, making logistics for arranging remotes a relatively simple matter. New York was the unchallenged pacesetter in offering the most origination points. But surprisingly, Chicago with fewer locations, may have been more influential. For no city inducted more important name bands into the winner's circle than "that toddlin' town." The leading ones included Guy Lombardo, Hal Kemp, Kay Kyser, Bob Crosby, Jan Garber, Ben Bernie, Horace Heidt, Shep Fields, Benny Goodman, Anson Weeks, Coon-Sanders, Freddy Martin, Dick Jurgens and Eddie Howard. *Down Beat,* in a big band retrospective, pointed to the four stepping stones the Windy City supplied: "(1.) win over a Chicago following and get located in a key spot;

(2.) entertain the wide audience within earshot of Chi sustaining radio broadcasts; (3.) then out to the hinterlands to meet the listeners on one-niters and theater tours; (4.) back to the 'name' Chicago spot until a coast-to-coast sponsored radio show was in the bag."[19]

Those leaders who were fortunate enough to land commercial radio shows never considered relinquishing their sustaining remotes. Sponsors evidently were not worried about over-exposure, figuring remotes were good promotional trailers for their bands' prime time properties. (For an indication of how big bands dominated late night network schedules 1935–1940, see Appendix on page 365.) The same table also portrays a gradual cutting-back toward the end of the decade. There were several reasons—some aesthetic and economic, and one that affected all healthy young American males.

By the early 1940s, the sameness Harold Miller detected in his WORK orchestra was afflicting the name bands. Listener ennui began setting in when many of the outfits started sounding alike. Fans who once lionized the maestros were now dividing their attention among other more varied fare on radio. Movies which had the Depression decade to spread their wings competed for attention as more entertainment dollars became available. Then too, popular music itself was slowly slipping out of the band-leaders' control and moving in the direction of singers. But an even more powerful force had moved centerstage. When the country went to war, the traumatic changes that altered American life had a profound effect on the big bands. Military obligations of leaders and sidemen (many of who were of draftable age), more lucrative defense plant jobs, transportation problems and wartime entertainment taxes—all contributed to dwindling population of bandstand tenants. Interest in dancing declined as male partners went off to perform to the sounds of different drummers. When radio went to war, programmers called on the depleted ranks of the big bands for the regular listening fare, and in addition, special shows with a patriotic flavor. Military installations often served as origination points for live broadcasts put on before appreciative men and women of the armed forces. (*Spotlight Bands*, a sponsored six-a-week live, prime time half-hour, featuring virtually every name band still going, originated from military bases in every part of the country for several of the war years.) For all practical purposes, however, the best years of the bands were behind them. They were not casualties of World War II. If anything, international events prolonged their life span a little longer; otherwise, radio would have ditched them sooner.

At their best, from their identifiable theme songs to their closing signatures, name bands were the first real stylists of popular music. They deserved much of the adulation showered upon them. Without radio, their influence would have been only a fraction of what it turned out to be. With radio and the name bands working together, millions of Americans became popular-music conscious. The easy accessability radio offered made the music name bands played Everyman's music. Without radio, those American classicists, the musical comedy composers, would have reached far fewer appreciative ears. Radio was the megaphone through which Cole Porter, Rodgers and Hart, and George Gershwin, were able to be heard and thus contribute to the musical appreciation of untold thousands.

At their worst, the big bands did little to explore new forms. They took the easy way out and committed the unpardonable sin of show business, namely, not knowing when to quit a successful formula. Big bands were the embodiment of Ralph Waldo Emerson's observation that, "Every hero becomes a bore at last."

NOTES

1. Orrin E. Dunlap, Jr. "Music Sets the Pace," *New York Times,* May 18, 1930, Section IX, p. 8.
2. ————. "Says Radio Chain Serves the Public," *New York Times,* January 19, 1930, p. 17.
3. KGIR Program Log. circa 1930, Montana Historical Society.
4. Ozzie Nelson. *Ozzie,* Prentice-Hall, (Englewood Cliffs, N.J.), 1973, pp. 86–87.
5. Author's interview with Harold Miller, October 29, 1980.
6. Abel Green, "Radio Rambles," *Variety,* July 2, 1930, p. 73.
7. ————. "An Appraisal," *Fortune.* September, 1932, p. 37, and *New York Times* Radio Program Log, March 8, 1932, p. 18.
8. Abel Green. "Ad Agency's VP Reber Sits on Top," *Variety,* August 8, 1933, p. 34.
9. *The Paul Whiteman Show,* December 7, 1933. McCoy Recordings, Reel 2424.
10. *Guy Lombardo on the Air,* circa 1935, Sunbeam Records, HB 308.
11. Gold. "Radio Report," *Variety,* September 24, 1934, p. 40.
12. "Voice of the Listener," *Radio Guide,* October 27, 1934, p. 10.
13. Land. "Radio Reports," *Variety,* April 6, 1936, p. 36.
14. Joey Nash. In Liner notes accompanying Richard Himber re-issue LP, Bluebird AXM2-5520.
15. *Ibid.*
16. *Anson Weeks at The Mark Hopkins,* 1932, Hindsight Records 146.
17. *Glenn Miller at the Cafe Rouge.* Radio Yesteryear Program No. 358.
18. *Bob Crosby and His Orchestra on the Air.* Aircheck Records 17.
19. George Hoefer. "How Radio Built the Bands," *Down Beat,* April 20, 1955, p. 144.

CHAPTER 5

Canned Music

IN RADIO'S FIRST DECADE, one operational dictum was declared inviolate. It decreed a live musical performance to be far superior to a recorded presentation. The derogatory term "canned music" was meant to imply all the shabby elements of third-rate broadcasting. The stigma connected with playing recordings on the air was not merely a case of arrogance flaunted by haughty operators who had network affiliations and the resources to do elaborate live local programming. The Federal Communications Commission even promoted the "live-is-better" cause. Recalling the licensing process of the early 1930s, pioneer broadcaster Harold Miller noted the FCC awarded prompt grants to new-station applicants who promised not to play recordings for their first three-year license period. Miller's WORK and other prospective licensees in his shoes agreed to this stipulation, thereby avoiding long waits, extra paperwork and the possibility of not getting a license at all. Pro-recording broadcasters (and they were in the distinct minority) knew their colleagues were Uriah Heeps of the airwaves. For indeed, the live-only advocates *were* using mechanically produced sound. It just went by a different name.

    Called *electrical transcriptions*, these were 16-inch discs on which a half-hour program (15 minutes to a side) could be neatly contained. Electrical transcriptions ("ET's" in broadcasting shorthand) were originally ⅛-inch thick and made of acetate. By the mid-1930s, they had been reduced to the thickness of a regular recording. Radio's use of ET's was an extension of their employment in the early movie sound process. Vitaphone had developed the 16-inch, 33⅓ rpm lateral disc and synchronized it mechanically with the projector to produce sound films. *Variety* reported the first use of transcriptions in broadcasting when it covered the appearance of ET inventor Harold J. Smith before the Federal Radio Commission—a step deemed absolutely essential, given that regulatory body's pro-live stance at the time.

Shunned at first, transcriptions did not make it to the airwaves until late 1929 when WOR broke the ice. The high-quality reproduction surprised many in the broadcasting-advertising fraternity and resistance was not long in breaking down. Within two years after their introduction, *Variety* estimated: a.) 75% of all stations were using ET's; and b.) in the year ahead, $11,000,000 would be spent on transcribed shows by such advertisers as Chrysler, Chevrolet and National Refining.[1] Broadcasters were thus able to put aside their *parti pris* about canned music as the cash register clanged out its melodious ring.

Advertisers were happy too. They found that by placing ET shows on stations, they were able to pinpoint select cities to accomplish specific marketing strategies, thus eliminating waste network coverages in places where they didn't need it. ET's also afforded advertisers the privilege of negotiating with stations for time periods of their own choosing, rather than having to take the abritrary time slots assigned by the network. Dance orchestras, the ruling class of popular music in the early 1930s, figured prominently in sponsor selections, Programs by dance outfits on electrical transcription were much like their live network counterparts: pop tunes of the day, interspersed within commercials and dialogue. One of the earliest of the genre, the *Sunny Meadows Radio Show,* presented in select markets in 1929, was named in contemporary fashion—after its sponsor, the Sunny Meadows Manufacturing Company, an appliance maker, located in Bloomington, Illinois. Each disc featured a 1920s-styled dance orchestra led by Ray Miller, a singer and a master of ceremonies named, not surprisingly, Sunny Meadows. Tunes played on the *Sunny Meadows Radio Show* were popular hits. One ET in the series featured these 1929 favorites:

Angry
You're the Cream in My Coffee
I Ain't Got Nobody
Sweetheart of All My Dreams
My Blackbirds Are Bluebirds Now
Caressing You
Royal Garden Blues[2]

Much of the program continuity was dreadful. Before listeners could hear a song, they often endured inane dialogue:

SUNNY MEADOWS: Ladies and gentlemen. Ray is about to make a confession and tell us about the sweetheart of all his dreams.

RAY MILLER: Pardon me, Sunny. I believe part of your announcement is misleading, simply because if I start making confessions over the radio—well, that would be just too bad.

SUNNY MEADOWS: You mean *bad* confessions, Ray?

RAY MILLER: Sunny, Sunny! That you should question my integrity! It isn't a confession. It's a melody called "Sweetheart of All My Dreams." Right, Boys?

BAND: RIGHT![3]

Transcribed pop music shows sometimes included a commentary by an expert in his field—usually on a current topic that had nothing to do with music. On an early 1930s ET series, for its Friendly Five brand, Jarman Shoes included an aviation commentator named Casey Jones. Freddie Rich, then the leader of the CBS house band, and His Orchestra provided the canned music. The *Friendly Five Footnotes on the Air* show was obviously supposed to entertain and edify. Freddie Rich and the boys took care of the entertainment with renditions in early 1930s dance band style. For edification, listeners to one program heard Casey Jones discuss the latest achievements in aviation: American Airlines' new service from Miami to Buenos Aires, cutting travel time from 23 to eight days; and Pan America's new winter trips to the West Indies ("By boat a Caribbean cruise takes some two to three weeks. By air, it can be completed in six days, covering 17 countries. The trip across the Caribbean now takes six hours.")[4]

ET popular music sponsors ran the gamut of American marketing, from the automotive giants to small cosmetic firms. Advertising agencies who produced the transcriptions rarely trusted the music alone to carry the show. On the big-budget ET's, there were short commentaries, guests, trips to exotic isles, whirlwind visits to expensive nightclubs, drop-ins to private penthouse parties. In the case of a mid-1930s show sponsored by Kelvinator, it was a "country club membership" that was evoked when the 15-minute show was over. Kelvinator's transcribed *Your Country Club of the Air* supplied words and music for a Depression fantasy aimed at housewives. Paul Douglas (who later gained fame as a Broadway and Hollywood actor) opened the show as follows:

> *Your Country Club of the Air* invites you to come and relax once again in one of its easy chairs or in one of its deep sofa lounges. Morton Gould and his Orchestra are here to play for you, and Donald Novis, the silver voice star of stage and radio is here to sing for you. So join us and make yourself comfortable.[5]

Cosmetics makers, one of network radio's earliest popular music sponsors, used transcriptions unstintingly. Low initial investment and low overhead were the lures that induced numerous fledging entrepreneurs to go into the cosmetics business during the Depression. Musical radio with its built-in romantic appeal to reach a women's audience, and its low cost, afforded unknown beauty products an opportunity for quick marketplace acceptance. Popular music transcriptions, placed in select markets, enabled lesser known brands such as Cheloni and Lavena to take on nationally-known makes. Both are names long since forgotten at cosmetics counters, but in the early 1930s in cities where their ET's were run, Cheloni and Lavena stood up to the giants in the powder puff derby. Cheloni Skin Rejuvenator, "that modern fountain of youth," sponsored Eddie South and His Orchestra in a transcribed pop music series. What made the *Cheloni Skin Program* unique was not the extravagance of its product claims ("to tighten up sagging facial contours . . . and bring back that double chin to more useful flattering lines . . . and wipe years from faces"). Cheloni's show was unusual for its time (1932) because it used a dance orchestra led by a Black, Eddie South ("The Dark Angel of the Violin"). South, a hot jazz violinist, like many musicians who had split musical personalities, laid on the schmaltz for the Cheloni show with a playlist of romantic ballads. Song announcements were low key and brief:

> ANNOUNCER: Here's a well-known sound, "Jealousy." Eddie South and his orchestra.
>
> or
>
> Now the "Dark Angel of the Violin," Eddie South and one of those delightful solos "Penthouse Serenade."[6]

For advertisers with limited budgets, those kinds of short introductions on ET programs were born of necessity. The wordier the script, the greater the chance for the announcer to blow his lines. In which case, the cumbersome recording machine that was used to cut the show on to disc had to be stopped and the entire production started all over again. Splicings, tape erasers and unlimited takes were luxuries unavailable in the recording field in 1932. In keeping talk to a minimum, producers were incorporating a rubric that foreshadowed Top 40 Radio's abhorrence of long-winded deejays. Standard openings for canned programs were scripted to get listeners into the music as quickly as possible. Harlow Wilcox's opening announcement for a transcribed package featuring Hal Kemp's Orchestra illustrates how no time was wasted in getting the show on the road:

> WILCOX: (Under Kemp's theme) Lavena, the new oatmeal treatment, which softens and beautifies skin, presents Hal Kemp and His International Favorites. Here's music that rests and relaxes. Our opening number—"This Is Romance." Wendell Mayhew sings.[7]

By the mid-1930s, transcribed dance music shows such as Hal Kemp's and Eddie South's were giving way to a different sort of canned entertainment. *Variety* called attention to a new trend in ET programming, noting "bigger budgets, better talent and greater variation of entertainment . . . the older procedure of buying one band, or singer (or combo), and then using them for a whole season is being supplemental by the "guest star" technique . . . Biggest guest star addict right now is Kroger Grocery and Baking Company, whose *House of a Thousand Eyes* is bankrolling the Bohemian Quartet, Dick Powell, Molasses 'n January, Frank Tours Orchestra, Lanny Ross, Walter O'Keefe and others."[8]

Detroit found particular favor with the ET mode of musical radio. Few months passed without Dodge, Chevrolet, Plymouth and Ford riding on station transcription turntables. Around the mid-1930s, one of network radio's star attractions, Fred Waring, signed with Ford to do a transcribed series. Bringing Waring into the ET fold not only represented a coup for Ford, it also told the world that the process of capturing melodies on disc with adequate verisimilitude had arrived. Otherwise, the musically fastidious Waring would have had no part of a music canning factory. The *Fred Waring Show* was the kind of advertising vehicle that local merchants loved, and this one especially endeared the manufacturer to the Ford dealer family. Some stations' uses of the discs, however, did not endear them to Fred Waring. The head Pennsylvanian learned that some stations were lifting out his material and building their own Fred Waring shows. Waring (whose frequent tiffs with broadcasters over the use of his commercial recordings enlivened Radio Row during the 1930s) made a test case of the issue by taking a North Carolina station to federal court. The judge, agreeing with Waring, issued a cease-and-desist order, alerting like-minded broadcasters to think twice before messing with the Pennsylvanians' discs.

Waring's plunge into ET programming, of course, spurred other car makers to get in the ET act. During the 1936 season, Dodge put on platter a pop music show starring such current favorites as Gertrude Neisen, Frank Parker and Kay Thompson. Such splashy variety-popular music packages were obviously of network calibre. And therein lay one of the problems. Transcribed programs were getting more expensive to produce, since the finished product had to match the live quality dispensed on NBC and CBS. Toward the end of the decade, the major networks had pretty well preempted choice time periods; desirable slots for ET's on local stations were getting harder to find. More and more national advertisers went shopping for network availabilities, as the NBC and CBS publicity mills continued to grind out sales success stories. Meanwhile, regional sponsors, the bread-and-butter accounts of ETland, were relying on stations to build live programs for them, thus avoiding the middleman transcriber.

Popular music shows on transcription, however, were far from passé after 1939. Scaled down in size to quarter-hour units, they made ideal insertions to fill in soap opera gaps and in the lucrative noon-hour and early evening local-station time spaces. The *Jack Berch Show* for Gulf products that ran on select stations during the summer months of 1939 was representative of this breed. Berch a song-and-patter man, who a decade later would become a network super-salesman for Prudential Life, was the featured artist on a breezy two-a-week stanza. Gulf's quarterhour format called for a mix of four pops and standards, all sung by Berch, backed by a three-piece combo (piano, organ and drums), two commercials, and light (often corny) banter of the star and the announcer. The following exchange between Berch and his announcer typified the dialog used between musical selections:

> ANNOUNCER: (After Berch's first number, "What's the Matter with Me"). Ah nice warblin', Jack old pal.
>
> BERCH: Why thank you, Johnny, old boy. For that bouquet, I shall go out into the orchard and pick you a nice, ripe, juicy peach.
>
> ANNOUNCER: Oh, swell. But do you mind if we make one stop before we go into the orchard?
>
> BERCH: Oh, certainly not, old man. Why?
>
> ANNOUNCER: Because I don't like to have flies buzzing around peaches. That's why I want to pick up a can of Gulfspray. (Then goes into commercial.) [9]

The *Variety* reviewer's report on the first of the Jack Berch Gulf series could have well applied to the majority of transcribed quarter-hour quickies that darted in and out of program schedules prior to World War II: "Nothing remarkable on these platters, but for the talent money spent, results should be OK."

Between 1942 and 1946 transcriptions were assigned a different role not contemplated in their original conception. Virtually all popular networks shows music and otherwise, (minus commercials) were shipped overseas and became the programming backbone of Armed Forces Radio Stations around the world. In the post-War period, as radio scrambled to cope with television, ET's appeared in various re-incarnations and new forms, both of which will be dealt with in Chapter 12. However, it would be remiss not to mention another family of radio transcription that flourished along side of the completely packaged variety.

When the Depression sent the commercial recording business into a reverse spin, there was another newly-developed source to which radio stations could turn when their needs called for recorded popular music. That source was specially-pressed 16-inch discs, available to radio stations only. Each transcription contained two to six tunes per side by the same artist—usually a name band. Under their contracts, stations received an agreed-upon number of new discs on a monthly or bi-monthly basis. One or more such transcription libraries were considered necessities at many stations; and even after commercial recordings became more frequent on American airwaves from the mid-1930s on, many stations continued to use material from their ET libraries—the idea being, that if all outlets were playing the same popular commercial recordings, the tunes on transcriptions would enable programmers to serve up a more varied playlist. Virtually every name band recorded for a transcription service. Reflecting the popular music world at large in the 1930s, there were few vocalists represented. Big bands were the *raison d'être* of ET libraries. Stations paid a yearly fee based on market size—or perhaps more often, based on the negotiating ability of the manager. Six companies dominated the transcription library field at the height of the big band era: C.P. McGregor, Standard , World, Associated, Langworth and RCA Thesaurus. Capitol, Vista and SESAC and several smaller firms came later. Bands switched back and forth between libraries, just as they did on conventional commercial labels. (Jimmy Dorsey worked for Standard, World and Associated beteen 1935 and 1945.) Because of contractural complications, artists sometimes used pseudonyms:

NAME BAND/VOCALIST	PSEUDONYMN(S)
Woody Herman	Wally Hayes
Will Hudson	Warren Hart
Bob Crosby	Bob Crosley or Bob Conley
Dorsey Brothers	Dale Brothers
Jimmy Dorsey	James Dalton
Benny Goodman	Bill Dodge
Glen Gray	George Gregory
Ray Noble	Reginald Norman or Ralph Norton
Red Norvo/Mildred Bailey	Ross Norman/Molly Baldwin
Chuck Webb/Ella Fitzgerald	Chuck Werner/Evelyn Fields
Larry Clinton/Bea Wain	Lennie Carson/Babs Warren

In July 1937, an RCA-Thesaurus station subscriber found as part of its March and July service these items by Art Shaw and His Orchestra:

ET #366 (March, 1937)

Love Is Good for Anything That Ails You
No More Tears
September in the Rain
The Mood That I'm In
Trust in Me
A Message from the Man in the Moon
Was it Rain
Swing High, Swing Low

ET #419 (July, 1937)

Whispers in the Dark
Don't Ever Change
If I Put My Heart Into a Song
Love Is a Merry-go-round
Till the Clock Strikes Three
The Moon Got in My Eyes
All You Want to Do Is Dance
It's the Natural Thing to Do.[10]

When interest in big bands declined, transcription library services responded by including vocalists and elements not directly concerned with music, as we shall see later.

In collectors' hands, in station basements, in archive vaults are thousands of the ancient over-sized 16-inch discs—recorded testimonies that when radio thought popular music, it always thought big. Ironically, canned music, regarded with scorn in earlier days, would one day be virtually the only kind of popular music on radio, and syndicators would enable broadcasters to serve it up push-button style.

NOTES

1. ———. "75% of All Radio Stations on Discs." *Variety*, December 24, 1930, p. 58. "11,000,000 Next Year for Radio Programs on Discs?", *Variety*, December 17, 1930.
2. *The Sunny Meadows Radio Show—1929*. Sunbeam Records MFC 14.
3. *Ibid.*
4. *Friendly Five Footnotes on the Air.* (vol. 2, 1932) Aircheck Records 14.
5. *Your Country Club of the Air.* McCoy Recordings, Reel No. 2643.
6. *Cheloni Skin Program.* McCoy Recordings, Reel No. 3502.
7. *Hal Kemp and His Orchestra—1934.* Hindsight Records, HSR 143.
8. ———. "More Showmanship in Transcriptions," *Variety,* February 26, 1936, p. 51.
9. *Jack Berch Show.* (circa 1939). Program No. 1004, Radio Yesteryear.
10. Joyce Music Studio Catalog. 1970, p. 72.

CHAPTER 6

Swing

"RADIO IS MERELY poor man's theater."

So went the canard that had been hung around radio's neck since early in the Great Depression. Pure nonsense, said a CBS presentation issued in late 1934. That network whose sales pitches had become the talk of Madison Avenue quoted Daniel Starch's "Ears and Income" to prove its point. Starch's study covering 88,462 homes found that: a.) workers earning over $5,000 annually listened to radio an average of four hours and 16 minutes daily; b.) those in the $2,000 to $5,000 range tuned in an average of four hours and two minutes; and those under $2,000 listened four hours and 38 minutes a day.[1]

CBS continued to issue elaborate brochure after brochure pinpointing radio's strength among all major sectors of the population—men, women, farm, urban. In all of them, the message to advertisers was the same: "There's money out there in America to be spent; pay no attention to the doomsayers." By the mid-1930s, such a positive line of reasoning was not without merit. President Franklin D. Roosevelt through his bold, legislative activism had rallied the country to believe the "only thing to fear is fear itself." Roosevelt's personal magnetism and his innovative, symbolic "Fireside Chats"—the first use of radio as political theater—helped restore confidence to a nation that only a few years before had been committed to despair. Musically, the dirge-like plaint of 1932, "Brother, Can You Spare a Dime," changed a few years later to the shiny optimism of "Things Are Looking Up." Relief payments and wages from government-sponsored work projects had pumped billions into the economy. Between 1933 and 1935 alone, even the Cassandras in the private sector could hardly deny there *was* cause for optimism. The following table shows some major indicators of economic recovery:

	1933	1935
Gross National Product	$39.6 billion	$56.8 billion
Manufacturing Production Index	$68 billion	$87 billion
Salaries and Wages	$28.7 billion	$36.3 billion
Unemployment	12,600,000	10,200,000

—Source: *Historical Statistics of the U.S.,* 1940, U.S. Government Printing Office.

In the advertising community, American business continued to find radio a strong marketing tool. Makers of packaged goods were particularly large users of the medium. Time sales for NBC and CBS in 1930 totalled $30,888,555. In 1935 (with the new Mutual chain chipping in less than a half-million) the networks grossed $56,862,753. Depression or no, the country still had to take baths, brush teeth, drive cars. And what was wrong if it treated itself to a carton of smokes and a case of beer every so often?

By the mid-1930s, even the naysayers in the entertainment world had accepted radio. There were no more holdouts. Talent agents in all the performing arts scrambled to get their clients exposed on network radio, either with shows of their own, or through guest-star appearances. New stars twinkled in the show biz firmanent, as others faded. In popular music, the established order was shaken by the arrival of a new music called *Swing.* Originally, the word had been coined to describe the rhythmic pulse, or exciting beat imparted to the performance of a song. Duke Ellington, in a 1931 composition, "It Don't Mean A Thing If It Ain't Got That Swing," stomped off the definitive word on the matter.

Swing, as musicians knew it, was the inherent property in the way Fletcher Henderson's Orchestra played a tune (hot) that differentiated it from Guy Lombardo's treatment (sweet). Both varieties were considered "jazz" in the 1920s. But the component that made one body of music, jazz, and the other, non-jazz (thereby hanging a tale for mis-naming an entire decade) was the inner rhythmic "heat" present in Henderson's way of playing, and missing in Lombardo's. White musicians who came to Roseland were enthralled mainly by the "swing" of Fletcher Henderson's band and imitated it freely.

Keeping in mind the *quality* (swing) imparted to a performance, the term took on another meaning in the mid-1930s. Swing came to mean a *body of music* that had an exciting rhythmic beat (usually 4/4), combined with select variations of traditional New Orleans music, all merged into the dance band format. Music etymologists Gammond and Clayton in their *Dictionary of Popular Music* spend four hundred words in pinning down an acceptable meaning of swing.* Their definition (narrowed down) as it applies to popular music in the 1930s could hardly be improved upon: "A kind of commercialized jazz as played by large bands, a mainly arranged music, often featuring soloists, but relying for its excitement on the overwhelming, biting effect of a number of instruments playing propulsively together with the frequent employment of riffs . . ."[2]

The period 1935–1945 is often referred to as the "Swing Era." That designation, conveying the impression that swing had taken over American popular music, does not square with the facts. What created this perception was the coming together of several forces around 1935—some social, some economic and some technological.

The selling of swing music represented the first multi-media hype in behalf of a popular music. The abating Depression found the sons and daughters of the middle class with more money in which to indulge their musical tastes. This obviously included college students, the important music trend-setters. Then too, there was the repeal of Prohibition in 1933 and the resultant shot in the arm for public dancing in ballrooms and nightclubs. The Duo Junior, a tubeless and speakerless record player, designed to be jacked into radio receivers, retailing for $16.50, made its debut. Record collecting thus became a hobby for many, and in turn helped sagging record sales. Juke boxes began to appear in coffee shops and taverns; the most popular among these congregating places for youth marked off small areas in their establishments for dancing. "Jitterbugs," "alligators," "hepcats" and "bobby-soxers," media code words, appeared often in the coverage of swing, with attention focusing on *dancing* aspects of the "new" music. In newspapers, magazines and movies, on radio and on the stage, the phenomenon was referred to as the "swing craze." Swing never achieved the pervasiveness of rock and roll—on the radio or off. But for a dedicated group of youth in the pre-war decade, it did become an important rallying point in American popular music.

Radio's part in introducing swing was a crucial one. The medium's appeal to conventional middle class tastes was apparent in the packaging of swing for its radio unveiling. For although Fletcher Henderson, Duke Ellington and other black swing bands were familiar to late-night tuners-in by the middle 1930s, radio's chosen vessel was white. Swing music, as middle America first heard it in early December, 1934 was nameless. It was carefully packaged as part of a coast-to-coast network program of "safe," familiar dance music. Chosen by the National Biscuit Company as

---

* Scholars and fans who seek to come up with precise definitions for one kind of popular music or another might well be advised to consider Fats Waller's profound advice. The story (perhaps apocryphal since Louis Armstrong's name has also been used) goes that the irrepressible Waller had been approached by a lady asking, "What is Swing?" Whereupon Waller is supposed to have replied, "Lady if you have to ask what it is, you ain't got it."

the vehicle to introduce its new Ritz Crackers, *Let's Dance* was a program of popular music that ran on NBC Saturday nights, from 10:30p.m. to 1:30a.m. Eastern time. The first hour featured Ken Murray's Orchestra, a sweet outfit that played standard commercial hits in the accepted manner of the day. Hour two showcased Xavier Cugat's unit, specializing in Latin rhythms. (It must not be forgotten that the dancing fever that enveloped in the country beginning in the 1920s required orchestras to mix tangos and rhumbas with fox trots; thus Cugat on the *Let's Dance* agenda was not at all off-beat programming.) For the final 60-minute segment beginning at 12:30a.m., in the least desirable time slot insofar as the populous East was concerned, McCann-Erickson, National Biscuit's advertising agency, selected a recently-organized band which played pop tunes—but in a "different" style from that ordinarily heard on commercial radio shows. Band number three had nailed down a spot in *Let's Dance* with less than a rousing display of confidence, getting there by a single vote from Mc-Cann-Erickson's jury. The leader of this band was a bespectacled 26-year-old clarinetist named Benny Goodman.

Goodman, who grew up in Chicago, took clarinet lessons when he was still in knickers and acquired a solid classical foundation. He also absorbed the music of New Orleans' black musicians who had started coming to the Windy City in the early 1920s. The young clarinetist was smitten by this "new" music, Jazz, the transplanted blacks were playing—its most noticeable characteristic being an exciting rhythmic beat. Benny Goodman was doubtless aware that the "jazz" Guy Lombardo and George Olsen were playing on the radio was not the same as the jazz of black players like Louis Armstrong and Joe "King" Oliver. At age 16, Goodman had become proficient enough to get a job in the reed section of Ben Pollock's band, an orthodox dance orchestra, where he remained for three years. During the Pollock years, Goodman recorded (sometimes as a leader) many sides of 1920s novelties and pop hits, including accompaniments for vocal favorites like Irene Beasley and Gene Austin. After leaving Pollock, Goodman served a valuable six-year hitch in the large network studio orchestras conducted by Freddie Rich, B.A. Rolfe, Al Goodman (no relation), Rubinoff and Johnny Green. This experience, together with an occasional Broadway pit band job, enabled Goodman to hone his recording skills and learn other tricks of the musical trade. Financially rewarding as the radio and recording studios were, however, they still seemed to Goodman to auger a lifetime career as a sideman. Those apprehensions began fading in the late 1920s, when through a fortuituous set of circumstances, the young pop musician met John Hammond*, the first of three men whose efforts in Goodman's behalf enabled him to become the Pied Piper of swing, and then its "king."

---

* The same John Hammond was to become Goodman's brother-in-law, and was to become the preceptor for Billie Holiday, Count Basie, Bob Dylan, Leonard Cohen, George Benson and Bruce Springsteen.

Thanks to a wealthy family background, John Hammond (a Yale dropout) was able to indulge himself in writing about the music scene, organizing recording dates, promoting the careers of his favorite artists—many of them Blacks—and in general, acting as a cheerleader for jazz, popular music and minority causes. Hammond's talent-scouting and encouragement were paramount when the idea of a Goodman-led band began to develop. Perhaps even more crucial, however, were some Hammond-supervised record sessions in which the Vanderbilt scion lined up leading Negro jazz artists (Coleman Hawkins, Frankie Newton, Chuck Berry, Art Tatum, et al.) to play with Goodman. The recording dates enabled the young clarinetist to benefit from the black artists' approach to music that most closely approximated his own. "For this," Goodman wrote in his autobiography, "the responsibility must be given almost entirely to John Hammond, who really put me back in touch with the kind of music [the Negroes] could play."[3]

Meanwhile, the big band Goodman had organized got what looked like the break it needed—an important New York engagement in Billy Rose's Music Hall. Three months later, however, Goodman was put on notice. Before he had too much chance to contemplate a winter of discontent, the *Let's Dance* contract materialized. Goodman's handlers touched all bases, from selecting the show's title and theme song to providing a budget for special arrangements. Theme music, upbeat and catchy, for the Goodman hour of the Nabisco show as a jazzed up version of Carl Maria von Weber's "Invitation to the Dance," appropriately retitled "Let's Dance," which Goodman adopted as his own trademark theme song for life. Thanks to the foresight of the producers, Benny Goodman encountered his second great benefactor, Fletcher Henderson. The *Let's Dance* budget was set up to include an allocation for special orchestrations, and the Roseland maestro whose own band-leading fortunes had been nipped by the Depression, was hired to turn them out. There were special scores by others, but it was the Henderson charts that transformed the "stock" arrangements used by the conventional dance bands of the day from their mundane predictability into swinging cameos with an infectious lilt, and still never strayed too far from the melody line. Of course, Don Redman had done this very thing for Henderson's own band a decade earlier. Fletcher Henderson, the arranger, went one step further, however. Where Redman's orchestrations were limited mainly to original pieces, Fletcher wrote for Benny Goodman swinging arrangements of currently popular pieces, heretofore unheard of. Goodman gives full credit for his initial success to Fletcher Henderson's arrangements, many of which were heard for the first time on *Let's Dance:*

> Up to that time the only kind of arrangements that the public had paid much attention to . . . were the elaborate ones such as Ferdé Grofe's for Whiteman. But the art of making an arrangement a band can play with

swing, I am convinced is an art . . . The whole idea is that the ensemble
passages where the whole band is playing together, or one section has the
lead, have to be written in more or less the same style that a soloist would
use if he were improvising. That is, what Fletcher could do so wonder-
fully was to take a tune like "Sometimes I'm Happy" and really improvise
on it himself . . . Without Fletcher I probably would have had a pretty
good band, but it would have been something quite different from what
it eventually turned out to be.[4]

Henderson arrangements notwithstanding, Goodman's portion of *Let's
Dance* was still basically pop music. With a few notable exceptions—items
such as "King Porter Stomp" and "Sugar Foot Stomp" in the jazz vein
that Henderson had taken out his own band's folio—playlists for *Let's
Dance* reflected the popular hits of the day. The program of January 5,
1935 was representative of the pattern:

Let's Dance (theme)
Love Is Just Around the Corner (Vocal, Buddy Clark)
I've Got a Feeling I'm Falling (Vocal, Helen Ward)
The Dixieland Band (Vocal, Helen Ward)
Serenade to a Wealthy Widow
Throwin' Stones at The Sun (Vocal, Helen Ward)
Honeysuckle Rose
Limehouse Blues
Night and Day (Vocal, Helen Ward)
Between the Devil and the Deep Blue Sea (Vocal, Helen Ward)
Stardust[5]

Although *Let's Dance* garnered a respectable 19.8 rating and was able
to earn a 13-week renewal into May, 1935, the show ignited no great
public acclaim for Benny Goodman and His Orchestra. But it did attract
the keen interest of one Willard Alexander, the third member of the tri-
umverate who shared in the selling of Benny Goodman. Alexander, a young
sometime-bandleader himself, had just graduated from The University of
Pennsylvania and joined Music Corporation of America, the giant band-
booking agency. The young MCA salesman persuaded his firm to represent Goodman's band—a not-inconsiderable sale in its own right, since
Music Corporation of America boasted a blockbuster roster of only the
very best-known dance bands, and all of them sweet. Willard Alexander
began booking his new client in the summer of 1935. When the band
bombed as the summer replacement for Guy Lombardo in the prestigious
Hotel Roosevelt Grill, Alexander deflected the I-told-you-so's of the MCA
front office and went ahead with a summer booking schedule. Alexander
sold the Goodman band to some key ballrooms across the country. At
each stop along the way, the story was the same, either: a.) crowds were
small; or b.) they were able to keep their enthusiasm under control. The

last stop in the tour was the Palomar Ballroom in Los Angeles, and on opening night, August 21, 1935, Goodman was about ready to throw in the towel:

> We took things kind of easy with the opening sets, playing some of the sweeter tunes and sticking to the softer arrangements . . . The crowd didn't seem very responsive. This went on for about an hour, 'till I decided the whole thing had gotten to a point where it was make or break. If we had to flop, at least I'd do it my own way. I called out some of our big Fletcher Henderson arrangements for our next set . . . the band dug in with some of the best playing I'd heard since we left New York. To our complete amazement, half the crowd stopped dancing and came surging around the stand . . . That first big roar from the crowd was one of the sweetest sounds I ever heard in my life.[6]

What Benny Goodman had experienced was a radio success story. *Let's Dance* had reached the West Coast in prime time and was able to attract a larger audience than in its 12:30–1:30a.m. Eastern time slot. In addition, several independent stations in the Los Angeles area, which of necessity featured recorded music, had been playing Goodman's newest releases. RCA-Victor, to which Goodman had recently switched, also gave the band's recordings the aggressive merchandising push for which this top-selling label was noted. The Goodman Era was underway.

Willard Alexander, whom John Hammond called "as important in Benny Goodman's early career as anyone," was soon directing traffic for the Goodman bandwagon. The selling of swing included the slickest marketing yet seen in popular music. As the figure around whom the swing hype was built, Goodman took it all in stride. The "King of Swing" byname never caused him to adopt the mannerisms affected by many other popular maestros. Benny Goodman, ever the stern musical taskmaster, displayed just enough affability to be accepted by an adoring public as a bona fide "personality." His shrewd business sense enabled him to capitalize on the swing fad through personal appearances, records, movies and a major prime-time radio show that will be described in detail in Chapter 8. So etched in the American consciousness is the Benny Goodman-swing connection that he has been able to keep his celebrityhood alive into the 1980s, conducting regular editions of The Traveling Nostalgia Swing Parade.

Benny Goodman has had to endure a lifetime of accusations for exploiting a Negro musical invention to make millions, while its creator, Fletcher Henderson, had to languish in obscurity. This "bum rap" does not square with the facts, for Goodman paid the arranger well and has been ever-unstinting in crediting Henderson for his contributions—both points often corroborated by Henderson. Without Goodman the popularizer, Fletcher Henderson the innovator would have been a forgotten name. Two generations later, thanks to Benny Goodman, echoes of Fletcher Henderson resound every time Doc Severinson kicks off the *Tonight Show* theme, or whenever Ray Charles's big band goes roaring into an opening set. Benny Goodman need never apologize for his relationship with black artists. Indeed, ever since his orchestra was less than a year old, when he had brought in Teddy Wilson and Lionel Hampton, no Goodman entourage has been long without black artists. On the night of his greatest triumph, his 1938 Carnegie Hall concert, Benny Goodman included members of the Duke Ellington and Count Basie orchestras. The historic significance of two black units and a white one on the same program at Carnegie Hall, playing popular music, was not lost upon commentators past and present. Long before social and legal movements focused on the civil rights issue, popular music demonstrated, at least in this dramatic instance, it was color blind.

The presence together of Goodman, Basie and Ellington at the Carnegie Hall affair suggests another point worthy of more than passing notice: of the many swing bands that emerged between 1935 and 1945, the three most successful ones—and the most durable—received their impetus via live radio broadcasts. We have already dealt with the medium's importance to Duke Ellington and Benny Goodman. Radio was no less pivotal for Count Basie in achieving his initial recognition.

William "Count" Basie, a young New Jersey musician, had absorbed the Harlem "stride"* technique of Fats Waller before becoming a pianist in a popular Kansas City-based band led by Bennie Moten in the late 1920s. The blues-drenched dance music played by Moten was favored by black dancers in the Southwest and became known as Jump-style, or Kansas City swing. After Moten's death Basie organized a nine-piece combo and fashioned its sound in Moten's strong, rhythmic "jump" tradition. Happy with any job he could find in the wide-open headquarters town of the Pendergrast political machine, Basie had to settle for work in some of Kansas City's toughest joints. Early in 1936, while Basie was playing in an all-night dive, The Reno Club, 500 miles away in Chicago's Congress Hotel amid the posh confines of The Joseph Urban Room, Benny Goodman was enjoying the first fruits of success. John Hammond, who had accompanied Goodman during that Chicago appearance, describes in his autobiography how he first encountered Count Basie:

> Having heard enough of Benny's music for the evening, I went out to my car, parked across the street from The Congress, not quite decided where to go next. It was cold as only Chicago in January can be, and I turned on my car radio. I had a twelve-tube motorola with a large speaker, unlike any other car radio in those days. I spent so much time on the road that I wanted a superior instrument to keep me in touch with music around the country . . . the only music I could find was at the top of the dial,

---

*Stride is a style of jazz piano playing in which the right hand plays the melody while the left hand alternates between a single note and a chord played an octave or more higher. It derives its name from the rapid alternate movements up and down the piano.

1550 kilocycles, where I picked up W9XBY, an experimental station in Kansas City. The nightly broadcast by The Count Basie band from the Reno Club was just beginning. I couldn't believe my ears.[7]

Hammond started writing rave reviews of the Basie's nine-piece unit in *Down Beat,* one of the period's pop music periodicals and regarded by its readers as the official publication of the swing movement. Hammond's enthusiasm rubbed off on Willard Alexander who took the band under MCA's wing. Goodman, John Hammond's other swing *cause celèbre,* meanwhile, joined the Basie cheering section by recording Basie's theme, "One O'Clock Jump" and using the Count's men on some record sessions. The trail blazed by Benny Goodman and Willard Alexander led to network remotes and a national following for the Basie orchestra. Expanding to 15 men, the Basie aggregation became a swinging juggernaut.

To hear the Count Basie band in full cry during the late 1930s was to hear the swing band incarnate. Chief chemist Basie compounded a rare prescription that began in his rhythm section. It was a new kind of rhythm, smooth and relaxed, accenting equally four beats to the bar in an even flow within the 12-bar blues framework. Superimposed on the rhythmic Basie base were loosely swinging ensemble passages and those obligatory swing punctuators, the short repeated staccato passages, called riffs. Basie's music, flowering as it did in the hospitable blues climate of the Southwest, was a source of inspiration for lesser combos who played an earthier and less polished kind of swing that eventually became known as rhythm and blues—which in turn was one of the essential ingredients in rock and roll. Although Basie never achieved Goodman's commercial success, he did develop a large loyal following of Blacks and a smaller congnoscenti of white middle class swing freaks. Basie's book, comprised mostly of originals, was a big band guide to swinging the blues. Unlike the rest of the popular swing maestros—white bands more than black—who paid regular homage to Tin Pan Alley, Count Basie stuck mostly with blues and hard-driving unfamiliar pieces. In short, the Basie band was not a split-personality band. No other swing band tried the Basie formula. All the rest who paraded under the swing banner were actually two groups in one—sweet *and* swing.

There were two reasons for this. First, was the music itself, rooted in the Hollywood-Broadway-Tin Pan Alley tradition. Many of the tunesmiths writing in the 1920s, 1930s and 1940s were European immigrants who had absorbed characteristics of operettas and other types of their native music and synthesized them in their writing. That the ballads they wrote comprised a large part of the nation's popular music can be gleaned by a quick glance at the top ten tunes of each of the first five years of *Your Hit Parade:* of the 50 songs on that catalog of tune popularity, 37 were romantic ballads. Swingdom could not ignore ballads. The second reason swing bands operated on two levels was radio. "Change of pace" was an expression heard often during big band broadcasts; programming strictures required it. Such tempo variations may be one reason why swing outfits were as popular on radio as they were. (In a later era when disco was touted as the "new dance music," its quick demise came about mainly because of the thudding monotony of its beat.) How well a swing band carried out its two-bands-in-one role became the standard by which it was judged.

George S. Simon who covered the big band beat for *Metronome* magazine called attention to this vital function from time to time. In a 1939 write-up of a Jimmy Dorsey remote broadcast, Simon said:

> The band not only swings to high heaven, but it's capable of producing a brand of sweet that'll make you think you're there. A year or so ago it could do neither well, chiefly because of arrangements that (1) had no definite swing pattern and (2) were none too interesting or mood-creating when it came to sweet.[8]

The networks themselves helped cultivate the notion that the whole nation was jumping and swinging after 1935. Fragments of two 1940 broadcasts illustrate how network remotes helped sell swing, the swing band and the location. The first, originating in March of 1940 at Frank Dailey's Meadowbrook (a mecca for white, middle-class college students) is from one of NBC's popular Saturday afternoon broadcasts called *Matinee at Meadowbrook:*

DORSEY ORCH: (Theme Song)

ANNOUNCER: Presenting that Sentimental Gentleman of Swing, Tommy Dorsey, his golden voice trombone and His Orchestra.

DORSEY ORCH: (Theme up and out)

ANNOUNCER: And good afternoon and greetings everybody. That familiar melody ushers in another full hour with that Sentimental Gentleman of Swing, Tommy Dorsey, his golden voice trombone, his versatile orchestra, with Frank Sinatra, Jo Stafford, and The Pied Pipers. This program comes to you from Frank Dailey's Meadowbrook, located on Route 23, The Newark-Pompton Turnpike in Cedargrove, New Jersey. Now this afternoon, the Meadowbrook is again packed with hundreds and hundreds of kids who jammed their way in here to hear Tommy Dorsey and His Orchestra.

DORSEY: Yes, Bill they make a mighty appreciative audience. You know, people think that youngsters today are all swing addicts, jitterbugs, alligators and so on. But that's not so at all. They've all gone back to liking nice simple, sweet stuff.

ANNOUNCER: Really Tommy?

DORSEY: Sure. Wait till we ask them. Kids, what would you like to hear? Sweet or swing?

AUDIENCE: SWING!

DORSEY: Fine thing, Bill. I thought you were gonna get them to say sweet so the boys and I could take it easy.

ANNOUNCER: Well Tommy, when they come here to hear you, they want to hear each tune played the way it ought to be played. You know they expect different arrangements to fit the mood of each tune because that's what you're famous for . . .[9]

Despite the foregoing, the next 57 minutes of *Matinee at Meadowbrook* included: two medleys of college songs; one medley of sorority tunes; three swing numbers; and the rest ballads.

Broadcast proceedings emanating from the Savoy Ballroom were often interlaced with jive talk and posturing by white announcers. Introductions such as this one from a 1940 Savoy Ballroom remote were not at all unusual:

ANNOUNCER: Presenting the Twentieth Century Gabriel, Erskine Hawkins!

HAWKINS ORCH: (Theme song)

ANNOUNCER: Well, there's that melody you like so well, "Tuxedo Junction." Tuxedo Junction," bringing us another program of jumping jive. Jumping jive with the Twentieth Century Gabe, playing that old trumpet of his, and of course, his boys surrounding him here. And here? Well, no other place than Swing Village, Swing Village in Harlem. And the locale, up in Harlem, of course. The old place itself, The Home of Happy Feet, the Savoy Ballroom, way up here on Lennox Avenue in the early 140s in New York City.

HAWKINS ORCH: (Theme up and out).[10]

To hear the announcer come on, one got the impression Hawkins and his crew were going to blast the roof off the Savoy. The half-hour program ended up, however, as a more or less routine swing card: two dragging ballads; two slow blues; and two jump numbers.

Swing bands paid high dues to reach exalted pinnacles like the Savoy and The Meadowbrook. The Tommy Dorsey's, the Erskine Hawkins's and their bands accepted the rigors of life on the road that went with the territory. Seventy-five dollars a week for a sideman was considered good pay. Occasionally a featured star instrumentalist might earn as much as 200 dollars weekly. Yet, during the Depression, these were the top jobs in popular music, and competition was keen. With the leaders, it was another

story. The top swing maestros, were astute businessmen; and their personal take was usually a well-guarded secret. But some idea of the money
involved may be gleaned from a random check of Glenn Miller of three
one-nighters during a Midwestern tour in the late spring and early summer
of 1941:

> June 22nd—5,500 persons @$1.10 each—Modernistic Ballroom, Mil-
> waukee
> July 1st—2,750 persons @$1.75 each—Meadow Acres Ballroom, To-
> peka, Kansas
> July 12th—6,000 persons @$1.25 male & $1.10 female—Aragon Ball-
> room, Chicago [11]

If a leader had a distaste for the commercial side of pop music, he was in
the wrong line of work. Artie Shaw, whose popularity put him at the head
of the swing parade for a year, was that kind of leader. A maverick, he
was outspoken in his disdain for the way the popular music game was
played.

Not unlike his contemporaries, Goodman, the Dorseys and Miller,
Artie Shaw had served his apprenticeship in network studio orchestras beginning in the late 1920s. In 1935, he put together a swing ensemble that
faltered because, as he soon learned, strings and swing did not mix well
together. By 1937, he had a modestly successful swing aggregation going,
but it failed to satisfy him—or his bookers. Ever the perfectionist, the clar-
inet-playing leader kept experimenting, and in mid-1938, Shaw felt he finally had the orchestra he had always wanted. It was a swing band, to be
sure. But there were differences. The new Shaw unit was not a powerhouse, yet it swung with a subtlety heretofore unknown in swing circles.
It projected none of Goodman's high energy ensemble passages, and none
of Basie's roaring pyrotechnics. Since Shaw and Goodman both played
clarinets, comparisons were inevitable. Years later, jazzman Cannonball
Adderley described the difference with two apt adjectives: Goodman played
hot swing; Shaw played *cool* swing.

Co-incidentally, the new-sounding Shaw outfit transferred to another
record label—a move that foreshadowed great changes in popular music
on radio. Artie Shaw's first recording under his new Bluebird contract was
a swing arrangement of "Begin the Beguine." The Cole Porter ballad itself
was intriguing, and given the subtle-swinging Artie Shaw treatment, the
recording became the first million-seller by a swing band. Not even Benny
Goodman could crack through that charmed circle. We have already observed the increased interest in record-collecting when the nation's economic health started showing signs of recovery. Radio stations that once
sneered at using phonograph records began to get the message: listeners
did not necessarily have to have their pop music served-up live-action style.
Toward the end of the 1930s, the perception of radio by the recording

industry was a mixed bag. Good sales of big band recordings, especially those by such as Tommy Dorsey and Casa Loma, had raised eyebrows on record row. Now, here was Artie Shaw with his million-selling "Begin the Beguine." In the retailing division of the wax kingdom, if a vote had been taken in 1938, however, the conventional wisdom that airplay was detrimental to record sales would probably have won out.*

Artie Shaw's appearance on the music scene signified more than the arrival of a new pop idol. He was a leader who had done his homework. In his autobiography he points out,

> Some way had to be devised to make [my musicians] sound good in spite of their inexperience. This could only be done through constant rehearsing, through careful arranging . . . and above all through time . . . There is nothing that can take the place of appearing night after night in front of audiences. The very tension that results from being aware of an audience is one of the biggest single factors that result in polishing the surface of a band . . . I can't think of a single band that has ever achieved and maintained success where this surface polish has been lacking. In other words, in popular music, mass acceptance can't be achieved without at least a surface flawlessness . . . The mass American public is by and large musically illiterate. There is always this engrossment with surface detail rather than intrinsic merit.[12]

Artie Shaw, a student of popular music, was aware of the growing importance of records. In his analysis of the anatomy of hits, he came to the conclusion that each successful record had a "clear transparency," arranged so simply that "even a lay listener could see all the way through the surface of the music right down to the bottom." Starting with "Begin the Beguine," Shaw imparted a needed "transparency" to the songs of the musical theater. He introduced to his young followers the melodies of Cole Porter, Jerome Kern, George Gershwin, Sigmund Romberg, Rodgers and Hart, Vincent Youmans. Thus, an important body of music received the exposure a Broadway stage in every city could not have delivered. Sweet bands had always leaned to this material, but it was through Artie Shaw's gently swinging versions of show tunes that swing may have left one of its most enduring marks on hordes of hepcats.

Not since Wendell Hall's "It Ain't Gonna Rain No More" had a recording been so vital to a popular artist's career as "Begin the Beguine" was to Artie Shaw's. Juke box and airplay of this and other Shaw recordings, network remotes and personal appearance demand heralded the new swing idol. By the end of 1938, Benny Goodman had been dethroned.

---

* Radio's role as a Depression escape-mechanism has often overshadowed its unsung contributions to the marketplace. *Variety's Radio Directory*, vol. 2, issued in 1938 reported Americans spent in the previous year $700 million for receivers, tubes, repairs and electricity. *Down Beat*, in the meantime, for the same year, estimated dance music grossed $80 million and employed 18,000 musicians on the road alone.

They called Shaw, the "King of the Clarinet," but everybody knew he had upstaged Goodman in every way. The Shaw band's surface slickness was enhanced by young Buddy Rich on drums who booted the band along with an insouciance that belied the "lift" he communicated. More recordings and remotes, a commercial radio show and movies made Artie Shaw the unquestioned pop music superstar of 1939. Then suddenly, late in the year, he turned his back on the whole business. He scrapped his band, and from a Hollywood bunker blasted the hype and hypocrisy of the music business. But his reasons, as he reveals in his autobiography, went deeper. They provide a revealing insight into the pop music performer as celebrity:

> I began to discover that this business of being a "big name" was a full time job. People insisted that I was "different" . . . People began to point at me on the street and ask for my autograph, stare at me and do all sorts of nonsensical things people generally do with those they themselves have put up on the curious pedestal erected for these freaks, these public personalities who have achieved success . . . The truth is I *was* a sort of side-show freak—that was the essence of my so-called celebrity.[13]

His fans and the radio music establishment castigated Shaw for his ingratitude. When he surfaced early in 1940, it was to go back on the attack. This time he was a participant in a *Radio Guide* "debate" with sweet band leader, Sammy Kaye. The point-counterpoint of the Shaw-Kaye exchange reflects not only Shaw's outspokenness, but how the band world was arrayed in two camps on the battleground of radio:

SHAW	KAYE
Radio is used strictly to hype bands. They worship the "Great God Mike."	The greatest thing that happened to the band business was radio. Radio has brought the music of the bands into the homes of millions.
Radio wires are the result of deals between hotels and booking agencies. A leader should not have to fight politics and corruption.	A bandleader doesn't fight politics and corruption. He fights competition from rivals who want hotel spots he thinks he ought to have.
What radio wants from the bandleader is a bunch of catch-phrases, slogans and wisecracks.	There isn't a wisecrack or catch-phrase invented that will make bad music good.[14]

Later in 1940, Artie Shaw returned to the band wars with another swing band which included a string section, and came up with his second million-seller, "Stardust." At the same time, Shaw formed a small jazz combo from within the big band and called it The Gramercy Five. Instead of a piano, the swing prodigal used a harpsichord in The Gramercy Five, producing an unusual, clanking sound that created the effect of a

chamber ensemble.* The Gramercy Five gave Artie Shaw his third million-selling record, "Summit Ridge Drive." Despite the avant-garde string
section in a swing band, and despite the cling-clanging harpsichord's re-
moval from antiquity to modern popular music, Shaw found the stardust
road a bumpy one this time. By 1941, with good bookings (including those
network remotes he found so distasteful), another hit record, "Frenesi"
and the addition of Negro trumpeter Roy Eldridge, "Artie Shaw and His
Famous Orchestra" regained only a small portion of its former glory, and
even less of its fame. The "clear transparency" Shaw himself had articu-
lated was missing. The orchestra some claimed was the best swing band
America had ever produced—even better than Benny Goodman's—had lost
its credibility in a sea of strings. For what it was worth, Artie Shaw may
have found consolation in watching two top competitors, Tommy Dorsey
and Harry James, copy his string-section idea.

Things were tough all over in the swing-leaning band fraternity at this
time. Like orchestras of other persuasions, the swingsters were afflicted by
the declining interest in big bands described in Chapter 4. During radio's
first two decades, music for dancing played by the big bands had dictated
the content and direction of American popular music. But, as with the bit
player of the theater, who ends up stealing the show—so in the sphere of
the Great American Bandstand, the Singer galaxied from the role of
"added attraction" to one of much stellar proportions, eclipsing even the
biggest bandleaders. Not only had a star been born, but a whole new con-
stellation was dominating the musical firmament. The music makers, like
dedicated astronomers, focused their telescopes on a rising class, the vocalists, whose talents would add the greatest sheen to their calling. The
result was a long and impressive list of discoveries—some meteoric—destined to capture the quixotic public fancy and introduce a new chapter to
American popular music entitled, "Crooners, Singers and Other Voices."

NOTES

1. ———. "Radio Not Merely Poor Man's Theater Is Thesis of New CBS Brochure," *Variety*, November 27, 1934, p. 38.
2. Peter Gammond and Peter Clayton. *Dictionary of Popular Music*, Philosophical Library,
(New York), 1961, p. 214.

---

* In network radio's heyday, a number of swing bands formed small jazz-oriented combos,
featuring men from within the parent organization. Paul Whiteman started the practice
with his "Jazz Wing." Others who followed included: Benny Goodman (trios, quartets,
quintets, sextets); Tommy Dorsey (Clambake Seven); Bob Crosby (Bobcats); Woody Herman (Four Chips). The band-within-a-band was an added attraction and gave its members
an opportunity for freer expression during a 20- or 30-minute interlude, after playing struc-
tured arrangements in the big band for several hours. Only one *regular* small swing-cum-
jazz combo, with no big band connection, was distinctive enough to land its own coast-to-
coast show. Oddly, it was a black outfit. John Kirby and His Sextet, whose program was
called *Flow Gently Sweet Rhythm*, was heard on CBS in a desirable time slot, late Sunday
afternoons in 1941, and for a short time after World War II.

3. Benny Goodman. *The Kingdom of Swing,* Frederick Ungar, (New York), 1961, p. 129.
4. *Ibid.* pp. 161–162.
5. D. Russell Connor and Warren Hicks. *BG on the Record,* Arlington House, (New Rochelle), 1969, p. 130.
6. Benny Goodman. *op. cit.* 198–199.
7. John Hammond. *John Hammond on Record,* Summit Books, (New York), 1977, p. 165.
8. George Simon. "Jimmy Dorsey Swings to High Heaven." Reprint of 1939 Metronome article, in *Simon Says,* Arlington House, (New Rochelle), 1971, pp. 127–128.
9. Tommy Dorsey remote broadcast. March 9, 1940, Joyce Music Studio, Tape No. 249.
10. "Erskine Hawkins/Cab Calloway 1940," Jazz Panorama 16.
11. John Flower. *Moonlight Serenade,* Arlington House, (New Rochelle), 1972, pp. 316, 318, 324, 328.
12. Artie Shaw. *The Trouble with Cinderella,* Collier Books, (New York), 1963, p. 276.
13. *Ibid.* pp. 304–305.
14. "Shaw vs. Kaye," *Radio Guide,* February 2, 1940, pp. 4–5.

CHAPTER 7

Crooners, Singers and Other Voices

WHEN THAT KINGPIN of popular music in the 1920s, the dance orchestra leader, wanted to feature a vocal chorus, he called on a sideman. Some maestros, unwilling to share the limelight with an instrumentalist, handled the words themselves. Either way, the renditions were often abominable—the song itself was a dreadful novelty (in which case showmanship dictated a hammy performance), or if the tune had intrinsic merit, it was quickly dissipated by the performer's limitations. Bing Crosby changed all that.

Originally intending to pursue a career in the law, Crosby and a fellow townsman, Al Rinker (Mildred Bailey's brother), formed a singing partnership and entertained in their native Spokane. Encouraged to go professional, they landed a job on the Fanchon and Mario vaudeville circuit in a show called, "The Sycopated Idea." A Paul Whiteman talent scout urged his boss to catch the Crosby-Rinker act, which he did. Whiteman had the boys ushered into his presence for an audition, and right then and there the duo became part of the Whiteman entertainment colossus. Another voice, Harry Burris's, made it a trio, and thus was born one of the classier singing groups of 1927, the Rhythm Boys.

Paul Whiteman's organization was an excellent training ground for Bing Crosby. It afforded him the kind of exposure that only the top theater, dance hall and night club dates could offer. Whiteman, however, found Crosby's attitude toward work too casual and sacked him in less than two years. When Crosby left Whiteman in late 1929, the other Rhythm Boys went with him. The trio took their own show on the road again—which,

100

considering the limited booking opportunities for their kind of act, meant vaudeville. Bing and his free-spirited colleagues had gotten valuable radio experience during the Whiteman stint. As part of the supporting cast on the Big Man's Old Gold CBS show, they had usually done several numbers in the one-hour weekly divertissement. Gus Arnheim, whose orchestra was playing at Los Angeles's Ambassador Hotel (the "in"-spot for the growing movie colony at the time) had followed the Rhythm Boys and liked what he heard. Since he also happened to be looking for an added attraction, he hired the Rhythm Boys. Their radio experience was the clincher because Gus Arnheim enjoyed a coveted radio wire that sent his music from the fashionable Cocoanut Grove to San Francisco and points north. Arnheim also recognized in Crosby the dominant figure of the trio and brought him front-and-center to solo on the nightly broadcasts. The trendy Hollywood crowd helped things along, and a minor cult movement for Bing and the Rhythm Boys sprang up during their California engagement.

Crosby's Cocoanut Grove popularity, meanwhile, led to another stroke of good fortune. In late 1930, he joined the Arnheim band to cut several sides as part of the bandleader's Victor contract. Among the sides was "I Surrender, Dear," a big favorite with Cocoanut Grove audiences—so big he sometimes had to sing it several times a night. A copy found its way aboard a luxury liner, among whose passengers was one William Paley, president of the Columbia Broadcasting System. In his autobiography, Paley tells how he happened to come across the record:

> I first heard Bing Crosby's pleasant baritone voice on the S.S. Europa . . . in June, 1931. Each time I circled the deck I would pass a teenage boy on a deckchair, listening to a phonograph recording of the same song, "I Surrender, Dear." One voice on that record stood out pure, dreamy, melodious with a unique phrasing of the lyrics. When I stopped to look at the record, there was the name in tiny print: "Chorus by Bing Crosby". . . . I cabled the CBS office: "SIGN UP SINGER BING CROSBY."[1]

When he returned to New York, Paley was "furious" to learn his associates had decided against the move because the word was out on the show biz grapevine that Crosby was unreliable. The CBS president took charge of the project at this point:

> I was not trying to buy reliability, but a unique and wonderful voice. Within a week, Crosby came in from the West Coast, but accompanied by a very able lawyer who had seen to it that NBC learned of my interest in his client. His price for Crosby, $1500 a week on sustaining time and $3000 a week when a sponsor was found. . . . was an outrage. . . . I negotiated as hard as I could, but we finally settled for his asking price.[2]

CBS installed Bing Crosby in radio's toughest time slot, 7:00–7:15 p.m., Monday through Friday, opposite *Amos 'n Andy*, which only happened to be the top-rated program on the air in late-summer, 1931. Bing's CBS debut was a disaster. He had a cold, and by trying to sing over it, he aggravated his pipes to such an extent he couldn't produce a sound. The premier show was cancelled with the standard "due-to-circumstances-beyond-our-control" disclaimer. Three nights later, same time, same network, that "unique and wonderful voice" appeared again. Crosby was not exactly the paragon of composure. He was "terrified" of New York itself, according to Agnes Law, retired Head Librarian, CBS Reference Library, who was present: "I recall taking material to the studio for his program. Everett, his brother and manager, was standing by while Bing was pacing the floor too petrified to open his mouth to sing. That continued for three or four attempts until he was underway."[3] The ensuing stream of letters and telegraphs signalled Bing Crosby an over-night star. From that point forward, the singer of popular songs could expect eventually to be on equal footing with the dance band. Indeed, the singer would henceforth not be merely a throw-in, but a needed member of the orchestra's table of organization.*

Bing Crosby's main talent—and he often admitted to modest natural gifts—was his ability to harness breathing and voice control, then project the proper delivery through the microphone. In short, Crosby's mastery was the mastery of the microphone. Around the time his radio career was taking off, microphone technology had advanced considerably, giving Bing another advantage in voice projection. Further, radio receivers had just come out with tone controls to balance upper and lower registers and regulate pitch. As Crosby's popularity increased, the expression, *crooning* (invented in the late 1920s to describe a style of interpreting a popular song, especially a love song) came into common usage. The term *crooner*, according to popular music etymologists Peter Gammond and Peter Clayton, was coined "when the frantic necessity to label the popular forms deriving from jazz was felt. It comes from the negro word meaning to sing a lullaby, [and denotes] a style which deviated from previous straight singing by copying jazz intonation and phrasing and employing a sensual tone from deep down in the throat and sliding up to the notes, rather than hitting them immediately."[4]

At the center of every fad or profound change in popular music, of course, stands one figure or group around whom the movement revolves—for followers and imitators. With crooning it was Crosby, and across the dial imitators came spewing out of those improved speakers. Although Bing Crosby and his crooning never became the *cause celèbre* of the Presley-rock and roll flap, reaction was sharp and shrill. Cardinal O'Connell of the Boston Archdiocese found this new way of singing a pop song one

---

* Rudy Vallee, the "personality," far outlived Vallee, the singer. Crosby was essentially a *singer*, despite his other show biz triumphs. Never an interpreter or "seller" of a tune, Vallee had a nasalized delivery that lacked the color, shading and naturalness of Bing Crosby's.

of the chief forces of evil in the land as of January, 1932. In an address before a thousand members of Boston's Holy Name Society, the Cardinal delivered an ecclesiastical right to radio's jaw, denouncing crooning as,

> Immoral and imbicile slush. A degenerate, low-down sort of interpretation of love. A love song is a beautiful thing in itself . . . But listen again with this new idea in your head and see if you do not get a sensation of revolting disgust at a man whining a degenerate song, which is unworthy of any American man . . . Instead of hearing good music over the radio, we have to put up with verse after verse of . . . that bleating and whining, with disgusting words, the meaning of which is a low-down source of sexual influence . . . It is a sensuous, effeminate luxurious sort of paganism . . . Think of the boys and girls who are brought up with that idea of music.* 5

A sure sign that crooning had arrived was the clamor it evoked in the press:

> As music it is atrocious . . . Of doubtful moral quality, and the slithering, sliding lounge-lizard voice of the crooner is anathema to so many that the radio enterprise is just now under an undoubted handicap of unpopularity with enough people to cause the manufacturers and program promoters to be concerned about their unseen audiences.
> —Washington *Evening Star*

> [Crooners] resort to vulgar suggestiveness. It is a gratuitous insult to that intelligent person which rightfully expects a better return for its expensive investment in radio equipment.
> —Springfield *Union*

> [The Cardinal's words] are certain to find an echo throughout the country.
> —Pittsburgh *Post-Gazette.* 6

Although the hubbub over crooning within the broadcasting family was mild compared to the rock and roll furor, there were regular flare-ups. WOR's program director found radio singing,

> far from what it ought to be. For the most part, it is nothing but untrained crooning that passes for singing . . . There is a deadly monotony about crooning that even the lowest morons must get tired of. But in spite of what we say against it, the ceaseless crooning goes on day after day, and those who have learned the trick continue to reap the rich harvest, while many better singers are driven to the point of joining the bread lines . . . The average crooner knows nothing about voice placement . . . He is not even interested in good artistry as long as he can hold his audience

---

* There is no account of whether the Cardinal, a decade later, objected to the film, *Going My Way*, in which a crooning padre, played by a crooner named Bing Crosby, stole the show—and won an Oscar.

with vocal tricks and mannerisms. And so radio has created a false standard of singing at the expense of real singing.[7]

Just as 1920s dance music, under the label "jazz," took its lumps when it pentrated the airwaves, so crooning became the focal point of the attack on musical radio in the early 1930s. Crooning was *the* buzz word, just as swing, rock and roll, and disco would become buzz words in other eras.* But through all the cant and clichés about crooning that often passed for valid criticism was a profound failure to appreciate the difference between good and bad singing on the radio. Bing Crosby was a *good* radio singer. His 15-minute daily recital of popular songs on CBS benefited from a conscious effort to stay away from over-production and cutesy continuity. It is inconceivable that a pop artist in a modern television series would receive on his/her first show such a simple introduction as this one of Bing's:

> ANNOUNCER: Here is the moment you've been waiting for. He's been the favorite of California. Here's Bing Crosby with "Just One More Chance."[8]

Within two months, Paley was able to pass Crosby's high tab on to a sponsor, the American Tobacco Company. Surprisingly, American's shrewd president, George Washington Hill, chose the firm's Cremo Cigars as the product he wanted pushed on the young singer's show, rather than Lucky Strike Cigarettes. Hill, the pioneer in harnessing cigarette advertising to the youthful appeal of musical radio, was pushing hard to retain Lucky Strike's newly acquired sales edge over Camel. In 1930, Luckies had moved ahead of Camel and Chesterfield. Much of the credit went to Hill's hard-hitting radio commercials presented in popular music settings. (We shall examine smoke-filled airwaves in detail in the next two chapters.) For Cremo, however, American Tobacco wanted Crosby. Possibly Hill had reverse sales psychology in mind, because at the time cigars were considered the delectations of older men; further, cigar-smoking was regarded by many to be an unsophisticated and unclean habit. What better vehicle than Bing Crosby, then, to alter that perception? The refreshing, young Crosby fit in well with Cremo's cleanliness pitch:

> Your eyes can't tell whether a cigar is clean or whether it is made by unsanitary methods. Smoke Certified Cremo and *know* that your cigar is clean. Cremo, made in the famous Perfecto shape, that is the mark of fine quality—is the only cigar in the world finished under glass. Fifty-six health officials endorse Cremo's crusade for cleanliness.[9]

Shortly after Cremo took over sponsorship, Hill, probably aware of the tough *Amos 'n Andy* competition on NBC, had the program moved to

---

* Words describing bodies of popular music always end up in song titles ("Sing Me a Swing Song," "Rock and Roll Is Here to Stay," "Disco Inferno.") For crooning it was "Learn to Croon (If You Want to Win Your Heart's Desire.")

7:15–7:30p.m. Eastern time. In the custom of the day, a second live broadcast was fed at 11:00p.m. to reach Western zone listeners in prime time. Top-of-the-line announcer David Ross, whose silken, soft voice complemented Crosby's romantic baritone nicely, was host and commercial spieler. The streamlined format mercifully had no provision for banter between Bing and/or Ross and/or the orchestra leader—only the theme, short introductions and titles, the songs, and the commercials:

ROSS: Bing Crosby—the Cremo Singer

THEME: (Crosby sings "Where the Blue of the Night")

ROSS: (Identifies show. Reads short commercial. Introduces first song.)

CROSBY: (Sings first selection)

ROSS: (Introduces second selection)

CROSBY: (Sings second selection)

ROSS: (Introduces instrumental by Carl Fenton and the Cremo Orchestra.)

ORCHESTRA: (Plays instrumental)

ROSS: (Reads Cremo commercial. Introduces final selection.)

CROSBY: (Sings final selection)

ROSS: (Closes show).[10]

Selections for a week in February, 1932 exemplify Crosby's reliance on the day's pop hits, with an oldie thrown in now and then:

February 1
Can't We Talk It Over?
* One of Us Was Wrong
Can This Be Love?
Goodnight Moon

February 2
Starlight
Was That the Human Thing To Do?
* Day Break
How Can You Say You Love Me?

February 3
With a Song in My Heart
I'll See You in My Dreams
* Without You
I Found You

February 4
Love, You Funny Thing
Ain't Misbehavin'
* How Long Will it Last?
The Cuban Love Song

February 5
Just Friends
There's Something in Your Eyes
* A Cottage Small
All of Me

February 6
My Woman
Snuggled on Your Shoulder
* Hits from 'Okay'
Beautiful Melody of Love [11]

(*) Indicates instrumental by orchestra

Crosby's unique talent for illuminating a song's lyrics started the country on its way to paying more attention to the words. After Crosby, bands followed suit, and in time, a performance without lyrics would become a radio rarity.* Crosby stayed with the fifteen-minute format through the 1932–1933 season on Chesterfield's *Music That Satisfies*. Subsequently, it was found those qualities that characterized Bing Crosby, the singer, could be translated into Bing Crosby, the total personality. Thus, once Crosby was accorded the one-a-week-prime-time treatment on the Woodbury program in the fall of 1933, America heard what was to be first of the well-calculated Crosby image, the enduring persona of the relaxed, easy-going performer—one that script-writers would find a joy to exploit. Lines for Bing could be fashioned on any subject including his personal life. This exchange between Ken Niles, the announcer, and Crosby on a 1934 Woodbury show was characteristic of many in which the public was to get selected peeks at his family, his golf game, his horses, his friends:

NILES: Ah, yes—twins. Say, have you learned much about them?

CROSBY: No, it's a new racket for me. But what would you like to know?

NILES: Well, tell me something about them. Anything!

CROSBY: Well, twins usually look alike, having been born more or less under the same conditions, and having no preference in the matter.

NILES: There you go, Bing!

CROSBY: Sure, and if they resemble the mother, they have what might be called a flying start in life.

NILES: What if they resemble the father?

CROSBY: Well, in that case, they should be held right end up and patted lightly on their respective backs.[12]

Throughout his long radio career, even after his shows were designated "variety," Bing Crosby never strayed from his popular music base. For the Woodbury show, there were generally three songs by Crosby, one by the Boswells, one by Bing with the Boswells, and an orchestra instrumental in each half-hour. Writers found his carefree manner useful for framing song lead-ins. The dialogue with Niles cited above continued and provided a graceful transition to the Boswells' number:

NILES: And after the twins grow up, what sort of careers do you have in mind for them?

---

* CBS's early evening block programing of popular music at the time, in which it followed Crosby with the Boswell Sisters, 7:30–7:45p.m., and Morton Downey, 7:45–8:00p.m., helped raise lyric-consciousness further and faster.

CROSBY: Well, I don't quite know. I hadn't thought about it. But if they were girls instead of boys, and triplets instead of twins, they could sing like . . .

BOSWELLS: (Humming and under for . . .)

CROSBY: Three girls with but a single fellow—harmony. And for many weeks to come—the Boswell Sisters![13]

By now Bing had become BING. An established show business figure, he had already appeared in his first feature-length film, the *Big Broadcast of 1932* *—an indication of Hollywood's recognition of radio. In a loosely-constructed plot, George Burns is manager of a radio station about to go under. Bing Crosby, the station's popular crooner, enlists the aid of his millionaire friend to buy the outlet and put on an all-star radio show. The "big broadcast" device is a means to trot before the camera top radio personalities of the day—Burns and Allen, Arthur Tracy (The "Street Singer"), Vincent Lopez and Cab Calloway and their orchestras, singer Donald Novis, and leading announcers Jimmy Wallington and Norman Brokenshire.

Starting in September, 1935, Crosby starred in the first of what was to be an eleven-year run, a music-variety program, the *Kraft Music Hall,* Thursdays at 10 p.m. on NBC. The *Music Hall's* weekly roster of talent and guest stars read like a who's who of the entertainment and sports worlds. When Ken Niles did the opening billboard for a show in early 1942, it was in the *Kraft Music Hall* tradition of star-studded line-ups:

NILES: The Kraft Music Hall, with Bing Crosby, Mary Martin, Victor Borge, Jerry Lester, John Scott Trotter and his Orchestra, the Music Maids and Hal, Madeleine Carroll, star of Paramount Pictures' *Bahama Passage,* Igor Gorin, famous concert baritone, and Slammin' Sammy Snead, one of the nation's colorful golf pros.[14]

In spite of that lengthy guest roster, the gags, the skits, the interviews, the obligatory exchanges of mutual admiration, Bing warbled 11 numbers, all popular songs, save one.

The infectious Crosby showmanship, it seemed, rubbed off on everyone. No less an intellectual than media critic Gilbert Seldes devoted a major piece in *Scribner's* to America's leading pop singer. Seldes seemed stunned, not only that a crooner could handle Proust, but that it would happen on radio:

---

* Hollywood often capitalized on radio's popularity in the 1930s and 1940s by producing pictures with broadcasting plots. There were the *Big Broadcasts of 1936, 1937 and 1938,* and dozens more. *Love Is in the Air,* released in 1937, featured a young actor, Ronald Reagan, in his first film role, a radio announcer.

When Bing Crosby spoke the name of Marcel Proust into the microphone on the night of August 6, 1936, more or less in honor of Miracle Whip, the long uneasy, half-scandalous affair between commerce and the arts was at last acknowledged. It was all the more definite because Mr. Crosby, introducing an ancient melody and using the words "remembrance of things past," might so easily have referred to Shakespeare instead; but airily, jauntily, with cold assurance and a good accent he pronounced the name which had been, a mere ten years ago, so alien, so perverse, and so exclusive. It was not a declaration of war; it was an announcement that the radio had embraced, or taken over the arts.[15]

On the local level, the Bing Crosby phenomenon was a boon to program directors who had time periods to fill. Crosby had switched to the newly-minted Decca label in late summer of 1934, a tremendous coup for the fledgling firm. Decca immediately began issuing a steady flow of Bing's platters, which gave stations (already owning a sizeable backlog of the crooner's songs on his previous labels) the kind of variety they needed. No other popular artist in the 1930s offered the depth of recorded material from which a station could draw in building a record show. Bing Crosby was the first popular artist on radio to find virtual unanimous local station acceptance around whom to build a complete program unit, whether in quarter-, or half-, or even full-hour, blocks. At WORK in York, where the station's all-live music covenant with the FCC was in force, Harold Miller acknowledged even his conservative Pennsylvania Dutch constituency was ready for a daily dose of Crosby crooning: "We didn't play recordings for the first three years we were on the air. But when we did start using them, the first program we put together with records was a daily 15-minute *Bing Crosby Show.*"

Some stations, not lacking in imagination (or gall), employed Bing Crosby recordings to implement a common radio subterfuge of the 1930s. They had the announcer introduce recordings in a manner that gave the listener the impression the music was live. The furor created by such artifice flared up from time to time, and depending which side of the argument you were on, it was either outright deception, or ingenious showmanship. *Variety,* in its ongoing coverage of the practice, tells how it was done in 1936:

> Copy has announcer open periods hailing 'em as entertainment by Crosby and then mumbling word "recordings." From then on warbler is addressed as though he were delivering songs in the flesh. Sample spiels: "Well, Bing, what are you going to sing for us today? . . . Let's see now. I notice we have you down to give us your rendition of _____." (And then at record's conclusion): "Fine work, Bing. You were never in a better voice, etc. etc." (And then as program nears end): "Just have time for one chorus of Bing's next song." (Then after orchestra on record barely gets through opening bars and time is up): "Sorry, Bing, we just couldn't squeeze that one in. We'll have to do it on tomorrow's program."[16]

It is difficult to over-emphasize Bing Crosby's influence on American popular music. Most popular artists owed their reputations and influence to youthful followings. Inevitably, not far behind, has come an older generation, inveighing and nay-saying. No so with Bing Crosby. Almost from the beginning, his appeal was universal, not limited to preferences governed by age or sex considerations. Radio, with its capability of reaching into the nooks and crannies of America, gave Bing Crosby's career the kind of firm base no other medium was capable of. He was the first popular singer to benefit from the mass circulation radio offered.

Imitators were unable to match Crosby's way with a song. Except for a freak accident, Russ Columbo who was hailed for a short while as Bing's chief competitor, might have come close. Hefty chunks of air time, recordings and a stint at leading his own orchestra brought Colombo to national attention in the early 1930s. His silken baritone voice and phrasing approximated Crosby's, so much so that some contemporary critics maintained it was Crosby who copied Colombo. Colombo, they said, who but for an "unloaded" pistol accident in 1934, would have de-throned Crosby and become the ultimate crooner.

But if no pop vocalist rose to challenge Bing Crosby directly, there were plenty who developed their own individual styles. Radio welcomed lots of them with open microphones. Even though network radio had become an important entertainment medium by the early 1930s, it continued to look to the older show business forms for singers. With their insatiable appetite for material, program producers were constantly on the prowl seeking new talent. From vaudeville or musical comedy stages of the late 1920s came tenors Morton Downey, Clark Dennis, Donal Novis and Kenny Baker, Singin' Sam (the "Barbasol Man"), Ruth Etting, Jane Froman, Irene Beasley and Gertrude Niessen. The Yale campus even sent two fair-to-middling crooner types to radio: Lanny Ross, singing emcee of the *Maxwell House Showboat,* a top network entry in the 1930s; and Barry Wood, who topped off his singing career as the lead male singer on *Your Hit Parade.*

Only one other singer besides Bing Crosby reached star status before ex-big band singers went out on their own to become the dominant force in musical radio. She was Kate Smith. Two generations have grown up since she made her initial impact on popular music through radio in the early 1930s. Almost 50 years later, she was still able to command media attention—first as a good luck charm singer of "God Bless America" at Philadelphia Flyers games, and later as the key figure in a real-life, front-page soap opera that found relatives quibbling over her estate while she languished in a nursing home. Without a svelte figure and other superficial glamor trappings Americans demand of their show biz favorites, Kate Smith came from the Broadway stage to Paley's Tryout Camp at CBS, singing just as Crosby did, in fringe time periods. Like Crosby, Smith had a stogie sponsor, Paley's La Palina, on her maiden network fling. She flourished throughout the network heyday, having a prime time show most every season beginning in 1931. When live radio went down the tubes, Kate Smith played network disc jockey for several seasons. She also did a successful daily talk show on the Mutual Network with her lifetime mentor-manager, Ted Collins. Her greatest claim to pop music immortality, of course, was her introduction of "God Bless America" in 1942. In the patriotic-schmaltz tradition, so vital a part of popular music heritage, the Irving Berlin tune became Kate Smith's, virtually sending to extinction her original theme, "When the Moon Comes Over the Mountain."

Despite the important groundwork they laid for singers when radio was a mass entertainment medium, Kate Smith and Bing Crosby were, nevertheless, aberrations because American popular music was dominated by name bands in those pre-War years. But because of Crosby, who almost single-handedly elevated the singer to equal status with the band, leaders found they had to carry featured vocalists to sell their organizations to the networks, theaters, and ballrooms. By the end of the 1930s, no name band was without a singer or a contingent of singers. Tommy Dorsey (with his blockbuster array of Frank Sinatra, Jo Stafford, Connie Haines and the Pied Pipers) and Glenn Miller (whose singing entourage included Ray Eberle, Marian Hutton, Tex Beneke and the Modernaires) dominated the category of swing-leaning (or swing-sweet) bands at this time. Their hits, like those of most big bands, became hits because of a singer's presence. As the name band era drew to a close, leaders found themselves playing second fiddle to their singers.*

One by one top names from big band vocalist camp defected, and before the exodus was over, a sizeable group of pre-rock and roll singers would claim membership in the Ex-Name Band Singer Alumni Association. Any number magnanimously credit their big band experience as the key factor in their later achievements. Frank Sinatra admitted his debt to Tommy Dorsey. In watching Dorsey master breath-control playing trombone, Sinatra says he learned how to adapt that essential art to the voice. Others acknowledge their basic training with big bands in different ways:

> BING CROSBY: How lucky I was! A small town fella working and consorting with all these musical giants in Whiteman's Orchestra. Inevitably something had to accrue to my own professional development. If nothing else, an appreciation of taste, style, and imagination.[17]

> PEGGY LEE: Band singing taught us the importance of interplay with musicians. We had to work close to the arrangement . . . I learned more about music from the men I worked with in bands than I've learned anywhere else. They taught me discipline and the value of rehearsing.[18]

---

* One singer, Dolly Dawn, who had won *Orchestra World's* poll as the outstanding band vocalist of 1937, received so much acclaim, the leader, George Hall, turned his orchestra over to her and signed on as Dawn's manager.

DORIS DAY: Being a band singer teaches you not only how to work in front of people, but also how to deal with them. You have to discipline yourself musically and in every way.[19]

The following table depicts the extent to which big bands served as training academies for leading names in the entertainment field. (A "Top Pop Record" is one that reached *Billboard's* best seller charts):

SINGER	BIG BAND BACKGROUND	NUMBER CAREER TOP POP RECORDS AS A SOLO PERFORMER, 1940–1978
Rosemary Clooney	Tony Pastor	18
Perry Como	Ted Weems	92
Don Cornell	Sammy Kaye	7
Bing Crosby	Paul Whiteman	70
Doris Day	Barney Rapp/Les Brown	30
Johnny Desmond	Gene Krupa/Glenn Miller	6
Mike Douglas	Kay Kyser	1
Billy Eckstine	Earl Hines	12
Ella Fitzgerald	Chick Webb	9
Merv Griffin	Freddy Martin	1
Dick Haymes	Harry James/Benny Goodman/ Tommy Dorsey	23
Al Hibler	Duke Ellington	1
Lena Horne	Noble Sissle/Charlie Barnet	1
Betty Hutton	Vincent Lopez	5
Kitty Kallen	Jimmy Dorsey/Harry James	3
Dorothy Lamour	Herbie Kaye	—
Art Lund	Benny Goodman	4
Helen O'Connell	Jimmy Dorsey	2
Peggy Lee	Benny Goodman	14
Patti Page	Benny Goodman	24
Frank Sinatra	Tommy Dorsey	81
Jo Stafford	Tommy Dorsey	31
Kay Starr	Charlie Barnet	25
Sarah Vaughn	Earl Hines	19
Dinah Washington	Lionel Hampton	17

—Sources for Top Record Data: *Top Pop Records, 1940–1955*, Joel Whitburn, Menomonee Falls, Wis., (1973) and Joel Whitburn *Top Pop Artists & Singles, 1955–1978.* (1979)

Before leaving singers of the big band era, mention should be made of another vocalizing form in radioland. Harmonizing duos, trios and

quartets sprang up within the dance orchestras, in a manner similar to solo
songbirds—instrumentalists (all male) who, more often than not, corned
up the already silly novelties they were handed. When Bing Crosby and
improved microphonic technology arrived to elevate the singer's status,
some leaders, caught up in the bigger-is-better syndrome, hired singing
groups to enhance their radio and theater prospects. From the late 1920s
until the close of the name band period, several dozen aggregations, representing musical styles as diverse as the Whiteman and Waring colossi
and Stan Kenton's carried vocal combos (male, female, or co-ed). The list
that follows includes some of the more prominent ones:

SINGING GROUP	NAME BAND
Skyliners	Ray Anthony
Rhythm Boys/Sportsmen	Gus Arnheim
Moonlight Serenaders	Tex Beneke
Bailey Sisters	Ben Bernie
Four Recorders/Three Strikes	Henry Busse
Rhythmaires	Bob Chester
Esquires/Pied Pipers	Tommy Dorsey
3 Earbenders/Charioteers	Eddie Duchin
Debutantes	Ted Fio Rito
Twin Tones	Jan Garber
Clarinaders	Benny Goodman
LeAhn Sisters/King Sisters	Horace Heidt
Kaydettes	Sammy Kaye
Barry Sisters	Wayne King
G-Noters	Gene Krupa
Modernaires	Glenn Miller
King Sisters	Alvino Rey
Top Hatters	Jan Savitt
Stardusters	Charlie Spivak
Lane Sisters	Fred Waring

A handful of songster groups hit the bigtime with no name-band ties
and managed to get radio exposure, either as feature acts or as guest artists: the Mills Brothers (14 career Top Pop records); the Boswell Sisters;
The Pickens Sisters (NBC's answer to CBS's Boswells); and the Andrews
Sisters (11 career Top Pop records). In drawing up the "perfect radio program" for a 1933 *New Yorker* piece, Ring Lardner listed the Revelers,
along with the Paul Whiteman and George Olsen Orchestras, and Fanny
Brice. One group, The Ink Spots (12 career Top Pop Records) has survived
personnel changes and numerous music fads and fashions to maintain a
loyal following through the 1970s.

Singers' domination of popular music was to last until the FM band began lighting up. The "beautiful music" format, stressing lush instrumentals, arriving on wings of FM song at the start of the 1970s, proved diversity was still the essence of American pop. Ironically, it was around this time Congress passed one of the most flagrantly discriminatory pieces of legislation in its history: banning cigarette advertising from the airwaves. A chorus of protests from the broadcasting and tobacco industries was for naught. For when the smoke screen was cleared away, musical radio had lost its patron saint. Not even George Washington Hill, marching into the national legislature's hallowed halls, leading B.A. Rolfe's blaring contingent, could have saved the day.

NOTES

1. William Paley. *As It Happened,* Doubleday, (New York) 1979, p. 74.
2. *Ibid.* p. 74.
3. Letter from Miss Law to author, December 14, 1980.
4. Peter Gammond and Peter Clayton. *Dictionary of Popular Music,* Philosophical Library, (New York) 1961, p. 56.
5. Quoted in "If the Crooners Could Hear." *Literary Digest,* January 30, 1932, p. 23.
6. *Ibid.* pp. 23 & 24.
7. Lewis Read. "Page for Singers," *Musician,* April, 1932, p. 16.
8. *Bing Crosby Show.* Museum of Broadcasting Tape No. R76: 0018. The Museum dates Crosby's premier CBS show September 2, 1931.
9. Larry F. Kiner. *Bing Crosby, 'Cremo Singer',* Published by Larry F. Kiner, (Kirkland, Washington) 1973, p. 7.
10. *Ibid.* pp. 7 & 8.
11. *Ibid.* p. 13.
12. *Bing Crosby on the Air.* Woodbury Program, September 18, 1934, Sandy Hook Records, 2002.
13. *Ibid.*
14. *Kraft Music Hall,* January 29, 1942, Spokane Records No. 11.
15. Gilbert Seldes. "Bing Crosby, Marcel Proust, and Others," *Scribner's,* October, 1936, p. 78.
16. _____. "WCBM, Balto Spieler Holds One-Way 'Conversation' with Crosby Records," *Variety,* April 29, 1936, p. 38.
17. Bing Crosby. Liner notes on "Early Rare Recordings," Biograph Records, BLP-C13.
18. Quoted in George Simon. *The Big Bands.* Macmillan, (New York) 1967, p. 33.
19. *Ibid.* p. 33.

CHAPTER **8**

Smoke Rings

WHEN CONGRESS LOWERED the boom on broadcast cigarette advertising at midnight, December 31, 1970, it ended the longest run of a popular music sponsor in radio history. Complete program sponsorship by then had long since disappeared in favor of select-market "spot" advertising. But to a generation that grew up when network radio was the leading source of mass entertainment, cigarette manufacturers were the major underwriters of live popular music. They packed their budgets with this programming to the extent that one could look over the roster of cigarette-sponsored music shows and get a pretty good notion of who were America's favorite artists at any given time.

With the rise of movies and print mass media that corresponded with radio's growth, cigarette smoking was portrayed to be not only socially acceptable, but entirely desirable: for men, blasé and dapper; for women, chic and symbolic of a new-found independence; and for both, worldly and sophisticated. George Washington Hill's radio pioneering in behalf of Lucky Strikes ignited the spark that fired the entire industry's interest in tie-ing popular music to the youth market.[1] By 1929, Saturdays at 10 p.m. on NBC, starring B.A. Rolfe's *Lucky Strike Dance Orchestra,* had become a national tune-in habit much like television's *Monday Night Football.* As one *Variety* review observed, "With a personnel of 35 men, Rolfe can do tricks with his instrumentations going in for handsaws, pig-slide whistles, novelty percussion and vibration combinations, in addition to the orthodox instrumental teams."[2]

Hill must have realized he couldn't have the field to himself forever. For while B.A. Rolfe's boys were blasting away on their pig-slide whistles, William Paley was masterminding a plan to bring to CBS a competitive musical attraction—and at the same time, land his first cigarette account. Paley's innately good programming judgment told him if CBS was the number-one network as his sales brochures claimed it was—remember, there were no ratings yet—then CBS ought to have America's *number-one* orchestra. And at the time this was Paul Whiteman who, except for some occasional one-shots, had avoided radio. Now Paley, the astute salesman, took over. He pitched a proposal for a weekly Whiteman extravaganza— not to Lucky Strike's leading competitors, Camel or Chesterfield, but to Old Gold, P. Lorillard's entry, running a weak fourth in the cigarette sweepstakes. The decision-makers at Lorillard said it was a deal if Paley could corral Paul Whiteman. La Palina's erstwhile buyer of radio time, turned seller, still had to convince Paul Whiteman. Undaunted in his pursuit, the youthful network head caught up with Whiteman playing at Chicago's Drake Hotel. In his autobiography, Paley relates the approach he used:

> During a break I introduced myself. A portly man with a great presence, Whiteman looked at me and laughed, "Young man, you don't think I'm going to do a regular program on *radio,* do you?" . . . I tried to persuade him of the advantages of a regular weekly program. He thought it would debase his reputation. We talked a bit and he went back to head his band. Then he returned and we talked some more. We talked until well after midnight . . . of the magic of radio, and of the vastly greater audiences than night clubs or Flo Ziegfeld had to offer. And we talked money. It was late night or near dawn when he said, "By God, you've sold me. I'll try it." [3]

Paul Whiteman's first program for Gold on the Columbia Broadcasting System was beamed across the country Tuesday night, February 5, 1929, 9–10 p.m. No previous musical radio show had been ballyhooed like this one. In May, a promotional tour mounted by private train, the "Old Gold Special," transported the Whiteman company cross-country to Hollywood, where the corpulent maestro was to star in a major film epic, the *King of Jazz.* Concerts were held enroute, with a principal stop at the Indianapolis Speedway, where the orchestra was towed around the track before the Memorial Day speed classic got underway. To modern audiences, conditioned by radio, television, personal appearances and other appurtenances of show biz-media hype, it may be difficult to comprehend the commotion instigated by a single radio series. As the Paul Whiteman-Old Gold Special steamed through the heartland, countless Americans experienced their first in-person encounters with entertainment celebrities. Quite simply what CBS and Old Gold had done was introduce the national promotional road show—a public relations stunt that would be used years later to promote all manner of advertisers' broadcast properties.

The Old Gold program itself was like its musical director—BIG. In trying to up-stage anyone who had ever played or sung a note into a mike, Whiteman shot the works. Every week's show was a Radio Special, with the Whiteman entourage at its very peak and star announcer Ted Husing spieling song introductions and commercials. Unlike B.A. Rolfe's Lucky Strike blast every Saturday night, the Old Gold hour was more like a concert *tour de force,* 1929 popular music to be sure, but invested with the high professional gloss Whiteman had spent a decade in perfecting. For Paul Whiteman was an entertainment icon, not just another orchestra leader, and any radio show in which he starred had to be worthy of his considerable reputation. From the Whiteman band book came the regular splashy arrangements, and to the program were added novelties and special effects. Whiteman's playlist for the broadcast of May 28, 1929, originating in Chicago, is indicative of what radio's first regular weekly music spectacular was like:

Diga Diga Doo
Canadian Capers
French Medley (Madelon, On The Boulevard, Ca C'est Paris)
My Dear Waltz Medley (A Smile, A Kiss, A Perfect Day, My Dear)
Hallelujah
'Till We Meet (Bing Crosby vocal)
O Ya Ya
Pickin' Cotton
Lady Fingers Medley: You're Perfect, Ga Ga, You Give Me Something to
    Live For (Crosby vocal)
Popular Medley: Doin' The Racoon, I Faw Down and Go Boom (Rhythm
    Boys vocal), My Mother's Eyes, I'll Never Ask for More
Red Hair and Freckles (Rhythm Boys vocal)
My Sin (Crosby vocal)
Sugar Is Back in Town
China Boy [4]

Was radio ready for Paul Whiteman? Perhaps not. It may have been that a full hour each week, crammed with production numbers was overdoing it, because the Old Gold show lasted only one season. But for all parties, it wasn't a bad deal at all: Whiteman came back, as he knew now he had to, in other seasons and in other formats; CBS had gained new prestige by bringing America's pop music giant to the medium; and for Old Golds, there was a handsome increase in sales. The following cigarette sales figures reveal how Old Gold (and Lucky Strike) benefited by sponsoring popular music on early network radio:

	1928	1929	1930
	(Sales in millions)		
Old Gold	6.50	8.30	8.50
Lucky Strike	27.40	37.00	43.20
Chesterfield	26.10	28.10	26.40
Camel	36.70	37.20	35.30[5]

Clearly, Chesterfield and Camel could no longer ignore the medium. During the next two decades cigarettes were to become popular music's dominant underwriter on radio. Sponsor identification meant sponsor *association* when a cigarette took on a radio show. In the 1930s, only a handful of brands existed—compared to 176 available in late 1979—and there were no participating sponsorships, since each cigarette had its own show. Listening to popular music on radio was construed to be a pleasurable experience,[6] so what better tie-in than with the pleasurable experience tobacco companies claimed for cigarette smoking? (R.J. Reynolds called its initial radio program the *Camel Pleasure Hour.*) The smoking pleasure parade that marched across American dials between 1930 and 1950 ultimately embraced the most predominant popular music figures of the two decades. Cigarette advertisers were never ahead of popular tastes. They waited until artists were established before signing them up, and then dropped them as soon as they thought the performers were wearing thin.

•   •   •

Radio criticism in the press through the early 1930s, except for *Variety* and a few other publications that reviewed specific programs, was for the most part comprised of sweeping generalizations. (e.g. anti-jazz and anti-crooning*) Therefore it came as somewhat of a surprise when a critic for a literary journal, *Forum*, in his first radio column cited three of 1932's cigarette-sponsored popular music programs among the finest on the air. He lumped them under the heading, "Lady Nicotine's Children":

> *Lucky Strike Dance Hour*—NBC Network, 10–11 p.m., Tuesday, Thursday, and Saturday 4 minutes 7 seconds of advertising, 13 minutes of Winchell, and the remaining time dance music. Brilliant showmanship makes each presentation glitter. Tune in if you like to dance and do not mind a diluted Winchell acting as a capper for Claney's [the announcer] unctuous remarks.

---

* In what may have been one of the first blows struck against musical radio's male tilt, Mrs. Elmer J. Ottaway, music chairman of The National Council of Women, claiming to speak for the Council's 5,000,000 radio-owning members, declared, "We do not like crooning and sentimental slush in vulgar songs by most jazz wheedling males." (Quoted in *Newsweek*, December 2, 1933, p. 34.)

Camel Quarter Hour—With Morton Downey and Jacques Renard Orch.,
CBS Network, Monday through Saturday, 7:45–8:00 p.m. 1 minute 45
seconds of advertising. 2 minutes of rubbish by the nation's great heart-
throb philosopher, Tony Wons, and remaining times divided between
Downey and orchestra . . . The music is smooth and worth hearing.

Chesterfield Quarter Hour—With Alex Gray, Nat Shilkret's Orch., Ruth
Etting or the Boswell Sisters, CBS Network, 10:30–10:45 p.m. Monday
through Saturday, and 10–10:15 p.m. Wednesdays and Saturdays. Less
than 1 minute of advertising, with no other interruptions . . . The most
enjoyable quarter hour of popular music on the air at the moment.[7]

Lady Nicotine eventually could even count among her children, Leopold
Stokowski and The Philadelphia Orchestra, Andre Kostelanetz and Lily
Pons. Classical music and cigarettes, however, were not considered good
blending, and popular artists remained the dominant strain in cigarette
companies' radio advertising mix.

Cigarettes, priced at around 15 cents a pack, were affordable antidotes to the Depression malaise that had engulfed the country. Americans
who couldn't afford magazines, or even newspapers, turned to radio; hence,
in the medium, cigarettes (and other packaged goods) found their most
efficient advertising. Whatever unknown health hazards cigarettes might
have had sealed within their white tissues, they did the country's economic
health no harm. Yet, strangely, there was a school of thought that claimed
otherwise. One of its leading spokesman was, of all people, a writer of
popular songs, Irving Caesar. He argued, in testimony before the FCC in
1934, cigarettes on radio were helping prolong the Depression. Caesar
maintained "tobacco, cosmetics, and patent foods, the backbone of the
radio industry," were keeping people glued to their sets, preventing them
from going out to stores and auto showrooms. Mr. Caesar's place in history is obviously more secure as a tunesmith than an economist:

> The American people cannot remain seated and listen to their radios . . .
> keeping them from visiting public places and destroying the necessity of
> demand . . . It is no more co-incidence that those very industries that
> employ relatively the least number of men . . . and thereby contribute
> least to the social wealth are the very ones that can afford the millions it
> takes to use radio as an advertising medium.[8]

After Caesar went back to song-writing, there were always other critics at the ready to pick up the cudgels against radio, popular music, and/or
cigarettes. But as the 1930s wore on, their words were dissipated as increasing amounts of popular music were wafted on clouds of smoke into
the ether. Songs themselves celebrated the cigarette. (Victor Herbert, as
early as 1908, had announced the connection in his composition, "Love Is
Like a Cigarette"). Tin Pan Alley, after tobacco and radio found each other,
evoked the exotic, the mysterious and romantic sides of smoking. Rudy

Vallee extolled "The Cigarette Lady" and Jerome Kern wrote "Smoke Gets in Your Eyes," the most famous of all the melodic encomia. Lyrics sometimes referred to romance-cum-cigarettes: "Here we are out of cigarettes"—"Two Sleepy People"; "A cigarette that bears the lipstick's traces"—"These Foolish Things." "Smoke Rings" was the theme song written expressly for the Casa Loma Orchestra when Camel Cigarettes introduced on radio the first of its long-running *Caravan* series. "Young America's Favorite," as it was billed at the time, the Casa Loma band enjoyed a three-season run on the *Camel Caravan,* beginning in the fall of 1933. The show garnered excellent ratings for its two-a-week prime-time shots, 10–10:30 p.m., Tuesdays and Thursdays on CBS.

What attracted Camel to Casa Loma was the band's ability to mix romantic ballads with up-tempo numbers. The inclusion of the latter, soon-to-be-called "swing" arrangements, scored in the Fletcher Henderson mode, foreshadowed important changes down the musical road and paved the way for Benny Goodman's acceptance. Regular radio wires to locations like Glen Island Casino and The Essex House had secured a dedicated college-age following for Casa Loma and made the band a natural for the *Camel Caravan.* It featured prominently a baritone crooner, Kenny Sargent, who helped popularize a group of ballads of the 1930s, including "For You," "Under a Blanket of Blue," and "It's the Talk of The Town." For change of pace, there were such "killer-dillers" as "Casa Loma Stomp," "Stompin' Around," and "Chinatown."

In the summer of 1936, when swing was celebrating its first anniversary of the Palomar explosion, Camel decided it was time to ditch Casa Loma and replace the band with a more current favorite. There was no doubt who should lead the *Caravan.* It had to be the swingmeister himself, Benny Goodman. The William Esty Company, Camel's ad agency, at first tried splitting an hour between Goodman and a sweet band, but eventually the *Caravan,* Tuesdays at 10 p.m. on CBS, settled into a swing groove and remained that way starring Goodman's band in prime time for three years. Insofar as pop music fans were concerned, the show was not without its faults. Advertising agencies, those program impressarios who controlled most of the networks' program schedules, were forever diluting musical radio with skits, guest comedians, movie actors and actresses, glee clubs, and the like. Few were the shows that America's number-one swing band got through without at least one "added attraction" sandwiched between selections. Still, each *Camel Caravan* managed to include six tunes by the Goodman orchestra and/or one of his small combos.

In its pitch to a young audience, the program was built around the collegiate theme. Everybody was addressed as "doctor," or "professor," and the audience, of course, was the "student body." Bill Goodwin, a leading personality-announcer of the day, was perfectly suited to join Goodman at the head of the *Caravan.* Not only did Goodwin deliver Camel commercials with an uncommon air of believability, the tongue-in-cheek scholasticisms he and Goodman exchanged seemed less hokey than much of the continuity prepared for many musical shows. Inexplicably, the program, shown as the *Camel Caravan* in newspaper program listings, did not always call itself that on the air. The "Swing School" reference, however, was always in the script, as the show of August 31, 1937 indicates:

> BAND: (Theme—"Let's Dance")
>
> BILL GOODWIN: (over theme) Camel Cigarettes presents *Benny Goodman's Swing School!* The Tuesday evening rally of everybody everywhere who gets a lift from the new pulsating music of youth—swing. Tonight the King of Swing presents the world's greatest swing band, The Goodman instrumental trio and quartet, the Camel Swing Chorus under the direction of Meyer Alexander, and our English fellow student, Pat O'Malley offers a little post-graduate work in swing, all brought to you by the makers of Camel Cigarettes.
>
> THEME: (up and out)
>
> GOODWIN: And here's the king!
>
> GOODMAN: Good evening, students. This is Benny Goodman, speaking for Camel Cigarettes. Welcome again to the Swing School.
>
> GOODWIN: What's on the blackboard tonight, Professor?
>
> GOODMAN: Well tonight, Doctor, we're gonna present a course in basic dancy rhythm. The opening lesson is a typical modern dance tune, "The Camel Hop."
>
> GOODWIN: Well, hop to it, pops![9]

References to college life were worked into the script to flavor song introductions like this one from the same broadcast:

> GOODWIN: And here's a rhythm that's very basic. By way of New Orleans honky-tonks and early jazz, it worked its way up to the Goodman Instrumental Quartet. "Vibraphone Blues," courtesy of the Board of Trustees, Doctors Hampton, Wilson, Krupa and the Professor . . .[10]

The *Camel Caravan* and other pop music shows aimed at young audiences afforded cigarette manufacturers an ideal way to re-inforce their print advertising, particularly when it included endorsements by famous personalities. The talking celebrity-head on radio lent a certain credibility to a personal endorsement. Ralph Guldahl, the golfer, was present in the Swing School session from which the previous fragments were excerpted:

> GOODWIN: Just imagine the stress a golf champion must play under. Or better yet, hear the words of Ralph Guldahl, winner of the 1937 National Open against a crack all-star field.

GULDAHL: I find that smoking Camels eases tension. Camels have one swell flavor. I'd walk a mile for a Camel.[11]

After Benny Goodman left it, the *Camel Caravan* rolled on into the early 1950s with Vaughn Monroe as its final leader. So attractive to Camel was the sponsorship of name bands, at one stretch, both Goodman and Bob Crosby were used.

By early summer of 1939, cigarette advertisers dominated name band sponsorship on the radio networks. These sponsorships shown in the following table reveal how cigarette advertisers cut across all orchestral styles—sweet, swing, sweet/swing:

BAND	SPONSOR
Bandwagon (various)	Fitch Shampoo
Larry Clinton	Sensation Cigarettes
Bob Crosby	Camel Cigarettes
Tommy Dorsey	Raleigh & Kool Cigarettes
Benny Goodman	Camel Cigarettes
Horace Heidt	Tums
Richard Himber	Studebaker
Hal Kemp	Griffin Shoe Polish
Kay Kyser	Lucky Strike Cigarettes
Guy Lombardo	Lady Esther
Matty Malneck	Pall Mall Cigarettes
Artie Shaw	Old Gold Cigarettes
Fred Waring	Chesterfield Cigarettes
Paul Whiteman	Chesterfield Cigarettes[12]

Before that fateful year of 1939 was over, Chesterfield beat out Lucky Strike for Glenn Miller who, except for the intervention of World War II, might have challenged Guy Lombardo (41 seasons) as America's all-time favorite radio name band. Miller, in the tradition of popular music idols, developed an enormous following in the pre-War period. What he had done was create a "trademark" sound required of every single artist or group to reach pop stardom—what Benny Goodman has called "a great sense of the commercial, of what could attract the average listener." Miller, an arranger-trombonist, was a contemporary of other name leaders who had served their apprenticeships in network studio orchestras of the late 1920s and early 1930s. He had experimented with various musical approaches throughout the 1930s. The one that clicked was quite uncomplicated: by using a clarinet on "top" of four saxophones (instead of the conventional alto or tenor saxophone leading the reed section), Miller achieved the sound he was after. On ballads, the clarinet-saxophone blending produced a heady romantic brew that cut across demographic lines. Miller, an astute showman, aware of the "swing thing," mixed in jump numbers and stompers in the right proportions. Mindful too of the need for visual appeal, he augmented the standard 13-man swing band with four additional instrumentalists, so that his up-tempo numbers could feature his orchestral sections in showy displays of repeated riffs, fading and re-appearing. But it was his romantic repertory that put the Miller band over. This was in tune with the mood of the country, as Americans watched the developments in Europe between 1940 and 1942. The yelling and whistling of Glenn Miller's studio audiences was a familiar sound to listeners who tuned in CBS, 10:00–10:15 p.m., Tuesdays, Wednesdays and Thursdays for three years starting in late 1939. Miller, serving as co-emcee (along with Paul Douglas and other first-team announcers) had a pleasing radio voice. Each *Chesterfield Show*—and that's what it was called—usually consisted of two romantic ballads and two swing numbers. Every so often there were "The Old-New-Borrowed-Blue" medleys. Usually the pieces played on the air were those Miller had recorded commercially. On the *Chesterfield Show* of October 30, 1941, it was three out of four:

(r) Stardust
(r) Chatanooga Choo-Choo
(r) This Is no Laughing Matter
    One O'Clock Jump [13]

Chesterfield couldn't have asked for a more merchandiseable radio show than Glenn Miller's. Playing ballrooms and theaters, the Miller band was a traveling billboard for the cigarette sponsor. In the spring of 1940 alone, there were prom appearances on the campuses of Bucknell, VMI, Virginia, Duke (twice), Hofstra, Penn State, Dartmouth, Temple, Union, Cornell and North Carolina.[14]

Concurrent with Glenn Miller, for more general appeal, Chesterfield presented Fred Waring, Monday through Fridays, 7:00–7:15 p.m. on NBC. Waring's program pointed up once more the ad agency-format problem—introducing non-musical elements into a popular music show. *Variety,* grumbling about the practice, didn't feel it made much sense to dilute Waring:

> Chesterfield bought the famous and expensive Fred Waring organization to broadcast 15 minutes of dance music every evening at 7:00 p.m. and then thought it necessary to gild the lily by including baseball scores, cutting two or three minutes out of a preciously short program . . . Why baseball scores? Because men are interested? What kind of baseball follower doesn't know the scores already by 7:00 p.m.?[15]

When Glenn Miller entered military service, his Chesterfield replacement was Harry James, who went into the traditional CBS popular music slot, 7:15–7:30 p.m. Waring held on to his early evening NBC serenade until the fall of 1944, when Perry Como moved in as the tuneful boniface on the new *Chesterfield Supper Club*. This was the vehicle that boosted ex-band crooner Como to stardom. Many a serviceman wondered how its host managed to warble nightly on the *Supper Club* while they had to be pre-occupied elsewhere. But such notions had little effect on the singer's popularity, and he went on to score some excellent ratings. Como's studied manner of easy-going delivery, a large studio orchestra, the Satisfiers, (so-named for Chesterfield's slogan, "They Satisfy") and Martin Block, the popular WNEW disc-jockey, as the announcer—all came together to earmark the nightly Como quarter-hour one of the better network wartime pop music shows. Here too, music sometimes had to take a back seat to variety elements. The name, "Supper Club," apparently offered justification—as guests popped in and out. Friday night, for example, was "Pick and Pat" night. Actors portraying two shiftless black stereotypes did several minutes each Friday. Their routines could easily have been lifted out of the nearest minstrel show. A portion of the Pick-and-Pat sketch on Como's November 30, 1945 *Supper Club* illustrates again how advertising agencies mis-trusted music alone to carry a program:

(Pick and Pat are discussing whether Pat should marry Ducky Pugh)

PICK: Well, I'se tellin' you one thing, son. You got to marry Ducky Pugh.

PAT: That settles it. I'se gonna jump off a high building.

PICK: You ain't gonna kill yourself, is you Pat?

PAT: Well, you talked me out of it. Ducky Pugh's got a rich aunt. Boy, she owns rabbit farms all over da country. She's a self-made woman. She started out with two rabbits, now she's got a million of 'em. She worked really hard. And boy, them rabbits wasn't loafin' either. . .[16]

When Perry Como signed off the *Supper Club* in 1949, Lucky Strike moved in to grab the time period. In its place, the musical heirs of G.W. Hill installed *Light Up Time,* starring Frank Sinatra and Dorothy Kirsten. It was one of network radio's last musical journeys down tobacco road. For his services on the five-weekly quarter hours, Sinatra, who was reported at the time to have staggering financial obligations, received $8500 a week. *Light Up Time* re-united Sinatra with his old employer, the American Tobacco Company, from whose fold he had stormed out in a huff a year earlier. The early evening Sinatra-Kirsten song recital lasted one season. Luckies were truly lucky for Sinatra. Not, of course, because of *Light Up Time,* which was to be relegated to the back of old-time radio trivia books after one season, but because it was on a Lucky Strike show that the singer got his first build-up as a solo performer. That program would have a permanent place in everybody's hall of fame because it introduced to popular music a concept that was to become the format of the future.

NOTES

1. In his study of the cigarette in American life, *They Satisfy,* (Anchor Press/Doubleday, New York, 1978) Robert Sobel states Hill's basic selling strategy in the straight-forward way the flamboyant American Tobacco president would have applauded: "Switch a middle-aged person from cigars to cigarettes and you might sell him the product for another twenty years. But when a teenager took to cigarettes, he might be a customer of the same brand for half a century. Figured at a pack a day, that came to 17,800 in a lifetime, and at fifteen cents each, $2670, or close to three years salary for the average worker of that decade." (pp. 104–105)
2. "Radio Rambles." *Variety,* February 20, 1929, p. 69.
3. William Paley. *As It Happened,* Doubleday, 1979, p. 66.
4. Richard Sudhalter. *Bix: Man and Legend,* Arlington House, (New Rochelle) 1974, pp. 383–384.
5. Letter of Catherine Preston, Librarian, Tobacco Merchants Association of the United States to author, May 29, 1979. Ms. Preston quoted Maxwell's *Historical Trends in the Tobacco Industry* as her source.
6. Prevailing perceptions of the relationship between broadcasting and advertising in the early 1930s can be gleaned from three key sentences from a lengthy internal memo of the D'Arcy Company, an advertising agency contemplating recommending sponsorship of a radio music program for its client, Coca Cola: "We must recognize that radio from the point of view of the great mass of listeners is purely a medium of entertainment. They turn to it to be amused, to be taken outside themselves . . . The listener's attitude is, strictly speaking, one which puts up with the advertising to get to the entertainment . . ." (Quoted in Laurence Dietz *Soda Pop,* Simon and Schuster, (New York) 1973, p. 129).
7. Darwin L. Teilbet. "What America Listens To," *Forum,* May, 1932, pp. 275–276.
8. Quoted in "Songwriter Turns Economist, Tells FCC Radio As Is Hurts Recovery," *Variety,* November 13, 1934, p. 41.
9. *The Camel Caravan,* vol. 2, 1937, Sunbeam Records, SB-147.
10. *Ibid.*
11. *Ibid.*
12. ———. "Name Bands Radio Spurt," *Variety,* June 7, 1939, p. 17.
13. John Flower. *Moonlight Serenade,* Arlington House, (New Rochelle) 1972, p. 365.
14. *Ibid.* pp. 156–180.
15. "Radio Reviews," *Variety,* June 21, 1939, p. 28.
16. *Chesterfield Supper Club,* November 30, 1945. Radio Yesteryear, *Listeners' Digest,* No. 39.

CHAPTER 9

"Your Hit Parade"

WHY HADN'T SOMEBODY thought of it sooner? Rank the top tunes of the day through some sort of regular survey and play them on the air. Every other phase of the culture and the marketplace was measured according to its standing with the competition—sports, sales, even politics—so why not popular music? The radio music box had ground away for 15 years before anyone considered setting up an "official" competitive evaluation of America's favorite songs and then presenting them on the radio. When the notion finally took shape in *Your Hit Parade,* it was accepted* as the national scorekeeper of what the leading hits of the land were and where they placed on the preference list. *Your Hit Parade* outlasted every network popular music program except Bing Crosby and Guy Lombardo. It also brought forth the basic design of Top 40, destined to catch the public's fancy just when radio needed it most.

Credit for originating *Your Hit Parade* has matter-of-factly gone to that tobacconist-cum-musicologist, George Washington Hill.[1] Such attribution may have been a common case of advertising agency magnanimity, wherein an agency dreams up ideas the graciously gives public credit to the client—but makes sure the trade knows who *really* had the idea. In all

---

*That acceptance, however, was far from unanimous. There were always some inquisitive souls who had the crude insensitivity to ask just *how* songs were chosen for the rankings. There was never a universal answer, as we shall see a few pages hence when we plumb the question.

likelihood, that was the way *Your Hit Parade* was hatched. Albert Lasker, head of the Lord and Thomas agency which handled the American Tobacco Company account, was personally in charge of keeping Hill happy. How many of Hill's ideas actually sprang from the brilliant mind of Albert Lasker will never be known. But Lasker's biographer, John Gunther, flatly states it was Lasker's daughter, Mary, who was the architect of *Your Hit Parade*.[2]

That a weekly network popular music program had so much staying power may have been more a testimony to the American preoccupation with numbers and rankings than to the promenade of talent that appeared before the *Hit Parade* microphone. *Your Hit Parade* (called *Lucky Strike Sweepstakes* when it went on the air) purported to be a weekly report card of the nation's favorite songs—nothing more. George Washington Hill considered the show an extension of those Saturday night dance sessions led by B.A. Rolfe. In the Hill style book, that meant snappy tempos and simple arrangements; using only the most popular songs would take care of his other imperative—that the music be familiar. *Your Hit Parade* debuted on the NBC network, Saturday April 20, 1935 at 8 p.m. Lennie Hayton led the first *Hit Parade* orchestra and singers through brassy, Hill-inspired arrangements. Ballads were treated with proper deference, but the up-tempo mood was established on the premier show and was never allowed to be anything else. Cigarettes denoted pleasure and listening to a popular music program should be a pleasurable affair. The opening theme, "Happy Days Are Here Again" was as up-beat as you could get; and so was the *Hit Parade's* signature theme, "This Is My Lucky Day." Both stayed around until the show left the air. Bracketed between "Happy Days" and "Lucky Day" were short song introductions, another of the opening show's hallmarks that varied little in the 24 years it played on radio and television. In fact, over the years there was little tampering with any part of the format. The show began by using the 15 songs it claimed were America's favorites. At various stages, seven, nine, or ten tunes made it to the winners' circle. In its final season of 1958, (foreshortened to four months) the list was cut to five. On volume one, number one, the announcer emphasized the egalitarian stamp imprinted on *Your Hit Parade*—and that, too, would never be rubbed off in its long run:

> ANNOUNCER: Once again the voice of the people has spoken to select the tunes of the *Hit Parade*. New Yorkers, Californians, Northerners, Southerners, Republicans, Democrats, men, women—120 million of you have told us what songs you want to hear this Saturday night. You've told us by purchasing sheet music and records, by your requests to orchestra leaders, by the tunes you listen to on your favorite programs. That's why the *Hit Parade* is *your* own program.[3]

Was the lofty preamble to each show a true report on the way the country's popular music preferences were tabulated? No one ever found out. Weekly *Hit Parade* song surveys were conducted with CIA-type secrecy by Lucky Strike's advertising agency. Whether the sampling methodology met the criteria of scientific public opinion research had always been the big *Hit Parade* question nobody could (or would) answer. All that ever leaked was that three yardsticks were used: record and sheet music sales and network play. Complicating matters was how each of those elements was weighted. Certainly sheet music in the 1930s was not the force in popular music that it had been in pre-radio days. In comparing *Variety's* weekly reports in those three areas with *Hit Parade* tabulations between 1936 and 1940, it is impossible to reach any final conclusions. Making valid comparisons was compounded by the fact that *Variety* did not publish all three sets of data for record, sheet music and airplay each week, nor were the seven days covered by the publication the same as those used by the *Hit Parade* in every instance. Random weeks selected from 1937, 1938 and 1939[4] indicate what wide fluctuations were possible, depending on how, when and where the surveys were made. For example, for the first week of April, 1937, *Your Hit Parade* listed "Boo Hoo" as the number one song; *Variety's* network airplay chart had it third. In 1938, "Ti Pi Tin" ended up the top tune on the networks as well as the *Hit Parade* for the third week in April that year. "Deep Purple," number five on the networks' playlist the week of March 4, 1939 was *Your Hit Parade's* choice for the country's favorite song. (For additional comparisons, see Appendix on page 367.)

No part of the *Hit Parade* legend has worn so well as the one alleging that all was not on the up-and-up in determining which tunes made it and which ones did not. Maestro Harry Sosnick who had two tours of duty leading the *Hit Parade* orchestra claims,

> There was a lot of money involved. There were pay-offs to get the "right" song up there. There were rumors of a lot of trickery to get the number-one song. It wasn't all legit either . . . they would take a canvass of record and sheet music stores. But there was a way of influencing the people who filled out the questionnaires. It's like the book business. I understand book publishers send secretaries out to buy their books to influence the *Times* lists.[5]

Sosnick involved bandleaders in some of the untoward maneuvers of *Your Hit Parade:*

> Questionnaires sent to every dance orchestra leader asked, "What is your most requested song?" If you could get to that leader, he didn't care what he put down as his most requested song if there was a little money involved . . . There were all kinds of ways of doing it.[6]

Irrespective of such unproven charges, *Your Hit Parade* was a reasonably accurate reflection of our predilection for hummable songs of romantic love and nonsense ditties. Nobody had to ask, "where's the melody?"

The cumulative American popular song repertory between 1935 and 1950 belonged to tunesmiths who toiled in the vineyards of Hollywood, Broadway and Tin Pan Alley. Composers Richard Rodgers, Sammy Fain, Harry Warren, Irving Berlin, Jimmy Van Heusen, Jimmy McHugh, Harry Revel, Ralph Grainger, Jule Styne and Cole Porter wrote of Septembers in the rain, stars falling out of heaven, sunburns at the shore, and things easy to remember/but so hard to forget. Lyricists Mack Gordon, Irving Berlin, Johnny Mercer, Leo Robin, Sammy Cahn, Al Dubin and Frank Loesser wrote of whispers in the dark, pockets full of dreams, fools rushing in, and blue rain.

During the years *Your Hit Parade* whirled through its weekly song sweepstakes, there was only *one* body of popular music—the same songs all the bands were playing live on the air, the same records that all juke boxes and radio stations were spinning. But even as *Your Hit Parade* was strengthening the concept of a single list of national hit tunes, seeds were being sown that would help scatter popular music to fragmented audiences, catered to by over 8000 radio stations.

Prior to 1941, all music had been licensed by the American Society of Composers, Authors and Publishers (ASCAP). Spurred on by Victor Herbert in 1914, a nucleus of composers and lyricists convinced the music establishment that legislation was needed to enforce the Copyright Act of 1909. That Act had set forth three noble provisions for writers and publishers of popular music: that they should be compensated for the *publication, recording* and *performance* of their works. The Act, however, provided little machinery for its enforcement. The Herbert lobby convinced Congress that tough legislation was needed, and ASCAP was on its way to becoming the first performing rights society in the United States. Radio, at first, seemed a natural ally to the composing and publishing fraternity and was permitted by ASCAP to broadcast music free of charge. By 1923, however, ASCAP recognized in the growing broadcasting industry a potential source of income, every bit as important as the dining salons and concert halls that had to cough up performance fees. In spite of the howls of protest, broadcasters paid their tribute to the ASCAP Caesar throughout the 1930s. Near the end of 1939, though, a greater impasse than usual developed over the new contract that was to take effect starting in 1941. The National Association of Broadcasters,* representing the networks and approximately 600 stations, was unable to come to terms with ASCAP.

For self-protection, the industry through its trade association decided to organize its own performing rights society, Broadcast Music Incorporated (BMI). The haggling continued through all of 1940, and when the year ended without an agreement, all ASCAP-licensed music ceased to be

---

* The NAB, by now, had become an important lobbying force in Washington. Philip Loucks, its managing director and legal counsel from 1930–1935, guided the association through some of its most difficult years.

heard on American airwaves. Thus, starting January 1, 1941, radio sent out a flood of BMI-licensed tunes and public domain (no license fees required) compositions, the latter as re-packaged items in popularized 1941 renditions.

Broadcasters and ASCAP finally agreed on a new contract late in the year, but BMI decided to continue as a performing rights organization. ASCAP at the time, with its strong New York-Hollywood axis and payments based on national network play, meant little to regional writers and publishers. BMI, on the other hand, included in its charter a provision to pay members for performances on local stations as well as for those on network shows. Re-arrangement of socio-economic patterns brought on by World War II and the post-war period saw great population shifts in the country. With such displacements came a rising interest in country and western, and rhythm and blues—two kinds of music that thrived first in their congenial regional settings and would then go on to become the national popular music of the United States and the world beginning in the mid-1950s. Writers and composers found the back roads charted by BMI more inviting than the Great White Way-Sunset Boulevard routes laid out by ASCAP. Consequently, the older licensing order gradually lost its near-monopoly status.*

Your Hit Parade, a child of the ASCAP-dominated era, however, had a way to go before it became a victim of the changing tastes in popular music. Indeed, the program enjoyed some of its best showings following the resolution of the ASCAP-BMI battle of 1941. The highest rating achieved in the 1930s was a 15.3 for the 1938–39 season. *Your Hit Parade* reached its peak during the World War II years:

SEASON	RATING
1942–43	17.1
1943–44	19.1
1944–45	17.8

—Source: *A Thirty-Year History of Programs Carried on National Radio Networks in the United States, 1926–1956.* Harrison B. Summers, ed., Arno (1971)

With the top nine or ten hits of the week, several "Lucky Strike extras" (the 1940s term for oldies), a boy and girl vocalist, and the rest of G.W. Hill's requisites, *Your Hit Parade* zipped through 45-minutes (1942

---

* After the great flush of BMI-licensed works, beginning around 1950, ASCAP could hardly be accused of applying the Hollywood-Broadway litmus test. Writers like Stevie Wonder, Bob Dylan, Carly Simon, Carole King, John Denver, Smokey Robinson, Marvin Gaye, Led Zepplin would all become card-carrying ASCAP members.

and 1944) or 30-minutes (1943) of the music decreed by the "voice of the people." By this time, the show had been on the air almost a decade—a long span in musical radio. When *Your Hit Parade* reached its peak rating in the 1943–1944 season, radio's captive wartime audiences may have been a major factor. So may have been the sponsor's choice of the featured male singer.

The timing was right for Frank Sinatra. He had left Tommy Dorsey's Orchestra late in 1942 to go out on his own and had just completed the obligatory Paramount Theater appearance when show biz lightning struck. Well-concocted portions of astute management and cunning press agentry had given Sinatra's career, in a short time, the kind of hype a showman like George Washington Hill appreciated. "Lucky Strike has gone to War," the cigarette commercials boasted—and so had many of the singers of popular songs. Hill examined the dwindling talent pool, and just as the American Tobacco Company had been Bing Crosby's first network sponsor, so the firm became Sinatra's initial network bankroller. Sinatra *was* the *Hit Parade* between February, 1943 and December, 1944.* Aided by noisy studio audiences and frequent press coverage, Sinatra's stints on the show became weekly media events. Little did the bobby-soxers who made up the bulk of his audience, squealing through the introductions and codas of his songs, think that two generations later, they would be convincing their spouses to plunk down the price of a week's groceries in Las Vegas to see one of his shows. His cause was aided by tunes tinged with wartime colorings: "Don't Get Around Much Anymore"; "They're Either Too Young or Too Old"; "No Love, No Nothin' ('Till My Baby Comes Home)"; "I'll Walk Alone"; "I'll Be Seeing You"; "You'd Be So Nice to Come Home To"; "I Heard You Cried Last Night"; "Long Ago and Far Away." Songs of that ilk always found favor with women separated from husbands and sweethearts in time of war; and given the way Sinatra caressed the lyrics, they had even more appeal. "Young Blue Eyes" played to a feminine constituency and they loved it. A less-adoring and snoopy press wondered regularly about Sinatra's 4F (physically-unfit for military service) classification. An ear problem, said the doctors, and "The Voice" (as the press agents dubbed him) was vindicated. No singer on *Your Hit Parade*, before or since, created the furor generated by Sinatra. Forty-eight different boy and girl singers, including some of the big names of the 1940s (Dick Haymes, Dinah Shore, Doris Day, Andy Russell, Dorothy Collins and Snooky Lanson) sang on *Your Hit Parade*, but none boosted the show's popularity as did the ex-Dorsey crooner.

By the time Sinatra began his second tour of *Hit Parade* duty, song stylists, mainly on records, had taken over popular music. The melodies of the hits—the essential point of *Your Hit Parade* in the first place—didn't sound right when performed by artists other than those who had recorded

---

*He returned for another hitch between September, 1947 and May, 1949.

them. Recordings of songs, often encased in special effects, echo chambers, etc., became the tuning forks of popular music; these were the versions the people wanted to hear. Still, *Your Hit Parade* went gamely on—as a simulcast, 1950–1953, and as a television-only production for its final six years. In the show's latter days, when tobacco manufacturers began bringing out new brands, American Tobacco Company introduced a *Hit Parade* cigarette. That brand outlasted the show, but not by much. *Your Hit Parade's* closing stanzas were often amusing (and sometimes pathetic) vignettes that found Dorothy Collins/Snooky Lanson/Giselle McKenzie/Russell Arms obliged to cope with the visual trappings required in television production. *Your Hit Parade* should have, in 1953, pulled down the shades on that "Doggie in the Window." Things went from bad to worse as the rising wave of rock swept over popular music in the 1950s. Not even a "Hound Dog" in 1957 was able to chase the show off the tube. It was not until two years later the show was mercifully put to rest. In its final years, *Your Hit Parade* won a Peabody Award and an Emmy. That a program so uniquely "radio" would win two of the most prestigious awards in television only attests to the sometimes strange goings-on in medialand. George Washington Hill would no doubt have relished the irony.

NOTES

1. So strongly was Hill identified as the guiding force of Lucky Strike's music shows, he was often mentioned right along with the talent. In a review of one early *Hit Parade* segment, *Variety's* critic detected the "hand and policy of George Washington Hill throughout. Hill proceeds on the theory that what is demonstrably in the public taste is good enough for him and Lucky Strike's radio program." (February 12, 1936, p. 50)
2. John Gunther. *Taken at the Flood,* Popular Library, (New York), 1961, p. 180.
3. *Lucky Strike Hit Parade.* Broadcast of July 20, 1935, McCoy Recordings, Reel No. 382.
4. John R. Williams. *This Was Your Hit Parade,* John R. Williams, (Camden, Maine), 1973, pp. 83, 89 & 95.
5. "Whatever Happened to Your Hit Parade?" Richard Lamparski interview with Del Sharbutt, Brank Buxton and Bill Owen. (Circa 1966). The interview co-incided with the publication of Buxton's and Owen's *Radio's Golden Age.* McCoy Recordings, Reel No. 1664.
6. *Ibid.*

CHAPTER 10

Comedy with Music

IN THE GLORY DAYS of networks, radio was America's all-in-one music box/theater/concert hall/vaudeville house/news center. Not surprisingly, the sole survivors in the Television Age are music and news. Yet, there remains a hearty hybrid with roots in network radio: the funny-man disc jockey. The modern deejay is an extension of the old-time radio comedian, working with recorded popular music, instead of live, between his routines. In post-television radio, a station with a comedian-disc jockey usually slots him in morning drive time, radio's prime hours. Recordings take a back seat to the jokes. Still, his show would be missing something without a few records now and then. For the network radio comic, popular music served much the same function.

After radio got off the ground and vaudeville re-treads became the medium's first funny men, popular music was recognized as a necessary prop. George Burns and Gracie Allen did their first radio comedy routines in one-minute segments with Guy Lombardo's Royal Canadians playing in the background. The year was 1930. Lombardo was at the height of his popularity on campuses. After three weeks of Burns and Allen jokes delivered over top of the "Sweetest Music This Side of Heaven," Burns was called into the office of John Reber, Radio Vice President, J. Walter Thompson Company. Thompson handled the Robert Burns Cigar sponsor's account and wanted to discuss with Burns audience reaction to the show. In his autobiography, Burns recalls the contents of a letter Reber read to him at that meeting. It was signed by 54 members of an Ivy league fraternity:

> Gentlemen: For the past two years every Monday night has been very special for us. It has been a tradition that we invite our girl friends over to the fraternity house to hear Guy Lombardo. However, for the past three weeks, out comes five minutes of these lousy jokes. May we point out if we want lousy jokes, we can get them from the same joke book they get them. Please stick to the music.[1]

As radio grew up and production values were better understood, producers worked out variations advantageous to comedian and orchestra leader alike. Ex-vaudevillian Ed Wynn's scripts called for dance band numbers that acted as separators between the comic's routines. Wynn, whose radio character the "Fire Chief" derived from his sponsor's Fire Chief Gasoline, was a high-rated feature on NBC's Tuesday night line-up in the mid-1930s, in much the same way Milton Berle a decade later dominated the time period on television, for the same sponsor. The writers used announcer Graham McNamee as Wynn's straight man. The orchestra, Eddie Duchin's, played hits of the day between skits. Song titles and Duchin's name were not always mentioned; in those instances, they simply followed Wynn's wrap-up punch lines for each sketch. Using that formula, the comedian concluded his opening routine on a March, 1935 show with the latest word on his aunt. (His aunt was a running gag.):

> WYNN: Oh, my aunt is really a mess, Graham. I'm sorry I mentioned her. I took her to a dress shop the other day, and the saleslady said to my aunt, "Would you like to try that dress on in the window?" My aunt said, "No, in the back of the store!"
>
> MUSIC: (Selection by Eddie Duchin Orchestra—in quick. No mention of song title or reference to Duchin.)[2]

Later in the same program, Wynn describes for McNamee the plot line for an opera the comic has written. An old maid, the central figure, has been pestering her doctor about her romance problem. The doctor observed that her latest haircut makes her look like an old man:

> WYNN: . . . . Now she gets mad: "I feel like shooting you for that". The doctor said, "You can't shoot me without a hunting license—I'm an Elk!"
>
> MUSIC: (Selection by Eddie Duchin Orchestra—in quick. No mention of title or reference to Duchin.)[3]

Duchin's orchestra usually played four or five short numbers per program.

Ed Wynn's radio efforts, like many comedy shows in the 1930s, were re-cycled vaudeville. Joe Penner, who had also come to radio from the older medium a little later than Wynn, however, employed a format that involved the orchestra leader as host. It is no surprise that on Penner's weekly half-hour, *Baker's Broadcast* (NBC), Sunday nights, Ozzie Nelson enjoyed better showcasing than Eddie Duchin received from Wynn. Ozzie Nelson and his vocalist-wife, Harriet Hilliard, were themselves one of the nation's leading attractions in the 1930s. Writers took advantage of this fact and had Nelson serve as low-key host. A representative show (May 13, 1934) came on the air in this manner:

THEME SONG: (Unidentified March)

ANNOUNCER: (Ben Grauer) *The Baker's Broadcast* brought to you by Fleischmann's Yeast in the United States and Canada. Presenting Ozzie Nelson and His Orchestra, with Harriet Hilliard. And starring Joe Penner.

PENNER: (Trademark laugh)

NELSON: Good evening, ladies and gentlemen. This is Ozzie Nelson speaking. I hope you enjoy our *Baker's Broadcast* for tonight. And I hope Joe does too. Our first number is the Harlem favorite, "Reefer Man."

ORCHESTRA: (Plays "Reefer Man")

NELSON: You're liable to find Joe Penner anywhere. Here he is helping out his friend in a music store. (skit follows)[4]

How much of the *Baker's Broadcast* popularity was due to Joe Penner, and how much to the supporting musical talent of Mr. & Mrs. Ozzie Nelson will never be known.[*] At the time, Ozzie, only a few years out of Rutgers, and still appropriately collegiate, with his new bride-vocalist, Harriet, personified an attractive and devoted couple sitting on top of the pop music world—a sort of 1930s Captain and Tennille. Listeners got one cooing-lovebird duet per *Baker's Broadcast,* in addition to a solo each by husband and wife. The Nelsons were not written into the Penner scripts. Yet, the sitcom *Ozzie and Harriet* who came after the musical Ozzie and Harriet certainly benefited from working on a major radio comedy program. It took a decade for Nelson's comedic flare to blossom, at which time he developed his situation comedy character, a sort of unflappable Ivy League Dagwood. Three of Ozzie Nelson's contemporaries in the band business did not wait that long, however, and preferred to stir in the comedy right on the bandstand.

Orchestra leaders Ben Bernie and Kay Kyser parlayed their innate grasp of comedy into careers that lent an extra dimension to their popular music labors. Dance bands led by Bernie and Kyser were more than adequate, but thanks to carefully constructed personas, they were able to straddle

---

[*] The show enjoyed high ratings both years Nelson and Hilliard supplied the music: 1933–34 season (35.3); and 1934–35 (30.3). Penner played on radio through most of the 30s with other bands. In his last season, 1939–40, he had slipped to a 9.0.

the worlds of popular music and comedy. Bernie's matriculation in the vaudeville prep school as a monologist-vocalist served him well when he turned to bandleading. Blessed with a deep, resonant voice suitable for the projection required by primitive microphones, Bernie parlayed his showmanship into early radio stardom. Adopting the sobriquet, "The Old Maestro," for himself, (he was born in 1891), and for his men, "All the Lads," Bernie fronted a band on a par with Vincent Lopez's and B.A. Rolfe's— no mean feat in the 1920s. In pre-rating days, he more then held his own in newspaper and magazine popularity polls.* When more scientific rating techniques arrived, the numbers showed the earlier polls were no fluke. During the 1932–33 season, Ben Bernie's weekly half-hour of dance music and banter rated placement in the year's top ten. Some of Bernie's best routines were built around a running "feud" between him and Walter Winchell, the show-business gossip columnist. Such cooked-up wrangles, if they caught on, were effective devices that script writers sometimes employed to heighten listenership. (Radio's most famous "feud," Jack Benny vs. Fred Allen, was kept alive throughout the network careers of both.) The contrived Winchell-Bernie hostility had enough mileage in it to extend the gag to two films, *Wake up and Live* (1937) and *Love and Hisses* (1939). Bernie's weekly radio show usually included six current hits, plus a guest star—quite often one that had something to do with popular music. The Old Maestro was able to project his unique personality—he was the star— through the home loudspeaker by means of Bernie-ese. This was a pleasant, casual, (sometimes ungrammatical) line of patter, tinged with a mild New York accent. Bernie did not belong to the bellylaugh/loud-guffaw school of comedy. Rather, he pegged his efforts on a low-key approach, illustrated in his words of welcome on a program heard in October, 1935:

> BERNIE: Yowsah, Greetings, ladies and gentlemen. 'Tis Tuesday. So 'tis. Time for the Old Maestro and all the Lads to watch their p's and q's, meaning pints and quarts of good old Pabst Blue Ribbon Beer. Yowsah! Well, Philadelphia is sure a great town. You know, last Saturday, I went around and visited all the old places of interest. And I really got historical. And last Sunday, I listened to Winchell and I really got hysterical. Well, once again we greet youse guys and gals . . .[5]

"Au Revoir, Pleasant Dreams," Bernie's sign-off, was one of the most personalized signatures heard on the air:

---

*Hyping for "good numbers" did not have to wait for the era of rating "sweeps." In the New York *Evening World's* 1925 radio popularity poll, word got out that Bernie's chief rival, Harry Richman, was buying *World* copies at the rate of $1000 worth a day to stuff the ballot box. An "appalled" Bernie invested a more modest sum to do the same thing. But when he saw Richman's "coupon plant" in action, The Old Maestro dropped out of the competition. (*Variety*, November 25, 1925, p. 1)

Au revoir, Pleasant dre-ams.
Think of us—when requesting your themes.
Until the next time when—
Possibly you may all tune in again,
Keep the Old Maestro always—in your schemes.
Yowsah, yowsah, yowsah.
Au Revoir—
This is Ben Bernie, ladies and gentlemen,
And all the Lads
Wishing you a bit of pleasant dre-ams.
May good luck—and happiness,
Success, good health, attend your schemes.
And don't forget—
Should you ever send in your request-a
Why, we'll sho' try to do our best-a
Yowsah.
Au Revoir, a fond cheerio.
A bit of a tweet-tweet,
God bless you—and
Pleasant dre-ams!

Bernie had a sponsored prime-time show through most of the 1930s. But his highly stylized manner (in which Bernie—the vaudevillian often outscored Bernie—the orchestra leader) was more suited to radio's greening years. When his popularity declined toward the end of the 1930s, there were, as always, new sounds and new voices swirling through the airwaves. Challengers in pop music never stopped pounding on the studio door and, in Bernie's case, swing bands, sweet bands, rippling rhythm bands, tic-toc rhythm bands, dixieland bands, singing song title bands made him virtually forgotten when he passed away in 1943.

Only one other popular music figure, Kay Kyser, was able to bat in Ben Bernie's personality/comic/bandleader league. Following in the path of other successful college band honchos, Kyser brought his University of North Carolina orchestra to radio in the early 1930s. He first drew attention through the employment of a gimmick to take care of song introductions—singing-song titles. They worked as follows:

VOCALIST: (Sings only first line including title) "Let's Build a Stairway to the Stars."

ORCHESTRA: (Plays one bar of tune)

ORCHESTRA: (Segues to Kyser's theme song, "Thinking of You" and under for . . .)

KYSER: Now here's one of the year's loveliest ballads, "Stairway to the Stars," sung by Harry Babbitt.

ORCHESTRA & BABBITT: (Do entire song).

Singing-song titles, however, were not responsible for bringing Kay Kyser's latent talent for comedy to the fore. It has been said the gimmick that eventually grew into his stock-in-trade came about by accident. According to the story, during a booking at Chicago's Blackhawk Restaurant, in order to boost slow Monday night business, Kyser incorporated a short pop music quiz in which patrons vied for small prizes. The idea caught on and ultimately developed into the long-running network hit, *Kay Kyser's Kollege of Musical Knowledge.* Kyser's soft Southern accent and self-deprecating manner (in reality, he was one of bandom's most business-minded hard noses) made him a perfect radio emcee. His adoption of the tag, "The 'Ole Professor," added that collegiate motif which pervaded the dance band business. Questions built around popular music were ludicrously simple. If contestants stumbled, which they often did, Kyser's sly hints yielded the answers. Kay Kyser's ability to ad lib often surpassed some of radio's professional comedians who were lost without their scripts. The 'Ole Professor never humiliated those bumbling contestants who seemed intent on making coast-to-coast fools of themselves.

Kay Kyser's Kollege of Musical Knowledge never strayed too far from its music base* even though it was perceived by some listeners more as a vehicle for Kyser's antics than a showcase for one of the country's leading dance aggregations. It was not until two or three minutes into the show that the leader came on. For unlike network television productions that open cold with a snippet of the action as a program tease, most of radio's coast-to-cast fare waded through a few moments of preliminaries—apparently in the belief that this wait added to the impact. In the case of *Kyser's Kollege,* it was a most effective device. The 'Ole Professor stood in the wings until the script cued his grand entrance. Wearing cap and gown, throwing kisses, waving and mugging, he approached the microphone amid cheers, whistles, and loud applause.

These were important elements to shows like Kyser's because live studio audiences provided a necessary lift for the performer. For those at home sitting in front of their radios, live studio audiences helped radiate an invisible glow, a show biz aura, that captured the listener's imagination. *Kay Kyser's Kollege of Musical Knowledge* is a good example of what live bigtime network musical radio was like in December, 1941:

ANNOUNCER: In a cigarette, it's the tobacco that counts!

AUCTIONEER: (Chants Lucky Strike's immortal logo)

---

* It's a good thing it did too. For as with all Lucky Strike musical shows, THE CLIENT, G. W. Hill, kept a sharp ear on proceedings.

ORCHESTRA: (Plays "Happy Days Are Here Again" for 30–40 seconds. Then fade for . . .)

ANNOUNCER: Lucky Strike presents *Kay Kyser's Kollege of Musical Knowledge* with a high helping of Hollywood hulla-baloo—$95.00 in prizes . . . *AND* that mighty flighty old blighter himself—KAY KYSER!

ORCHESTRA: (Kyser's theme song, "Thinking of You" for 30 seconds, then fade for . . .)

KYSER: Evening' folks. How y'all? Well, class night comes to town, and scholars come to class, all ready to take these exam hurdles with fun and fame along the way, and high finance at the finish.

ANNOUNCER: Pardon me, Professor. But before class, one of the students asked if I'd give you an apple.

KYSER: An apple! Why certainly, let the little fellow come forward.

ACTOR: Here it is, teacher. But you'll have to bob for it.

SOUND EFFECTS: (Water splashing to convey impression Kyser fell into container)

AUDIENCE: (Loud laughter and applause)

KYSER: (Wiping face and shaking off water) A fine way to start class, chillun! But while we mope around here, what say to a bit of required bobbin'? Do the Big Apple and Yes Dance!*

ORCHESTRA: (Plays "Sing Halleljuah," introduced by singing-song title).[6]

Following a second tune and a commercial came the first quiz sequence. In the show described above, contestants were asked to identify "Oh, How I Hate to Get up in the Morning" and "You're in the Army Now." Several quiz sequences were formatted for each show—all built around musical questions. Seven or eight songs by the Kyser band and his vocalists per hourly broadcast helped make this one of network radio's highest rated pop music offerings. *Kyser's Kollege* remained on the air through the mid-1940s. A television version lasted one season, and soon thereafter Kyser retired from show business to enjoy the considerable fruits of his radio harvest.

A black version of *Kay Kyser's Kollege of Musical Knowledge* may have been what the NBC-Blue Network had in mind when it introduced *Cab Calloway's Quizzicale* in 1942. For whatever reasons, *Quizzicale* failed to achieve the fame of *Kyser's Kollege,* Cab Calloway was not one of them. The energetic bandleader-emcee had paid his dues when his organization replaced Duke Ellington's Cotton Club revue in 1931. His "Hi-de-

---

*The "Big Apple" was a dance of the period, and "Yes" was Kyserese for "Let's."

hi-de-ho" trademark became a well-established radio logo, and his band was the spawning ground for future jazz greats Dizzy Gillespie, Cozy Cole, Milton Hinton, Chuck Berry, Tyree Glenn, Quentin Jackson and Danny Barker. Throughout the 1930s, Cab Calloway was a presence—on the air, and off. When name bands were the dominant force in popular music, Cab Calloway was the only black leader to emcee a prime time network show, albeit short-lived and unsponsored. In the summer of '42, Wednesday nights on NBC-Blue, listeners to the *Cab Calloway Quizzicale* heard the standard big production open:

> SOUND: (Drum rhythm)
>
> BAND: It's right!
>
> CALLOWAY: Now is it false or true?
>
> BAND: It's true!
>
> CALLOWAY: Wait a minute! Wait a minute! (Drums out) How do you know it's true?
>
> ACTOR #1: Why, man, it says so on the radio! On that program—now what was that program?
>
> BAND: CAB CALLOWAY'S QUIZZICALE!
>
> ACTOR #1: Yeah, man! That's the one, *Cab Calloway's Quizzicale.*
>
> ACTOR #2: Ummmmmm—Hmmmmmmmmmm. It's a natural.
>
> ORCHESTRA: Calloway's theme song, "Minnie the Moocher." Cue audience applause after Cab yells.)[7]

Next came a sub-introduction:

> ANNOUNCER: Yes, indeed, ladies and gentlemen, it's Harlem's weekly battle of brains—*Cab Calloway's Quizzicale*—coming to you this evening from New York, and featuring the original Harlem experts and thinkers along with the uptown music of Dr. Calloway and the band. And in keeping with the high I.Q. level of the *Quizzicale,* Dr. Calloway opens with a geography lesson entitled, "Idaho."[8]

It took another sequence before Calloway had a chance to get into the meat of his act. Following "Idaho," came yet a third introduction:

> ANNOUNCER: Now he could talk when he was two weeks old.
>
> ACTOR #1: That's being real smart.
>
> ANNOUNCER: He could quote Shakespeare before he was five!
>
> ACTOR #2: Oh, that takes brains!
>
> ANNOUNCER: So naturally when he grew up—

ACTOR #1: He must have done real well.

ACTOR #2: Yeah! How'd this fellow turn out anyway?

ANNOUNCER: How did he turn out? Why he turned out to be the head
man of the *Quizzicale.* And here he is, the Doctor himself—CAB
CALLOWAY![9]

Questions directed at the four contestants per *Quizzicale* were of comparable complexity to those on *Kyser's Kollege.* (Sample: "Define these three
words—sinkers, spuds and suds"). Of the four tunes allocated to the orchestra, Calloway sang three. When his dance band days were over, the
"Hi-de-hi-de-ho" man created for himself a second career on the musical
stage and night club circuit. He was the only black leader to do so. (Billy
Eckstine's host-band career was limited to singing.) Fundamentals learned
in the pop music-radio prep school did Cab Calloway no harm, as thousands familiar with his roles in two hit Broadway musical comedies, *Hello,
Dolly* and *Bubblin' Brown Sugar,* can attest.

Another way in which popular music worked hand-in-hand with radio comedy was the use of the orchestra leader as comic foil to the top
banana. Phil Harris was a popular bandleader in the early 1930s, but his
reputation as a comedian far out-distanced his fame as a baton-waver.
Harris's orchestra first came to national attention because of the leader's
reputation as a radio singer who didn't own a singing voice—a circum-
stance made possible with the advent of the microphone. His above-average musical crew was rounded out with the obligatory girl vocalist—in
Harris's case, Leah Ray, the future wife of Sonny Werblin, MCA principal
and later a leading figure in New York sports circles. Phil Harris and His
Orchestra joined Jack Benny in 1936. Harris's "Hi ya, Jackson!" became
a much-copied greeting across the country. Benny's writers used the raspy-
voiced musical director sparingly at first, although the Phil Harris character was established as soon as he came on the show. Harris's persona was
that of a flip, relaxed and mischievous fellow, who enjoyed nothing more
than putting Benny down. On a show from this period, a typical Benny-
Harris exchange included Harris's heckling of Benny. The orchestra leader
has just told the comedian he thought Fred Allen was very funny—meaning funnier than Benny:

BENNY: Phil, you're still on probation with me. If you don't behave
yourself, I'll make you take back that watch you gave me for Christmas.

HARRIS: OK, where is it?

BENNY: Well, just be careful, that's all.[10]

Gradually, Harris's bandleader role was subordinated to that of a fully-
developed, alcohol-inclined, egotistical roué who insulted Benny at every

turn. His was the key supporting role. On one program, Harris had just returned after a two-week absence:

HARRIS: Hi ya, Jackson!

BENNY: Oh, hello Phil.

HARRIS: Hey, Jackson, let me look at you. Your stay in Palm Springs did you a lot of good. You're two inches taller.

BENNY: What?

HARRIS: You're taller!

BENNY: Oh, darn it! I forgot to take off these high-heeled shoes. But Phil, no kidding, I sure missed you.

HARRIS: I know!

BENNY: What?

HARRIS: You need me, Jackson. You need me.

BENNY: What do you mean? I got big laughs, didn't I?

HARRIS: Yeah, you got laughs. But there was something missing. You know, your program without me is like a Persian rug—it looks good, but it just lays there.[11]

Harris carried his predilection for comedy to further heights in developing, with his wife, Alice Faye, a well-rated radio situation comedy that ran from 1946 until 1954 on NBC.

Like Jack Benny, Bob Hope invented a persona for one of his bandleaders. Skinnay Ennis, who had perfected a breathless singing style ("Got A Date with an Angel") in Hal Kemp's Orchestra for over a decade, became a fixture of Hope's wartime shows. The antithesis of Harris's wise guy, Ennis's low-key, Southern gentleman was a perfect foil to Bob Hope who came on with a brash, staccato delivery. Unlike Phil Harris whose musical contributions to the *Jack Benny Program* were secondary, Ennis sang a number or two each week on the Hope series—as did the show's songstress, Frances Langford. Hope's writers regularly wrote Ennis into the script, referring to the bandleader's string-bean stature using such surefire bits as these:

HOPE: And it's really windy here in the shore of Lake Michigan. Skinnay Ennis walked out on the beach today and stretched his arms. Ten minutes later, they shot him down over Gary, Indiana.[12]

and . . .

HOPE: Just a second, Colonna. I want you to meet my buddy. Hey Ennis! Colonna—this is Skin.

COLONNA: I beg pardon.

HOPE: I said this is Skin.

COLONNA: Yeah, and why didn't you put someone in it?[13]

After Les Brown's "Band of Renown" took over the musical chores on The *Bob Hope Show*, the replacement maestro served no comedic function.

On the *Edgar Bergen—Charlie McCarthy Program*, an Americanized British bandleader, who was the show's musical director, also ended up with a key supporting part in numerous scripts. Ray Noble had come to the United States in the early 1930s, planning a tour with his popular English dance band. Encountering insurmountable union problems, he organized a dance orchestra manned by leading American musicians instead, and for a while enjoyed bookings at such prestigious haunts as New York's Rainbow Room. By the time Noble was chosen for the Bergen-McCarthy show, he was leading a nondescript dance outfit.* His importance to the show was dramatic, rather than musical, portraying a scatterbrain, bumbling Englishman whose crisp accent played well off the earthier lines of Charlie McCarthy. A representative skit on a 1937 show involves a golf game. At several points in the script Noble asks to play through the foursome of McCarthy-Bergen, Announcer Bill Goodwin and guest W. C. Fields. Each time Noble is denied. Finally, in desperation:

NOBLE: Oh, I say, chaps, could I please play through?

BERGEN: What are you in such a rush about?

NOBLE: Well, I really should get home—you see my house in on fire.

FIELDS: There's nothing nicer than coming home to a warm house. Where was I?[14]

Three or four selections, usually two featuring the cast's permanent girl singer, were used to accessorize the weekly Bergen-McCarthy hour.

• • •

Choosing a name band to dress up a comedy/variety program was often a harrowing experience in network radio. It called for an extra measure of diplomacy on the part of the advertising agency. One adman, speaking for his fellow Madison Avenue toilers, called the process of selecting an orchestra,

"Sponsoritis" in its most virulent form. There may be presidents whose wives, children, and other assorted relatives who do not know "all about

---

*Ray Noble was one of the more prolific songwriters in the big band leader fraternity. A number of his compositions have become standards and rank with the best of the 1930s pop output: "Goodnight Sweetheart," "The Very Thought of You," "The Touch of Your Lips," "I Hadn't Anyone 'Till You."

music." There may be sales and advertising managers who do not rave
about a certain band ("A swell unit, not well known, but positively terrific") . . . But if there are such folks, I never seem to find them.[15]

The adman went on to bemoan the high cost of dance orchestras for shows,
attributing a large part of the problem to the need for special arrangements, complaining that "radio consumes music faster than composers can
grind it out."

The importance that ad agency producers ascribed to adorning their
variety/comedy packages with popular music during network radio's heyday is apparent in the following table:

COMEDIAN	BANDLEADER	SINGER
Jack Benny	George Olsen, Ted Weems, Frank Black, Don Bestor, Johnny Green, Bob Crosby, Phil Harris	Frank Parker, Michael Bartleft, James Melton, Kenny Baker, Larry Stevens, Dennis Day, Sportsmen Quartet
Fred Allen	Lon Katzman, Peter Van Steeden, Lennie Hayton, Al Goodman, Ferde Grofé	DeMarco Sisters
Eddie Cantor	Rubinoff, Cookee Fairchild, Louis Gress, Georgie Stoll, Jacques Rinard, Jimmie Greer	Dinah Shore, Robby Breen, Deanna Durbin, Margaret Whiting
Bob Hope	Al Goodman, Red Nichols, Skinnay Ennis, Les Brown	Judy Garland, Gloria Jean, Doris Day, Frances Langford
Edgar Bergen/ Charlie McCarthy	Robert Armbruster, Ray Noble	Donald Dixon, Anita Ellis, Dale Evans, Anita Gordon
Burns & Allen	Guy Lombardo, Jacques Renard, Ray Noble, Paul Whiteman, Meredith Wilson	Milton Watson, Tony Martin, Jimmy Cash, Dick Foran
Abbott & Costello	Will Osborne, Skinnay Ennis	Marilyn Maxwell, Connie Haines
Red Skelton	Ozzie Nelson, David Rose	Harriet Hilliard, Ozzie, Anita Ellis, 4 Knights
Robert Benchley	Artie Shaw	Helen Forrest, Tony Pastor
Ed Wynn	Eddie Duchin	Lew Sherwood

During the wireless medium's reigning years as a major force in mass
entertainment, producers stuck close to the popular music mainstream. With
one rare exception, however, network radio managed to showcase jazz—
of all things—in prime time. With the help of brilliantly written scripts,
featuring tongue-in-cheek continuity, the program was not distinguished

for pulling down big ratings, but it shone luminously through the drabness of most of network radio's pop music. The show was called the *Chamber Music Society of Lower Basin Street*. Using wry, mock-serious phraseology, the program's writers raised the radio script-writing art to an unheard-of level in the late 1930s and early 1940s. Following the establishment of theme song, "Basin Street Blues," came the show's introduction, written with whimsical exaggeration and delivered with stuff-shirt overtones. A characteristic opening comes from a program heard in July, 1940:

> ANNOUNCER: Tune in both ears to the *Chamber Music Society of Lower Basin Street*, formed to preserve the music of the three B's—barrelhouse, boogie-woogie, and the blues. Among the musicologists foregathered here on this gladsome Sunday afternoon are Maestro Paul Lavalle with his Virgin Pine Woodwinds, Dr. Henry "Hot Lips" Levine with his Dixieland Symphony of eight men and no female, Mademoiselle Dinah Sore, our one-woman torchlight parade. As our special guest, we have the celebrated Lionel Hampton Quartet. And as our intermission commentator, a famous musical authority whose name will be known to all of you as soon as you hear it. But the Society is being called to order by our chairman, Dr. Gino Hamilton who now raises his gavel, and makes a pass at the table.[16]
>
> SOUND: (Three knocks on wood).

The Society "chairmanship" alternated between Milton Cross, the legendary Metropolitan Opera commentator, and Gene Hamilton, an NBC staff announcer, both of whom lent the proper air of contrived pomposity to the proceedings. Hamilton was narrator for the program mentioned above, on which "My Gal Sal" received this send-off:

> HAMILTON: . . . We would like Dr. Henry Levine to give us his Dixieland reading of an early American classic. The work was written as a chamber concerto with a disfigured bass, and it features a solo by Dr. Levine on trumpet, Professor Aloysius on sliphorn, and Professor Louis Evanson on clarinet. Listed as Opus 33, first door to the left, the work is popularly known as "My Gal Sal."[17]

Every song received a similar preamble. For "Stardust," the Society chairman had the following introduction:

> HAMILTON: . . . As we have often told you, Fellow Members, the ten musicians in Maestro Paul Lavalle's Chamber Group play a total of 36 woodwind instruments, including the flageolet. The flageolet is, I'm sure you read, a small flute played in one hand while, the other beats a drum. When Maestro Laval made his super-modernistic arrangement of "Stardust," he wrote in a part for flageolet. However, as he already had a drummer, he was not able to locate a one-armed flute player. The part was transformed from piano and is played on

this occasion by Professor Mario Umberto Janero. Here then is Maestro Laval's Concerto for Orchestra and One-Armed Flute Player,
"Stardust." [18]

That the *Chamber Music Society of Lower Basin Street* managed to find a
place in the NBC schedule over three seasons is remarkable, considering
that its subtle mien was not designed for mass tastes.

• • •

When the radio laughter died down in network studios and the comedians moved to television, popular music's role on video comedy shows
changed drastically. In the first place, comedy in television is entirely different. Comedy-variety programs are plugged in as "specials," and except
for Johnny Carson, no attempt is made at week-in, week-out frequency.
Orchestras and singers, except as special guests, on television's big comedy-variety shows (not to be confused with sitcoms) are nothing more than
production necessities.*

By the time the radio comedian had been condemned to Fred Allen's
"treadmill to oblivion," network executives, who also had television fish
to fry, knew that not all their radio affiliates were going after television
licenses. There were still some radio operators left who felt there was a
place for radio in the communications spectrum. But where? The bands
were disappearing one by one, and so were the comedians. Funnymen who
had already arrived on the tube were making cracks about radio's demise,
prompting some radio partisans to request that the networks lower the
boom on ingrate ex-radio comedians. Winds of change were indeed swirling through the airwaves. The signs were everywhere. Clearly, the plight
of radio after 1948 was no laughing matter.

NOTES

1. George Burns. *The Third Time Around,* Putman, (New York), 1980, p. 116.
2. *The Ed Wynn Show.* March 26, 1935, Radio Yesteryear, Program No. 769.
3. *Ibid.*
4. *The Baker's Broadcast.* May 13, 1934, Museum of Broadcasting, Tape No. R76: 070.
5. *The Ben Bernie Show.* October 15, 1935, Mark 56 Records, No. 755.
6. *Kay Kyser's Kollege of Musical Knowledge.* December 10, 1941, Museum of Broadcasting, Tape No. R77: 0385.
7. *Cab Calloway's Quizzicale.* June 10, 1942, Broadcast Pioneers Library script.
8. *Ibid.*
9. *Ibid.*
10. *The Jello Program, Starring Jack Benny.* circa 1937, Museum of Broadcasting, Tape No.
    R77: 0450.
11. *The Jack Benny Program.* April 25, 1948, Nostalgia Lane Records, No. PB0261.
12. *The Pepsodent Show.* May 5, 1942, Radio Yesteryear, Program No. 3641.
13. *The Bob Hope Show.* December 18, 1945, Radiola Records, No. MR1060.

---

* The only major exception turned out to be Leader Doc Severinsen on the *Tonight Show.*

14. Ross Firestone, ed. *The Big Radio Comedy Program,* Contemporary Books, (Chicago), 1978, p. 196.
15. Kenneth L. Watt. "One Minute to Go," *Saturday Evening Post,* April 2, 1938, p. 85.
16. *Chamber Music Society of Lower Basin Street,* July 14, 1940, Radio Yesteryear, Reel No. 617.
17. *Ibid.*
18. *Ibid.*

By the early 1930s, the radio
music box had become a necessity. Shown here is one of
the first radio-phonograph-
recorder combinations.

The first commercially successful "spread band" radio receiver was introduced by RCA
in 1938. With eight push buttons, domestic and shortwave
bands, phonograph connec-
tions, it retailed for $200.

LISTENERS HAD A CHOICE OF "SWEET" AND SWING AS THE BANDS PLAYED ON THROUGH THE 1930S

Ozzie Nelson
Ozzie Nelson's show business career "took off" when his band was chosen to open the new Glen Island Casino, New Rochelle, N.Y. in 1930.

Jan Garber
Like many name band leaders, Jan Garber had an identifying tag. He was "The Idol of the Airlanes."

Anson Weeks
One of the few name bands to start on the West Coast was fronted by Anson Weeks ("Let's go dancin' with Anson!") Weeks' home base was The Peacock Court of San Francisco's Mark Hopkins Hotel.

Red Norvo
Norvo led one of the less heralded swing bands of the 1930s. Together with his wife, vocalist Mildred Bailey, they adopted the billing, "Mr. and Mrs. Swing."

Sammy Kaye
From the campus of Ohio University came Sammy Kaye. Listeners were invited to "Swing and Sway with Sammy Kaye." However, there was little "Swing" and more "Sway" as Kaye led one of the 1930s top "sweet" bands.

Tommy Dorsey
"The Sentimental Gentleman of Swing" hit big time radio when he was sponsored by Ford in the summer of 1936. But it was his *Raleigh-Kool Show* on NBC (1937–1939) that made him a national favorite.

(All photos courtesy Steve Tassia)

BENNY GOODMAN, "The King of Swing," and vocalist, Frances Hunt, in a crowded studio during Benny's first season on the *Camel Caravan*.

WILLARD ALEXANDER. Young Alexander convinced his bosses at Music Corporation of America, the leading talent agency of the big band era, to stick with Benny Goodman through his band's early adversity. Alexander later left MCA to form his own booking agency.

With or without his orchestra, Benny Goodman was a frequent guest artist on network music and variety shows. By the time he appeared on CBS's *Songs by Sinatra* in early 1946, singers had taken over popular music.

Bing Crosby, "The Cremo Singer," on CBS, 1931.

A Thursday night fixture on NBC for over a decade beginning in 1935, Bing Crosby as host for the *Kraft Music Hall* delivered some of the network's best ratings.

Jimmy Dorsey, Tommy's older brother, became more noted for leading the band that featured songbirds Helen O'Connell and Bob Eberly than for serving as the first musical director for Bing Crosby's *Kraft Music Hall*.

Scores of entertainers such as comedienne Cass Daley appeared with Crosby on the *Kraft Music Hall*. However, through the years, the program was essentially a showcase for Bing, the singer.

150

Glenn Miller
Chesterfield beat Lucky Strike
to the punch for sponsorship of
Glenn Miller and Orchestra late
in 1939.

When lesser known cigarette brands such as Sensation wanted better identity in the marketplace, they often chose a name band. Larry Clinton and His Orchestra broadcast for Sensation on NBC in 1939.

The *Camel Caravan,* a long-running big band network series under R.J. Reynolds sponsorship, began on CBS in 1933 with the Casa Loma Orchestra. The show's theme song, "Smoke Rings," became so popular, the orchestra adopted it as its own theme melody.

Bob Crosby
Bob Crosby, Bing's younger
brother, and His Orchestra, replaced Benny Goodman on *The
Camel Caravan* in 1940.

(Courtesy Bruce Davidson)

Many popular music shows in the 1930s were strong enough to attract big name guests. On one Tommy Dorsey *Raleigh-Kool Show* in 1938, (l. to r.) Jack Benny, Dick Powell, Ken Murray, Bing Crosby, and Shirley Ross joined Dorsey for a jam session.

(Courtesy Dave Dexter, Jr.)

Woody Herman
Old Gold in the mid-1940s was a sponsor of Woody Herman's Orchestra, considered by many the "last of the great swing bands."

(author's collection)

Lloyd Schaeffer (l.) was one of several musical directors for Perry Como's *Chesterfield Supper Club* which held down NBC's traditional 7:00–7:15 p.m. pop music block between 1944 and 1949.

152

(Courtesy Steve Tassia)

Johnny Green

Your Hit Parade reached in many directions for its stars. Johnny Green, composer of such standards as "Body and Soul" and "I Cover the Waterfront," and a former dance band maestro, led the show's orchestra for a time during the 1930s, before he settled in the Hollywood studios. Yale graduate Lanny Ross, who gained his original radio fame on the *Maxwell House Showboat*, was the featured *Hit Parade* male singer for the 1938–39 season.

(author's collection)

Lanny Ross

BANDSTANDS WERE THE FOCAL POINTS OF POPULAR MUSIC IN THE 1930s

(Courtesy Steve Tassia)

(Courtesy Steve Tassia)

(Courtesy Steve Tassia)

In top photo, Hal Kemp (legs crossed, seated on left), who organized his band at the University of North Carolina became a radio favorite. Skinny Ennis, Kep's drummer and vocalist, (seated on right) left in 1938 to form his own orchestra and starred on Bob Hope's show.

In center photo, Ace Brigode (standing, center) and His Virginians were popular on radio around 1930. Note potted palms at rear and megaphone on left. In photo on left is Don Bester (center) who gained additional popularity for his orchestra by serving a stint on the *Jack Benny Program.*

154

(Courtesy Merle Hildebrand)

The arrival of swing in the mid-1930s stimulated the record collecting hobby. Recordings such as those shown helped increase not only the popularity of the bands and singers themselves, but focused attention on a rising new personality of musical radio—the disc jockey.

BLACK BANDS OFTEN OUT-SWUNG THEIR WHITE COMPETITORS, BUT ONLY A FEW MADE IT BIG

(Courtesy Merle Hildebrand)

Steeped in the Kansas City blues tradition, Count Basie has led the quintessential black swing band since 1936.

(Courtesy Steve Tassia)

(Courtesy Steve Tassia)

Jimmie Lunceford
Swing outfits were called on to excel as dance units and also as "show" bands for theater appearances. None surpassed Jimmie Lunceford's swinging aggregation.

Louis Armstrong
Armstrong, whose contributions were fundamental to the development of swing, enjoyed popularity in the 1930s more as a radio and movie personality than as a swing maestro.

Paul Whiteman had to be sold on the merits of radio by young William Paley of CBS. After Whiteman's debut on that network in 1929, the portly leader moved his large unit to NBC where most of his programs were heard during the 1930s. "The Jazz Wing" was a small band-within-a-band that Whiteman used to perpetuate his title, "King of Jazz," which he was not.

Below: In the selling of swing, leaders used every opportunity to incorporate the word—just as Whiteman had done with the word, jazz. But in the case of the "Swing Brass Section" of Mal Hallet's Orchestra, the label was correct: Hallet led one of the better swing bands of the era.

(Courtesy Dave Dexter Jr.)

SWING BRASS SECTION FEATURED WITH MAL HALLETT ORCHESTRA

(Courtesy Steve Tassia)

157

BANDS FEATURED FEMALE THRUSHES
. . . In Groups

(Courtesy Bruce Davidson)

TD's Pied Pipers

(author's collection)

Alvino Rey's King Sisters

. . . and as Singles

(Courtesy Steve Tassia)

Leah Ray

After Bing Crosby, girl singers, too, became obligatory fixtures in the name band entourage—in groups, and as singles. Radio broadcasts of the 1930s often gave them build-ups as big as their parent organizations. In top photo on opposite page, Jo Stafford (third from left), was a featured soloist with Tommy Dorsey, as well as a member of the Pied Pipers. Frank Sinatra (on Stafford's right) in same photo was not part of the Pipers, but joined them from time to time. Alvino Rey gave the King Sisters (bottom photo opposite page) their show business start with his big band. Leah Ray sang with Phil Harris's Orchestra in the early 1930s. Mildred Bailey warbled as a single before and after her swing band days. Ella Mae Morse parlayed in 1942 record hit made as a big band singer ("Cow-Cow Boogie" with Freddie Slack's Orchestra) into a career as a single.

(Courtesy Dave Dexter, Jr.)

Mildred Bailey

(Courtesy Dave Dexter, Jr.)

Ella Mae Morse

159

POPULAR MUSIC PACKAGED WITH RADIO NETWORK
COMEDY WAS STYLIZED BY A VARIETY OF ARTISTS

(Courtesy Steve Tassia)

Ben Bernie

Ex-vaudvillian Bernie, who led a successful dance orchestra, developed a knack for comedy and became a radio star.

(Courtesy Steve Tassia)

Phil Harris

Harris's comedic talents ultimately won out over his bandleading interests, and led to his own NBC show with wife, Alice Faye.

(Courtesy Dave Dexter, Jr.)

Kay Kyser

Bandleader-comic Kay Kyser, was the star of NBC's *Kollege of Musical Knowledge.*

(author's collection)

Cab Calloway

Duke Ellington's successor at the Cotton Club in 1931, Calloway created a "personality" for himself early in his bandleading career that included comedy, singing and dancing.

(author's collection)

Dennis Day

Irish tenor Day sang the obligatory one selection on the *Jack Benny Program*, but his popularity derived more from the role Benny's writers assigned him—that of an innocent whose feigned naiveté caused Benny no end of exasperation.

By 1933, many broadcasters had installed turntables capable of playing 16-inch transcriptions.

RCA Thesaurus was a pioneer in producing special library material on transcriptions for station subscribers.

A decade is a long time in popular music. In the top photo, Red Nichols was riding the radio name band crest of the mid-1930s. Ten years later, singers such as Dick Haymes, (r.) and Helen Forrest (c.) had taken over. Gordon Jenkins, (l.) was music director. Their show for Autolite was one of the last "blockbuster" popular music programs on network radio.

Part Three
(1948-1954)

A DECLARATION OF
INDEPENDENTS

*The mill cannot grind
with the water that's past.*

—George Herbert

CHAPTER 11

Network Fade-out

WHEN MILLIONS OF service men and women returned to civilian life in the mid-1940s and dialed around for popular music, they were reasonably sure of what they might find. Overseas veterans were able to stay in touch by means of stateside programs provided by the Armed Forces Radio Service. Purists may have objected to the AFRS's deletion of commercials, and the real radio freaks may have considered themselves treated as second-class citizens hearing shows—shipped on transcriptions—a month or more after they were broadcast in the States. But, by and large, American men and women in the farthest outposts around the world, some of whom had been there four years, were grateful they could tune in a "touch of home" abroad. Popular music was an especially big item on AFRS stations overseas. Drama, comedy and other kinds of programs required concentration, not particularly appropriate for the peripatetic military listener. If for no other reason than its ready availability, pop music often ranked ahead of magazines, movies and other diversions that were supposed to boost morale. Thanks to AFRS, the ex-GI didn't come back a complete pop music ignoramus.

Veterans returning to civilian life had a big hand in shaping music tastes in the 1930s. They were the young males in their late teens and early twenties—a segment that has always greatly influenced the direction of pop music. Now, four and five years later, their intensity of interest in popular music had diminished in favor of such concerns as careers, housing, education, marriage, children, divorce and inflation.

165

Veterans, however, were not so pre-occupied they couldn't join their fellow citizens in helping make the sun shine on radio row by buying new radios at a record clip. The expected post-War set-manufacturing boom was right on schedule. (See table next chapter). From a pre-War high of 13,000,000 receivers made in 1941, assembly lines pushed out 17,000,000 in 1947 alone, plus another 3,200,000 for autos. As far as advertising was concerned, sponsors still put the big bucks on the networks. Billings to clients that had reached a previous high of $81,744,395 in 1942, soared to $122,723,098 in 1948—the all-time record sales year for networks. In programming, network radio was still the hottest ticket in town. A popular network radio show from the night before could stir up coffee shop and office talk the next day.

But if the society was changing with the re-entry of 14,000,000 veterans, so were America's listening habits. Dramatic shows by now had become the overwhelming favorite network entertainment form. The following table, charting major prime time network programs per season, by types, shows this trend developing since 1935. The table also indicates why their aides were keeping network executives away from open windows in skyscrapers around 1955:

SEASON	COMEDY	VARIETY	POPULAR MUSIC	DRAMA
1935–36	11	6	39	17
1940–41	9	8	18	39
1945–46	15	12	25	57
1950–51	9	5	12	52
1955–56	1	1	3	12

—Source: *A Thirty-Year History of Radio Programs, 1926–1956.* Harrison B. Summers, ed., Arno, 1971.

Popular music shows out of New York and Hollywood in the first post-War years continued to wear the unmistakable gloss of big-time mass entertainment. Advertising agencies still ran the show, from hiring the script writers who put clever words in the mouths of the stars, to deciding whether the middle commercial should be 35- or 65-seconds. Programs were still designed for single-sponsorship, one of network radio's strongest arguments for a client's marketplace identity. Advertisers followed the tradition established early in musical radio by using safe, mainstream artists whose songbooks bulged with the works of the Broadway-Tin Pan Alley-Hollywood composers. Old favorites were still the networks' meal tickets—Guy Lombardo, Phil Spitalny, Fred Waring, *Manhattan Merry-Go-Round, Album of Familiar Music, Your Hit Parade, Waltz Time.* If the musical Hooperatings could not match those of the dramatic and comedic blockbusters, they were, as the Mad Avenue folk like to say, at least "respectable."

The take-over of popular music by vocalists that so marked this period was easily discerned on network programs: by the middle of the 1940s they had all but replaced big bands. The trend to singers that had started with Bing Crosby, and worked its way ever so slowly through the 1930s, began to pick up momentum when Frank Sinatra left Tommy Dorsey's Orchestra to go out as a single in 1942. Following a break-in stanza on *Your Hit Parade,* Sinatra got his own show in 1945. *Songs by Sinatra,* Wednesdays at 9 p.m. on CBS, followed the network formula: name performer, full orchestra, supporting vocal group or singer, familiar songs that reflected a studied mix of standards, current pops, novelties. Songs used on a Sinatra program in November, 1946 encapsulate what a network popular music program was like in radio's final years of prime time entertainment:

"Let It Snow, Let It Snow, Let It Snow"
"I Concentrate on You"
"Glory, Glory Hallelujah"
"Zip-A-Dee-Doo-Dah"
"The House I Live In"
"You'll Always Be The One I Love"
"Why Does It Get So Late So Early?"
"Falling in Love With Love"
"Night and Day"
"Put Your Dreams Away"[1]

Emphasis on the music dictated that continuity on such programs be lean and spare. In order to squeeze in 10 to 12 selections, three commercials, open and closing themes, and credits—all in a half-hour—show scripts, such as the one for *Songs by Sinatra* in January, 1946, were tightly written, and tried to avoid getting in the way of the music,

SINATRA, (Finishing show open) . . . This evening belongs to Jerome Kern.

MUSIC: (Sinatra sings) "I Won't Dance."

SINATRA: Don't twist my arm, 'cause that won't work. Keep it mellow. But most of all, keep it Jerry Kern.

ORCHESTRA: Establishes first bars of "Who". . . .

JANE POWELL (Guest): I didn't know Mr. Kern wrote that.

SINATRA: His range was wider than a keyboard as the Pied Pipers will attest right now.

MUSIC: (Pied Pipers) "Who."

SINATRA: One of the loveliest of Kern's songs, Jane, is "Smoke Gets in Your Eyes." It's a shame Jerome Kern's not here to hear your lovely voice.

MUSIC: (Powell) "Smoke Gets in Your Eyes."

SINATRA: Mighty swell, Jane. That was beautiful.

POWELL: Thanks, Frank. Now it's your turn for this song from Jerome
Kern's *Sweet Adeline*. . . .[2]

Before the 1940s ended, in addition to Frank Sinatra, Dinah Shore, Ginny Simms, Vic Damone, Tony Martin, Gordon MacRae, Dick Haymes-Helen Forrest, Vaughn Monroe and Eddie Howard joined the popular singer brigade that landed their own shows in prime time network slots. Yet the highest rated (a 20 Hooperating) network popular music show of the transition years included none of the above. It was network radio's Last Great Blockbuster, and it came when the network's swan song had already begun. It was created more out of necessity than anything else.

ABC, the youngest of the networks, in scrambling for advertising dollars, was unable to compete with CBS and NBC because it couldn't deliver the prestigious station line-ups of its well-entrenched rivals—a splendid position for trying something "different." So it was in the spring of 1948, the third major radio network brought forth on the American continent *Stop The Music*. Installed by ABC Sunday nights, opposite NBC's two comedy heavyweights, Edgar Bergen-Charlie McCarthy and Fred Allen, *Stop the Music* almost literally stopped the country between 8 and 9p.m. Radio, which had always been able to generate conversation pieces had done it again. (As it turned out, this was the last network one.) The chief ingredient that made *Stop the Music* a national phenomenon was older than radio, older than music. It was good old fashioned greed. The simple format consisted of a studio orchestra and singers performing tunes the listening audience had a chance to identify for shots at enormous jackpots. That a person's chances of being called were 25 million to one mattered not a bit.

Stop the Music was an instant hit. Fast-paced for 60 bang-bang minutes, the show opened with one or two up-tempo numbers, followed by a commercial, then the first contest sequence. In order to qualify for a whack at naming the mystery tune, a contestant first had to identify a disarmingly simple one. Bert Parks, the bubbling emcee, then commanded maestro Harry Salter to give the downbeat for the orchestra to sail into the mystery song, while singers Kay Armen and Dick Brown hummed the portions containing the giveaway words. Somewhere in the middle of the number, Bert Parks shouted, "STOP THE MUSIC!" For correct identification, a contestant could win a jackpot worth between $10,000, $25,000 or more. In March, 1949, by naming the mystery tune, a listener collected plunder valued at $32,250—including: a $1000 bond; a Kaiser sedan; $1500 tax payment; $1500 men's wardrobe; $1500 women's wardrobe; $1000 worth of groceries; a new kitchen; paint job for the house; living room set; fishing outfits; year's supply of shaving lotion; candy, haircuts; piano; necklace; two motorcycles; silver and fireplace sets; two great Danes; $500 cowboy boots; $3000 rug; record library; $2500 watch; and an ermine coat.[3] Fred Allen, whose ratings were demolished by *Stop the Music,* took out insurance guaranteeing an Allen listener $5000 if he was called by *Stop the Music.* The show prompted Allen to deliver a scorching commentary on the state of radio in the late 1940s:

> Giveaway programs are the buzzards of radio. As buzzards swoop down carrion, so have giveaway shows descended on the carcass of radio . . . Radio started as a medium of entertainment . . . The networks that once vied with each other to present the nation's outstanding acting and musical talent are now infested with swarms of hustlers . . . If I were king for one day, I would make every program in radio a giveaway show; when the studios were filled with the people who encourage these atrocities, I would lock the door. With all the morons in America trapped, the rest of the population could go about its business.[4]

Fred Allen's description of the fate of the network comedian at this time, "treadmill to oblivion," could have applied to many musical programs as well. Yet ironically, one of radio's most successful "pure" pop music shows came during the period when networks were fading out.

Club 15, 7:30-7:45p.m., Eastern time, Monday through Friday, enjoyed a five-year run on CBS, a loyal sponsor in Campbell's Soups, and the benefit of a good lead-in, the sprightly *Jack Smith-Dinah Shore Show,* 7:15-7:30p.m. The quarter-hour dinner-time musical-offering idea stretched back to William Paley's use of Bing Crosby, Kate Smith, et. al. in the CBS schedule between 7 and 8 p.m. Before *Club 15* ended the strain, many of the pop artists of the 1940s and early 1950s appeared before its microphones—Bob Crosby, Jo Stafford, Margaret Whiting, Patti Clayton, The Andrews Sisters, Dick Haymes, Evelyn Knight. Jerry Gray, former arranger for Artie Shaw and Glenn Miller, was musical director. Budgeting for Gray's big band was an indication that Campbell's Soups and CBS were still interested in the aura of bigtime show biz and were not about to compromise by trimming the standard show orchestra down to combo size, a not uncommon practice at the time. *Club 15,* an effervescent 15 minutes, bounded merrily along with consistency on every one of its five nights. Show continuity was sometimes sophisticated, sometimes corny, always upbeat, and never out of sync with the music. A typical fast-paced comedy bit was this exchange between Bob Crosby ("Head Man of *Club 15*") and Jo Stafford:

CROSBY: Say Jo—Jo Stafford.

STAFFORD: Yes, Bob?

CROSBY: Say, did you like riding a merry-go-round when you were a kid?

STAFFORD: Not much.

CROSBY: Why?

STAFFORD: Never got me anywhere.

CROSBY: Oh! Gee, I'll never forget my first merry-go-round ride. A little girl had a pass. There I was sitting on a horse, going around and around, with her running beside me.

STAFFORD: Running?

CROSBY: Sure, the pass was only for one.

STAFFORD: So you rode?

CROSBY: Oh, sure. Gee, my mother told me that running after a merry-go-round caused Bing a lot of trouble.

STAFFORD: Why?

CROSBY: Got him started following the horses. And I've been broke every since!

ORCHESTRA: (Hits intro to next number)[5]

Campbell's Soup commercials were frequently integrated and featured Del Sharbutt, *Club 15* announcer, one of the last of the deep-voiced types the network favored. Sharbutt who performed more as a comedian than a straight man was often written into the script and ended up with many of the punch lines. *Club 15's* adaptations of popular music to enhance commercial messages were models of selling-as-entertainment. The following example was taken from the *Club 15* show cited above:

SHARBUTT: Once upon a time there were two lovers, Valencia and Roberto. But they quarreled.

STAFFORD: We've been going together for 15 years, Roberto, and you still haven't asked me to marry you.

CROSBY: Well, a man needs time to think things over.

STAFFORD: I'll do anything to make you happy.

CROSBY: You will?

STAFFORD: I will.

CROSBY: Well then, listen—(Sings to tune of "Valencia") Valencia! Give me soup for lunch today And I will wed you right away.

STAFFORD: (Sings) Roberto, I will do that thing for you, Cause it's my luncheon favorite too!

BOTH: (Sing) Quick to serve and such a treat, Oh soup for lunch that can't be beat . . . (After several more quatrains . . .)

SHARBUTT: So they got married and joined the millions of people who eat soup for lunch every day.

VOCAL GROUP: (In quick run-off, sing Campbell's "MMM-Good" song).[6]

But not even *Club 15* with its classy corn and buoyant spirit could stop the decline of interest in network radio's pop musicales. By the time *Club 15* was getting ready to close shop in 1953, the show had been reduced to a three-a-week strip and its rating fell to a 5.7, almost half of its 1948 high. In *Club 15's* final season, only three other major network popular music programs could claim sponsors: *Vaughn Monroe and His Orchestra* (Camel); *Your Hit Parade* (Lucky Strike); and The *Mindy Carson Show* (Buick).

Television's tidal wave had rolled over night-time schedules to such an extent, that in the fall of 1955, only a scattering of drama and comedy staples were still around. (When CBS had practically thrown in the towel four years earlier to announce advertising rate cuts of 10% for programs after 1p.m., it came as no surprise. What did shock many inside and outside of broadcasting was CBS President Frank Stanton's candor: "We have gotten only one legitimate piece of new radio business since July, 1950.")[7]

Three of the networks, by 1955, had retained a few hardy perennials: CBS—*Suspense, Gunsmoke, Johnny Dollar, Our Miss Brooks;* NBC—*Dragnet, People Are Funny, Truth or Consequences, Fibber McGree and Molly, The Great Gildersleeve;* Mutual—*Counterspy, Wild Bill Hickok, Gangbusters.* ABC had cleaned virtually all dramatic properties out of its schedule and went into several different directions. For all four radio networks, it was not their finest hour: in 1947, 97% of all AM stations on the air were network affiliated. Eight years later, the number had plummeted to a shocking 30%.

In their desire to prove to their affiliates they intended to stay in business, all four networks plugged some of the prime time holes with big bands. It seemed strange to find dance orchestras once again ensconced between 8 and 11p.m. But there they were—Guy Lombardo, Lawrence Welk, Sammy Kaye, Dick Jurgens, the Dorseys, Henry Jerome, et al. Through these golden oldies, the networks were perhaps trying to salvage older listeners who might defect from television to get *their* kind of popular music—music that had virtually vanished from the airwaves. With the exception of a few public service "sponsors," such as the Treasury Department, which picked up talent costs, the dance orchestras brought the networks no revenues. Stations that once touted their affiliations often cut away from the network to fill with recorded music. Early in 1954, NBC acknowledged the awful truth. As of February first, it cancelled all band remotes, for as *Variety* reported,

The web discovered most of the affiliates were not accepting net offerings, preferring to fill time with local disc jockeys on the theory that they come closer to knowing the musical pulse of their individual listeners . . . Dee-jays spend considerable time programming a show, maintaining a healthy balance between current pop tunes and standards and the bill of fare is apparently more palatable to late night audiences.[8]

Network daytime adjustments to radio life in the television age were less jarring simply because networks never supplied much music in pre-night time hours to begin with. Network option time during the day had always been the province of soap operas, homemaker hints, quiz and va-riety shows—*Arthur Godfrey Time* and the *Breakfast Club* being notable examples of the latter. Paradoxically, it was during its last years as a mass entertainment medium that one of network radio's most stunning popular music shows, *Fred Waring Time,* appeared in the daytime. It will be dealt with at this point, not because it was typical daylight radio fare—for it most assuredly was not.

Fred Waring Time was simply the best of all Waring's broadcasting excursions—in radio or television. And since no survey of popular music on radio can aspire to cover the main currents without reflecting upon the Waring phenomenon, this seemed the logical place to explore a Waring radio undertaking. In references to Fred Waring elsewhere, it was observed he was an artist of strong feelings. His encounters with broadcasting and advertising agency middlemen are legendary. With his penchant for show-manship and attention to detail, it is somewhat surprising to find him tak-ing on the staggering responsibility of five weekly half-hour productions. Yet, in the mid-1940s *Fred Waring Time* arrived in NBC's morning sched-ule. By that time, Waring had long since scrapped the dance band format in favor of a musical company that could perform on several levels. *Fred Waring Time* had all the trappings of night-time, big-time radio. Spon-sored by Johnson's Wax and the American Meat Institute, the Waring-NBC gambit was one of the major underwritings of musical radio, daytime or nighttime. A generous budget made it possible for the Pennsylvanians to maintain their personal appearance schedule and gain further exposure by originating from different parts of the country. Polished production, a Waring trademark, was never more apparent. Listeners tuning in NBC on a weekday fall morning in the late 1940s might well have mistaken the hour for 10p.m. a decade earlier:

ANNOUNCER: It's 10 o'clock and time for Fred Waring—Fred Waring to bring out the beauty of a song.

WARING GLEE CLUB: (Singing) Bring out the beauty of a song.

ANNOUNCER: Johnson's Wax to bring out the beauty of the home.

WARING GLEE CLUB: (Singing) Bring out the beauty of a home.

ANNOUNCER: The makers of Johnson Wax present Fred Waring and the Pennsylvanians to brighten your morning.

WARING GLEE CLUB: (Singing) I hear music—I hear melodies.

ANNOUNCER: Here's your Monday and Wednesday host for Johnson's Wax, your fall semester professor—Fred Waring.

(Applause)

WARING: Hello everybody. Thanks for coming. Today the Pennsylvanians are in Kahn Auditorium on the campus of Northwestern University, broadcasting from Evanston, Illinois . . . (Waring continues his opening remarks, referring to the up-coming Northwestern-UCLA Rose Bowl game, and introduces the first musical selection, "A Salute to Northwestern.") *

Waring's radio programs were eclectic in a way no other popular music organization tried to match. There were show tunes, folk songs, pop hits, patriotic airs, light classics, special-occasion religious pieces, college fight songs. Selections played on the Evanston origination were typical: "Yours Is My Heart Alone," "I May Be Wrong," "My Darling, My Darling," an elaborately orchestrated "Billy Boy," and "Going Home." Fred Waring, who served as his own on-air host, regularly violated one of the caveats of popular music: he sought to increase the listener's knowledge. Conventional wisdom had always warned against mixing "education" and entertainment, but Waring's disregard for such warnings never detracted from his popularity; in fact, his illuminating program notes may have been a magnet that drew many listeners who felt the head Pennsylvanian was expanding their music education. There is an illustrative Waring mini-lecture on the Northwestern broadcast:

WARING: (after identifying the next song, "Going Home"). . . . This tune was written in Iowa where we played last night. "Going Home" is part of the *New World Symphony,* written by the Czech composer, Anton Dvořák. During the year Dvořák taught in New York, he spent his summer vacations in Spillville, Iowa on the Mississippi. And it was there that he found the inspiration for his greatest work. The orchestra plays and Jane Wilson sings, "Going Home." [9]

Fred Waring violated most of the shibboleths of popular music. Even when his orchestras were competing with conventional dance outfits of the 1920s and 1930s, he eschewed playing anything on the basis of popularity alone. A tune might be popular, but unless it passed the Waring litmus test, it did not get on the air. By the mid-1940s, the Waring entourage had become exclusively a concert organization with emphasis on glee clubs and choruses. By means of his choral showcases, he carved out a special niche in the entertainment field. As the symbol of middle-brow pop, Waring

---

* Throughout his 60-year career, Waring never severed the campus connection established in the 1920s when his band catered to the college crowd. Years later, whether broadcasting from a campus or from a studio, Waring programs often had a collegiate flavor.

never left any fuzzy images as to where he belonged in the music spectrum. A long line of Waring alumni—those who performed with the Pennsylvanians and those who matriculated at his Shawnee-on-Delaware workshops—are a special group who have added to the rich diversity of American popular music's colorful mosaic. The product that has distinguished Fred Waring's traveling choral repertory company was a "minority" music, to be sure. Yet it survived for six decades the trendy onslaughts of one musical fad after another. In broadcasting, Fred Waring's métier was network radio. When television became the chief source of mass entertainment, he made the transition. No 27-inch screen could encompass the Waring style, however, and his shows enjoyed only mild success. The Pennsylvanians were always at their best in the theater—the theater of the mind, radio.

By the time Waring had run his course on radio, the networks revitalized a program concept that had served them well in earlier years. Quarter-hour strips of pop music across the board were shoved into holes along the network dikes. Highlighting a singer, a three-or-four-piece combo and an announcer, the pop music quickie appealed to the network—because of low production costs, and because it lent at least a modicum of credibility to the notion that the network was still a supplier of live entertainment.* For the affiliate, the 15-minute cameo re-inforced the claim that its network was still the source of live entertainment. Many varieties of the species popped in and out of schedules during network radio's latter days. Lanny Ross, Kate Smith, Curt Massey-Martha Tilton, Jane Pickens and Gloria Parker were among the names called on to render musical first aid. Some like Jack Berch were established network artists and kept right on warbling into the 1950s. Berch, a midday fixture, first on NBC, then ABC, was a latter-day song-and-patter man who sang three or four snappy numbers and exchanged small talk with the announcer in a manner reminiscent of his syndication days.** Affiliates, however, were becoming increasingly apprehensive over the incompatibility of a Jack Berch with their own disc jockeys. The Age of the Disc Jockey had arrived by now; it was just a matter of finding the right ones to fit the right time slots.

Billboard's 1954 Disc Jockey Poll revealed that of the 109.4 hours the average station was on the air each week, 63.8 hours—or 60%—were devoted to record shows. This trend "reached its greatest acceleration in the last two years during which period television pre-empted from network radio the position of top programming and advertising medium . . ."[10] Nobody in broadcasting was surprised at the figures released in *Billboard's*

---

* Actually, this format had never completely disappeared. As late as 1946 when network radio was still alive and well, the quarter-hour strip served as a good vehicle to showcase new talent, e.g. Gordon MacCrae, 4:30–4:45p.m. on CBS.

** Veteran Prudential salesmen consider Berch somewhat of a legend, marveling at the way his commercials pre-conditioned "the lady of the house" to line up on the Prudential's side when the salesman got husband and wife together to make his pitch.

poll. But the highlights of a confidential study prepared by the William Esty Company, one of the country's largest advertising agencies, and released at the same time, sent shock waves up and down ad row. Esty predicted that "by 1956 regular [network] operations will be virtually eliminated." [11]

Esty's forecast came close to hitting the bull's eye. For by 1956,* only a few soap operas were still around together with some odds and ends like *Monitor*. In the mid-1950s, the only value a station could put on its network affiliation was quality news coverage. What remained of daytime network-originated popular music was a parade of Saturday afternoon dance orchestras. Which is what may have inspired NBC to go the dance band route weekdays. With much fanfare NBC announced on July 30, 1956, the debut of *Bandstand,* two solid hours of big bands, 10a.m. to 12noon, Monday through Friday. Name orchestras to appear on separate programs included the Dorsey Brothers, Benny Goodman, Les Brown, Freddy Martin, Harry James, Xavier Cugat, Guy Lombardo and Louis Armstrong, plus guest performers from Hollywood and Broadway. In their paean to old time radio, former network executives Sam Slate and Joe Cook recall a poignant moment in connection with *Bandstand:*

> Bert Parks had just finished reading through the script in NBC's Studio 6-A. In the fifteen minutes before airtime, we talked about the shows he had emceed over the years—*The Camel Caravan, Stop The Music*—and the excitement these programs used to generate. He looked out into 6-A's auditorium. It was only a third filled . . . Bert smiled and asked, "Did you ever get the feeling that the whole business is sliding into a lake?" [12]

Bandstand was gone in less than a year. And so were most other network popular music shows. Bert Parks, in his dire prediction, however, failed to reckon with the infinite possibilities of the radio music box. Like many doom-mongers at the time, Parks must be forgiven for failing to concede the possibility that the Network Phoenix might rise from the popular music ashes. *Bandstand's* demise was not network radio's swan song. It only signalled a hiatus.

Notes

1. Albert I. Lonstein and Vito Marino. *The Compleat Sinatra,* Cameron Publications, (Ellenville, N.Y.) 1970, p. 232.
2. *Songs by Sinatra.* Broadcast of January 23, 1946, Radio Yesteryear, Program No. 5528.
3. Robert Warnick. "Jackpot," *Life,* March 28, 1949, p. 104.

---

*Two long-running network daytimers, Don McNeill's *Breakfast Club* and *Arthur Godfrey Time* did hang on considerably longer. ABC stuck with the *Breakfast Club* (9a.m., E.T.) until 1968; CBS kept *Arthur Godfrey Time* four years longer. Although both shows had served as showcases for many pop artists over the years, their longevity was due more to the dominance of their personality-hosts.

4. Fred Allen. *Treadmill to Oblivion,* Atlantic, Little, Brown, (Boston), 1954, pp. 217–219.
5. *Club 15.* McCoy Recordings, Reel No. 1721. (undated).
6. *Ibid.*
7. ———. "Cut Rate Radio," *Newsweek,* April, 1951, p. 101.
8. ———. "Band Biz Setback with NBC Calling It Quits on Remotes," *Variety,* January 20, 1954, p. 47.
9. *Fred Waring Time.* Broadcast of November 29, 1948, McCoy Recordings, Reel No. 643.
10. Paul Ackerman. "Disc Jockey Dubbed Radio's King by Station Managers," *Billboard,* November 13, 1954, p. 1.
11. *Ibid.*
12. Sam J. Slate and Joe Cook. *It Sounds Impossible,* Macmillan, (New York), 1963, p. 231.

CHAPTER 12

Playing It by Ear

HILLTOPS AND MOUNTAINS across post-War America bore witness that the expected radio station building boom was underway. New towers punctuated the skyline from Maine to California. As of January, 1940, there were 765 licensed AM stations of record. Eight years later the number had more than doubled. The static-free spectrum, frequency modulation, went into 1948 with 458 occupants. But when you mulled over the good investment possibilities of radio around that time, you were really talking *AM*. FM stood for *fine music,* a sort of licensed Muzak the farsighted owner thought he ought to have—just in case FM ever "took off."

Original outlay to go into the radio business after World War II was not prohibitive for the small investor, especially in secondary markets. Certainly the personnel and equipment needed to run a station in virtually any size market, large or small, were nothing compared to the staff and printing presses required to start a newspaper. Of the dozens of enterprises that might be expected to cash in on post-War prosperity, a radio station had to be rated at an eight or a nine. Risk capital could be minimized if the investor wanted to forego building a plant to house the station. All he need do was rent space in an office building. For after all, brick and mortar were never the most important parts of a radio station's assets—the license granted by the Federal Communications Commission was. Add, then, to the low initial investment and overhead, visions of enormous profits—often based on tales of stations as wartime money machines—stir in the inevitable fascination of entering a branch of show business, and the rush for new sets of call letters was on. So what if cautious bankers did raise the question of television? Radio was here and now. After obtaining a license in the mid-to late 1940s, $100,000 or less could put you in the wireless business. Later on, if you wanted to add the "magic lantern," it was assumed radio licensees would be the logical applicants for television grants.

To many a newly-arrived post-War broadcaster, his discovery that he had to deal with a cadre of middlemen—Washington attorneys and consulting engineers—could not dissolve the euphoria of getting in "the business." Nor was he greatly concerned that his newly-minted program schedule required filling 12 to 18 hours a day with listening fare attractive enough to hold a fickle public. For the station operator who had a network between 1946 and 1950, his affiliation was still a big plus. But even without an ABC or CBS or NBC or Mutual button to press, the record library-newswire parlay was gaining favor around the industry—with some observers so crass as to say the networks were finished, and the music-and-news combination was the radio wave of the future. Prophets of doom, meanwhile, were arriving daily on the broadcast scene. They did not like what they saw for radio in the years ahead. But television? Ah—that was ticket! Billing figures bore them out. Time sales for television in 1950 increased 229.2% over those of 1949.

Still, there were no reports of any radio operator going to the almshouse. Radio billings overall in 1950 were up 6.9% compared to the previous year, with local time sales up 11.6%. Another sign that forecasts of radio's death were greatly exaggerated appeared in the figures of set sales. Between 1950 and 1955, when television pre-empted radio's claim as the primary source of mass entertainment, radio sets out-sold television receivers by comfortable margins. (See appendix on page 368.) By the end of the decade, such comparisons would be irrelevant, however, for the two media would no longer be competitive in the same way.

Programming the average radio station from the late 1940s through the mid-1950s called for several pairs of rose-colored glasses, lots of faith, and an ownership that was philosophical about shrinking bottom lines. Old-line and new syndicated program services offered drama and comedy to fill the gaps left open by network defections. It was the E.T. program* idea coming back to gain a new lease on radio life—only this time there was more than canned music. Hollywood (for a price) made its bid to help radio in its hours of need when the mighty Metro-Goldwyn-Mayer formed a Radio Attractions division. The MGM blockbuster package was not cheap, but if those prime-time voids were to be filled with network quality shows, why then broadcasters should expect to lay out some dough. Big dough. Of course, the only way a station could re-coup its investment was

---

* These should not be confused with transcription libraries, whose stepped-up use during radio's darker hours we shall explore presently.

through selling the shows to local advertisers. MGM lavished great care in the preparation of its ET's so that local merchants' messages could be blended into the program fabric as smoothly and unobtrusively as possible. Many a program director in 1949 went all out to sell his station manager on buying MGM's radio package. The features were chips off the venerable movie company's production block, quickly indentifiable, star-laden, and did not contain one musical show—except for radio versions of MGM musical extravaganzas:

SHOW	STARS	WEEKLY FREQUENCY
The Hardy Family	Mickey Rooney, Lewis Stone	Half-hour
Adventures of Maisie	Ann Southern	Half-hour
MGM Theater of the Air	Major artists	Hour
Story of Dr. Kildare	Lew Ayres, Lionel Barrymore	Half-hour
Crime Does Not Pay	—	Half-hour
Good News from Hollywood	George Murphy	3 Quarter-hours
Hollywood, USA	Paula Stone	5 Quarter-hours
At Home	Lionel Barrymore	2 Quarter-hours [1]

MGM's stiffest competition in the syndicated field was Ziv Radio Productions. This pioneer firm, which had been around almost as long as Sam Goldwyn's *non sequiturs*, stepped up its sales efforts to convince stations that the way to program in the dawn of the Television Age was with more network-type mysteries (*Boston Blackie, Philo Vance*), more adventure (*Cisco Kid, Lightning Jim, Bold Venture*, this one starring Lauren Bacall and Humphrey Bogart), and more soap operas (*Career of Alice Blair, Dearest Mother*). To capitalize on the rising McCarthy-Red hysteria, there was *I Was a Communist for the FBI*. Ziv even brought back the delightful *Easy Aces*. In addition to the dramatic shows for local sale, the veteran syndicator trotted out a stable full of canned music entries in the ET sweepstakes. Ziv's pop music line-up was 1930s radio all the way, but hundreds of stations plugged them in during the late 1940s and early 1950s:

SHOW	STARS	WEEKLY FREQUENCY
Pleasure Parade	Vincent Lopez Orch., w/Modernaires	5 Quarter-hours
Showtime from Hollywood	Freddy Martin Orch.	5 Quarter-hours
Barry Wood Show	w/Margaret Whiting	5 Quarter-hours
Sincerely, Kenny Baker	w/Buddy Cole	5 Quarter-hours
Guy Lombardo Show	w/David Ross	Half-hour
Wayne King Show	w/Franklyn MacCormick	Half-hour [2]

The Ziv Company's experience in the field paid off in these not-quite-ready-to-ditch-prime-time-type radio programming years. By 1947, with its 24-show inventory, Ziv was already reported to be grossing $10,000,000 a year. Assult forces of specially-trained Ziv salesmen went knocking on radio station doors. Their pitch: based on market population, stations pay Ziv a per-program fee (usually no less than $50.00 per half-hour show in the smaller cities); and contracts must be signed for no less than a 26-week cycle. Station time costs were added to the syndication fee, and for that, advertisers received three commercials per half hour show, two per quarter-hour feature, plus opening and closing sponsor identification. As one candid radio sales manager said, "I don't know if our Ziv features solved any of the advertisers' problems, but they sure solved a lot of ours."

Discs containing program features produced by Ziv, MGM and others had benefited immensely from improved technology since the days of Freddie Rich's *Friendly Footnotes*. Bing Crosby's move from NBC to ABC via transcription in 1946 had added further respectability to the concept. During the late 1940s and early 1950s, a modest spurt of interest in completely contained program features on ET (a la *Sunny Meadows*) was detected. Harry S. Goodman Productions could claim such advertisers as Nehi, Swift and Company, H.J. Heinz, Wildroot and Robert Hall. The Borden Company dropped its CBS show, *County Fair* in 1950 in favor of syndicated programs placed locally. In the spring of 1949, several hundred stations in the larger markets vied to carry a 26-week series, The *Sammy Kaye Chrysler Showroom*. Produced by Chrysler's advertising agency, McCann-Erickson, and sent to stations on standard 16-inch transcriptions, the two-a-week *Showroom* quarter-hour was so well produced, it could not be distinguished from a live network program. It was so popular with Chrysler dealers, many of them lobbied for an additional 26-week cycle, but it never came to pass.

•   •   •

If a label for this time of uncertainty in radio were needed, it might well be called "The Scrambling Years." Programmers scrambled for original ideas; they scrambled for ways to turn attention away from the boob tube; they scrambled for ways to save money. They even welcomed the government's supply of popular music. Out of Washington, compliments of Uncle Sam, around this time came a flood of transcribed shows, paid for from the budgets of various agencies and the military services. They were sent free of charge to virtually every radio station in the country. The transcriptions, featuring name talent, included drama, comedy, and most of all, popular music. Stations received credit for public service time to include in their FCC commitments. One or two minutes per program were alloted for low-key pitches extolling the virtues of the "sponsoring" organization. Notable were the U.S. Air Force's *Serenade in Blue* and the U.S. Treasury Department's various series of *Guest Star*. *Serenade in Blue,* a slickly-produced vehicle for the Air Force's dance band and used for recruiting and p.r., lasted from 1946 to 1976. The National Guard's pop music vehicle was *Let's Go to Town*. However, the transcription series that represented the high-water mark of the government's use of popular music for sugar-coated public service was *Here's to Veterans,* a slick package of approximately 500 shows that lasted into the 1950s. The discs were recorded at the major networks and produced with the same polished professionalism accorded commercial offerings. Radio stars appeared in *Here's to Veterans'* versions of their network programs with occasional appearances by guest Sunset Boulevardiers. VA files contain details only on the first 130 shows that ran until 1950 and of that number, 80 were devoted to popular music. They provide an accurate summation of America's pop preferences between 1946 and 1950. Most of the key maestros, vocalists and personality bandleaders who were featured on popular network shows were featured during *Here's to Veterans'* four-year run.

In the darker days of the early 1950s, when radio station managers weren't involved in looking for ways to cut expenses, or fielding advertisers' cancellations on the telephone, they were with their program directors trying to figure out where on earth radio was headed. For now they saw through the tube darkly. The main reason was their fixation with relating to radio in terms of mass entertainment. Some enlightened managements sensed immediately the only way to go against television was to rely on more recorded popular music, to clean out the dead program wood, and turn to the turntable. Other operators moved more cautiously. Reliance on recordings, however, could not have come at a more inopportune time.

Things were chaotic in the record business. In 1948, Columbia had introduced its 33 1-3 rpm non-breakable, microgroove, long play recording. Six months later, RCA Victor, rejecting Columbia's lp disc, introduced a seven-inch, microgroove, non-breakable record, engineered to spin at 45 rpm. So here was radio caught in the crossfire of the "battle of the speeds." Not only that—there were also all those 78 rpm records, some dating back to the 1920s and 1930s, lining station library shelves.

But if the grooves caused confusion in the late 1940s and early 1950s, the kind of music that went into them was even more bewildering. "What exactly was the popular music mainstream?" the more thoughtful program people were asking. There was no mainstream, of course—just the trickle of several rivulets. The only music programming policy that made any sense was to play it by ear: a little of this, a little of that. If anyone had spotted some kind of trend in popular music, he was keeping it a well-guarded secret. What better time, then, to announce the return of the big bands? "They're Playing the Bands Again," a feature story in *Billboard* declared early in 1953:

> The [big band] revival is not limited to a few stations and deejays, but is
> widespread and on stations all over the country . . . The interest in dance

bands is also pointed up by network programs (featuring) top works from
the Hollywood Palladium . . . Tradesters point out that the last great era
of the 1930s followed a period which was notable for such vocal stars as
Bing Crosby, Russ Columbo and Rudy Vallee.[3]

Aside from drawing a rather debatable parrallel regarding the big band
era, *Billboard's* report of the bands bounding back in 1953 was indicative
of more smoke than fire. Ever since they went away, big bands were always "coming back." Beginning around this time and once very few years,
through the 1970s, a big band trend was said to be developing. Actually,
when the *Billboard* forecast was made in 1953, there were those who might
have argued that the big bands never went away. The Dorsey's, the Goodman's, the James's were still around, as were a number of newly-organized
post-War bands. In the latter group were five maestros who sought to
retain the dance band format, and at the same time strike out on innovative paths heretofore ignored by pop music.

Ray McKinley, who (with Will Bradley) was co-leader of an early
1940s swing band, brought in Eddie Sauter, an avant-garde arranger of
the name band era. McKinley had hoped Sauter's adventuresome scores of
conventional pop tunes and clever originals would spark interest in a return to the bands.

Another leader, Boyd Raeburn, experimented by adding french horn,
harp, flute and english horn to the standard dance band instrumentation,
but his music often sounded as though he were more interested Milhaud,
Ravel and DeBussy than in bread-and-butter popular dance music.

Claude Thornhill, whose arranger, Gil Evans, later became the darling
of jazz trumpeter Miles Davis's fan club, played around with ideas similar
to Raeburn's.

Oddities like the glockenspiel, a toy trumpet, sleigh bells and triangles
were the forté of the experimental Sauter-Finegan Orchestra. Sauter-
Finegan benefited from a massive push by RCA Victor for whom the
band had recorded a number of long-playing albums. RCA had also just
announced its new "living sound" high fidelity consoles, and by a tie-in
with its record division, hoped that the Sauter-Finegan menagerie of off-
beat instruments would show off the record players to good advantage.

Stan Kenton ("Innovations in Modern Music") had led a conventional
big band since 1941. Always striving for something "new" without forsak-
ing his dance orchestra base, Kenton harrumphed bravely into the 1950s,
never quite sure whether to be a band, available for concerts, or for dances.

Big band loyalists—their ranks dwindling by now—who tuned in a
station playing McKinley, Raeburn, Thornhill, Sauter-Finegan and Kenton, formed cheering sections for the five innovators, because "they were
at least trying to keep the band flame alive." One by one, all except Kenton, a prolific composer and master-showman, fell by the wayside. He
was, at his passing in 1979, still a "name" attraction to a hard core of
nostalgia buffs and to hundreds of dedicated college musicians who en-

rolled in his regular workshops. Surprisingly, Stan Kenton's music received airplay on more than a handful of AM and FM stations starting in the early 1960s. He did it by establishing his own corporation, through which he acquired title to most of his Capitol albums and re-issued them on his own Creative World label. These, together with newly recorded material, sparked a Kenton revival that was still going strong until his death in 1979. By that time, however, his hard-sought image as a musical icono-clast and as an ombudsman keeping an eye on the prevailing popular music establishment came across more like an embittered elder statesman. Kenton had always thrived on controversy, and it was not until he passed away that most of the music world learned of his right-wing political pro-clivities. But unlike many other artists—of the leftist and the rightist per-suasions—Kenton at least was not guilty of injecting messages into popu-lar music.

Whatever bandstand charisma prolonged Stan Kenton's career, it was only because he stayed out of step with prevailing musical modes. Had he, in the final half of the 1940s, opted to go head-to-head with other name outfits who stuck around with the orthodox big band format, Kenton would have probably ended up writing film scores. Some of the bands which did plow bravely on managed to come up with occasional hits in those disor-dered days of popular music in the late 1940s and early 1950s. Bands that did have hits had them only because: a.) their records were showcases for their singers (Sammy Kaye—"Roses," 1950; Kay Kyser—"On a Slow Boat to China," 1948); or b.) because of the leader's own singing (Eddie How-ard—"Maybe It's Because," 1949; Vaughn Monroe—"Ballerina," 1947); or c.) for their novelty effect (Art Mooney—"I'm Looking Over a Four-Leaf Clover," 1948). The following table tells graphically how singers gradually came to dominate popular music in the post-War period:

NUMBER OF
TOP SELLING RECORDS
SINGERS AND BIG BANDS
1946–1950

	SINGERS	BIG BANDS	MISC.
1946	39	24	4
1947	54	27	4
1948	98	34	10
1949	122	43	9
1950	115	40	7

—Source: *Top Pop Records, 1940–1955,* Joel Whitburn, Menomonee Falls, Wis. (1973)

Clearly, by 1950 singers had taken over. This situation irked many program people whose ideas of popular music were rooted in the big band years. The "battle of the speeds" was bad enough, and now the need to put up with vocal artists—many of whom possessed highly stylized mannerisms—created numerous cases of turntable trauma in radioland. For this reason, hundreds of stations turned to an old ally—the transcription libraries. Many stations had made only limited use of their transcription libraries during radio's halycon days. But now that turmoil marked the music scene, libraries could at least supply safe, middle-of-the-road material, they reasoned. Alert to radio's problems in a marketplace where television had elbowed its way in, transcription services stepped up their inventories of production aids to supplement regular popular music releases. In 1951, a subscriber to RCA's Thesaurus Library had on hand the following:

BASIC LIBRARY: Approximately 5000 selections

MONTHLY RELEASE: No less than 52 new musical selections each month. Hit tunes released in advance of their popularity.

WEEKLY SCRIPTS: Continuity for 25 program series. 73 individual shows per week. Material enough for 20 full hours of broadcasting.

PRODUCTION AIDS: Voice tracks, theme music, mood music, sound effects, vocal cues, time and weather jingles.[4]

Thesaurus's 1951 artist list, among others, included:

BANDS	COMBOS	SINGERS
Sammy Kaye	Art Van Damme	Hank Snow
Vincent Lopez	Johnny Guarnieri	Dolly Mitchell
Xavier Cugat	Knickerbocker Four	Carson Robinson
Hugo Winterhalter	Novatime Trio	Jimmy Wakely
Music of Manhattan	Sons of the Pioneers	Louise Carlyle
Russ McIntyre		Slim Bryant[5]

As late as the mid-1950s, a Thesaurus subscriber could still find in his new releases selections typified by Sammy Kaye and His Orchestra—material that, save for improved recording fidelity, could have been issued 10 or 15 years earlier:

RECORD NO.	SELECTION	TYPE	TIMING
1919 H	East of the Sun	Fox Trot	2:15
1919 J	Let Me Call You Sweetheart	Waltz	2:19
1919 K	I Cried for You	Fox Trot	2:12
1919 L	September in the Rain	Fox Trot	2:34
1919 M	My Silent One	Fox Trot	2:30[6]

In addition to RCA Thesaurus, Standard, World and Langworth were still issuing monthly selections by such name bands as Tommy Dorsey, Harry James and Les Brown. Most ET services stayed in business well into the 1950s. *Radio Daily, Yearbook, 1951* listed 67 transcription companies, most of whom were selling some kind of popular music.

Meanwhile, as local stations scrambled to cope with the music mess, low staff morale and decreasing revenues, the industry was wary of statements by television-possessed network executives, the gist of which was "never, no never, will we desert radio." * In conference room deliberations, in the two-by-four offices of smalltown stations, in trade paper articles, from the podiums of conventions, radio's agenda for the future could be summed up in a word: SURVIVAL. No matter how the subject was approached, the central issue remained: radio must do something television cannot do. And that "something" meant, as everyone knew, recorded popular music. Lots of popular music. In 1954, there were 3101 AM and FM commercial stations on the air, and of that number, 1337 were network affiliates. Which meant an awful lot of stations had already learned to make do without network offerings. But there was one which did it better. That station had been programming *only* popular music and news for two decades. Its call letters, WNEW, New York, were probably the best known set of call letters in America.

NOTES

1. Metro-Goldwyn-Mayer Radio Attractions display ad. *Radio Annual/Television Yearbook*, 1951, p. 544.
2. *Ibid.* (Frederick W. Ziv Radio Productions display ad, inside cover.)
3. Paul Ackerman. "They're Playing the Bands Again," *Billboard*, February 28, 1953, p. 54.
4. *Op. cit.* pp. 792–783. RCA Recorded Program Services display ad.
5. *Ibid.*
6. RCA Thesaurus Cue Sheet 2-C, December 1955–January 1956.

---

* This sort of soothing, early 1950s balm was probably uttered as much for the FCC's benefit, as for assuaging disgruntled affiliates.

CHAPTER 13

Music and News

ONE DIDN'T HAVE to be a programming professional to realize radio had to make major adjustments in the early 1950s. Where once stood those mighty console radios, television screens now set American parlors aglow with lightning fury. Everybody said, "Music and News—it's the industry's only salvation!" When the more knowledgeable of the radio clan talked about music and news generically, what most of them had in mind was MUSIC and NEWS—WNEW New York-style. Long before the one-eyed monster had fixed its steady gaze on the media landscape, enterprising operators had studied WNEW, then a 10,000-watter at 1130 on the dial.

For years WNEW had thrived right in the middle of the nation's network capital, playing records and running news on the hour and half-hour, 24 hours a day. As early as the late 1940s, alert radiomen were studying WNEW's operation. Owners and managers came to New York regularly and set up tape recorders in hotel rooms, hoping a closer examination of the WNEW *modus operandi* could yield the secret alchemy of the music and news potion. Good business strategy had always dictated, "Study a winner." If there was one station the depressed network affiliate wished to be in this time of radio melancholy, let it be WNEW. In 1950, on sales of $2,870,600, the outlet's gross profit was $839,600, a whopping 25% return. Envious station executives diagnosed the WNEW tapes back in their own shops, and for hours on end, they listened and listened. What *was* the WNEW magic?

Music and news. It sounded so simple. Had WNEW's potential imitators studied the station's history, they would have discovered its success was a curious mix of intuition, excellent management, good timing, a little luck and a certain chemistry every radio station must have if it wishes to lead the pack.

The WNEW chemistry started working shortly after the station was established in the depth of the Depression. Milton Biow, a successful ad-man, Arde Bulova, a successful watch man, and a third investor put WNEW together in 1934 from a conglomeration of New Jersey stations and moved the operation to New York. Before the station was a year old, it acquired a manager who had never held a job in management, one whose only accomplishment was to play an excellent game of golf. "An institution," Ralph Waldo Emerson wrote, "is the shadowed extension of one man." In WNEW's case, Emerson might have added "—or woman." For that manager was a woman, Bernice Judis. WNEW, as it grew through the 1930s and 1940s bore the imprint of her tastes and convictions.

Miss Judis scored her first broadcasting coup, not in popular music, but in news. In the spring of 1935, when Bruno Hauptmann was being tried for the Lindbergh baby kidnapping, Judis not only wanted to compete with the networks, she wanted to beat them. The problem was how to get the microphones close to the courtroom for putting the latest news on the air? Milton Biow, the WNEW co-founder, describes the Judis solution in his autobiography:

> [She] sent six men to study the problem thoroughly. They finally reported we could put our microphone right in the courthouse itself . . . in a cubby hole in the corridor outside the courtroom and use a long enough cord to bring it right up to the door. The networks needed much more room for all their engineers and equipment, so they rented space a block away . . . We would be on the air before the others could even reach their microphones . . . We thought of it and the networks didn't, so we beat them by a mile. People found out fast—and WNEW got the listeners.[1]

Scooping the networks on Lindbergh bulletins gave WNEW credibility. However, something else was included throughout those long hours between reports on Hauptmann's fate while the station maintained its vigil at the Flemington, New Jersey courthouse.

During trial recesses, a newly-hired announcer named Martin Block played recordings—but with a gimmick. Block conjured up an imaginary dance hall with a "revolving bandstand," on which alternating dance bands took their turns. He invented a crystal chandelier and other trappings to create the imagery of a ballroom. Initial listener reaction was good. In one instance, an early test of the pulling power of Block's record show was a Father's Day offer. Women could get a box of cigars for their husbands at a dollar box. Next morning, there were already 150 envelopes in the WNEW mail. The *Make Believe Ballroom* quickly became an entity and was officially opened for business, mornings 10 to 11:30a.m. and early evenings, 5 to 7p.m.

When WNEW's new owners had taken over, one of their first moves was to feature live remotes, called the *Dance Parade,* from spots around New York. Thus, with the *Make Believe Ballroom* and *Dance Parade* foundations, Judis built a program schedule composed entirely of popular music. She also threw in 15-and 30-minute periods here and there for aspiring pop singers who jumped at the chance for exposure in New York.* Here and there were a few periods devoted to news. Such a program idea in the mid-1930s, even for New York, had to be *tres avant-garde*—or sheer naiveté. According to John Van Buren Sullivan, former WNEW vice president and general manager, who had begun at the station as a salesman under Judis, it was neither:

> She had a feeling—an idea. It was that all the little independent stations in town were trying to emulate the network stations. Those that had affiliations carried network programs eighty percent of the time. And when they were on their own, they had book reviews and recipe shows, interviews, shopping ideas, and cooking hints. And Bernice Judis's conviction was that women at home who had to plan the meals and do the shopping and wash the dishes didn't want to hear about homemaking all the time. Her idea was they might like music—popular music. And the only way to get popular music in those days was by records, because musicians were expensive for a small station that didn't have any great bankroll.[2]

Radio, it must be remembered, was a very conservative business in its first 30 years, and the thought that programming should be plumbed except along network lines was *lese majesté.* Not only did Judis go ahead with her idea of an all popular music format, she realized WNEW's stature might even be enhanced—at small cost—by being musical 24 hours a day. Thus was born all-night radio. At WNEW it was called the *Milkman's Matinee,* with its first host, Stan Shaw. Judis's timing for an operation built on popular recordings was excellent, since it coincided with the growing phonograph record collecting hobby.

Choice of records to be heard on the air was left to the announcers for their individual shows. But if Judis heard one she thought didn't fit the "WNEW sound," she was certain to register her displeasure. Jack Sullivan recalls her protesting more than once,

> "Dammit! What's that? What's the matter? That stinks!" Then she and the program director or announcer would have a big argument, and maybe the record would stay and maybe it wouldn't. What she was concerned

---

* One such warbler who commuted from Hoboken, New Jersey had been compensated in carfare money for the trip from his home to the WNEW studios. When he approached G.M. Judis for a weekly fee, she told him to get lost. The singer's name was Frank Sinatra.

with was not whether she liked the record, but whether it fit the WNEW sound. This was the Bernice Judis idea that really made WNEW. It was her great taste—her subjectivity, really. She would say, "I don't care how popular that performer is in Texas or Canada, that's not for us. Don't play it." There it was again, that feeling, that "This is WNEW. We're playing for a certain kind of person. We're playing for five million radio homes in three states, and we want to have a taste, a standard, and for those that don't like it, let them go somewhere else."[3]

Judis's "great taste" in setting WNEW's musical standards was hardly enough, however, to make it a prosperous independent when network stations were ruling the radio roost. What went *between* the records was as important to Bernice Judis as the music. "Entertain, and while entertaining, *sell*" was ever the battle cry to her announcers. When an opening occurred, the replacement ritual was something to behold. First off, network announcers need not apply. Prospects who submitted to the agonizing WNEW audition—in front of the station staff—were selected only if they demonstrated a unique mix of talents: a rare quality of voice; an uncommon ability to ad lib; and an extraordinary acumen of showmanship. For those who survived and made it to Judis's first team, commercials could seldom be read "straight." Rather a "copy platform" delineating the advertiser's main sales points were left to the announcer to adapt to his own style, to modify, from time to time, in meeting demands of the season, the weather, the time of day, his own mood. What's this? *Announcers* taking liberties with advertisers' commercials! *Advertising agencies* are the creators, aren't they? Don't advertising agencies insist on writing their clients' copy? Once more, violating the canons of the industry, Judis instructed her time salesmen to hold fast and require agencies to supply only copy points from which announcers could ad lib, rather than accept the carefully-honed commercials Madison Avenue turned out for network shows.

In a few years, Judis's stars would be called *disc jockeys*. No one could have foreseen in the early 1940s that their greatest impact was yet to come. All she was doing in WNEW's first decade was offering counterprogramming with records and "personalities," placing "her big guns," as Jack Sullivan put it, "in the daytime because the networks had their big guns at night."

Another Judis innovation that opened new trails for radio was her incorporation of news digests on the hour, within the all-music format. Prior to this, newscasts presented by local stations generally followed the quarter-hour morning-noon-early evening-late night pattern. In recalling the origins of Judis's WNEW music-and-news fusion, Jack Sullivan said,

All credit must go to Bernice Judis. Here again, her astuteness was in evidence, because three weeks after Pearl Harbor, she signed a deal with the *New York Daily News* to carry five minutes of news on the hour, around the clock. They set up a sixteen-man radio desk down at the *Daily News*. They compiled the news and wrote five-minute newscasts and put them on a teleprinter over to the station which had the final editing proviso. And so was born the slogan, "The Original Station for Music and News."[4]

In October, 1952, Bernice Judis was officially certifed a SUCCESS, meeting all requirements for induction in to the *Fortune* business pantheon. When the *Fortune* hunter zeroed in on WNEW, the result was a gushy panegyric to a "rattling good business organization, aflame with the kind of sales fervor that has been too scarce on the business scene . . . Patently, WNEW must have something on the ball that enables it to turn back television so handily."[5]

But *Fortune* only confirmed what many broadcasters already knew: There was Bernice Judis in the most competitive market, operating her picture-less money machine; and out there they were, across the nation in a radioland that was echoing tales of dwindling audiences and shrinking profits. WNEW had certainly proven that even in those dark days of the early 1950s, popular music must, in one way or another, figure in radio's future. But how? Just because the WNEW method worked in New York did not necessarily mean it would play in Peoria. Still, it was precisely in the garden of bandstand/ballroom recorded music the first seeds of radio's rebirth were sown—out in the heartland. Creativeness, Bernice Fitz-Gibbon the ad whiz has said, is "turning up what is already there." In the mid-West, a creative broadcaster began turning up what was already there. Before he got through, America would be turning on to radio again.

NOTES

1. Milton Biow. *Butting In: An Adman Speaks Out,* Doubleday, (New York), 1964, pp. 131–2.
2. Author's interview with John Van Buren Sullivan, December 4, 1980.
3. *Ibid.*
4. *Ibid.*
5. ———. "Radio's Little David Doesn't Fear TV," *Fortune,* October, 1952, pp. 133–134.

TWO WHO FLOWED WITH THE TIDE . . .

(author's collection)

(Courtesy Bruce Davidson)

Former big band thrush Jo Stafford became a star of *Club 15*. She is shown here with composer-singer, Johnny Mercer.

Bing's younger brother, Bob, gave up his band and became "head man" of *Club 15*, one of the last of the early evening live network pop music shows, ending a CBS tradition begun with the *Cremo Singer*, in 1931.

AND ONE
WHO HELD OUT . . .

(Courtesy Dave Dexter, Jr.)

Maverick leader Stan Kenton kept a big band together until his death in 1979. Here he mops his brow after a CBS remote from the Hollywood Palladium in the mid-1940s.

With the expected post-World War II boom came such technological advances as magnetic recording tape. Progressive stations were quick to install Magnecorders, the first professional tape machines, in the late 1940s (shown on the left).

The advent of television saw radios getting smaller, as table models replaced consoles.

With the onslaught of televison after 1948, stations resorted to more popular music. Many outlets supplemented their conventional record libraries to get more musical variety by resorting to transcription services. Most of material on ETs was not available on commercial recordings.

(Courtesy Hy Daley)

Frederic W. Ziv was a major producer of "open-end," slick, (and expensive) pop music shows on transcription for sale at the station level. Stations found such programs useful in plugging the holes left by network defections in television's wake.

The Sammy Kaye Show in 1949 gave some broadcasters a strong feeling of déjà vu. The twice-weekly, quarter hour reminded them of those lavishly produced ET programs of the 1930s.

(Courtesy Hy Daley)

(Courtesy Hy Daley)

Even the federal government was in the ET act. A number of agencies used canned music programs after World War II to reach specific target audiences.

Martin Block, who brought the *Make Believe Ballroom* idea from Los Angeles to WNEW, New York, gave the station's first manager, Bernice Judis, a base on which to build the first successful radio station to rely only on recorded popular music and news.

Below: Because of its location (New York) and its heavy pop music identity, WNEW launched successful promotions based on popular music stars. Kicking off "Benny Goodman Day" in 1946 are (l. ro r.) Mrs. Alice Goodman, Goodman, Manny Sachs, Columbia Records executive, and Art Ford, host of *Milkman's Matinee.*

(Courtesy WNEW)

(Courtesy Warren Hicks)

Part Four
(1955—1980)

BORN AGAIN

In what is new and growing there
is apt to be something crude, insolent,
even a little vulgar which is shocking
to the man of sensitive taste;
quivering from the rough contact,
he retires to the trim gardens of the
polished past, forgetting they were
reclaimed from the wilderness by men
as rough and earth-soiled as those from
whom he now shrinks in his own day.

—BERTRAND RUSSELL

CHAPTER 14

Rock, Roll and Top 40

WNEW's success in the face of television's rising tide was an aberration. The station's programming roots were, after all, in recorded music, rather than in network variety. Almost two decades of such fare had positioned WNEW firmly in listeners' minds. And New York was, after all, the show biz capital of the world. A radio station could survive in New York with even a small fraction of the audience, but out there in Radioland USA, it was an entirely different matter. Although the industry knew by the early 1950s that radio's only hope for survival rested on music and news, the malaise that spread over broadcasting was less the result of recognizing WNEW's uniqueness than in accepting the notion that if network radio died, all radio was dead. A few broadcasters, however, refused to accept the canard that radio could not thrive in the coming Television Age. Not surprisingly, the broad idea of a foundation to rebuild radio's crumbling mansion, came not from the networks, but from the WNEW model.

In 1949, the Storz Brewing Company of Omaha, which had acquired the city's pioneer station, KOWH, (established 1922) placed Todd Storz in charge of the station. On that decision rests much of the medium's rejuvenation, for it was Todd Storz's bold and innovative Top 40 format that ushered radio into its modern era. Top 40 Radio, however, did not spring full blown from the mind of Todd Storz one day in 1949. The building process was one that involved careful planning and help along the way from several bright young associates. Storz's initial programming concept was built along the lines of WNEW's segments of recorded popular music, featuring vocal artists and big bands—although there was some classical and country mixed in from time to time. KOWH, for a while, also carried play-by-play broadcasts of the Omaha's minor league baseball team. Ken Greenwood, who was a student at the University of Nebraska around that time—he later joined the Storz organization—recalls listening to KOWH in the early days of the Storz regime. Greenwood commuted regularly from Lincoln to Omaha where he was a staff musician at KFAB. He had become interested in what was going on at KOWH. However, he is quick to point out, the form that came to be known as Top 40 was fairly conventional radio at the outset:

> As it was originally conceived, Top 40 was a broad-based, broad-audience, musical concept. Keep in mind, it spun out of the bandstand concept which was fifteen minutes of Doris Day, fifteen minutes of Guy Mitchell, fifteen minutes of the Four Lads, maybe fifteen minutes of a Harry James, or a Ray Anthony, or a band of that time.[1]

Greenwood remembers that the next step in the evolutionary process was a housewife-hit parade-type program of recorded popular music between 9 and 11 a.m.; and that the concept of playing pop hits had become established by 1953, catapulting KOWH from dead last among six rated stations in Omaha to first. However, at this juncture, Top 40 was still some distance away from being the well-defined format that would stir the sluggish blood of listeners and give radio a new lease on life. In 1953, the Storz interests, (now known as the Mid-Continent Broadcasting Company) acquired WTIX, New Orleans, "because Todd wanted to try the idea in a major market with a full-time facility. This is what Storz did when he bought the little station (I want to say it was on 1490*) 250 watts, in New Orleans, and by that time, they were into their Top 40 concept."[2] Ex-Storzman Bill Stewart, who had originally competed against WTIX (and whose Odyssey we shall subsequently follow in more detail), agrees with Greenwood's assessment—up to a point: "The first purely Top 40 music was on WTIX . . . They called it 'Top 40', but it really wasn't."[3] According to Stewart, "The important thing was the excitement factor. Music was important, and it grew more important a year or two later."[4] Whatever it was, within a year WTIX had followed the rating success of KOWH. In 1954, Mid-Continent purchased WHB, Kansas City (10 kw day/5 kw night on 710 kc), the company's first choice facility. Following the Storz pattern of cleaning out as quickly as possible all remnants of old time radio in order to incorporate a full menu of popular music and news, the new owners dumped WHB's Mutual Network affiliation and the broadcasts of the Kansas City Blues, then in the American Association. The KOWH and WTIX ratings stories were repeated.

---

* It was 1450 kc.

Meanwhile, changes were taking place in popular music that impinged significantly on Top 40 Radio. Ken Greenwood, who had become so fascinated with what he had been hearing in Omaha, took a sales job at the new WHB. He recalls that when he got there,

> Early Top 40 as we knew it was a musical concept that was almost entirely mature, or adult, performers. The teen performers didn't enter the picture at all in those days. The first record I remember that caused any consternation at all in the radio station was Bill Haley's "Rock Around the Clock."[5]

⌐ Gradually, by the mid 1950s, as other rock and roll recordings burst on the scene, popular music had become a pastiche. Elvis Presley, Bill Haley and Jerry Lee Lewis were co-mingled with what Ken Greenwood called

> "Bread and butter" records: Sinatra, Perry Como, Doris Day, Patti Page, Rosemary Clooney, Steve Lawrence and Eydie Gorme. Popularity heavily favored bread and butter artists . . . Then we went through a period where, very slowly, the established artists were pushed off the playlist. You could just see it happening if you sat back and looked at it over a period of a year or so . . . Most of your hot stuff would be the rock stuff. Some of the program directors who really weren't sure they wanted to play that much rock in those days would sort of pray for a new Andy Williams.[6]

"Some program directors," however, did not include Robert Todd Storz. The incisive Storz did not allow his own ideas of taste to enter into what popular music should be played on his radio stations. Bill Stewart, who had come to KOWH in the mid-1950s, remembers the music "research" he and Todd Storz did in those days:

> We would go into the bar across the street from our place in the Kilpatrick Department Store Building on 16th Street in Omaha—this happened many times—and we'd notice the waitress would be serving drinks all evening while the same songs would come up on the juke box over and over. Upon cleaning up, she'd go over and put a half-dollar in the juke box to listen to the *same* record she'd been listening to all evening, six more times! That happened many times. I remember Todd and I having lunch together at the Omaha Athletic Club, sitting there in the Grille, while people went over to the juke box having sixty songs on it. Four songs might be rock and roll while the other 56 were Perry Como, Glenn Miller, Frank Sinatra. It was the rock and roll songs that kept coming up. They'd be 40 and 50 year old people playing them.[7]

To those observations of human behavior, Stewart added his own insights. He tells how he made an earlier discovery which he shared with Storz, and out of which came the ultimate musical distillation of Top 40, that of playing the same hits over and over:

> I taught radio and speech at Emerson College in Boston. Summertimes, I would take a couple of weeks and go round the country to see what other disc jockeys were doing. At that time, 1953, the hottest disc jockey, and my idea of the best deejay that ever lived was Bill Randall in Cleveland. I spent about a week listening to him and six other disc jockeys of WERE. In those days, when a record was a hit, there would be about eight covers on it. It was the number-one station in town and I got the impression there was something radically wrong with the station. If you listened to it for twenty-four hours you would hear one song by Jo Stafford, for example, on the 6 to 10 show. Then you would hear it on the 10 to 2 show by Perry Como. Then Bill Randall, 2 to 6 would come with a version by the Four Lads. Phil McClean would come on in the evening, and he would have another version. Then the all-night guy would have still another version. So it seemed as though we were listening to six different radio stations. It occurred to me that was wrong.[8]

By the time Mid-Continent had invaded the North (WDGY, Minneapolis—1955) and established a beachhead in Miami (WQAM—1956), Storz had added refinements to his format. It had become by now *de rigueur* to incorporate a 24-hour operation in the station's new look. Aside from big-city powerhouses, signing-off between 1 and 5a.m. had become accepted radio practice. Newscasts were moved to :55 to get the jump on everybody else's news-on-the-hour. Top 40 was in full bloom. Predictably, copycats quickly tried to duplicate the Storz invention. The great majority were unsuccessful. Would-be imitators, much to their surprise, discovered Top 40 Radio was a finely-tuned instrument with which they were unprepared to play. The copyists learned that Top 40 was more than spinning 40 records over and over, more than buying joke services for their disc jockeys, more than unleashing clever sound effects.

At the interior of Top 40 was a basic management understanding of the importance of nuances—nuances of timing, of sound reproduction, of listener empathy. Nothing was left to chance. Top 40 Radio was quality-controlled all the way, beginning with an orientation for the entire station staff on what to expect. It covered such items as how salesmen should sell the new concept and how the station telephone operator should handle complaints about the music. Deejays were not allowed to enter the format without thorough training, including dry runs. Many jocks were sent to serve short observational internships at successful Top 40 stations. Studying training tapes of the best of Top 40 was mandatory before a disc jockey was allowed on the air. Every Top 40 operation had its lists of do's and don'ts. Newsmen and air personalities were being taped continuously and their work critiqued frequently on the following points:

Air Personalities

Fast-paced delivery to create excitement and enthusiasm.

Absolutely no dead air.

Never use the word "record"—substitute "Music," or "song," or "tune."

Never offer a negative comment about a record.

Talk over instrumental introduction of a record—but don't step on lyrics. Talk over last sounds of tune's coda.

Promote. Promote. Promote—the next newscast, the next weathercast, the new contest, the new disc jockey, etc.

Specified minimum number of time checks, weather reports, station call letters and personality's name per hour. (See clock)

All recorded elements must be separated by the "live" voice of the personality; thus, no segueing of commercials.

Air personalities are not allowed to take outside calls during their shows.

Personalities should strive to spend three hours of show preparation for every hour on the air.

Newsmen

Delivery style should be punchy and authoritative.

Write with colorful and "emotional" adjectives.

Use minimum of twelve stories per five minute newscast.

Be alert for bulletins and interrupt during the playing of a record if necessary.

Use sound to enhance a story—if it doesn't impair journalistic integrity.[9]

Many Top 40 stations had a model clock-hour disc jockeys were expected to follow. These were not cast in cement, and clock hours could vary from station to station. The key was *showmanship,* and since all other branches of the performing arts blocked out their elements by using stage directions, positions, etc. why not the record show host? The figure on the next page represents a typical Top 40 clock hour:

1. Time checks, quickie promos, brief weather mentions separated commercials.
2. 20 Call letter mentions, five personality mentions per hour.
3. Pick Hit and Number One record played once every three hours.
4. Top 10 rotated every three hours.
5. 11–20 rotated every four hours.
6. 21–40 rotated every six hours.
7. One "extra" played in alternate hours.
8. Clock shows 14 commercials. Sponsored news & weather forecasts brought total to limit of 18 commercial units per hour.[10]

The Top 40 format was often criticized for making of the disc jockey a mechanical figure, an automaton from whom all humanness was drained.

A Typical Top 40 Clock Hour

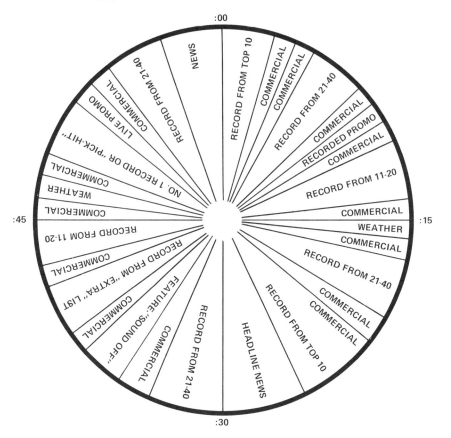

It is true: a Top 40 jock was required to keep his engine running throughout his entire show, maintaining the same level of intensity the third hour as the first. But the smart Top 40 operators knew listener attention could be focused as much on the music presenter as on the music. Radio, after all, is the only form of show business offering daily potential for spontaneity, and the creative disc jockey could enhance the Top 40 format (well-structured though it was) in ways that five new Elvis Presley records in the top 10 could not. Bill Stewart, who worked with many a jock, agrees:

> In the days of the real Top 40, there were a lot of great personalities who helped make Top 40 what it was. I don't think they got the credit. I think that's greatly overlooked. I think of people like Herb Oscar Anderson who in his own way was a great personality . . . there were a lot of people like that. There were people in Cleveland, in New York. Joe Smith

in Boston was a very Top 40 jockey. A lot of people were. They don't get credit. I think music *was* important. But if you had to allocate a percentage, music was 40%, promotion was 20%, and personality was the rest.[11]

But the care and feeding of disc jockeys and newsmen were only a part of the meticulous attention to detail exerted by committed managements of Top 40 stations. Engineering became a handmaiden of programming. Prior to Top 40, equipment and how it was used was often regarded as a necessary evil. With the advent of Top 40, the chief engineer became an equal in the station hierarchy. Before most operators went with the Top 40 format, they replaced much of their existing equipment, sometimes including even transmitters that had lots of mileage left in them. Reverberation units were installed to give the station a "big" sound; records were transferred to tape cartridges to eliminate scratches from constant use; special teletype clatter was crafted to be played behind newscasts to lend an urgency to news; filter mikes and other sound devices were built by engineers to give select disc jockeys "character" voices and alter egos—these and other implementations created for the Top 40 Radio an aural ambiance* envious and unimaginative competitors couldn't have figured out in a thousand years.

Then there was the promotion. Especially the promotion. There was at work a system of understanding between the Top 40 station and its audience that some unique, offbeat promotion or contest might turn up at any time: a putting-golf "tournament," featuring city celebrities vs. the station's air personalities; a donkey race among the disc jockeys on Kentucky Derby day; the formation of disc jockey softball and basketball teams to play high school faculties and hospital departments for charity; the creation of special names for the disc jockey staff ("Sensational Seven," "The Good Guys"). Although the big blockbuster promotion (whose origins we shall explore momentarily) never went out of style, it was the small listener-participation contests that scored highest: over-the-air on opening day of baseball, a trivia call-in using simple baseball questions, with game tickets as prizes; the "outside" contest—most unique Jack-o-Lantern using station call letters, with winner treated to "night on the town" with disc jockey host. Still, Top 40 promotion never strayed too far from its popular music base. Thousands of Top Tune sheets, distributed to record stores and other select outlets weekly, with the station's call letters served as the imprimatur for an official listing of the area's favorite music. Record hops, emceed by the disc jockeys and station-sponsored concerts, featuring name

---

*The creation of the transistor by Bell Laboratories in 1948 was a boon to radio in general and to Top 40 stations in particular. A top 40 station's sound was easy to identify on the dial and came through unmistakably even on small speakers. The Electronic Industries Association reported close to two million sets were sold between January, 1956 and July, 1957.

artists helped maintain the symbiotic bond between popular music and the Top 40 station.

There is an important connecting link between Top 40 Radio and musical radio of the 1920s and 1930s. When the radio-nurtured big bands died, so did much of the interest in dancing. The beat of rock rekindled that aspect of popular music. And with the big bands gone, dancing had to be based on recorded music. But what recorded music? Obviously, the "new" popular music heard on the radio. Enter the disc jockey—and another great promotion opportunity for the Top 40 station.

This was the phenomenon of a man on the air three or four hours a day, playing Top 40 hits becoming a celebrity—of sorts. In truth, the jock was not the "personality," the records were. However, if he could appear at a "record dance" (shortly to be re-termed "hop"), he was an instant personality. This did not mean that he had no responsibilities. Music had to be programmed, not just played. The wise (and probably experienced) disc jockey quickly realized that the true magnet was the recorded music. The music kids heard on the radio—on the Top 40 station. So, whereas their parents had swooned to "Star Dust," their sons and daughters close-danced to Elvis and "Love Me Tender." Or instead of jitterbugging to "Little Brown Jug," the new generation danced to the earthy "Dancin' In The Streets."

Although certain hop records became standard fare, the most requested and popular discs at record hops were those most frequently played on the radio. Proof: When "hops" were at their peak—not only in schools, but in fire halls and churches—it was not the on-the-air disc jockey who drew the crowd (as ego-shattering as this may have been), it was the small "hop-box," containing approximately 40 hit records. There were times when Top 40 stations supplied emcees for as many as 17 hops a weekend. Most stations couldn't supply this many people. But the kids wanted to dance to Top 40 music. So, if disc jockeys weren't available, station receptionists or typists were sent. They could be "Miss Unknown of 1958," but if they had a "hop-box," they were instant successes. Hops became such a phenomenon that one top selling record used record hops as its central theme: Danny and The Juniors recording of "At The Hop." Thus, the radio-dance music kinship, begun with remotes from the ballrooms of the 1920s, enjoyed a resurgence by way of Todd Storz's new-fangled format.

Around the time Storz was getting Top 40 off the ground, Gordon McLendon, a Dallas-based group broadcaster was making his own contributions to the format. Storz and McLendon met from time to time to discuss the state of the industry and share ideas. It was not uncommon for McLendon employees to leave for a Storz job, and vice versa. When the first Storz-sponsored Disc Jockey Convention took place in Miami in 1958, Gordon McLendon was the keynote speaker.

There was little debate as to who invented Top 40—that credit had generally gone to Todd Storz. But when it came to the Compleat Top 40, Top 40-cum-Pizz-Zazz, Top 40 Pure and Undefiled, Gordon McLendon whipped up the *chef d'oeuvre.* Following World War II, McLendon had established the Liberty Broadcasting System, a sports chain he had hoped would be a challenge to the four major radio networks. McLendon's forte was the reconstructed football and baseball game. Key game information was received in a Dallas studio via Western Union ticker, and against a backdrop of recorded sound effects (stadium organ, bats cracking, crowd noises), McLendon re-created games that were many times undistinguishable from the real thing. During the LBS re-creations, "The Old Scotchman," as McLendon called himself on the air, honed an already-keen imagination that served him well after he turned to Top 40. When the ticker stopped, McLendon remembers, it called forth special improvisatory revelations:

> I would have a dog run on the field and I would describe it at great length, waiting for the ticker to be resumed and the wire fixed in whichever park it was located. Or we'd have a fight going on in the stands between two tough customers. I'd describe the fight for about thirty minutes and no one would wonder why the police didn't break it up.[12]

The television boom of the early 1950s spelled the end of the Liberty Network and McLendon began building a group of radio stations. He had no doubts about which way he wanted to go:

> Television had left to radio only two things that radio could do either as well as, or better than television—it seemed to me at least, and that was music and news. For that reason, economics forced me to grab at those two things, music and news. I don't know why the average fellow who was in radio those days didn't do the same thing. It was the only logical thing to do. I'm given credit for a lot of things economics forced me to do.[13]

McLendon superimposed on the Top 40 format a lamina of razzle-dazzle promotional stunts that earned for him the label, "P.T. Barnum of Broadcasting." He admits,

> I *was* flamboyant. But of necessity. A fellow named C. E. Hooper, who ran the dominatn rating service at the time, listened to us when we had first started our new format. He said, "Gordon, I've listened to it, and you're doing everything right but one thing, and you've got to do yet". Well, I thought I was doing it all right. Be he said, "You've got to promote. You've got to have a lot of promotions on the air." Thus was born what I believe to be the modern, all new Top 40 format . . . Todd Storz did a variety of it, but not with as much promotion. KLIF was the first station to do it with flamboyance and razz-ma-tazz.[14]

McLendon's promotions, of course, helped to get listeners back to radio: The $50,000 KLIF Treasure Hunt; The KLIF Mystery House Number; The KLIF Mystery Telephone Number—there were dozens. McLendon recalls one with particular glee, The KLIF Money Drop:

> A group of us—Bill Stewart who was then program director, myself, Don Keyes, a few others—got on one of the top floors of the Adolphus Hotel. All of us spent about two hours blowing up an enormous number of balloons. And at the height of traffic about 5 o'clock in the afternoon, we started dropping these balloons. I guess we dropped about a thousand of them. Traffic was totally stopped. Naturally, in those days, we had not alerted the police. And we had some mad, mad police officers on our hands. But KLIF got to be well known as a result.[15]

There was also a more sober side to the Gordon McLendon Top 40 genre. His newscasts often contained stories heavy with issues. Early in the game, he involved his stations deeply in news and public affairs: KLIF was the first station, he maintains, to editorialize; the first station in Dallas to offer sustained coverage of election returns; the first to do continuous coverage of breaking news events; and the first outlet to send out mobile news units. Bill Stewart claims it was a mobile news unit that really put KLIF's Top 40 on the map to stay:

> The first thing that turned KLIF around was on the Friday night after I got there . . . I was doing 3 to 7 on the air and after I got off for a sandwich, I went out with the guy who was running the mobile news unit . . . We were driving around the Oak Cliff section and we heard a police call, a robbery in progress about two blocks from where we were. So we sped around the corner. We were the first ones on the scene. The guy was distraught. I jump out with a mike in my hand . . . and ask the guy what happened, he says, "Well this f___ guy came in with a f___ knife and held it, to my f___head and _____." I said, "Hold it. Wait a minute." I went to the unit and told the guy, "Give it to me." We had this big news open with a siren and everything, "First News First—KLIF takes you to the scene of news as it happens." He gives it to me. I go back to the victim and say, "Can you repeat what happened, sir?" And he repeats it verbatim . . . When it was over at quarter to nine, we got three phone calls complaining about what was said. This was an indication to me nobody was listening. So I went down to the *Times Herald* and the *News* and got an ad in the paper that said: "Oops, Sorry!" It was edged in black and on the obituary page. It said "KLIF wishes to apologize for the unfortunate language used last night at 8:44, but in covering news stories, the emotion of the moment is sometimes" . . . and it went on like that. The ad ran in the Saturday papers, and by Monday the phone lines were down from people calling to hear what was said . . . Well that made the station overnight . . . If it weren't for that we wouldn't have been able to pull 15 or 25,000 downtown two or three Fridays later when we threw the money out the window . . .[16]

Two other group owners, the Bartell chain, headquartered in Milwaukee, and Plough, the Memphis drug company, also developed Top 40 versions of their own in the 1950s. By the end of that decade they, together with Storz and McLendon, were operating a total of 33 Top 40 outlets. These alone would have been sufficient to declare Top 40 Radio the new wave of broadcasting. But another development, starting around 1956–57, was to assure that no region in the country would miss its wallop. It came as no surprise that various employees intimately familiar with the interior of Top 40 Radio should take it elsewhere—to introduce the concept to old-line operations, or to use it at stations they themselves had acquired. The Storz and McLendon groups were particularly vulnerable since their stations did Top 40 best. But it was the former Storz acolytes who left the fold to fan out across radioland that contributed most to the further spread of the gospel according to Top 40. Many of them also eventually rose to leadership positions in the industry.

Jack Thayer, who had joined Storz as a disc jockey at WDGY,* went on to become that station's manager. Following a stint as manager of WHK, Cleveland, Thayer moved to KLAC, Los Angeles, where he introduced two-way talk radio. He later became president of NBC Radio, and following that, general manager of WNEW, New York. Charles Murdock, a former disc jockey and program director at WQAM, ultimately became general manager of WLW, Cincinnati. David Croninger, ex-WQAM program director joined the Metromedia Chain and was promoted to manager of both WIP, Philadelphia, and WNEW, and served for a time as Metromedia's president. Ken Greenwood left his sales job at WHB to build his own group, the Dandy Broadcasting Company, which included KLEO, Wichita, KDEO, San Diego, and KQEO, Albuquerque and WPEO, located in the smallest city of the acquisitions, Peoria. WPEO represented a watershed of sorts, for until then, Top 40 Radio's stunning results were registered in medium-to-larger markets. Greenwood had no idea how Top 40 would play in Peoria. He soon learned: that paragon of middle Americanism was no different from the rest of the country—WPEO zoomed ahead in the ratings and dominated Peoria radio for a long time.

Several ex-Storzmen joined Robert Eastman at ABC Radio for his noble experiment of 1957–58, in which he tried to convert the Top 40 recorded popular music concept to a live one. When ABC gave up on the idea, Stephen Labunski, who had come to the network by way of managing WDGY, joined WMCA and introduced Top 40 to the Big Apple—where it played just as well as it did in Peoria. Labunski also served as president of NBC Radio for a number of years. Arthur Carlson was a salesman at WDGY, and after leaving ABC, joined Susquehanna Broadcasting Company, eventually becoming its Senior Vice President, Radio

---

* The WDGY line-up at that time also included one Bill Armstrong, who was to become better known as U.S. Senator William Armstrong, a Republican from Colorado.

Division, and building that group's line-up to seven AM and seven FM properties.

Ralph Beaudin, who had been in the Storz farm system at KOWH, was also in the faction who went with Eastman to ABC. He, however, stayed at ABC and spearheaded that network's expansion of owned-and-operated radio stations, and was ultimately responsible for the revolutionary "4 Network" concept ABC introduced in the mid-60s.[17] ABC Radio, when it acquired KQV, Pittsburgh, in the late 50s, sent Ralph Beaudin there for the Top 40 transfusion, and while he was not able to knock off the solidly-entrenched KDKA, he at least turned KQV around, and sent ABC on its way rejoicing in 1960 to acquire WLS-WENR, Chicago. This situation posed an interesting problem. Here was an oldline 50,000 watt facility, known half the time as WLS, during which it beamed its programs to a farm audience, and the other half as WENR, going after urban listeners. WLS's reputation for programming to the vast mid-West farm population dated back to the early 1920s. Sears, Roebuck had been the original licensee of WLS (for *World's Largest Store*). In 1928, Sears sold the station to the *Prairie Farmer* which continued programs with rural appeal. WLS was the home of that radio barn dance fountainhead, the *National Barn Dance,* from which flowed dozens of imitations, and the first one to go coast-to-coast. Would Beaudin and ABC dare to plow under this mid-West farm institution and switch to Top 40?

The answer was not long in coming. The WLS-WENR conference room was crowded one morning with the station's management team, awaiting the arrival of the archduke who would preside over ABC's new Chicago Archduchy. The room Beaudin would soon enter also served as a repository for artifacts, plaques and memorabilia, most of which reflected WLS's close farm ties. Beaudin, who had deliberately planned a late entrance, came into the conference room carrying a hammer. Without a word, he approached a ceramic bull sitting in the middle of the table. In one fell swoop, he severed the phallus of the bull. Stunned silence. After which Beaudin's cryptic announcement: "This is my way of telling you we're cutting off all our farm programming blocks." He retired the WENR call letters, retaining WLS. The new WLS's ascent out of second-division Chicago radio, to outstanding ratings and profits within a year, was the talk of the industry.

The season of sweet content was late in coming to WLS. For those operations on whom Top 40 had smiled much earlier, the reviews were, nevertheless, mixed. True, on the bottom line where it counted most, "the newest thing in radio since networks" was a box office smash. But, within, broadcasting, an internecine war of words broke out. Established American institutions do not like boat rockers, and when these brash, young Top 40 operators hit the airwaves with their *arriviste* stations, they kindled the wrath of the rulers of the kingdom. By the mid-1950s, the traditionalists and the upstarts had at it—with a vengeance. It was impossible to go to a broadcasters' convention or pick up a trade paper without one side or the other releasing a verbal fusillade. In one of the most slashing intra-mural attacks radio had known, Robert O. Swezey, general manager of WDSU New Orleans, an old-line NBC affiliate, addressed the 1956 convention of the Amrican Women in Radio and Television, vitriol dripping from every word. Probably smarting over Storz's WTIX, New Orleans success, Swezey blasted

> the trend into simple routine patterns of news and music, all playing over and over again the same few pop tunes and reading the same news, fresh from the tickers, at regular intervals. Many of these stations are, as you know, run on mechanical formulate; their service is much more comparable to wired music than the type of service we have always accepted as good radio . . . news and music operation should be recognized for what it is—a different, lesser type of service—and some sort of modified, or second class license with appropriate conditions and regulations . . . It distresses us who have known radio in its good days, and its glorious moments, to think of it being debased, and to see it sink into the blaring, senseless mediocrity of the juke box. For the quick-buck boys who have never thought much ahead of the next spot announcement, this may be hunky-dory. They had just as soon sell old bones as fresh flowers. But for the rest of us, this does make a difference, and only as we make a determined and intelligent effort can radio have any significant future . . .[18]

Surprisingly, the leading rebuttals to Mr. Swezey's unprecedented tirade did not come from Top 40 stations. In a letter to *Variety* the following week, William B. McGrath, managing director of the venerable Boston independent, WHDH, was not ready to relegate Top 40 stations to the back of radio's bus:

> Some of these so-called juke boxes have made their competitors "Nielsennervous," for apparently television has made the radio audience seek alternatives the networks do not now supply . . . It is pompous of anyone to propose that a station featuring music and news operate under a "second class license" for then one might fall victim to the proposal that a network affiliate, unable to sense the personal preferences and needs of its audience during chain broadcasts, might only be entitled to a tertiary license.[19]

Richard D. Buckley, president of WNEW, the pioneer music and news outlet, endorsed the Declaration of the Independents in the same issue of *Variety* and defended the format of music and news for presenting

> any single owner or group with the greatest opportunity to program according to the public taste and perform a maximum amount of public

service. Evidently, the American public prefers this type of radio because all research indicates independents moving into number one position in listening audience in many markets throughout the country.[20]

Sharp as these exchanges were, they were the stuff of nursery rhymes compared to the furor that was to come. For at that time, rock and roll was still an embryo on radio. As Ken Greenwood had said, early Top 40 music was Perry Como, Patti Page and Doris Day. Only a few rock and roll tunes such as Bill Haley's "Rock Around The Clock" and "Heartbreak Hotel" and Don't Be Cruel" by Elvis Presley were on Top 40 playlists in 1955 and 1956. The term was gaining a little radio attention though; a tune with the expression in the title, "Rock and Roll Waltz" by Kay Starr had even made the 1956 charts—although it was far from being rock and roll music.

Radio, inexorably intertwined with popular music, could not expect to stay above the coming battle over rock and roll for long, and when the flak started flying, Top 40 would have to take the brunt of it. For now though, the barbs at Top 40 would still concern its *methods,* rather than its *music.* Meanwhile, out on the barricades, the word war over rock and roll was already underway. In Birmingham, in March 1956, segregationist leader Asa Carter, executive secretary of the North Alabama White Citizens Council, charged that the National Association for the Advancement of Colored People had "infiltrated" Southern white teen-agers with rock and roll music. Carter said he would ask juke box operators to throw out "immoral" records in the new rhythm. Coin music distributors countered that this would mean eliminating most of their hits.[21] A few days earlier in Hartford, Connecticut, after a rock and roll concert where police arrested 11 youths for unruly conduct, Dr. Frances J. Bruceland, a noted psychiatrist, called rock and roll a "cannibalistic and tribalistic form of music" and a "communicable disease—another sign of adolescent rebellion."[22] Jack Gould, respected radio-TV critic of the *New York Times,* in reviewing Elvis Presley's first appearance on the *Ed Sullivan Show* in September, 1956, found him "unpleasant" and his singing "singularly distasteful." Gould labeled CBS's "selfish exploitation and commercialized overstimulation of youth's physical impulses . . . a gross national disservice."[23] Returning fire from the pro-camp, Dr. J. McAllister Brew, in an article entitled "There's Nothing Wrong with Rock and Roll," appearing in the British Medical Association's *Family Doctor,* thought it was the Roaring 20s all over again. And if "those former days of the Charleston were less violent and anti-social," according to Dr. Brew, it was because that was a "less violent age . . . the irritations caused by the young [of the '20s] was confined to a relatively small group of well-to-do . . . Today the adolescent enthusiasms are more widespread simply because more young people can afford to get 'sent' by the fashionable craze of the moment."[24] Broadway's Richard Rodgers, while not offering a spirited defense of the music, at least knew its origins, and admitted its number-one troubadour performed a public service. Rodgers told *Etude,* "Rock and roll's melodic and structural origins . . . spring directly from the blues, while its heavy, insistent beat is indebted to Gospel music . . ." As for Elvis, "he serves a useful purpose where kids are concerned and I think it's a good one. They release a good deal of energy watching Presley . . ."[25]

The arrival of rock and roll is sometimes cited as being out of sync with the 1950s, often called a "bland decade." This does not square with the facts, for the 1950s were a time of social upheaval in America. One need not agree completely with Haynes Johnson's dark view of those years, but his assessment should remind us the decade was hardly "bland." Johnson called them

> Years of fear and tension, repression and intolerance . . . on a major scale. They were the years of Joe McCarthy and character assassinations, of Korea and the human wave infantry assults . . . of the most rigid expressions of the Cold War mentality, of a strain of political viciousness, virtually unmatched in this century . . . of the organized crime syndicate (Mafia) and its connection with political corruption . . . the civil rights revolution that would transform much of American life . . . building the confrontation between the federal government and the states in September, 1957 in Little Rock . . . [Years] that saw racial violence stain the land in the aftermath of the Freedom Marches and burning of buses in the South . . .[26]

Whatever part rock and roll played in the general social and cultural revolution is open to debate; however, it was to become the most pervasive force in American popular music.

Around 1958–59, when rock and roll became the *sine qua non* of Top 40, the main battleground shifted to radio. Prior to that, only Alan Freed and a few of his imitators were featuring a steady rock diet. Musically, Top 40 Radio had never been *avant-garde;* its credo had always been "Play the hits." Which is what Top 40 stations continued to do as the new music caught on. As more and more rock and roll tunes made the playlists, protests against Top 40 Radio reached fever pitch. Top 40 operators were snubbed at Rotary meetings and denounced in letters to the editor. Anonymous hate calls to Top 40 stations were common ("When are you going to get off that nigger music and play something good?" "The Communists are behind that music."). The author recalls an incident at a state broadcasters' convention that illustrates the fear and loathing of Top 40 Radio at the time. The manager of a Top 40 station and his wife were waiting at the dining room entrance to be seated for breakfast. At a table nearby, with his fashionably attired wife, sat an owner whose station had been taking a clobbering from the one represented by the unseated manager. "Hey," the disgruntled owner bellowed, loud enough for at least half the diners to hear, "Why don't you guys get in a pissing contest with a skunk?" *

Newly-coined dersive sobriquets for the Top 40 format entered the radio lingo: "rockers," "schlockers," "teeny-boppers." Bad-mouthing of rock and roll had truly become broadcast establishment chic. In Baltimore, WITH program executive Richard Covington called Top 40 playlists "sick," and declared, "It's time that stations got off the 'sick list'." [27] In St. Louis, KWK announced it would take a week to play all of its rock and roll records one more time, and then break each one with a sharp snap, clearly audible to the listeners. KWK manager, Robert T. Convey averred rock and roll "has dominated the music field long enough. The majority of listeners will be surprised how pleasant radio listening can be without rock and roll." [28] KSFR, San Francisco offered to the public free window stickers containing the station's slogan, "I kicked the Junk Music Habit by Listening to KSFR," with owner-manager Al Levitt declaring, "Everyone has been talking about rock and roll music, but no one has done anything about it until now." [29] WISN, Milwaukee dramatized its "non-rock, anti-Top 40" policy by deliberately playing five hours of rock tunes, then burning 200 records in the station's courtyard, and commemorating the occasion by including a picture of it in a sales brochure with the caption, "WISN finds a good place for 'Top 40' records." [30] At KDEN, Denver, station breaks were often preceded and followed by, "Help stamp out Rock and Roll. Patronize KDEN advertisers and KDEN, Denver's first station now busily engaged in stamping out rock and roll." [31]

The most blistering attack, the one that was to focus national attention on the subject came from, of all places, a record company. Mitch Miller, a Columbia A & R man—obviously oblivious to the egalitarian nature of American popular music that found some listeners enjoying his "Sing-a-Long" product, while others regarded the genre insipid—looked upon Top 40 programming and found it wanting. In a speech in early 1958, entitled "The Great Abdication," before a broadcasters' group including many disc jockeys and Top 40 executives, Miller's attack reached a new high in shrillness:

> To say you've grossly mishandled this great, fat money-maker—radio—would be understating the case. Some of you have made the man who killed the goose that laid the golden egg look like Bernard Baruch. You carefully built yourself into the monarchs of radio and abdicated—abdicated to the corner record shop, to the eight to 14-year olds; to the pre-shave crowd . . . .[32]

---

* The same owner's station, two decades later, would be merrily cranking out "album oriented rock" in unrestricted doses.

Miller urged the broadcasters to lift the scales from their ears and appeal to the audience that wants "variety, musicianship and more sophistication in their music." What Miller was doing, of course, was merely carrying on a tradition of cant and cliché that had started in the 1920s with "jazz," had passed through crooning and swing, and was lumped under a call for more "quality" popular music on radio.

Miller's attack had hardened the positions of advocates in both camps, something akin to the gun-control debate. Todd Storz repeated, as he had so often, the doctrines of Top 40:

> Our desire is that our stations shall please the majority of the people the majority of the time . . . Our format was built on the premise that is not within our province to dictate by censorship, programming tastes to the American public . . . We felt that a control of music to the extent that we could not play certain selections because they did not meet with our wholehearted approval would be very akin to thought control . . . We also believe the public has a great appreciation for a really progressive sounding operation. This means rapid-fire production e.t.'s, a top news department, and most important, disc jockeys who can attain and keep a loyal audience following.[33]

Dick Pack, vice president, Westinghouse Broadcasting Company (the first establishment chain to adopt many Top 40 policies), speaking before the National Association of Broadcasters' programming conference, excoriated station managers who were "musically middle-aged":

> Deejay, top hit, juke play have become dirty words. Irresponsible criticism labeling music and news stations as "radio's best generation" has hurt the whole broadcasting industry . . . We live in a democratic nation and radio is a democratic industry. There is room for different tastes and opinions in both. Other media don't berate their members for a touch of corn. All magazines can't be *New Yorkers,* and all newspapers can't be the *New York Times.*[34]

When the payola scandals of 1959–60 broke (a topic to be pursued at length in Chapter 17), musical radio in general, and Top 40 stations in particular, were belted with volleys of innuendo. "See," the traditionalists chortled gleefully, "we told you so. The only way that rock and roll gets on the air is through somebody paying somebody off." The fact that only a handful of disc jockeys were found guilty did little to mute the debate. But the more strident the criticism, the more Top 40 operators stuck by their guns. "Nobody likes us but the people," one of them observed.

By the end of the decade, Top 40 Radio continued to gain ground. It was still possible in mid-1958 to turn a pumpkin into a silver slipper. This was nowhere better typified than in the Scranton-Wilkes-Barre, Pa. area, where Susquehanna Broadcasting Company acquired WARM (from the William Scranton family). In spite of its excellent facility (5 kw at 590 kc) WARM had floundred near the bottom of the Scranton-Wilkes-Barre heap. Following the Top 40 transfusion, the situation was dramatically reversed. Early WARM ratings told loud and clear a now-taken-for-granted story: like other stations which received the proper Top 40 injection, it zoomed to the top of the Hooperatings. (For a detailed breakdown, see Appendix on page 369.

Despite such documentation, WARM and most of its Top 40 compatriots had difficulty at first in convincing advertisers. Until *they* were convinced, rating victories would be pyrrhic. "Nothing happens in America," it has been said, "until somebody sells something." And because buying decisions are often made on the emotional level, salesmen of Top 40 stations encountered many stonewalling clients. For many advertisers, like other Top 40 haters, refused to buy time. Bill Stewart recalls an artifice that helped win more than one local advertiser over to a Top 40 station:

> We'd have a salesman go out and talk to these people and say, "we have 50% of the audience here in Omaha." They'd say, "Yeah, but they're all kids." So the salesman would come back and say I was over at Kurtz Furniture Store yesterday, and this guy is spending "a lot of money on KFAB," a middle-of-the-road station. "I've got to have something to prove to this guy that we have listeners." So we came up with the "Secret Word." The next day, every half-hour, the disc jockey would say, "the Secret Word is Charlie Kurtz." That's all he would say. People would call Kurtz up and asked, "What does this mean? I hear your name on the radio." Or he'd run into the same thing at church on Sunday: "I heard your name on the radio a few days ago and nothing else. What does it mean?" Then our salesman would go back the following Tuesday and hear, "You guys must have listeners. A hundred people asked me about that."[35]

Secret words may have been fine on Main Street, U.S.A., but on Madison Avenue they would never fly. Yet, if radio's re-birth was to be complete, it had to be acknowledged and supported by national advertisers. Following the advertiser exodus from network radio to television, advertising agencies that controlled millions of dollars had to be convinced, not only that Top 40 Radio was the proper environment for their clients' commercials, but indeed that radio itself was not a horse-and-buggy medium in the Jet Age. To Robert E. Eastman fell much of the task of proselyting Madison Avenue to "modern radio." Early in 1958, Eastman organized a national sales team located in major buying centers to go after national advertising budgets in behalf of the stations he represented. Eastman's timing was right: just when the show-me denizens of Madison Avenue needed to be won over, along came Bob Eastman and his assault force of "young tigers" to admit to the national advertising community that, "Yes, Top 40 Radio is the mother lode of popular hits, but it is also a *primary medium.*"

Bob Eastman, a former NBC page, was the vice president at John Blair Company when that firm represented many of the Storz and Mc-Lendon stations. He understood Top 40 from top to bottom. So much so, he was sure the concept could be transferred successfully to live network radio. In the summer of 1957, Eastman became president of ABC Radio and installed big studio orchestras and vocalists performing cover versions of current hit songs. Name emcees were also included in a last-ditch effort to save traditional live network radio programming. Eastman's live-shows stayed on board until the following spring when ABC scuttled the works—including its creator. Eastman feels the ABC executive apparatus ("except Ed Noble who owned the business prior to his demise") was committed to the Eastman's return-to-live radio idea:

> Leonard Goldenson and the rest of the people were willing to give it a fair trial, except at that particular time they were having a struggle, trying to carve out a niche in television. Their primary cash flow at the time was from the theater business. They had several hundred theaters scattered across the United States which came into the deal in the American Broad-casting-Paramount merger. The cash flow from the theater business was supporting the building of a TV operation, and also supporting what we were trying to do on the radio side. In the summer of our first year of endeavor, the country was struck with the Asian flu epidemic. The flu cut down very sharply on theater attendance, and consequently the whole operation. The money we were expending, attempting to build a radio product therefore became expendable. As the cash was cut off, our enterprise which we'd hoped would bloom into something significant, was chopped off at the ankles, not by anybody—call it circumstances, or fate.[36]

After the ABC's Lord High Executioner gave Eastman the bad news, he lined up a list of predominantly Top 40 stations for representation. Top 40 couldn't have had a better sales emissary at the time (1958) because the concept was spreading—and so were the cries to throw the heathen out of the radio temple. Eastman's name fortunately carried some clout on Madison Avenue. His heavy-with-Top 40 list* told the ad world: If a gray emminence like Bob Eastman stakes his professional reputation on this new musical radio, then there must be something to it. Not that Madison Avenue galvanized quickly and rushed to place Top 40 alongside of baseball, hot dogs, apple pie and Chevrolet—far from it. Not even Bob Eastman and his team of "young tigers" (many of whom he had hired away from low-paying advertising agency jobs) were able to gain instant legitimacy for Top 40 at the agencies where the big bucks were dispensed. Quickly, Eastman and Company gained the reputation as "The Top 40

---

* Other station representative firms, particularly John Blair & Co., had Top 40's in their fold. But Blair's list was more varied and included more stations' whose musical persuasions leaned more to middle-of-the-road than Eastman's.

Rep," "The Rock and Roll Rep." Eastman maintains that was good: "It gave us a label which was better than being ignored. We met it head-on. We said, 'It's here, it's real, the people are listening to it. The ratings prove it. You got to believe in it.' We didn't sell it halfway."[37] When his salesmen trotted up and down Ad Row with the huge ratings of their Top 40 stations, many of the shops who normally worship at the numbers shrine countered by saying, "Ratings were only one phase of the time-buying process." Bob Eastman recalls the kind of reception he and his men received:

> When one station came into rating prominence in their market, you went into the agencies and showed them the ratings as proof. There would be four or five other stations from the same market knocking it. They would derisively say, "Well, we're sure the ratings are there, but they're all kids. It won't last." There were many clichés that came out of the competition. But it *did* last and it wasn't only kids; it was also the mothers and fathers who were listening to this programming. There was a great deal of evidence that surfaced from the local level where they could measure sales more readily that this programming was not only generating ratings in the marketplace, but was viable as a sales-producing medium. Gradually, the screams of the competition trying to tear it down failed and we generated believability, and the national advertisers, sometimes kicking and screaming, bought it.[38]

When Bob Eastman's competitors descended on ad agencies, playing tapes of representative Top 40 programming, it was difficult to mount a defense. Many agency people, like those listeners-at-large who recoiled at the sound of Top 40, found their sensibilities offended. This was particularly true when rock and roll records began dominating Top 40 playlists. Their revulsion began with the term itself, for "rock and roll"* certainly had sexual connotations. Then came the hallmark of rock and roll—rhythm. Prior to rock's arrival, popular music was a synthesis of straight-forward rhythm, "pretty" melodies and colorful harmony. Rock and roll was so primal and raw; counterpoised with Jerome Kern's or Richard Rodgers's elegant refrains, its dominant rhythm strain was bound to shake up the musical world.

---

* Alan Freed is generally credited with having coined the expression. The melding of Negro rhythm and blues with white country (hillbilly) music to form the fusion called rockabilly, and gradually, rock and roll, sent philologists and sociologists scurrying about, trying to pin down the term's origin. They needn't have gone any further than blues singer Trixie Smith's 1922 recording of "My Man Rocks Me With One Steady Roll." Jazz etymologist, Robert Gold in his *Jazz Lexicon* includes a citation from the April–June, 1927 *Journal of Abnormal and Social Psychology:* "The majority of the expressions in the blues relating to the sex act are sung from the point of view of women and are mostly concerned with the quality of movements made by the male during coitus. [In] 'My Man Rocks Me with One Steady Roll' the woman boasts of the steady movement with which her man executes the act." (Robert Gold. *A Jazz Lexicon,* Knopf, New York, 1964, pp. 255–6.)

The oft-told Elvis Presley story beginning with the Sam Phillips' Sun sessions that produced "That's All Right, Mama" (written by bluesman Arthur "Bit Boy" Crudup) hardly requires repetition; nor is a re-telling of the saga of Carl Perkins's "Blue Suede Shoes" necessary. Suffice it to say, those seminal rockabilly records were distinguished, first and foremost, by a pre-dominant beat. Radio is sound—and sound only—and it was Top 40 Radio, with its obsessive concern for sound that provided such a congenial aural environment for the beat of rock and roll. As early as 1926, an English radio critic, Gordon Lea, had hypothesized that rhythm in sound is the best radio. As was previously mentioned, Top 40 Radio had become a workable format before Elvis Presley and Buddy Holly, but it was rock and roll that made the Top 40 sound really "pop." The driving rhythm of rock fit snugly into the unity and consistency of Top 40. For if it was one thing that Top 40 compounded, it was unity—all components (commercials, public service announcements, the excitement) were compatible with the music. The Gestalt was greater than the sum of the parts.

Spawned by the rock and roll phenomenon, the record collecting hobby got a shot in the arm—by a new generation, a new speed (45 rpm) and the new tinier disk. It was part of the Top 40 approach to "break" (introduce) new records on the air; and it was very important for fans to rush out and buy copies to play at home. Just as Benny Goodman, Artie Shaw and Glenn Miller, 20 years earlier, had enhanced their careers by getting airplay for their records, so would the new popular music idols. Record collections that began in the 1950s with such rock anthems as "Shake, Rattle and Roll" (Bill Haley), "Maybellene" (Chuck Berry), "Rebel-'Rouser" (Duane Eddy), "Peggy Sue" (Buddy Holly) and "Only You and You Alone" (Platters), extended into the '60s to include "The Twist" (Chubby Checker), "She Loves You" (Beatles), "Where Did Our Love Go" (Supremes), "Be My Baby" (Ronettes), "Nights in White Satin" (Moody Blues), "Like a Rolling Stone" (Bob Dylan), "Soul Man" (Sam and Dave) and "Light My Fire" (Doors). The very names of rock groups conferred an extra colorful dimension on the Top 40 format. Even Shakespeare would have been hard pressed to know what was in names that often came out plant, vegetable or mineral:

ANIMAL	VEGETABLE	MINERAL
Animals	Cream	Big Brother & The
Beatles	Bread	Holding Co.
Blackbyrds	Dante & Evergreens	Braso Ring
Blue Oyster Cult	Grapefruit	Consumer Rapport
Byrds	Grass Roots	Cystals
Chipmunks	Hot Chocolate	Italian Asphalt Co.
Crickets	Jelly Beans	Ohio Express
Crow	1910 Fruit Gum Co.	Pacific Gas & Electric
Eagles	Peaches & Herb	Shells

ANIMAL	VEGETABLE	MINERAL
Flamingos	Peppermint Trolley Co.	Stones
Iron Butterfly	Raspberries	
Monkees	Strawberry Alarm Clock	
Stone Poneys	Sugarloaf	
Stephen Wolf	Wild Cherry	
Turtles		

Since musical fashions always go in and out of style, it was inevitable that Top 40 itself would change. A decade is a long time in popular music and by the mid-1960s, when Top 40 reached a ripe old age, some of its mechanics decreed an overhaul.

The body shop foreman who directed the re-building was one Bill Drake, nee Philip Yarborough. Drake had become Drake so his disc jockey name would rhyme with WAKE, the Bartell Atlanta outlet where he served his "modern radio" basic training. A transfer to Bartell's KYA (San Francisco) exposed Drake to the key KYA slogan used as the peg on which the station hung much of its promotional gimmickry—"Radio KYA—Boss of the Bay." Drake's next stop was KYNO, Fresno where he constructed his own version of the KYA—Boss model. Ratings victories that toppled the Fresno competition led to an association with KGB, San Diego, where Drake served as a consultant, once again grabbing on to radio's holy ratings grail. Meanwhile, Drake, who had earned the reputation as a program miracle worker was summoned into the presence of Thomas O'Neill, president of General Tire and Rubber Company, owner of the RKO stations, who told Drake, do thou likewise to the group's floundering properties in Los Angeles (KHJ) and San Francisco (KFRC). And so it came to pass in 1965, Boss Radio received its most prominent showcase. Los Angeles is more than a tough radio market—it is the Western capital of show biz, where for every person wishing a new entertainment venture well, a thousand hope it falls flat on its face.

The Drake Formula was a rousing success in Los Angeles. KHJ became the ultimate Boss station, prototype for hundreds of attempted clones. Starting with the station's location, "Boss-Angeles," everything was "Boss." Bill Drake distilled the essence of Top 40: he declared dead air a felony; he decreed more rapid-fire talk by disc jockeys; he dropped the traditional 40-song playlist down 10 to 30—that is, "Boss 30"; he reduced the allowable 18 commercials per hour (the FCC quota) to an iron-clad 12. Bill Drake enforced time limits for deejay patter between records and other program elements. KHJ's claim that it played "much more music" could hardly be met, Drake felt, if disc jockeys yakked on endlessly. From the enemy camp, where had risen such unflattering cries as "Dreck Radio," came word that Bill Drake had gone so far as to install a studio light—to flash when a disc jockey, overcome with even a mild case of *flux de bouche*, chattered on beyond seven seconds. Not so, said Drake, just another case of false witness-bearing. He defended his philosophy of less talk and more music:

> There were a lot of guys that talked a lot. A lot of people think they can only be personalities if they talk a lot. And they don't take into consideration what they're saying. I took the attitude there's a vast difference between personality and somebody who just talks a lot . . . I believe heavily in personalities and we've always tried to nurture and encourage that. We would make allowances within the format . . . So we allowed some people to do it, and we didn't allow others to do it. We would allow it if a jock demonstrated he was capable of handling it. But if they weren't . . . what do you accomplish by allowing them to keep talking? [39]

The following typical sequence by KHJ disc jockey, "The Real" Don Steele (a name subsequently adopted by others across the country) times out to 16 seconds. If the words struck the un-Bossed as meaningless babble, they at least proved Drake allowed exceptions to the seven-second rule:

> STEELE: Three o'clock in Boss Angelese! And gey HEY, thitz me, the Real Don Steele, a billion dollar weekend there, and you're looking out of sidewalk call; I got nothing but groovy those groovy golds. We're gonna fit Chuck out here on a fractious Friday boy, got to get a set outside that (unintelligible word resembling blowing bubbles in a glass of water) jumbo city. (Pause) Take a trip. When you chase 'em, daylight. [40]

Drake never flinched from his belief that brevity was the soul of radio wit:

> A lot of stations had weather jingles, but most of them were thirty seconds long. I cut it down to just "KHJ Weather." As far as "Golden," I didn't want "Gold Record," "Golden Oldie," or any of the longer terms. I wanted to say just "93/KHJ Golden," and cut it like a weather jingle. [41]

Within a year KHJ, initially dubbed "Drake's Folly," was indeed boss of Los Angeles radio. So impressed was Tom O'Neill that he appointed Bill Drake program vicar of all the RKO Radio realms in the land. Later in the 1960s, the maverick consultant joined Gene Chenault, a California station owner, to form Drake-Chenault, and specialize in syndicated radio programs and station consulting.

By the time Bill Drake went to KHJ, his wonders to perform, doctrinaire Top 40 (i.e. of the Storz and McLendon genus) was getting more competitive. Musical radio—indeed, all radio—was growing. The medium had proven it could thrive in the television age. An AM or FM station license, especially with the scarcity of TV channels, became the hottest show biz ticket in town. Musically, new sounds were happening too. The British Invasion and the Motown Sound were further proof rock was not going to go away. Stations that formerly vowed, NEVER!, were actually dabbling in such fare as "I Hear a Symphony" (Supremes) or "Yesterday" (Beatles). Adult dancing to rock and roll, started by Chubby Checker's Twist, had lent more legitimacy. In 1965, came The Frug, The Jerk and The Monkey to take their places alongside the Charleston and the Big Apple. That year, *Time* discovered what Top 40 Radio stations had been saying all along:

> The boost for big-beat music has come, amazingly enough, from the adult world. Where knock-the-rock was once the conditioned reflex of the older generation, a surprisingly large segment of the 20- to 40-year olds are facing up to the music, and what's more, liking it. Mostly, the appeal is its relentless beat . . . It may seem monotonous but it is utterly compelling to the feet. The result is rock and roll has set the whole world to dancing . . .[42]

The more popular rock and roll became in the 1960s and 1970s, the more new spin-offs emerged. The more rock radio grew, the more stations there were to play it. There seemed to be a piece of rock for almost everyone:

Country Rock/Rockabilly	Soft British Rock
Good Time Rock	Jazz Rock
Folk Rock	1970s Hard Rock
Motown Sound	1070s Mellow Rock
Surfin' Rock	San Francisco Sound
1960s Hard Rock	Disco

So the beat went on. And like the Twelve Tribes of Israel which sprang from a common ancestor, certain men born of Top 40, struck out in new directions in the 1960s and 1970s. Top 40 was the source of the strength that led them to seek new radiolands of milk and honey. With them they brought a certain set of expectations, as one form of rock radio begat another:

BILL DRAKE: Leaves Top 40 KYA, San Francisco; takes Boss Radio along to "consult" KGB, San Diego, then to KYNO, Fresno where both are smash successes.

BILL DRAKE: "Consults" RKO-General's KHJ; Drake also introduces first Top 40 to FM on RKO-General's WOR-FM which evolves into 99X.

TOM DONAHUE: Leaves KYA to discover underground (progressive) KMPX-FM, then moves to KSAN-FM bought by Metromedia group which installs rock format on its other FM stations: WNEW-FM, New York, KMET-FM, Los Angeles, and WMMR-FM, Philadelphia.

BUZZ BENNETT: Leaves KGB, goes "across the street" to KCBQ, and beats Drake with "Q" format; goes to Pittsburgh and introduces frequency used in call letters-13Q.

BOB PITTMAN: Leaves WRDQ-FM, Detroit (rock) to go to WPEZ-FM, Pittsburgh (rock) to WMAQ, Chicago (country), to WKQX-FM, Chicago (rock) to WNBC; Pittman succeeded by Bob Sherman, ex WCAU-AM Philadelphia, and WNBC-AM pass mighty WABC in "broad-appeal contemporary sound."

LEE ABRAMS: Leaves WMYQ-FM, Miami (rock) for ABC o & o WRIF-FM, Detroit; meets Kent Burkhart, former WQAM p.d., at WQDR-FM, Raleigh, (rock) where they introduce "Super Stars" AOR format and form consultant firm.

Other hybrids (See Genealogy Chart Appendix on pages 372 & 373) and additional appurtenances, on both the AM and FM bands that had no direct linkage to Top 40, owed some debt to trail blazers Storz and McLendon. Even the True Unbelievers who would go spinning off this earthy coil still contemptuous of Top 40 Radio could not deny that the format and its offspring got America back in the radio habit again. Through the station proliferation of the 1960s and 1970s, *all* radio benefited from the lesson Top 40 had taught so well: that when inventiveness and imagination, nourished by an enlightened management, were brought to bear, *any station* could benefit.

Take the matter of promotion. Not just the razzle-dazzle of a McLendon Circus Maximus, but the everyday garden variety. The Top 40 bible declared that in the beginning are the call letters: *Do something with those legally-required, mundane audio identification tags.* That promotion must start with the call letters was part of the holy writ of Top 40 Radio. It didn't matter whether the station had been assigned an awkward set (WDGY), or whether it was blessed with a naturally promotable combination (WARM). What could be clumsier than WDGY? When Storz took over the Minneapolis outlet, the surrounding promotion came out as "Wee-Gee." Needless to say, Top 40 WARM offered so many obvious built-in promotional opportunities, it boggles the mind. A partial listing of only a handful of propitious call letters reveals the value of those important four-letter franchises:

In a word . . .

KING, Seattle
KATE, Albert Lea, Minn.
KITE, Terrell Hills, Tex.
WAKE, Valparaiso, Ind.
WANT, Richmond, Va.
WAVE, Louisville
WIFE, Indianapolis

WINK, Ft. Myers, Fla.
WIRE, Indianapolis
WORD, Spartansburg, S.C.
WORK, Barre, Vt.

For kicks . . .

KICK, Springfield, Mo.
KIKN, Sinton, Tex.

KIKS, Iola, Kansas
KIKX, Tucson
KIXS, Kileen, Tex.
KXXX, Cobby, Kansas

Quick radio . . .

KWIQ, Moses Lake, Wash.
KWKK, Dardanelle, Ark.
WQXI, Atlanta
WPDQ, Jacksonville, Fla.
WQIK, Jacksonville, Fla.

In tune with weather . . .

KFOG, San Francisco
KOOL, Phoenix
WARM, Scranton–Wilkes-Barre
WIND, Chicago
WHOT, Campbell, Ohio
WRRM, Cincinnati
WSUN, St. Petersburg, Fla.

Sound the Z . . .

KWIZ, Santa Ana, Calif.
KZAM, Bellevue, Wash.
WINS, New York
WINZ, Miami
WIZZ, Streator, Ill.

Kissing radio . . .

KIIS, Los Angeles
KISS, San Antonio
KIST, Santa Barbara
KKIS, Pittsburg, Calif.
KKSS, St. Louis
KYSS, Missoula, Montana
KSNN, Pocatello, Idaho
WKIS, Orlando
WKSS, Hartford, Conn.

When it came to call letters, however, the most creative wrinkle of all was the singing station identification. Not surprisingly, this impactful innovation received its greatest impetus from Top 40 Radio. The Storz and McLendon stations did not originate the idea, but it was in the hands of those standard bearers who rocked the cradle of modern radio that the singing station break became institutionalized. Bob Eastman, Top 40's most enthusiastic Madison Avenue lobbyist, recalls one serendipitous day in the middle 1950s, when the singing station identification entered his life. Eastman was still with John Blair Company, the national sales firm whose station list at the time included many Storz and McLendon properties. Pete Schloss, WWSW, Pittsburgh, had come to town with a reel of tape he was most anxious to play. Bob Eastman assembled the Blairmen for an audition of something called "musical ID's":

> To my knowledge, these were the first musical station breaks. They were very catchy and defined in jingle form all the elements of programming on the radio station. I got very excited about these and asked Pete who did them. He said it was Ginger Johnson, the fellow who did the original Pepsi Cola jingle. He had teamed up with Eric Siday to put the jingle package together. I asked Ginger to give me right of first refusal in every market in which we had a station . . . Station after station bought the jingle ID's, maybe 20, and almost overnight there was another huge jump in ratings.[43]

Station promotion of every kind was intricately woven into the fabric of the McLendon and Storz versions of musical radio. Some years later when Top 40 had become a museum piece cloaked with the mantle of trivia and radio headed in other directions, this ceased to be true. Most of the free-wheeling spontaneity that marked much of Top 40's promotional hoopla had been replaced by promotion that: a) emphasized other media advertising, which for many pop music stations means creating logos specially dressed up for print and television ads; b) de-emphasized listener participation; c) observed more restrictive parameters, e.g. eliminating "treasure hunts" to avoid problems with local police, or even the FCC. In a real sense, the promotion *was* the Top 40 format. The medium and the message were one.

Top 40 Radio's golden years were 1955–1965. After that, the gradual splintering of rock and the growth of FM rendered the concept obsolete. But the seismic shift that Top 40 started will be felt as long as there is popular music on radio. It was airy, feisty, pungent, brash, sassy, provocative, exciting. Radio needed that.

NOTES

1. Author's interview with Ken Greenwood, January 20, 1981.
2. *Ibid.*
3. Author's interview with Bill Stewart, March 30, 1981.
4. *Ibid.*
5. *op. cit.* Greenwood interview.
6. *Ibid.*
7. *op. cit.* Stewart interview.
8. *Ibid.*
9. WSBA Program Guidelines, October, 1957.
10. *Ibid.*
11. *op. cit.* Bill Stewart interview.
12. Gordon McClendon interview by KLIF, Dallas, June, 1980.
13. *Ibid.*
14. *Ibid.*
15. *Ibid.*
16. *op. cit.* Bill Stewart interview.
17. The blunt and outspoken Beaudin, who had developed a reputation as a sort of *enfant terrible* of Top 40, had the burst of insight that was responsible for a vast overhaul of traditional network radio. It was Beaudin who conceived the idea that a single corporate network entity might originate four distinctly different network "feeds" to appeal to different target audiences. ABC adopted the plan and thus emerged the American Entertainment Radio Network, American Information Network, American Contemporary Network and American FM network. A detailed account of ABC's four-network scheme, and how Beaudin presented it may be found in Sterling Quinlan. *Inside ABC*, Hastings House (New York) 1979, Chapter 9, "That Crazy Radio Idea," pp. 121–132.
18. Guy Livingston. "Swezey Hits 'Quick-Buck' Boys Who Debase Radio to Jukebox Level," *Variety*, May 2, 1956, p. 25+.
19. William B. McGrath. Letter to *Variety*, May 9, 1956, p. 40.
20. Richard D. Buckley, Letter to *Variety*, Ibid.
21. ———. "Segregationist Wants Ban on 'Rock and Roll'," *The New York Times*, March 30, 1956, p. 39.
22. ———. "Rock-and-Roll Called Communicable Disease," *The New York Times*, March 28, 1956, p. 33.
23. Jack Gould. "Elvis Presley: Lack of Responsibility Is Shown by TV in Exploiting Teen-Agers," *The New York Times*, September 16, 1956, Section 2, p. 13.

24. Quoted in Dorothy Barclay. "British Expert Unrocked by Current Music Trends," *The New York Times*, March 1, 1957, p. 26.
25. Albert J. Elias. "Richard Rodgers on Current Trends in Popular Music," *Etude*, April, 1957, p. 23.
26. Haynes Johnson. "Eyes Shut, Clock Unwound, Seeking Shelter in Shades of the Past," *The Washington Post*, September 30, 1980, p. A3.
27. ———. "Balto Station's 'Top 40' Blast," *Variety*, August 27, 1958, p. 43.
28. ———. "Rock 'n' Roll Opponents Are Due for Big Break," *The New York Times*, January 13, 1958, p. 49.
29. June Bundy. "DJ's Dramatize R & R Sneer Campaign Via Colorful Tactics," *Billboard*, April 21, 1958, p. 1.
30. *Ibid.* pp. 1 and 4.
31. *Ibid.* p. 4.
32. Herb Schoenfeld. "Deejay: Performer or Puppet?," *Variety*, March 12, 1958, p. 60.
33. Quoted in interview, "Radio Formats: What is Radio?," *U.S. Radio*, May, 1958, p. 22.
34. ———. "Westinghouse Broadcasting Exec Scolds Broadcasters," *Billboard*, November 3, 1958, p. 6.
35. *op. cit.* Bill Stewart interview.
36. Author's interview with Robert E. Eastman, January 28, 1981.
37. *Ibid.*
38. *Ibid.*
39. Interview with Bill Drake by editors of *Radio and Records*, in special supplement, "The Top 40 Story," September, 1977, p. 32.
40. Arnold Passman. *The Deejays*, (New York), MacMillan, 1971, p. 288.
41. *op. cit. Drake interview.*
42. ———. "Rock 'n' Roll: The Sound of the Sixties," *Time*, May 21, 1965, p. 84.
43. *op. cit.* Eastman interview.

CHAPTER 15

FM and The Format Explosion

AMERICANS HAVE BECOME so accustomed to their own inventiveness and to the contributions of science, that they have long since ceased to marvel at the "better mousetrap." By the mid-1960s, the better mousetrap of broadcasting was FM, or frequency modulation. For listeners, FM spelled out a Fresh Milieu of more varied programming, and for broadcasters, it meant Fresh Markets to enhance their standing in the media family.

Beginning in the early 1960s, the technology influencing the direction and reception of popular music on radio was properly in tune with the Jet Age. Advancements in studio and transmitter equipment, together with the arrival of the transistor and magnetic tape, contributed significantly to improvements in the delivery of sound. But no technical development in the colorful saga of the Great American Music Box—for the listener, for the broadcaster, and for the music maker alike—struck with greater impact than FM. Few scientific achievements, in or out of broadcasting, were ever beset with greater frustrations and disappointments, however. That struggle—compounded by unbelievable governmental, legal, and even corporate maneuvering, and ending in tragedy and triumph—was waged by one man who prevailed, yet never lived to see the full flowering of his invention.

FM was the brainchild of Edwin Howard Armstrong, a brilliant Columbia Univeristy engineering professor. Armstrong had distinguished himself as a key radio pioneer, contributing to the invention of two vital circuits—the regenerative, or feedback, circuit and the superheterodyne— both basic to modern radio and television transmission and reception. He had come up with the FM idea around 1933. When he took his scheme for an experimental station to the Federal Communications Commission in 1935, he was met with a maze of bureaucratic obstacles. The competitive chicanery he encountered, particularly from RCA, would have beaten an ordinary scientist. Then there were the major networks which had vested interests in their standard AM, or amplitude modulation, operations; they scorned the notion of a second mode of broadcasting. Only the threat of taking his idea to a foreign country enabled Armstrong to get an experimental outlet on the air in 1939. Operating on 7.5 meters with a 40 kw transmitter, Armstrong's station, W2KMN, at Alpine, New Jersey, demonstrated beyond all doubt the superiority of an FM signal.

In elementary terms, Professor Armstrong's frequency modulation invention enables the amplitude (strength) of transmitting waves to remain constant, while his circuitry varies the number of times the wave vibrates; this variation coincides with the transmitted sound. Amplitude modulation, on the other hand, *varies* with the strength of the transmitted wave to agree with the sound (music) being transmitted. (See accompanying figure.) An FM receiver is thus able to filter out distracting electrical noises caused by thunderstorms and man-made devices. This, plus the wider-moving FM wave, makes possible a fuller frequency range and lends a more natural aura to the music.

Despite the demonstrated superiority of FM, Armstrong was far from realizing unqualified acceptance of his new system. Nevertheless, he continued to conduct virtually a one-man crusade in FM's behalf. While spending his own money for further improvements—he enjoyed an independent income from previous patents—he also traveled far and wide, making speeches to spread the FM gospel. Before 1939 ended, Armstrong had sufficiently impressed 150 brave souls to file applications with the FCC for FM stations; they were, however, vying for only five allocated channels. Opposition from the RCA-NBC combine and CBS meanwhile continued, as they labeled the entire FM concept impractical and economically unsound.

In 1940, such criticism was somewhat blunted when a new FCC Commissioner, James Fly, took over as chairman. Under Fly's leadership, the Commission fostered a policy that favored the development of FM over television. (RCA at the time was pushing hard to get TV moving.) This was the big boost Edwin Armstrong needed. In a little over a year

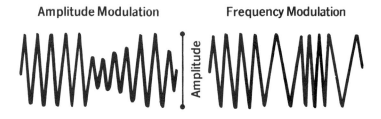

Amplitude Modulation   Frequency Modulation

after Fly became chairman, there were approximately 500 FM station applications for him and his fellow commissioners to consider. As of mid-1943, 74 stations were authorized to operate. By then, however, radio, like everything else, had gone to war; transmitting equipment and receiver manufacture were virtually halted.

In recalling his early FM days, Donald Flamm, pioneer AM-FM station operator, affirms that the FM road was not paved with gold:

> In 1943, my associate in the ownership of WPAT, Patterson, N.J., and I applied for an FM license and went on the air shortly after purchasing a large tract of land on High Mountain in North Haledon, one of the highest land points in Passaic County, 879 feet above sea level. But like many others at the time, we found the operation of FM a severe drain on our resources and on our staff. Besides, advertisers were not ready to use it as an advertising medium.[1]

Following World War II, Armstrong and his partisans expected the anticipated peacetime boom would prove their long-awaited shot in the arm. Such was not to be, for no sooner had the country returned to normal than the big television push was on; established AM station owners were either too busy trying to get into television, or too busy fighting it. Throughout the post-War years, many FM licenses were returned to the FCC or, as Donald Flamm puts it, "sold at ridiculously low prices." Those operators who did hang on to their FM franchises either duplicated their AM signals or, if they did offer separate programming, presented what came to be known as "wall-to-wall music," which could mean anything from classical to a popular variety, usually string-drenched melodies in the Mantovani mode.

It was during this period that FM came to stand for *fine music*. The term was not altogether complimentary, because whenever an FM advocate pointed out that the medium *could* be a viable advertising medium, he was promptly reminded that FM's *real* potential was as a commercial-free source of uninterrupted music—fine music, that is. It was also fashionable to refer to FM's product at this time as "elevator music." Poignantly, these years that saw FM's fortunes at their lowest ebb also found its inventor's affairs reaching a precarious state. From the first stirrings of his creative genius, Armstrong had gotten involved with one patent litigation after another. Most of his patents had expired by 1950, and the press of legal fees, plus declining health, had caused him great despair. Early in 1954 he committed suicide, an act that provided a melancholy counterpoint to the depressed state of radio—all radio, AM and FM at the time. Had he lived, Edwin Howard Armstrong would have been astounded at FM's incredible growth.

From the time of Armstrong's tragic end, it took almost a decade for the great FM leap to begin. The medium wasn't exactly standing still before then, because there was steady expansion starting in the late 1950s. But by 1965, as the following table indicates, broadcasters were putting their money on FM:

DATE	AM AUTHORIZED	ON AIR	FM AUTHORIZED	ON AIR
January 1, 1965	4,077	4,009	1,468	1,270
January 1, 1966	4,129	4,049	1,657	1,446
January 1, 1967	4,190	4,121	1,865	1,643
January 1, 1968	4,249	4,156	2,004	1,753
January 1, 1969	4,300	4,237	2,114	1,938
January 1, 1970	4,344	4,269	2,651	2,476
January 1, 1971	4,383	4,323	2,795	2,636
January 1, 1972	4,411	4,355	2,971	2,783
January 1, 1973	4,431	4,382	3,162	2,965
January 1, 1974	4,448	4,395	3,360	3,135
January 1, 1975	4,477	4,432	3,617	3,353
January 1, 1976	4,513	4,463	3,752	3,571
January 1, 1977	4,536	4,497	3,969	3,743
January 1, 1978	4,569	4,513	4,130	3,972
January 1, 1979	4,599	4,549	4,310	4,089

—Source: *Broadcasting Cable Yearbook; 1980*

If there was any doubt that the broadcasting fraternity regarded the 1970s as the decade of the FM music box, the comparison of AM and FM station authorizations should put it to rest: while FM's were up by almost 40%, AM's had increased by only 6%.

Listeners obviously liked what they were hearing, as set sales sky-rocketed 20-fold between 1960 and 1980. The following table depicts that dramatic growth:

YEAR	SET SALES (EIA)	SETS IN USE (year end) (millions)
1980	42,147,000	350.0
1979	37,834,000	320.0
1978	41,300,000	300.0
1977	38,637,000	270.0
1976	27,956,000	240.0
1975	27,800,000	220.0
1974	33,900,000	190.0
1973	32,852,000	160.0
1972	35,417,000	135.0

YEAR	SET SALES (EIA)	SETS IN USE (year end) (millions)
1971	28,700,000	110.0
1970	24,280,000	93.0
1965	7,582,000	30.0
1960	1,994,000	6.5

—Source: Electronic Industries Association and
Radio Advertising Bureau

Nor was the dramatic rise of FM isolated. By 1970, except for a few markets, most of the country showed penetrations of over 50%. Those with penetrations 70% and over are listed in the following table:

MARKET	% PENETRATION
Akron, Ohio (2 county metro)	81.8
Atlanta (5 county metro)	71.0
Baltimore (5 county metro)	75.7
Bay City, Mich. (metro)	72.8
Beaumont-Port Arthur-Orange, Tex. (2 county metro)	70.6
Binghamton, N.Y.-Pa. (3 county metro)	76.3
Brevard County, Fla. (Cocoa county)	83.8
Buffalo, N.Y. (2 county metro)	70.9
Burlington, Vt. (Chittendon county)	73.8
Chicago, Ill.-N.W. Indiana (8 county area)	80.4
Cincinnati, Ohio-Ky.-Inc. (7 county metro)	71.1
Cleveland (4 county metro)	78.6
Columbus, Ohio (3 county metro)	72.9
Dayton, Ohio (4 county metro)	81.3
Des Moines, Iowa (metro)	73.3
Detroit (3 county metro)	81.1
Erie, Pa. (metro)	74.4
Evansville, Ind.-Ky. (3 county metro)	79.6
Grand Rapids, Mich. (2 county metro)	75.3
Greenville, S.C. (2 county metro)	72.8
Hamilton-Middletown, Ohio (metro)	74.9
Harrisburg, Pa. (3 county metro)	72.9
Houston (5 county metro)	73.3
Indianapolis (8 county metro)	73.3
Kansas City, M.-Kan. (6 county metro)	70.6
Lansing, Mich. (3 county metro)	70.2
Lawrence City, Mass.	71.7
Los Angeles (2 county area)	75.1

MARKET	% PENETRATION
Lowell City, Mass.	75.5
Madison, Wis. (metro)	74.1
Manchester City, N.H.	70.6
Milwaukee (4 county metro)	77.8
Muskegon-Muskegon Heights, Mich. (metro)	74.9
Norfolk-Portsmouth-Newport News Hampton, Va. (metro)	70.8
Philadelphia, Pa.-N.J. (8 country metro)	84.1
Phoenix (metro)	88.2
Rochester, N.Y. (Monroe county)	76.8
Sacramento, Calif. (3 county metro)	74.7
Saginaw-Bay City, Mich. (2 county metro)	77.8
San Bernardino-Riverside, Calif.	72.7
San Diego (metro)	72.1
Shreveport, La. (2 county metro)	72.6
South Bend, Ind. (2 county metro)	70.5
Steubenville-Weirton, Ohio-W.Va. (3 county metro)	78.4
Syracuse, N.Y. (3 county metro)	70.7
Toledo, Ohio-Mich. (3 county metro)	73.8
Topeka, Kan. (metro)	72.6
Utica-Rome, N.Y. (2 county metro)	70.5
Washington, D.C.-Maryland-Va. (7 county metro)	79.0
Wheeling, W.Va.-Ohio (3 county metro)	71.1
Wilmington, Del.-Md.-N.J. (3 county metro)	72.6
Youngstown-Warren, Ohio (2 county metro)	76.1

—Source: Pulse, Inc. *FM Penetration Study,*
1969

By 1980, FM had achieved a 95% penetration of U.S. households.

What caused this startling turn to FM? Why, in the face of AM radio's ability to prove its resilience, its ability to thrive in the television age—especially the Top 40's—did this happen? Wasn't it AM radio where the nation had turned for the "new" music of Elvis and the Beatles and Chubby Checker?

One of the reasons was economic. As the following table indicates, families with incomes of $10,000 or more in 1956 made up only 8% of the nation's population. By 1960, the number had almost doubled, and by 1970, over one-half of all families were in the five-figure circle.

Much of the economic fuel that helped propel the rock and roll/Top 40 engine was at work in the rise of FM. Lower-middle and middle class youth with money to spend continued to contribute to the expansion of interest in popular music, and hence the furtherance of the record-collecting—which by now had extended beyond the boundaries of a mere hobby. If a collecting fever gripped rock and roll fans, it was a phobia that accompanied the building of a record collection triggered by the rise of FM.

FAMILY INCOME

PERCENT DISTRIBUTION BY INCOME LEVEL

YEAR	NUMBER (1,000)	UNDER $3000	$3,000 TO $4,999	$5,000 TO $6,999	$7,000 TO $9,999	$10,000 TO $11,999	$12,000 TO $14,999	$15,000 AND OVER
	1	2	3	4	5	6	7	8
1970	51,948	8.9	10.3	11.8	19.9	12.7	14.1	22.3
1969	51,237	9.3	10.7	12.3	21.7	13.0	13.7	19.3
1968	50,510	10.3	12.1	14.5	23.4	12.5	12.4	14.7
1967	49,834	12.6	12.9	16.2	24.4	11.9	10.7	11.4
1966	49,065	14.1	13.7	17.7	24.6	11.5	9.3	9.3
1965	48,279	16.1	15.6	18.8	24.2	10.1	7.6	7.6
1964	47,835	17.6	17.0	19.8	23.2	9.5	6.9	6.3
1963	47,436	18.5	17.7	21.3	22.5	8.3	6.2	5.4
1962	46,998	19.9	19.1	22.4	21.0	7.6	5.3	4.9
1961	46,341	21.4	19.9	21.9	20.7	6.6	4.6	4.6
1960	45,456	21.7	20.3	23.7	20.0	6.2	4.4	3.7
1959	45,111	22.7	21.8	24.2	18.9	5.4	3.7	3.1
1958	44,232	24.1	24.6	24.4	16.8	4.7	2.9	2.4
1957	43,696	24.5	25.9	24.8	16.4	4.0	2.5	1.9
1956	43,497	25.6	27.4	23.5	15.6	3.5	2.5	2.0

—Source: *Historical Statistics of the U.S.*, U.S. Department of Commerce, Bureau of Census, 1975.

Stereo had made its debut around 1960, and with it came an entirely new ball game. Suddenly the 45 rpm recording seemed ancient alongside a stereo long-playing album containing four to seven selections per side. Recordings cut by the two-channel process and played on stereo equipment created a thrilling new listening experience. Sound became an end in and of itself. Ears that grew accustomed to stereo would henceforth not be satisfied with recordings cut for monophonic reproduction. Artists, no longer constricted by the two-and three-minute straight-jacket of 45s, could stretch out to performances of 15 minutes or more.

Nor was the stereo phenomenon, begun in the early 1960s, entirely the province of youth. Parents, pestered to buy stereo sets or components, themselves soon discovered the enhancement of sound afforded by two-channel reproduction. They in turn started long-playing album collections of their own. It is interesting to note that in 1961, two years after stereo had proven itself, the top five selling long-playing albums included two original cast packages (*Camelot* and *The Sound of Music*) and a film soundtrack of (*Never on Sunday*). Elvis Presley had to be satisfied with seventh place (*G.I. Blues*), and only one other rock group, The Platters

(*Encore of Golden Hits*) showed up in the first 25. With stereo rigs, of course, came FM receivers as standard features. No longer were there references to "radio-phonograph combinations." The "in" thing was a *sound system;* it was a sure sign of middle class chic in the American home of the early 1960s.

Another major influence contributing to FM proliferation was its availability for counter-programming. By the early 1960s, Top 40 imitators had multiplied like rabbits up and down the dial. Unfortunately, most of them were wretched, ersatz copies. Owners, not understanding the interior of the *real* Top 40 station in the first place, and unwilling to make the financial commitment if they did, unleashed their crude imitations on the airwaves. Hiring low-paid announcers and incorporating all manner of dreadful sound-effects, they literally drove many listeners away—to FM. The highly professional Top 40's of course weathered the onslaught of the shabby copycats and later adjusted to the realities of FM. Starting with its wobbly, uncertain status, FM was perceived as the "less-commercials band" on the dial. When it became a viable advertising medium, enlightened operators refused to let success spoil it and instituted rigid policies limiting the number of spot announcements per hour. (We shall presently pursue the matter of formats in detail.)

FM also got a helping hand from Washington in 1968 when the Federal Communications Commissions issued regulations requiring separate programming for AM and FM in the first 50 markets. What looked at the time like another specimen of bureaucratic meddling to plague broadcasters turned out to be a blessing in disguise. Operators, thus prodded, were that much further along with separate FM identities when the medium "took off" in the 1970s.

And take off FM did. Success stories had become commonplace by the late 1970s. The leading indicators (audience growth and earnings) were so positive that, had such forecasts been made 10 or 15 years earlier, they would have been considered the ravings of a madman. Conditioned by the medium's first uncertain years, industry forecasters had traditionally approached FM's future with caution. For example, when a 1963 Harvard University study predicted FM passing AM by 1975, Michael Hastings, President of WBCN-FM, Boston, recalling typical reaction at the time, declared: "I was the idiot of my class. Everybody told me this was the best way of going broke . . . In 1963, we were the laughing stock of the industry."[2] But as everyone knows, there's nothing funny about money, and those with designs on buying an FM station, were advised to please bring plenty of it. In 1979, KBPI-FM, Denver, was sold for the record price of $6.7 million. The top price paid for an FM outlet (KBRE, Houston) just four years earlier was $2.5 million. In 1978 alone, 16 stations sold for over $1 million each. The following table, showing representative re-sale prices of FM stations when they changed hands in the 1970s, left no doubt that FM was a box office smash:

STATION AND LOCATION	PREVIOUS PURCHASE PRICE	YEAR	RE-SALE PURCHASE PRICE	YEAR
WLYF-FM, Miami (Formerly WWPB-FM)	$ 325,000	1970	$6,060,000	1978
KOAX-FM, Dallas	1,700,000	1976	7,000,000	1980
WTAN (AM & FM Combo), Clearwater, Fla.	750,00	1976	3,700,750	1980
WEZW-FM, Wauwatosa Wisconsin (Milwaukee Suburb)	170,000	1971	3,000,000	1978
WLAK-FM, Chicago	400,000	1970	4,200,00 (12,250,000– new price tag)	1978 1981
WMOH-AM & WYCH-FM (Combo), Hamilton, Ohio	550,000	1975	600,00 for WYCH-FM	1979

—Source: Ted Hepburn Co.

The message of set sales, penetration and station selling prices was loud and clear: FM had finally arrived.

By 1980 it was not unusual for FM listening to exceed AM's in many markets. Arbitron, using its Spring, 1980 "sweep" data, found FM grabbing 51.4% of the audience in its first ten radio markets. The following table indicates FM's audience in relation to AM's shares in the Top Ten:

MARKET	TOTAL NO. STATIONS	NO. OF FM STATIONS	SHARE	
			FM	AM
New York	47	24	48.0	43.8
Los Angeles	45	22	48.1	43.4
Chicago	34	20	50.8	42.3
Philadelphia	24	13	53.3	36.1
San Francisco	44	27	47.0	44.0
Detroit	25	16	57.0	30.2
Boston	30	13	40.4	47.1
Washington, DC	30	16	60.8	29.0
Dallas-Ft. Worth	27	15	63.7	30.1
Pittsburgh	30	15	44.6	49.1
Average	34	18	51.4	39.5

—Source: Spring, 1980 Arbitron Radio Survey
Metro Persons 12+ Mon–Sun 6AM–MID

The significant rise in FM acceptance has cut across all age groups. In its continuing national studies of trends, Statistical Research, Inc. (RADAR) found FM listening up dramatically since 1973, in all time periods, among all demographic groups.

With all the foregoing evidence of FM's burgeoning good fortune, there was never any question its success was spelled M-U-S-I-C. Historically, everyone had always perceived it as the music side of the radio band. Yet, after nearly two post-War decades, FM had not shed the "fine music" tag. But in 1967, sparks started flying from a San Francisco FM station that would ultimately change that image. Oddly, the nature of this new development in musical radio—the first one since Todd Storz's invention—bore several uncanny resemblances to the way Top 40 started on AM radio almost 15 years earlier: both were by-products of dazzling bursts of insight on the part of several persons; both were launched by non-Establishment types; and both were ultimately accepted as fit for membership in the family of established, big time media.

There was also a connecting link between Top 40 radio and the new FM muscial concept. His name was Tom Donahue, an announcer at KYA, the San Francisco "Boss Radio" station in the Golden Gate City. Donahue had resigned his disc jockey job at KYA, rebelling at such assignments as broadcasting from a teenage fair. The unemployed Donahue had already adopted what was euphemistically referred to as an "alternate life style." (San Francisco, by 1967 home of the Haight-Asbury District, had become the symbol for hippies, Vietnam War protestors and the drug culture). How FM was instrumental in ushering in a new concept of musical radio does not exactly fit your standard American Research and Development plan. Donahue's wife described in *Rolling Stone* what took place:

> Tom and I were sitting around with our Telegraph Hill neighbors, smashed on his birthday, playing records for each other: The Doors, Judy Collins, all kinds of records no one played on the radio. Tom said, "Do you realize that we sit here every night and smoke dope and play records for each other? I wonder why nobody's done this on radio? . . . I don't know what made him think of calling FM stations, which at the time were inconsequential. I guess he figured FM people were the only people dumb enough to do it. He called around until he found a station in San Francisco that had its phone disconnected, and that, my friends was KMPX, formerly jazz station KHIP.[3]

KMPX was housed in the basement of a warehouse, and thus arrived the term *underground radio*. KMPX's programming appeal to the San Francisco sub-culture was in tune musically and emotionally with its listeners and consequencly laid the groundwork for the "target audience" concept that was to become standard trade jargon in the 1970s. Tom Donahue portrayed the format as embracing

FM SHARE OF ALL RADIO LISTENING
1973–1980 LEVELS AND TREND

	Persons 12+			Adults			Persons 35+			Persons 18–34			Teens		
	1973	1980	Percent Change	1973	1980	Percent Change	1973	1980	Percent Change	1973	1980	Percent Change	1973	1980	Percent Change
M–F															
24 hr. day	27	57	+111%	28	55	+ 96%	24	44	+ 83%	34	68	+100%	23	74	+222%
6A–M	28	57	+104	28	55	+ 96	25	44	+ 76	34	68	+100	23	74	+222
6A–10A	21	48	+129	21	46	+119	18	37	+106	26	60	+131	18	67	+272
10A–3P	31	59	+ 90	31	58	+ 87	27	48	+ 78	36	69	+ 92	26	76	+192
3P–7P	29	60	+107	30	58	+ 93	28	49	+ 75	33	69	+109	22	75	+241
7P–M	33	64	+ 94	35	61	+ 74	29	47	+ 62	42	74	+ 76	27	76	+181
Weekend															
24 hr. day	30	59	+ 97	31	56	+ 81	28	46	+ 64	35	70	+100	26	73	+181
6A–M	30	58	+ 93	31	56	+ 81	29	46	+ 59	34	70	+106	26	73	+181
6A–10A	22	47	+114	22	45	+105	20	38	+ 90	26	61	+135	21	66	+214
10A–3P	31	59	+ 90	32	57	+ 78	31	48	+ 55	33	70	+112	28	72	+157
3P–7P	33	61	+ 85	34	59	+ 74	33	51	+ 55	36	70	+ 94	28	74	+164
7P–M	34	65	+ 91	37	63	+ 70	32	49	+ 53	42	76	+ 81	26	76	+192
M–S															
24 hr. day	28	57	+104	29	55	+ 90	25	45	+ 80	34	68	+100	24	74	+208
6A–M	28	57	+104	29	55	+ 90	26	45	+ 73	34	68	+100	24	73	+204
6A–10A	21	48	+129	21	46	+119	19	37	+ 95	26	61	+135	19	67	+253
10A–3P	31	59	+ 90	31	58	+ 87	29	48	+ 66	35	70	+100	27	74	+174
3P–7P	30	61	+103	31	59	+ 90	29	49	+ 69	34	69	+103	23	75	+226
7P–M	33	64	+ 94	35	61	+ 74	30	48	+ 60	42	75	+ 79	26	76	+192

—Sources: 1973—RADAR 9, Spring 1973
1980—RADAR 22, Spring/Fall, 1980
Statistical Research, Inc.

the best of today's rock and roll, folk, traditional and city blues, raga, electronic music, and some jazz and classical selections. I believe that music should not be treated as a group of objects to be sorted out like eggs with each category kept rigidly apart from the others . . .[4]

The kind of radio Donahue was describing, with its music mix, was by Donahue's own admission, "old time" radio. As the format evolved, its concentration on rock led to a gradual phasing out of the word, "underground," and the introduction of the label, *progressive rock.* (The term, "rock and roll" by this time had become obsolete; the handle for that particular music was now simply, "rock"). Whatever its name, Donahue's new FM approach on KMPX was enormously successful. In 1968, a policy difference with ownership led to a strike and the eventual dismantling of Donahue's staff and format. That he was on to something, however, was evident. In 1968, he was hired by the important Metromedia Group to program the chain's KSAN-FM in San Francisco and KMET-FM in Los Angeles.

Metromedia's imprimatur on progressive rock sent signals through the broadcasting world that FM should be recognized as bona fide radio and could stand on its own by carving out carefully identified program niches. Slowly at first, with certain hours set aside, then gradually whole day parts, and finally the entire day, progressive rock was putting life into the FM band. A *Billboard* survey in 1968 carrying the heading, "Progressive Rock Gives Life to Dead-Weight FM Radio Stations," revealed overwhelmingly positive audience reaction from such disparate markets as Salt Lake City (KLUB-FM), Dallas (McLendon's KNUS-FM), and Cincinnati (WEBN-FM). At WHFM-FM, Rochester, mail and phone response prompted the station to play progressive rock on a 24-hour basis, six months ahead of schedule. WEFM-FM, Winchester, Virginia reported after trying several formats, progressive rock was "the answer," with revenue up 100%.[5]

As progressive rock continued to sweep across the FM dial during the late 1960s and early 1970s, it did not follow the circumscribed music strictures for which Top 40 was renowned. There were no "policy books" to go by in this new music free form. Some stations stuck to the original Donahue eclectic approach. (One school of programmers held that even Greek, Mexican or country music was OK for the progressive rock environment, so long as it was "outstanding".) Others said the format should include only rock and rhythm and blues. Still others maintained it was necessary to include with the *de rigueur* rock, some conventional pops and oldies offered on AM stations—although purists scoffed at this notion.

Progressive rock never did settle into one crystal-clear, easy-to-nail-down music groove. Its chief characteristics that might be called universal included: playing selections mostly from albums to capitalize on stereo sound; featuring new music without regard to record sales; running cuts regardless of length (some ran 15 minutes or more*); severely restricting the number of commercials; and de-emphasizing the disc jockey, allowing limited talk between the musical selections. George Duncan, general manager of WNEW-FM, New York, a Metromedia outlet which had grabbed the progressive rock format when WOR-FM abandoned it after a short run, pointed out the changing nature of popular music, using the progressive rock as an example. Duncan observed that WNEW-FM's playlist included only two hits from *Billboard's* "Hot 100" in the station's initital progressive phase, but two years later, WNEW-FM was playing 68 of the top 100. According to Duncan, the "program philosophy had not changed, but kinds of songs that made the charts had."[6]

Progressive rock on FM was certainly the big radio story of 1968. Each week the trade press reported additional stations switching to what they hoped would be the next big musical trend. Lest operators get any ideas that here was a low-cost kind of boutique "free-form" radio, *Billboard* cautioned the industry to bear in mind,

> a progressive rock radio station has to be better than an ordinary radio station. The reason is: Its listeners, so far, are above the common breed— they're doctors, lawyers, college students, young adults who are bored with regular radio, ex-classical music fans . . . This has been strongly pictured by the flow of letters to progressive rock stations . . . One of the key elements is taste.[7]

Compared to doctrinaire, tight-playlist Top 40 AM radio, progressive rock *was* free form. And therein lay much of its appeal. Undoubtedly the infinite musical possibilities of frequency modulation would have been "discovered" sooner or later, but progressive rock was the catalyst in the FM upheaval. Just as Top 40 induced listening not only to its own innovative offerings, but to *all* AM radio at the time, so progressive rock awakened interest in the *entire* FM spectrum. Adventuresome managements, seeing the excitement one specific FM musical approach had stirred, tried other avenues, including not only music but some of the conventional fare AM radio had relied on since its beginnings. America's fascination with radio was heightened now that there were two dials to explore. Sales of FM receivers that had jumped from 1.9 million sets in 1960 to 24.3 million a decade later was evidence for even the most skeptical partisans who had waited so long for FM to succeed. The ubiquitous transistor radio that

---

* Interestingly, around this time, progressive rock was changing the nature of some of the music on AM pop stations. When lengthy cuts such as Richard Harris's "McArthur Park," The Doors long version of "Light My Fire," and the Temptations "Cloud Nine" became hits, they could not be ignored by AM stations which claimed to play the hits. Top 40 hit radio, of course, thrived on short cuts, and the longer-song development was not taken lightly.

had proven such a boon to AM's rebirth had come on the scene by the mid-1960s in the form of AM/FM portable receivers. (In 1968, AM/FM portable transistor sets were retailing as low as $14.98 and $19.98.)

AM radio which had seemed an impregnable pop music fortress started showing noticeable cracks in the late 1960s. FM radio, which had always been perceived as a music medium—albeit with that "fine music" millstone hung around its neck—was demonstrating how wide a swath American popular music could cut. The music wars were on. AM-FM competition livened up to open the 1970s as the struggle intensified between stations on opposite parts of the dial, and between stations on the same band. Programmers were exploring "target" audiences, attempting to appeal to their specific desires. The idea was to cater to the myriad music tastes of a diversified population that had not only grown in number, but also in its awareness that variety is indeed the spice of life. Broadcasters began adding new expressions such as "MOR" and "AOR" to their trade lingo, while re-working their ideas of constituted beautiful music or oldies—or even POPULAR MUSIC itself. Everybody in broadcasting, it seemed, was in search of a *format*.

The format. It was a hold-over word from old time radio to describe the outline or sequence of elements for an individual show. Every program required a format, whether it was formally written on paper or not. For network radio shows, the format came before the script. In the case of a comedy-variety half-hour, for example, a format was blocked out to indicate the number of sketches and routines featuring the star, how many musical selections and commercials and where each was to appear in the script. Thus, in the *Baker's Broadcast,* starring Joe Penner, Ozzie Nelson and Harriet Hilliard, the format might appear as follows:

Theme
Show Open—Ben Grauer
Ozzie Nelson Intro
Music—selection by orchestra
Joe Penner skit
Commercial
Music—Ozzie & Harriet duet
Music—Ozzie vocal
Joe Penner skit
Commercial
Music—Ozzie & Harriet duet
Commercial
Ozzie Nelson—closing remarks
Public Service Announcement—Ben Grauer
Show close—Ben Grauer

For a routine quarter-hour of pop music on a local station, there was a format; for a five-minute newscast, there had to be a format. When Top

40 burst forth on the dial, we observed the format employed to structure the *entire* output of the broadcast day. Indeed, Top 40 outlets were often demeaningly referred to by envious competitors as "format stations." Eventually, every single station on the air, AM and FM, would have a format, and music formats would far out-number all other kinds.

If Top 40 aroused format awareness, FM raised musical radio's format consciousness. Broadcasting's pre-occupation—its obsession, really—with formats in the 1970s worked to an advantage that listeners never dreamed possible only a few years earlier. Musical format choices were as available as cereal brands on the grocery shelf. By the end of the decade, every city and town in the country had access to at least a half-dozen music formats. Industry-wide, it was possible for a station to choose from a smorgasbord totaling 133, of which all but six could lay claim to being "popular" music in one respect or another. Devising formats became the basis for an industry in itself, as syndicators scrambled for musical niches to fill. Musical "trendies" were in their glory as they added new terms to the trade jargon. We shall attempt nothing of the sort, except to individualize the major music format classifications generally accepted in the industry. However, before we embark on that task, it is necessary to trace briefly the format phenomenon.

Prior to the early 1970s, the most-asked musical question was, "What kind of music do you play?", not "What is your format?" Music stations were perceived (and labeled) Top 40 or middle-of-the-road (MOR), or in an alternate categorization, "rockers" and "non-rockers," since Top 40 had become synonymous with rock and roll. In order to delineate further musical differences among stations, The Katz Agency, a station representative firm, in 1964 issued a "Radio Field Guide." Katz's Guide laid out lines of demarcation attempting to classify music stations on a spectrum, ranging from Top 40 to the most conservative "quality music" approach. Although there was nothing official about the Katz Guide, it did provide a fairly good idea of how musical radio was perceived at the time.

Another endeavor that sought to nail down music format descriptions had wider industry distribution than Katz's Guide, but noble (and scholarly) as that effort was, the confusion continued. Standard Rate and Data Service, a publication that issues updated separate books monthly for radio and television stations, magazines and newspapers, for a number of years carried a music Glossary in the front of the radio book. Prepared by two Northwestern University professors, SRDS's Glossary and Chart also included a chart pigeonholding music types. (See Appendix, page 375). Among SRDS's interpretations were these:

Popular Music

Music considered to be primarily of entertainment value to a relatively large general public. Commercial success is not necessary. Under the broad heading, Popular Music, fall these categories:

Current Hits. Popular music regardless of type which are currently commercially successful. Other terms include "Top 20," "Top 40," "Top Hits" and "Pop Hits."

Trend Music. Popular music that fits technically into one of the other categories, but because of its association with a particular trend, fad or era is classed by itself. This does not apply to current trends (see above). *Examples:* "Roaring Twenties Music," "Cha-Cha," "Barbershop."

General Popular Music. Popular music which is not suitably classed as "Rock," "Folk," "Country and Western," "Jazz because it contains a mixture of several different styles.[8]

By the mid-1970s, SRDS had sensibly given up definitions, and began the practice of listing only terms used to describe formats. (See Appendix on page 376). SRDS's "Descriptive Terms/Music and Format" delineation became the ultimate format listing; it demonstrates the proliferation that has taken place in musical radio.

In spite of hybrids and cross-pollinations, a sort of loose consensus within the radio, syndication and recording industries has existed since the late 1970s. Thus, it is possible to refine principal format-types under the following classifications:

MOSTLY FM

Beautiful Music. Primarily an instrumental form, characterized by lush arrangements of the "standard" repertoire and contemporary hits, with heavy emphasis on strings. It draws from the most catholic sources because of its need to feature songs that have a predominant melody. Considered by programmers the ideal background music, this format is comfortable with compatible arrangements of material from George Gershwin and Jerome Kern to a Doobie Brothers hit. *Typical artists:* 101 Strings, Frank Chacksfield, Anita Kerr, Mantovani, Andre Kostelanetz and Percy Faith. Beautiful Music was one of the first formats to evolve in the effort to counter-program against progressive rock. Its ability to survive fads has been excellent; however, a scarcity of new product began showing up in the late 1970s as record companies curtailed releases that fit this format. (The recording industry, a highly promotional business, has traditionally tended to favor the "hot" pop artists of the moment.) Syndicators and the more affluent station users, seeking to replenish their inventories, have had to turn to orchestras in England, France and Canada for customized renditions, many costing as much as $1000 per selection.

Easy Listening. A somewhat more hip version of beautiful music. This format highlights contemporary popular music which has eliminated such inconsonant elements as overdone guitar or percussion punctuation. Easy Listening can be all instrumental, or it can include a blending of instrumentals and vocals. It is a more foreground music and less predictable than Beautiful Music. The Easy Listening playlist could range from cover versions of hits such as Billy Joel's "Just the Way You Are," Lynn Anderson's "Rose Garden" and Paul Simon's "Kodachrome" to the movie soundtrack single, "Ballad of Easy Rider." In addition to removing any harsh ingredients that might have characterized originals, Easy Listening cover arrangements dig out the melody. *Typical artists:* Bert Kaempfert, Lalo Schifrin, Ferrante and Teicher, Ray Conniff, Vic Damone, Perry Como and The Carpenters.

Album Oriented Rock More commonly known by its trade initials, AOR. A complete child of FM, this format began there and has stayed there. It is the metamorphosed progressive rock format that started life as underground radio. Characterized by heavy amplification, hard guitar instrumentation and loud vocal stylings, AOR stresses group sounds, although some vocalists qualify. Following in its progressive rock ancestral tradition, AOR places great emphasis on music, usually down-playing disc jockey involvement in the format. Some AOR stations, however, have fashioned modified versions allowing deejays a higher degree of participation. When this occurs, such personalities must have sharply defined personas, compatible with AOR's aggressive music, and suitable for exploitation in outside promotions that appeal to the station's youthful audience. *Typical artists:* Led Zeppelin, Molly Hatchet, Pat Benatar, ZZ Top and Leonard Skynyrd. By the late 1970s, a further synthesis of AOR began taking place in the form of an avant-garde rock. It did not fit tidily into the AOR bag, so the depiction progressive rock was dusted off and pressed into service once more. The "new" Progressive Rock is marked by a greater willingness to experiment with new sounds and artists. This music is often less inclined to feature heavy guitar amplification. It might also be called "adult free form rock." Here seemed to be the easiest pigeon hole in which to place Punk and New Wave Rock.

MOSTLY AM

Middle-of-the-Road. Usually steamlined to MOR. This designation sprang up as a code word used by sales departments of stations competing with Top 40s in that format's heyday. With the format proliferation of the 1970s, it became apparent there wasn't much of a road left to be in the middle of. Nevertheless, even though MOR became an anachronism by 1980, it is retained in the format lexicon, if for no other reason than to understand the forms that have replaced it. (See below). The basic MOR songbook is distinguished more by its artists than by the songs they sing since it is primarily vocal. MOR music is in a traditional mode of high-lighting soft standards folded into conservative orchestrations. *Typical artists:* Tony Bennett, Frank Sinatra, Robert Goulet, Jerry Vale, Steve Lawrence/Eydie Gorme, Barbra Streisand and Herb Alpert.

Adult/Contemporary and Pop/Adult*. Often used inter-changeably, these are difficult terms to pin down. When FM moved in on AM's music turf, it became obvious that the older medium had to make adjustments. In the nation's largest cities, select stations dropped all popular music and turned to News or News/Talk. But for the vast majority of AM'ers, these two highly specialized (and expensive) formats were impractical. Many old-line AM stations, including some former Top 40 leaders, then switched to an amalgam of pop music and news/sports/information. Not being able to compete with FM's music image, such AM operations, knowing they still had to maintain a music base, adopted the term *Pop/Adult* to describe what they did. Generally, the more this format concentrated on news and information, the more likely it would be called *Pop/Adult*. The more an avowed adult-appeal station played up its music, the more likely it could be considered *Adult/Contemporary*. It is particularized as soft, modern popular music, featuring more youthful lyrics than Easy Listening, minus guitar and percussive harshness. *Typical artists:* James Taylor, Melissa Manchester, Neil Diamond and Barry Manilow.

BOTH AM & FM

Country. Frequently (and incorrectly) called Country and Western. The tacking on of "Western" makes the designation a misnomer. Western music should properly be reserved for the songbooks of Gene Autry, Roy Rogers and Pat Buttram. *Country* is actually two musical forms: The first is Urban Country, country lyrics set to popular contemporary arrangements; the other is the root form. Traditional Country features twangy guitars and "lyin'-dyin'-cryin' " lyrics. Both types derive from a synethesis of bluegrass and what was once called hill billy. Purists, in describing the dichotomy, decry the dilution of traditional country music by elaborate orchestrations and other "modern" trappings. They point out that in so doing, Country has "crossed-over" to the pop mainstream, and therefore is no longer worthy to be called "Country"—a matter to which we shall give

---

* Some in the industry do not accept this delineation, and when we come to charting format popularity, we shall find it necessary to accept *Adult/Contemporary* as the name of this format.

detailed treatment in Chapter 16. In spite of this conflict, Country is the only body of popular music since 1955 that has been able to span the generation gap. *Typical Urban Traditional artists:* Ronnie Milsap, Crystal Gale, Dolly Parton and George Jones. *Typical Traditional Country artists:* Mel Tillis, Merle Haggard and Emmy Lou Harris.

Black. Once called "race music" and later "rhythm and blues," the black music format often varies from city to city. In all cases, however, it does reflect a jazz and disco influence. This format, an outgrowth of Motown-Memphis-Philadelphia soul music, is also known as Contemporary Urban or Popular Urban. The raised consciousness of black culture, a by-product of the Civil Rights movement of the 1950s and 1960s, has seen a decided veering-away on black stations of stereotyped, jive-talking disc jockeys who pretty much programmed music according to their personal tastes. Nowhere is the new black format better demonstrated than in New York, where WBLS spent most of 1980 on top of the rating heap. *Typical artists:* Teddy Pendergrass, Kool and the Gang, and Earth, Wind and Fire.

Disco. The format that capitalized on the disco craze. Disco, at its apogee, was a phenomenon around which erupted an entire body of cultural icons. Essentially a dance music, disco served as a point of departure for special night club franchises and clothing designs—and, of course, radio formats. The hype that accompanied disco's frenzied invasion of the entertainment scene was as insistent as the music's heavy amplification. Estimated by the *New York Times* to be a $4 billion business in early 1979, the fad and format had fizzled out by mid-1980. Recognized by the pounding beat of its bass drum punctuations and its swirling orchestrations, disco's layered sound began spewing out of radio speakers around 1975. From coast to coast, AM and FM operators, demonstrating the zeal a new pop music form is always capable of inspiring, switched to disco. Some 100 stations were estimated to be disco-formatted while the craze was at its peak. Artists with such exotic names as Chic, Sylvester, Evelyn Champagne, Voyage, and Dr. Buzzard's Original Savannah Band helped to enhance the touch of contrived decadence that the fad affected. Many broadcasters were put off by the music's overtones of drugs and homosexuality. Nevertheless, disco's influence was reflected in 1979's list of number-one singles: for 26 weeks of the 52, a disco tune was on top. All of a sudden, everybody looked up and there was a disco station in first place in America's largest market—and an FM station at that. WKTU-FM. New York, had roared past some of the most vaunted call letters in broadcasting and stayed there through most of 1979. After disco-mania simmered down, WBLS-FM (see above) topped WKTU in Arbitron's October–November 1979 survey and maintained a slight edge until September 1980 when WKTU, by de-emphasizing disco and moving closer to the urban popular sound, was back on top again. When WKTU's owners decided to offer the station for sale early in 1981, with a price tag of $15.5 million, hardly anyone in the trade blinked an eye.

Top 40. In a real sense, this format's validity had been diminishing since the FM-sparked format expolosion of the mid-1970s. Yet, a goodly number of stations clung to the belief it was possible to continue the spirit—if not the letter—of the venerable Top 40 concept and maintain it as a viable format. The die-hards circumscribed a broad-appeal rock, avoided the extremes of AOR, featured tunes containing young-adult-oriented lyrics set to non-offensive musical production,—and said, "See-Top 40 lives!" Record sales, as in the old Top 40 rulebook, constituted the major research for their playlists. *Typical artists:* Doobie Brothers, Steely Dan, Paul McCartney and Wings. Late in 1980, the influential trade paper *Radio and Records* interred its Top 40 department and announced a replacement that it claimed more accurately represented a format shaped by playing only the hits. In suggesting the designation, "Contemporary Hit Radio," the publication reminded hit-oriented stations,

> Top 40 radio has changed so dramatically in the past few years that the term "Top 40" doesn't say enough about what your station's format is. Contemporary Hit Radio does. Your station plays the hits, not the Top 40 hits necessarily, but the hits . . . Sales are still relatively important to most stations but those figures are no longer the sole determining factor in playlist design. Research in all its many forms has found new fans within the contemporary radio community . . . If disco music is happening, then your station should recognize that. If new wave is a factor, your station might play the hit new wave product . . .[9]

Cautious managements and bandwagon jumpers alike watch format performances very carefully. Format A's meteoric rise in Market Z may or may not be significant. Trends in musical radio follow no predictable pattern. "Stay alert!" is from page one of the survival manual. So crucial is the format, one publisher prints a "Shopping Guide" twice yearly. Issued by the popular newsletter, *Inside Radio,* the Guide offers national perspectives to its readers (mostly top management) possibly contemplating format changes. The following sampler was offered early in 1981:

> *Fusion-Rock*—Blend of album rock, singles . . . tough format to copy. One false move and its album rock or Top 40.
>
> *Country*—Will work as it always has in south-west and west and at WHN's and WMAQ's where management successfully read its nuances . . . Urban Country will fail . . . It's disco with hats and boots.
>
> *Adult Contemporary*—Benefits from death of traditional rock format as listeners grow older. Emphasis must be on mainstream music . . .
>
> *Album Rock*—Suffering from lack of real rock musical trends . . .
>
> *Rock*—(Sometimes called Top 40, 30, or 20). It's on its deathbed . . .

Beautiful Music—There will always be a market for this format . . .But stay away from it if two other stations . . . are already doing it.

Oldies—No real indications that U.S. population is getting nostalgic for oldies of fifties, sixties, or seventies.

Big Band—Excellent for stations desperately in need of alternative programming.[10]

Were *Radio and Records* and *Inside Radio* merely engaging in esoteric verbal gymnastics? Not at all. The game of the format name is a deadly serious matter. With over 8000 stations engaged in musical radio, each trying to carve out a piece of turf, formats have become as blurred as their names. Middlemen—trade papers, news letters, syndicators, consultants, rating services—have as many conflicting ideas on formats as do the stations they serve. The nearest the industry comes to have an arbiter for format descriptions is Arbitron. This is the rating service that overwhelmingly dominates radio research. Although several other firms compete in this vital area, it is Arbitron that carries the authority to make it the recognized "numbers ruler of the airwaves." Arbitron's listing, from which stations must choose one that describes their format best, includes 16 generic species:

Beaut. Music/Easy List.	Big Bands/Oldies
Contemporary Top 40	Non/Commercial
Contemporary Rock	Classical
MOR/Personality	Country
Religious/Gospel	Disco
Black/Soul	Jazz
Hispanic	AOR
News/Talk/Info	R & B

As for listeners, they couldn't care less. When it comes to musical radio, they do not listen to formats, or to stations—they tune in their *favorite music.* To stations that play what listeners like most obviously must accrue the most benefits. America's tastes in popular music, even though catered to in such an incredible variety—compared to the 1930s when one body of music prevailed—are still capable of being gauged. The sole means of learning which kinds are most preferred at any given time, of course, must come through ratings. (We shall give ratings closer scrutiny in Chapter 18.) Since ratings measure the relative popularity of stations, the formats of these station become the standard by which tastes are evaluated. To quantify pop music popularity, rating data for stations using the same (or similar) formats in a given number of markets are combined and a composite picture derived. Simmons Market Research Bureau has done such studies on a national basis. The following table shows the relative strength of formats by age and sex nationally in 1980:

	18+ %	18–24 %	25–34 %	35–44 %	45–54 %	55+ %
1980 **SEX/AGE COMPOSITION OF AUDIENCE** **BY RADIO FORMATS**						
Men						
Adult Contemporary	100.0	20.0	30.1	17.8	14.8	17.3
All News	100.0	12.3	18.2	17.7	25.1	26.7
AOR/Progressive	100.0	43.6	35.6	11.5	6.4	2.9
Beautiful Music	100.0	10.5	16.9	19.9	21.5	31.2
Black	100.0	28.5	21.7	21.3	8.7	19.8
Classical	100.0	7.6	24.2	22.9	23.1	22.2
Contemporary/Disco	100.0	30.2	31.2	18.3	10.8	9.5
Country	100.0	14.7	26.6	22.3	16.3	20.1
Golden Oldies	100.0	17.1	35.6	25.0	7.4	14.9
Middle of The Road	100.0	16.1	21.9	18.5	18.9	24.6
Religious	100.0	14.6	16.8	15.1	19.5	34.0
Soft Rock	100.0	35.9	27.3	25.6	4.0	7.2
Talk	100.0	13.0	16.6	21.1	20.8	28.5
	18+ %	18–24 %	25–34 %	35–44 %	45–54 %	55+ %
Women						
Adult Contemporary	100.0	22.2	27.9	16.5	13.6	19.8
All News	100.0	7.3	18.8	13.7	22.5	37.7
AOR/Progressive	100.0	46.0	25.0	12.0	8.6	8.4
Beautiful Music	100.0	13.4	19.5	15.9	20.9	30.3
Black	100.0	35.6	29.6	12.4	7.3	15.1
Classical	100.0	16.7	19.6	13.4	28.2	22.1
Contemporary/Disco	100.0	29.6	30.6	18.8	9.7	11.3
Country	100.0	14.3	21.5	18.6	17.2	28.4
Golden Oldies	100.0	26.3	33.6	12.4	13.9	13.8
Middle of The Road	100.0	12.6	18.8	18.0	17.3	33.3
Religious	100.0	11.3	22.8	12.9	12.1	40.9
Soft Rock	100.0	35.7	37.5	17.8	4.0	5.0
Talk	100.0	8.3	11.3	13.3	18.7	48.4

—Source: 1980 *Media & Markets,* Simmons Market Research Bureau, Inc.

McGavern-Guild Radio, a national sales representative for radio stations using Arbitron audience estimates, has tracked formats regularly in the Top 25 markets. The firm's research department has refined its data to include preferences for day parts by age and sex. In the accompanying table preferences are shown for all persons 12+:

TOTAL PERSONS 12 + MON–SUN 6A–MID TOP 25 MARKETS
THE MCGAVREN GUILD FORMAT STUDY

	'75	'76	'77	'78	'79	'80
Adult Contemporary	—	—	—	12.0	19.3	20.4
Top 40	19.3	19.5	19.9	14.1	7.9	9.2
Disco	—	—	1.5	2.6	3.4	1.1
Mellow	—	—	1.4	1.4	1.5	.14
AOR	—	—	6.1	8.2	9.9	12.5
Progressive	7.2	7.7	4.2	1.4	.5	.1
MOR	17.0	17.4	13.9	9.7	7.1	4.5
Good Music	15.7	15.5	14.9	13.6	14.5	14.8
Country	6.9	6.7	7.3	7.6	7.7	8.7
News	4.8	5.2	5.2	5.8	6.5	6.4
Black	5.6	5.0	4.4	4.5	5.3	2.7
Talk	3.5	3.3	2.9	3.0	2.5	4.0
Classical	1.6	1.4	1.3	1.3	1.3	1.7
Oldies	1.1	1.2	.4	.2	.7	1.3
Spanish	—	—	1.6	1.6	1.7	2.0
Jazz	—	—	—	—	.6	.7
Urban Contemporary	—	—	—	—	—	3.5
Big Band	—	—	—	—	—	.4
Music of Your Life	—	—	—	—	—	.2
Others	17.3	17.1	15.0	13.0	9.6	4.4

—Source: McGavern-Guild, Average of all Arbitron Reports Each Year

Interestingly, the wide choice of music formats gave rise to the development of listening alternatives. Non-music formats—talk, news, or a
combination of news/talk—are represented in most of the nation's top 25
markets. In Philadelphia, KYW, an all-news station, had led the ratings
race consistently beginning in the late 1970s. Over the same period, KABC,
Los Angeles, with its all-talk—that is, mostly listener call-in shows—has
enjoyed number-one status.

Another means of assessing format popularity is by calculating the
number of stations devoted to each. For its annual yearbook, *Broadcasting*, "the industry bible," includes a format check-off selection in a questionnaire sent to every station. *Broadcasting Yearbook's* list of choices
(different from Arbitron, Simmons and McGavern-Guild) includes seven
basic music formats: Beautiful Music, Black, Country and Western, Golden
Oldies, MOR, Progressive and Top 40. All stations returning questionnaries with selections indicated are so listed. By compiling these listings,
we may trace format usage between 1974 and 1981 according to what
stations who returned questionnaries say they are:

	1975	1976	1977	1978	1979	1980	1981
Beautiful Music	277	384	537	609	585	647	657
Black	152	246	256	245	240	239	189
C & W	1559	1733	1808	1860	1919	1881	2103
Golden Oldies	122	184	189	187	184	163	200
MOR	2167	2480	2513	2655	2703	2803	2745
Progressive	345	404	443	502	567	644	603
Top 40	378	1503	1547	1451	1547	1555	1522
	5000	6934	7293	7509	7745	7932	8019

—Source: *Broadcasting Yearbooks* 1975, 1976, 1977, 1978, 1979, 1980, 1981.

Behind radio's format fixation is the unmistakable desire to gain a competitive edge. Given the twists and turns of the trendy pop music business, what was "hitsville" yesterday, can be "shantytown" tomorrow. If a musical think-tank springs a new format (or the variation of an old one) in Salt Lake City or New Orleans, a hundred floundering stations across the country are candidates to pounce on it. Copyrighting a format is virtually impossible, and as soon as something different pops up, it is apt to be copied within weeks. Monkey-hear-monkey-do knows no market restrictions. In big city or small, the clone bug bites with frequent regularity. The imitation contagion it carries is incurable in musical radio. By no means, though, are all format switches made simply to copy a winner elsewhere. Ownership changes, shrinking market segments, personnel and/or financial problems, and competitive pressures may prod managements to make the big move. Generally, the larger the market, the more intricate and profound the process. Corporate entities are often involved in major market stations, and corporate entities do not make format changes *a priori*. So critical is the format issue that the Supreme Court ultimately had to make a ruling regarding changes. The Court decided in March, 1981, switches by licensees could be made at will, and that the Federal Communications Commission was correct in not getting involved in format disputes.[11]

Preparing for a format change requires first a psychological tooling-up. Audience and market research is usually the required prologue to any format replacement. When the exact kind is chosen, ownership poses a key question: Will the station management that reigns over the current format be compatible with the new one? Format changes leave in their wake obituary columns filled with station employees who have been considered incompatible by the home office when it has been decided to switch to a new format. Once the station's dramatis personnae is agreed upon, attention turns to *product* (should the station purchase thousands of albums and program the music itself, or should it turn to a syndication service?) and *promotion* (how much for newspaper, billboard, television advertising?).

Mainly FM's soaring 1970s have accounted for the tide of format changes that have become commonplace on the dial—a phenomenon the industry predicts will continue for the rest of the century. In simplest terms, format alterations are either evolutionary or revolutionary. Outstanding illustrative examples may be found in New York, Washington and Los Angeles, where in 1980 three stations made fundamental alternations that serve as prototypes of the format-change syndrome.

New York City has never been listed as the "typical" American town. Yet, what has taken place in musical radio there has been duplicated across the country. Although there are variations in the scenario, the turn-to-FM-for-music theme is the same. WABC, the AM rock behemoth that rode roughshod over all pop music contenders in New York City for almost a decade and a half, was passed in the ratings race in 1978. (WKTU-FM and WBLS-FM had much to do with it.) By the end of 1980, its fall from numbers grace found the WABC powerhouse that once claimed to be "the most listened-to-station in North America" in ninth place. Adopting a policy of deliberate gradualism, WABC opted to veer from a heavy-music regimen (where announcers were constantly admonished to "shut up and play the music") to a music-and-information mix. The former much-more-music giant of Gotham expanded its news, traffic and weather information—and in a symbolic demonstration that it aims to fulfill its advertising claim ("New York's Radio Station"), signed up to carry Yankees' baseball. Reflecting the awareness that a popular music base will always be critical to an AM Top 40-turned-Pop Adult, a WABC program executive declared: "Music is the lifeblood and future of this station . . . WABC will evolve as opposed to starting out with a bang in a new format . . . Our goal is to be entertaining and informative, to reflect what's going on in the lives of our listeners." [12] In less than a year, WABC went all-talk.

Format renovation of another kind was typified in the fall of 1980 by a mildly revolutionary adjustment on the FM band in Washington, D.C. FM's flowering, as we have seen, was early in arriving in the nation's capital where listeners quickly become conditioned to a variety of formats. Washington, D.C. FM has always been hard-ball FM. WJMD-FM (on the air since 1943) had gone along since 1970 as one of several stations, sharing a portion of the Beautiful Music-Easy Listening pie—and losing 40% of its audience in the process. By the spring of 1980, when WJMD had dropped out of Washington's top 10 into 13th place, the home office proclaimed, "Enough!" WJMD, licensed to SJR Communications, owners of WKTU-FM, installed as program director the former high-rated morning man of their high-rated New York outlet, Paul Robinson. Out went Mantovani, Percy Faith and the Hollyridge Strings. In came Billy Joel, Melissa Manchester and Paul McCartney—and Frank Sinatra, and Judy Garland,

and Nat King Cole, and Johnny Mathis. Beefed-up news and $250,000 in technical improvements completed the transformation. But it was the music that signalled the "New 94." Robinson's goal in mixing vocalists of the past 30 years with those of a more contemporary bent was to design a format that had special appeal in a market where half the population is estimated to be between 25 and 49. Product was no problem since Robinson brought his own collection of over 3000 albums to start things moving. WJMD's innovative mixture was decided upon, according to its preceptor, because it "emphasizes romance and that will never go out of style. Plus, it provides a great opportunity for family members to become exposed to each other's type of music." WJMD research, according to Robinson, revealed a "shrinking base" in Washington, D.C. "Something had to be done; there was an absolute need to contemporize this station. We'll become the variety show of Washington radio. Remember, they laughed at Ed Sullivan, too." [13]

No format change causes more excitement in a market—or in the trade—than the abrupt change. Nowhere was this better exemplified than at KHJ, Los Angeles. The same KHJ that introduced to Western civilization Top 40's ultimate rarefaction, *Boss Radio*. Incredible as it seemed, KHJ—*Capo di tutti Capi,* The Boss of all Bosses—switched to the country format late in 1980. To mark the occasion, the station called attention in a full-page ad to the changing characters of popular music, noting a "whole new kind of song" had emerged, "coming from a long tradition." KHJ, "the station we all grew up with," closed the rock garden and looked toward what it hoped would be the greener pastures of Country. (See Appendix on page 377.) KHJ was the fourth Los Angeles station to switch to Country within a three-week period in the autumn of 1980.

Further north, that same fall, KSAN, San Francisco's monument to FM rock, saddled up for a run with Country. With a change in call letters to WMMS—a not unconventional move when a format switch occurs— the old KSAN became San Francisco's only Country-formatted FM station. In Dallas a little later, at KLIF, where the McLendon cradle first rocked Texas, the switch was to Country too. So it was at Storz's WQAM, Miami, one of the original Top 40 citadels. Everywhere, it seemed, stations were galloping to Country: WNOE-FM, New Orleans; KILT-FM, Houston; and WKHK-FM, New York (formerly WRVR-FM), where a big brouhaha broke out when new owners dropped a long-running jazz music policy. TM Programming, a syndicator, said sales doubled in 1980 for its "TM Country" automated format.

The country division of radioland's format factory surely worked overtime in 1980, but that was nothing new. Country had been going to town for years—long before KHJ decided "we all grew up to be cowboys."

NOTES

1. Donald Flamm. "FM and How It Grew from Expensive Toy to AM's Chief Rival," *Variety,* February 13, 1980, p. 106 and 140.
2. Quoted in "FM: The Great Leap Forward," *Broadcasting,* January 22, 1979, p. 32.
3. Raechel Donahue. "Underground Radio Surfaces," *The Sixties,* Random House/Rolling Stone Press, (New York), 1977, p. 216.
4. Tom Donahue. "AM Radio: Stinking up the Airways," *The Rolling Stone Rock 'N' Roll Reader,* ed. Ben Fong-Torres, Straight Arrow, (New York), 1974, p. 673.
5. Claude Hall. "Progressive Rock Gives Life to Dead-Weight FM Radio Stations," *Billboard,* April 20, 1968, p. 22.
6. Caroline H. Myer. "The New Respectability of Rock," *Broadcasting,* August 11, 1969, p. 46D.
7. Claude Hall. "Progressive Rock Listeners Do Wash," *Billboard,* July 27, 1968, p. 44.
8. James Hopkins and Theodore Ashford. "Music Glossary," *Spot Radio Stations,* Standard Rate and Data Service, October 1, 1968, p. 11.
9. John Leader. "It's Contemporary Hit Radio!," *Radio and Records,* September 12, 1980, p. 24.
10. *Inside Radio,* January 12, 1981, p. 3.
11. F.C.C. v. WNCN Listeners Guild, No. 79-824, March 24, 1981. The format *cause célèbre* that produced the landmark decision, began in 1976 when WNCN-FM switched from classical to rock music. Uniting to protest the change disgruntled followers of the old format formed a "listeners guild." In its 7-2 vote against format by fiat, the high court ruled it was entirely proper for the Commission not "to grasp, measure and weigh the elusive and difficult facts involved in determining the acceptability of changes in entertainment format. To assess whether the elimination of a particular format would serve the public interest, the Commission would have to consider the benefit as well as the detriment that would result from change."
12. Quoted in Colby Coates. "ABC Radio's N.Y. Flagship Rebuilds with More Than Talk," *Advertising Age,* September 22, 1980, p. 78.
13. Quoted in Dennis John Lewis. "Beautiful Music Format Takes on New Meaning," *Washington Star,* December 29, 1980, p. C-2.

CHAPTER **16**

Country Goes to Town

ON THE MYTH-LITTERED media landscape, one myth stands taller than the rest. It is this: in each branch of the American culture, a monolithic force, made up of a few individuals, or organizations, or institutions, determines what we shall hear or see—or believe. Thus: many normally cynical persons accepted the thesis that the Nixon-Agnew problems derived from collusion of "liberal media," comprised of the television networks, the newsweeklies, the *New York Times* and the *Washington Post* and *they* did those poor fellows in; or that a cabal of pointy-headed Eastern liberal types control U.S. foreign policy and *they* are responsible for any Communist gains. For our television fare, the *they* changes, but the myth applies nonetheless: we get only what *they* force down our throats. In pop music, it should be plain by now, the musical by-products of our pluralism are so diverse, no single force on earth can dictate what becomes popular—or when—and what doesn't. There is no better proof of this than in the realm of country music. Despite the fact that it was on radio from the beginning, over four decades were needed for Country to make it to the American popular music mainstream. Radio's role in guiding it there cannot be overstated.

What ultimately emerged as "modern country"—the only kind a radioman means when he says his station plays Country—had its roots in the early songs the English, Scottish and Irish brought with them when they settled in the hills of the Virginias, the Carolinas, Kentucky and Tennessee. Intermingled with their native songs were Negro blues and even sacred strains. Out of this rich diversity grew a repertory of "heart" tunes, "event" songs (e.g. "The Sinking of the Titanic"), hoe-downs and religious pieces. These songs achieved their first degree of prominence in the 1920s when trailblazer recordists took their primitive gear to the hills. The recordings they made were often the only means that mountaineers had of learning about such events as Lindbergh's flight, Floyd Collins's demise in a cave, or the Scopes evolution trial. Only a small minority of hill folks, however, were able to hear the recordings. Radio was to be the agent that unified the growing audience for "country music"—something it was never called in its formative years.

Some of the earliest old-time music the isolated mountain people heard on the air—those fortunate enough to get near a radio—was also played by artists at fairs, picnics and political rallies. Using musicians of this ilk, WSB (Welcome South Brother), Atlanta built a roster of performers. One of the first such artists to make a significant impression on the pioneer Georgia outlet was Fiddlin' John Carson. A showman of the first order, Carson, like his fellow musicians, recognized that exposure on WSB afforded him an opportunity to plug personal appearances—a back-scratching arrangement that would later become part and parcel of live hillbilly music on radio—and to be heard by recording talent scouts. Fiddlin' John Carson's 1923 recording of "Little Old Log Cabin in the Lane" was the first country hit.

By the mid-1920s, the success of Carson's recording led to stepped-up activity by record companies to sign up rural artists.* Valuable as these efforts were, however, it was through another route blazed by radio that country music made its biggest splash in the 1920s and 1930s: the radio barn dance was a major force in coalescing the growing body of country fans. Not actually put together for dancing purposes at the points of origin, barn dance programs were showcases for groups of musicians who performed as repertory companies. Featuring an array of instruments that included banjos, violins, double fiddles, kazoos, washboards, harmonicas, mouthharps, mandolins in solo and group settings, the barn dance was essentially a program of happy-time music. Square-dance calls were part of some stations' barn dance shows, giving listeners the opportunity to dance at home. A barn dance could also have comedians or barbershop quartets—there was nothing rigid about a format. Credit for originating the idea is generally given to WBAP, Fort Worth, Texas. Ironically, WBAP did not stick with the concept very long, although the station later became strongly identified with the country idiom by presenting such performers as The Red Chain Bohemians, Traffic Cop and the High Octanes—and its

---

* The sagging record business at this time, following radio's impact, prompted the recording industry to be especially interested in cultivating specialized markets to offset losses in their "general" product line.

most famous one, W. Lee "Pappy" O'Daniel, who went on to become governor of Texas.*

To WLS, Chicago, must go the recognition for launching the first block-buster of the breed, The *National Barn Dance*. Beginning life as the *Chicago Barn Dance*, in April, 1924, it was conceived by a Memphis newspaper reporter, George D. Hay, who had turned to announcing on WMC in that city and was later wooed to WLS. Riding through the heartland on the 50,000 watts of WLS, (under Sears-Roebuck ownership[1]), the Saturday night show, aired 7:30 p.m. to midnight, C.S.T., quickly became a favorite in many of the 48 states. When Sears sold WLS to the *Prairie Farmer* in 1928, it had no bearing on the show; in fact, its best years lay ahead. So much had the program's popularity grown that, starting September 30, 1933, one hour weekly was carried on NBC-Blue and sponsored by Alka Seltzer. The *National Barn Dance* alumni society includes many familiar names in the country and western field: Gene Autry (who was on the show between 1930 and 1934); Arkie, the Arkansas Woodchopper; Johnny Bond; Homer and Jethro; Patsy Montana; Lulu Belle and Scotty; Red Foley; Uncle Ezra; the Hoosier Hotshots; Eddie Peabody; Pat Buttram (The Sage of Winston County, Alabama); Louise Massey and the Westerners; and Smiley Burnett. Some artists who went on to adopt non-Country personas included Fibber McGee and Molly and George Gobel. Expressions flowing from the show became national catch-phrases ("Are you ready, Hezzie?" "Give 'em a toot on the tooter, Tommy").

After the network portion was dropped in 1946, the *National Barn Dance* remained on WLS until 1960 when Ralph Beaudin arrived with his terrible swift sword. It got a reprieve of sorts by moving to WGN, Chicago and lasted in a diluted form until 1970. In a tearful obituary on the occasion of the final WLS show, the *Chicago Daily News* lamented that "the new WLS management had decided on an around-the-clock menu of music-news-weather with six new disc jockeys [to] give WLS a more desirable 'metropolitan image' . . . The rock 'n rollers were on the march and radio was reeling from the beat."[2]

Network radio was also responsible for raising the nation's country and western consciousness through another important show. It would not only outlast the *National Barn Dance*, but become the enduring symbol of country music. The *Grand Ole Opry* came to NBC from Nashville in 1939, six years after the *National Barn Dance* had been established for many country followers as the Saturday night listening habit; yet by the mid-1940s, that head start had been dissipated. The reason one survived and the other didn't is told not in mournful numbers. For since both shows were heard Saturday nights a half-hour apart, their rating histories indicate an almost even-draw:

---

* In a further note of irony, WBAP, considered one of the nation's leading country stations, did not adopt that format on a 24-hour basis until 1970.

SEASON	NATIONAL BARN DANCE	GRAND OLE OPRY
1941–42	10.0	11.2
1942–43	12.6	9.7
1943–44	8.9	11.5
1944–45	11.8	9.5
1945–46	10.6	11.8

—Source: *A Thirty-Year History of Programs Carried on National Radio Networks in the United States, 1926–1956.* ed. Harrison Summers, Arno, 1971.

There is another linkage between the two shows. After *Chicago Barn Dance* founding father, George D. Hay, had been at WLS as chief announcer for a year, he was offered the position of station director for Nashville's new outlet, WSM. Hay was at the station only six weeks when he inaugurated the *WSM Barn Dance.* Billing himself as the "Solemn Old Judge," the 30-year old executive quickly built the show into a popular local feature. WSM had just joined the newly-organized NBC network and scheduled Hay's show at 10 p.m. Saturdays, following the *Music Appreciation Hour,* hosted by the celebrated musicologist, Dr. Walter Damrosch. Later, Hay recalled how radio was responsible for the unique parody that came to identify America's most enduring symbol of country music:

> Dr. Damrosch always signed off his concert with a minute or so before we hit the air with our mountain minstrels and vocal trapeze performers. We must confess that the change in pace and quality was immense. But that is part of America—fine lace and homespun cloth . . . Out of the loudspeaker came the correct, but accented words of Dr. Damrosch: "While most artists realize there is no place in the classics for realism, I am going to break one of my rules and present a composition . . . which depicts the onrush of a locomotive . . . After [Damrosch's] number and sign-off, [We said] for the next three hours we will present nothing but realism . . . We will call on DeFord Bailey with harmonica to give us the country version of his "Pan American Blues" . . . At the close of it, your reporter said, "For the past hour we have been listening to music from the Grand Opera, but from now on we will present the Grand Ole Opry."[3]

The *Opry's* radio network run lasted from 1939 to 1957, with the original sponsor, Prince Albert Smoking Tobacco, staying on until the end. WSM's microphones, however, remained, and the festal Saturday night broadcasts continued. When WSM and family celebrated the *Opry's* 55th anniversary late in November, 1980, no one doubted for a moment WSM would be airing the centennial celebration. Nor could anyone doubt the *Grand Ole Opry* would remain the academy that stocks the Country and

Western bigtime. No round-up of American popular music can ignore the following performers—all of whom cut their show business eye teeth at the *Grand Ole Opry:*

Roy Acuff
Jack Anglin
Eddy Arnold
Ernie Ashworth
Bobby Bare
Margie Bowes
Rod Brasfield
Jim Ed Brown
Archie Campbell
The Carlisles
Mother Maybelle
  Carter
Johnny Cash
Lew Childre
Zeke Clements
Patsy Cline
Jerry Clower
Stoney Cooper
Cousin Jody
Cowboy Copas
Betty Jack Davis
Skeeter Davis
Little Jimmy Dickens
Roy Drusky
Everly Brothers
Lester Flatt
Red Foley
Duke of Paducah,
  Whitey Ford
The Four Guys
Curly Fox
Fox Hunters
Larry Gatlin
Don Gibson
The Glaser Brothers
Billy Grammer
Jack Greene
George Hamilton IV

Hawkshaw Hawkins
David Houston
Paul Howard
Ferlin Husky
Ed Hyde
Sonny James
Jim and Jesse
Jimmy, the Vagabonds
Johnny and Jack
George Jones
Grandpa Jones
The Jordanaires
Claude Lampley
Wilma Lee
Little Rachel
Hank Locklin
Lonzo and Oscar
Bobby Lord
Charlie Louvin
Ira Louvin
Bob Luman
Loretta Lynn
Uncle Dave Macon
Barbara Mandrell
Uncle Joe Mangrum
Sam McGee
Ronnie Milsap
Bill Monroe
Clyde Moody
George Morgan
Jimmy Newman
The Osborne Brothers
Texas Ruby Owens
Dolly Parton
Minnie Pearl
Stu Phillips
Ray Pillow

Ray Price
Jeanne Pruett
Del Reeves
Jim Reeves
Tex Ritter
Marty Robbins
Texas Ruby
Fred Schriver
Earl Scruggs
Jeannie Seely
Jean Shepard
Asher Sizemore
Ralph Sloan Dancers
Connie Smith
Smokey Mountain Boys
Hank Snow
Stringbean
The Stoney Mountain
  Cloggers
Mel Tillis
Ernest Tubb
Justin Tubb
LeRoy Van Dyke
Porter Wagner
Billy Walker
Charlie Walker
Stanley Walton
Weaver Brothers
Kitty Wells
Dottie West
Jim Widener
Curly Williams
Don Williams
Hank Williams
The Willis Brothers
Del Wood
Marion Worth

Vital as the *Grand Ole Opry* has been to the country cause, what started taking place in Nashville recording studios in the mid-1960s lent even more impact to the rise in popularity of the country music format.

We shall give that phenomenon more scrutiny shortly, when we return to the *Opry's* birthplace and probe the "Nashville Sound." But for the moment, we must go back to the 1930s, to the live musical radio era when the medium's use of Country was widespread, and when the music was still called "hill billy," or "rural," or "old time."

Following the lead of WLS and WSM, stations around the country created barn dance broadcasts of their own. Although they never achieved the fame of the *National Barn Dance* and the *Grand Ole Opry,* local versions attracted loyal followings and contributed to the spread of the music. Many such broadcasts were features of powerhouse outlets—often with clear channels—for this was a time before every town of 5000 population had a station of its own, a time when regional coverage was the only way millions could be reached by radio. *Jamboree* on WWVA, Wheeling, West Virginia, ranks right behind the *National Barn Dance* and the *Grand Ole Opry* and completes the Big Three of barn dances. Like the *Opry, Jamboree* went into the 1980s still kicking its heels with a live Saturday night broadcast. So keyed in on Country had the industry become that in 1978 an hour of the show was picked up by Mutual for coast-to-coast airing as *Jamboree USA.* WWVA's inaugural *Jamboree* program was heard in January, 1933, and thanks to the station's 50,000 watts and 1170 dial setting, could be heard regularly in 18 states and six Canadian provinces. Due to *Jamboree's* early success, WWVA adopted the slogan, "The Friendly Voice from Out of the Hills," dedicated to a policy of "Bringing Country to the Country." Yet, surprisingly, it was not until 1965 that the outlet adopted a 24-hour country format.

As the popularity of barn dance broadcasts spread, stations located in metropolitan areas, rather than country hotbeds, built their own packages. Heard mainly on Saturday nights, there were variations from station to station—on the KVOO (Tulsa) show, for example, Bob Wills and his Texas Playboys, featuring "Western Swing," were special favorites—but the sound of fiddle, banjo, mandolin, harmonica and happiness permeated all of them. The following table listing some of the better known barn dances on the air on the 1930s is evidence that the strain knew no geographic limits:

STATION AND CITY	SHOW
KMOX, St. Louis	*Hill Billy Champions* *
KSTP, Minneapolis	*Sunset Valley Barn Dance*
KVOO, Tulsa	*Saddle Mountain Round-up*
WBT, Charlotte	*Crazy Water Crystals Barn Dance*
WFIL, Philadelphia	*Sleepy Hollow Ranch*
WHAS, Louisville	*Renfro Valley Barn Dance* *

---

* *Hill Billy Champions* and *Renfro Valley,* along with *Corn Cob Pipe Club, Dude Ranch, Carson Robinson's Buckaroos, Plantation Party, Shady Valljy Jamboree* and *Hayloft Hoedown* had network runs of varying lengths, but none was ever any real challenge to the *National Barn Dance* and the *Grand Ole Opry.*

STATION AND CITY	SHOW
WHN, New York	*WHN Barn Dance*
WHO, Des Moines	*Iowa Barn Dance Frolic*
WLW,Cincinnati	*Boone County Jamboree*
WOWO, Fort Wayne	*Hoosier Hop*
WRVA, Richmond	*Old Dominion Barn Dance*
WSB, Atlanta	*WSB Barn Dance*

Barn dances and jamborees were by no means the sole radio carriers of the country idiom in the 1930s and 1940s. Another pipeline to fans was the endless array of artists heard on local stations.

In all parts of radioland it was possible to hear Country played and sung by individuals or combos. The music was invariably branded "hill billy." Its performers were frequently typecast as shiftless, ne'er-do-well hayseeds who spoke with Southern-cum-Western accents, in a language as sloven as their grooming. Artists often went out of their way to cultivate this image in the same manner Blacks sometimes played along with the stereotype of the "darky" who ate watermellon and loved to dance. Any veteran broadcaster whose station carried a hill billy show can produce an instant anthology of anecdotes about the musicians who were usually colorful, sometimes talented and professional, often unpredictable—and, in select situations, followed by a retinue of groupies. Country and Western shows on local stations in the 1930s and 1940s were usually live and could range from quarter-hours to full-hour blocks, morning, afternoon or night. They could be heard on small-market stations such as Michigan's WEXL, Royal Oak and WFXD, Flint, where Skeets MacDonald and Little Jimmy Dickens, respectively, served their apprenticeships, and on big powerhouses like WBZ, Boston, KDKA, Pittsburgh and WHAM, Rochester, when Bradley Kincaid introduced mountain songs to the metropolitan Northeast. They could be heard on WMT, Cedar Rapids, where Tom Owens and his Cowboys serenaded regularly, and on WHAS, Louisville, where Randy Atcher's Swinging Cowboys sent their stomping sessions out over that pioneer outlet's big coverage area.

At WORK, York, Pennsylvania, where the station's first three-year covenant with the FCC forbade playing recorded music of any kind (and where a network affiliation was not to come until 1937) old time-rural music was crucial. Harold Miller, recalling his program problems of the Depression, was unflinching in crediting two outfits who helped get the station over the hump:

> We had difficulty in filling a whole day. Those were the early years and things were rough. We had two hill billy groups on the station for quite a while. They did three things for us: they filled time; they made people aware we were there; and they brought in money because they were spon-

sored. The *Happy Johnny and Handsome Bob Show* was our introduction to this sort of thing. Johnny and Bob were sold out. Then came *Cousin Lee and his Boys,* sponsored by Texas Crystals. We had an hour of each in the morning and an hour in the afternoon—that was four sponsored hours all day.[4]

Crazy Water Crystals, deeply committed to country music at the time, wanted to blunt Texas Crystals' efforts, and since all four hours were sold out, Miller tried to find another group to fly the Crazy Water banner. The search proved futile, so the resourceful program director created the WORK Hill Billy Trio. He found two semi-professional singers to join him, had his staff orchestra leader, Bernard Hochberger, provide fiddle backgrounds, and Crazy Water Crystals had its answer to Texas Crystals. Miller confessed his trio had a limited repertory, remembering,

> There were many reprises of "Red River Valley" and "Brown Eyes, Why Are You Blue?" Of course, we were no match for Happy Johnny and Cousin Lee. When *they* were on the air, we used to fill the balcony-mezzanine as well. They were good for the station, and we were good for them. They made personal appearances in the area every night—even jammed the churches when they played there.[5]

By the time country music was standard fare on the WORK's and the WMT's, another more limited, but nevertheless influential ground swell was making itself felt. It was the growing awareness, particularly in the academic community, of the uniqueness of the entire mountain folk culture. Scholars in the 1920s had already begun their probings into the balladry, the language, the crafts and the literature. Carl Sandburg's *American Songbag,* published in 1927, had covered folk songs from all sections, but gave prominence to those from the mountain regions. As the 1930s wore on, grants for university research increased, while government subsidies were provided to support such indigenous enterprises as quilt-making and wood-carving. Only the arrival of World War II slowed down the rising tourist trade to the Smokies and like regions. A pinnacle of sorts was reached in 1945 when Aaron Copland won the New York Music Critics' Award and the Pulitzer Prize in music for *Appalachian Spring.*

Mr. Copland's discovery of old time music that inspired him to fold fiddlers' tunes and Shaker motifs into *Appalachian Spring* certainly represented a landmark in American music. But for the average pop listener, Copland's composition predictably had little impact. As described earlier, the mid-to-late-1940s began the period of transition for popular music and for radio. Millions of returning servicemen and women, now four or five years older and otherwise pre-occupied, understandably had an insentient attitude toward popular music. In this connection, a tiresome cliché has been repeated *ad nauseum:* GI's, according to the transplant scenario, absorbed country music heard on stations surrounding military bases in the

South and Southwest; they developed a taste for it; and then they returned to their homes in northern metropolitan areas; and lived to become country fans forever after. There is, however, no substantive evidence to support this. A transplanting did occur, but its root cause was economic, not musical. The attraction of better pay in northern factories was the magnet that pulled thousands of rural dwellers out of the South. For example, Akron, Ohio, home of the rubber companies, was for West Virginians a particularly inviting destination. In parts of West Virginia, it was said, they taught "readin', writin', and Route 21 to Akron." And country music was part of the migration to the city.

Another influence in the spread of Country was less noticeable. It involved the arrival of a new clan of country *chanteurs* who eschewed the stereotypical mannerisms and baggage (the twang, the knee-slapping, the "gully-washer" songbook and the "git-tar"). In the forefront of this movement were performers such as Eddy Arnold, Marty Robbins, Tennessee Ernie Ford, Jim Reeves and Jimmy Dean. But even as Country and conventional pop were taking their first uneasy steps in coming closer together during the early 1950s, countervening forces were pulling them in opposite directions. The fall of the networks and the general decline of live local radio were anathema to country music and its musicians. Yet, perhaps the most telling blow of all was the "desertion" by one of their own. Elvis Presley and rock and roll, while not sweeping country music off the radio, certainly dealt it some telling blows. Although the *Grand Ole Opry* had been removed by NBC, that hearty perennial remained on WSM, and Nashville was still the capital of country music. But, as far as radio was concerned, even though hundreds of stations continued to program some form of Country, the medium had become pre-occupied with Top 40 and rock and roll by the late 1950s. And so had many country performers. This was reflected in concessions many of them made to the "new sound" pioneered by Elvis Presley. In trying to move closer to the styles of the newly acclaimed rock and rollers, however, they found themselves on the horns of musical dilemma: on one hand, they might attract the new breed of fan whose first taste of Country had come by way of Memphis; and on the other, they would surely turn off their traditional followers. Aware that the dichotomous split could develop into something more serious, the country music industry, in the early 1960s, orchestrated (so to speak) a deliberate change in the sound of the music. Out were fiddles, double fiddles, mandolins, harmonicas, washboards and banjos; in were background vocal groups and 20-piece orchestras of violins and horns. The "Nashville Sound" had arrived in American popular music; it would not be long until its influence would be felt on radio.

No precise definition for the Nashville Sound has ever been formulated. Generally, it is characterized by a "feel," starting in a tightly-knit rhythm section and enhanced by a "laid-back" mood created by Nashville studio musicians whose playing together over the years has enabled them to develop an empathy for each other. Getting to the interior of the Nash-

ville Sound, *Down Beat* properly credits the key role of the Nashville recording studio engineer:

> An engineer has the same involvement . . . as the artists, players, or pro-
> ducer. Since there is only a very small amount of freelance engineering in
> Nashville (although that trend seems to be changing) almost all engineers
> are committed to working at a "studio." As a result, the engineer tends
> to be as concerned about the studio's success or failure, or the condition
> of the equipment in the facility as are the owners. Making a record in
> Nashville is a unison effort between the artist, producer, engineer, and
> musician.[6]

Without the Nashville Sound, there could have been no country format.
As soon as the Nashville blender began processing country music, it was
ready for middle American tastes. Don Nelson, general manager at WIRE,
Indianapolis (a pioneer *modern* country station) when it gained early recognition with its high ratings, maintained the Nashville Sound was paramount:

> When Nashville broadened its base, when it changed the product, that
> made it possible for country music stations to succeed . . . It's important
> that we realize the big successful radio stations did not *make* Nashville,
> Nashville made these stations.[7]

Like Top 40, country radio was destined to get its tryout in smaller
markets before it would hit the majors. By the mid-to-late-1960s, a time
when Top 40 imitators were swarming all over the dial, and a time when
more new stations, including FM'ers, were coming into the aural jungle,
attention focused on a handful of larger-market operations that had made
a switch in formats and were setting a style with an innovative format
they called *modern country*. They included KRAK, Sacramento, KSON,
San Diego, WJJD, Chicago, and KAYO, Seattle. Jay Hoffer, program director of KRAK when that 50,000 watter changed formats (in 1962), made
it clear success could only come when a front office made a commitment
that country radio required the same principles of sound management as
any other kind:

> We tried to apply the modern techniques of radio, meaning format radio,
> and superimpose that onto a country structure. Country radio before this
> time was a very loose arrangement. There was a lot of yak on the air
> from what we heard of the small country stations around the area. There
> was a lot of visiting, that kind of crap. And they played whatever the hell
> they wanted. It became apparent to me . . . that all these guys had their
> own particular prejudices . .[8]

The professionalization of the format by radio and the modernization
of the music in Nashville studios led to a proliferation of full-time country
stations that would have astounded even George Hay. Between 1978 and
1980 alone, 384 stations turned Country:

YEAR	FULL-TIME COUNTRY* STATIONS
1961	81
1963	97
1965	208
1969	606
1971	525
1972	633
1973	764
1974	856
1975	1116
1977	1140
1978	1150
1979	1434
1980	1534

—Source: County Music Association

Another factor in the country radio boom has been FM. Country music, of course, started out as a province of AM. But with the expansion of FM, it was only a matter of time before operators were to discover it played well there too. How FM Country had become one of the fastest growing parts of radioland is nowhere better illustrated than at WFMS-FM, Indianapolis.

Until the fall of 1976, WFMS had programmed the "Sound of Your Life" (Beautiful Music) format. The station was one of a dozen or so AM and FM outlets sharing the radio audience of Indianapolis. They wore the format tags shown in the following table:

STATION		FORMAT
WFMS	(FM)	Beautiful Music
WIFE	(AM)	Rock
WIBC	(AM)	MOR (News and sports image)
WNAP	(FM)	Rock
WNDE	(AM)	Adult Contemporary
WTLC	(FM)	Black
WXLW	(AM)	MOR
WXTZ	(FM)	Beautiful Music

*The alert reader will have noted the disparity between these figures and those in Chapter 15. Both sources, the Country Music Association and *Broadcasting Cable Yearbook*, compile their data from information supplied by stations in response to questionnaires. The larger number listed by *Broadcasting* is probably due to that publication's status as the "industry bible," and hence prompts a higher ratio of returned questionnaires than that of CMA.

STATION		FORMAT
WFBQ	(FM)	AOR
WIRE	(AM)	Country (Some news and sports)
WATI	(AM)	Beautiful Music
WBRI	(AM)	Religious
WNTS	(AM)	News and talk

In September, 1976, WFMS switched to Country, even though WIRE had gotten there first. Larry Grogan, WFMS manager, explained the reason behind that move:

> WIRE was the only game in town. It "broke" all the new [country] releases. The station also had high visibility within the trade press—*Billboard's* Country Station-of-the-Year—three or four years; Major Market Country D.J.-of-the-Year; etc. The fact is, as we saw it they had a "variety" station. Plainly, a wide open opportunity existed in Indianapolis for a country music FM. We wanted to maximize that opportunity by playing Country on stereo FM radio. Our long-range goal was to establish ourselves as "The Country Music Station in Indianapolis." [9]

While not the first FM station to go Country—a few had done it earlier—WFMS was the first to do so in the Midwest. The WFMS switch was a bellwether situation. Politically and culturally conservative, Indianapolis has never been the place to look for striking changes. WIRE, after all, *was* Country, and as everyone always knew, "you can't change those stubborn Hoosiers." How well WFMS succeeded may be seen by charting the ratings of Indianapolis between 1976 and 1980. WFMS's five-year audience gains are all the more impressive, for they came even as most competitive stations lost listeners. For those that showed increases, they were small ones:

	April/ May 76	Oct/ Nov 76	April/ May 77	Oct/ Nov 77	April/ May 78	Oct/ Nov 78	Spring 79	Fall 79	Spring 80	Fall 80
WFMS	1.4	4.1	5.2	7.0	8.8	5.6	7.1	8.4	7.4	9.0
WIFE	7.6	6.4	6.5	5.1	4.8	5.3	4.9	3.4	2.9	1.8
WIBC	13.1	14.2	15.1	15.8	18.0	19.4	17.5	15.9	15.7	15.6
WNAP	8.6	8.3	11.6	9.3	9.3	9.2	8.9	8.1	7.1	9.9
WNDE	6.7	7.7	6.3	7.4	7.0	6.7	6.0	5.4	5.3	5.0
WTLC	18.2	8.5	9.1	8.6	8.2	7.2	8.8	9.8	9.2	9.3
WXLW	3.8	3.8	4.0	3.0	2.5	2.9	1.7	1.3	2.0	.5
WXTZ	18.4	13.2	12.3	15.0	13.7	13.7	13.6	13.5	12.5	10.3
WFBQ	4.4	5.3	5.0	3.9	6.0	6.5	8.7	9.9	6.7	7.4
WIRE	13.3	11.9	11.6	10.2	9.0	7.5	11.9	9.5	8.8	9.3

—Source: *Arbitron Radio Estimates in the Arbitron Market of Indianapolis.*

By the time WFMS and other C & W stations had chalked up rating successes, the image of the country listener-as-clod had virtually vanished. The general acceptance of Country as a valid popular music and the growth of country-formatted stations in the Northeast, where cultural icons get their most scrutiny, have been major factors in regarding the typical country music fan as something other than a tobacco-chewing ancient farmer or an overalled mountaineer. Country stations in the 1960s encountered the stereotype image regularly and they knew that only as they demolished it, could they gain advertisers, for without advertisers, country radio would have little credibility. It was not easy. One station manager, perhaps speaking for his country compatriots, told *Television/Radio Age,* "In 1967, we found a great deal of prejudice toward the format from advertisers with products that would be considered oriented to higher income groups, or groups with higher education levels." [10] In 1976, to counter such resistance the Country Music Association commissioned research in 16 markets. The results revealed country listeners were not backwoods hillbillies who should be relegated to the marketplace badlands. In education, income and buying habits, country listeners, according to the CMA-Arbitron study, were not much different from the country at large. More extensive research on a national basis was conducted as part of Simmons Market Research Bureau's 1980 study of media and markets. The results are shown in the following table:

COUNTRY LISTENERS TO COUNTRY MUSIC RADIO STATIONS

(Percent composition of country music audience—6 a.m.–midnight, Mon.–Fri. cume)—vs. percent composition of U.S. population)

	% Country Music Listeners	% Total Population
By Age		
18–24	14.5	17.9
25–34	24.2	22.6
35–44	20.6	16.2
45–54	16.8	14.8
54–64	12.6	13.5
65+	11.4	14.9
By Education		
Graduated college	11.8	14.8
Attended college (1–3 yrs.)	13.8	16.5
Graduated h.s.	38.4	38.2
Attended h.s.	17.4	14.9
Did not attend h.s.	18.6	15.6
By Occupation		
Professional/technical	8.3	10.7
Manager/administrator	6.3	7.2

	% Country Music Listeners	% Total Population
Clerical sales	15.2	14.7
Craftsman/foreman	12.3	8.3
Other employed	23.2	20.0
Not employed	34.7	39.0
By Household Income		
$25,000+	26.0	31.1
$20,000–$24,999	12.3	12.7
$15,000–$19,999	19.1	13.8
$10,000–$14,999	20.6	19.8
$ 5,000–$ 9,999	12.3	13.5
Under $5,000	9.7	9.2

—Source: Simmons Market Research Bureau 1980 study of media and markets.

But if controversy surrounding the image of country station listeners had subsided, the flap over the music itself picked up in intensity. By the late 1970s, the "crossover" debate was going hot and heavy: throughout the entire industry they were asking the musical question, "Will crossover songs dilute the 'purity' of Country?" In a special report from Nashville, *Stereo Review* concluded "things have reached the point where in some musical quarters, 'cross' and 'over' are two brand-new dirty words."[11] Grand Ole Opry singer Ernest Tubb spoke for purists when he complained, "An artist singing with a 30-piece orchestra with a violin section just isn't country music. Now the violins are all right if they're played like a fiddle . . . The stations say they can't play it ['real' country music] because the companies won't make it. Each of them is passing the buck. They're both wrong. They're both to blame."[12] Jean Shepard, another Opry veteran, lamented, "You can't tell the pop radio stations from the country stations."[13]

Actually, the idea of conventional country artists having hits that crossed over to general popularity is not new. ("Ghost Riders in the Sky," Number 1 in 1949; "The Tennessee Waltz," Number 2 in 1951; "The Battle of New Orleans," Number 2 in 1959; "Honey," Number 7 in 1968.) In the 1950s and 1960s, many country artists appeared on the "regular" hit charts—Eddy Arnold, Flatt and Scruggs, Jeannie C. Riley, Roger Miller, the Statler Brothers, Donna Fargo, Sonny James, Buck Owens, Faron Young and Webb Pierce, to name a few. Very little was heard about it then in radioland. But with the spilling of Country into the popular mainstream in the 1970s, it became fashionable for broadcasting symposia and trade papers to apply one litmus purity test or another. The general press discovered crossover and it became an obligatory buzz word in most stories having to do with C & W. Nearly everybody, it seemed, was getting into the crossover act, from Country to pop, and vice versa: Kenny Rogers one day up and dropped his folk-rock group, the First Edition, and took the Country oath; Charlie Rich's "Behind Closed Doors" was a blockbuster pop hit; Willie Nelson glided effortlessly from Irving Berlin and Hoagy Carmichael to Kris Kristofferson; the Nitty Gritty Dirt Band teamed with the "king of country music," Roy Acuff, to do an album; pop artists Tom Jones, The Carpenters and Engelbert Humperdinck made the country charts; Emmy Lou Harris, a pop artist, crossed the narrow divide and declared herself "Country"; Dolly Parton went the other way; Eddie Rabbit hopped back and forth with no difficulty; John Denver and Olivia Newton-John won top country music awards; country-rock can be the only appropriate label for the Bellamy Brothers, Dr. Hook and Charlie Daniels; Loretta Lynn and Teddy Pendergrass cut a sound track album together; Soulful James Brown performed at the *Grand Ole Opry,* of all places; and perhaps the mutation that left fans on both sides of the aisle mute—Porter Wagoner, after five years of obscurity, suited up in his rhinestone livery and put together an act that included disco and rock. Confusing as these meldings were, without the fusion, country radio could never have made its big leap in the 1970s.

Still, the country and western "movement" has also benefited from multi-media input. Hollywood took notice and out came such films as *The Electric Horseman, Coalminer's Daughter, Urban Cowboy, Honeysuckle Rose, Outlaw Blues* and *Hard Country.* Media re-cycling that saw such country-cum-pop hits such as "Ode to Billy Joe" and "Harper Valley PTA" parlayed into movies would pick up in tempo. Television, which has had a wobbly relationship with pop music, discovered even with slicked-up showbiz, down-home played well on the tube. C & W specials[14] were erupting all over the place, and rare was a week that a talk show didn't feature an artist of the genre. A Southern President elected in 1976 (whose White House guest list was replete with country performers) and a Western chief executive chosen in 1980 did the cause no harm. A "new patriotism" that re-affirmed basic American values was in evidence after Vietnam, Watergate and Iran to provide a friendly habitat. Whether such patriotic surges merely afforded escapist nostalgia, and can stand up to the vaunted "reality" of country and western music, remains to be seen.

Country music on radio should stay strong as long as it continues to fuse with regular pop, for it was only when Country broadened its base that the real spread took place. Buddy Killen, president of Tree International, Nasville's largest music publisher, put the matter in terms as simple as the lyrics to a country song. In an outlook-for-the-1980s survey, Killen told *Variety,* he thought, "country music will always sustain. You can bombard it with all different styles, but the basic style will always be there. I think there's something for everybody."[15]

Musical radio, of course, can never return to the halcyon *Hit Parade* days when only one body of popular music existed, but Country may end up coming closest.

NOTES

1. The giant retailer made sure its catalogue users were reminded of recordings by WLS artists. In the 1927 edition, there appeared with lists of Silvertone Records (at 39 cents each), under the heading SELECTIONS BY WLS RADIO STARS, the following copy: "We have now made it possible for you to hear your favorite WLS radio star on your phonograph. A record is always at hand; ready to play when you so desire." *1927 Edition* of the *Sears, Roebuck Catalogue.* ed. by Alan Mirken, Crown Publishers, (New York), 1970, p. 692.

2. Terry Turner. "Exit Radio's Oldest Show: National Barn Dance Dies After 36 Years," *Chicago Daily News,* April 30, 1960, p. 38.

3. WSM Souvenir Pamphlet. (undated)

4. Interview with Harold Miller.

5. *Ibid.*

6. Sam Zambuto. "The Nashville Sound Is Alive and Well," *Down Beat,* April, 1980, p. 35.

7. ———. "There's New Life in an Old Radio Art Form: Country Radio Has Come to Town in a Big Way," *Broadcasting,* September 18, 1972, p. 32.

8. *Ibid.* p. 30.

9. Interview with Larry Grogan, March 24, 1981.

10. Dan Rustin. "Station's Report That New Sound Is Pretty as Ring of the Cash Register," *Television/Radio Age,* June 28, 1971, p. 25.

11. Noel Coppage. "Is Country Going to the Dogs?," *Stereo Review,* November, 1978, p. 99.

12. ———. "Industry Deserted Country Music, Says Ernest Tubb," *York Dispatch,* April 1, 1980, p. 24.

13. Joe Edwards. "Mutation Music: The Marriage of Country and Pop," *Sunday Patriot-News, (Keystoner)*, September 16, 1979, p. 8.

14. The major television networks presented 21 prime time country music specials in 1979, double the 1978 number. Among the higher rated ones: *CMA Awards Show* (CBS, 10/8/79, 22.4); *Smokey and the Bandit* (NBC, 11/25/79, 31.8); *John Denver and the Muppets* (ABC, 12/5/79, 23.2) Source: Country Music Association.

15. Lee Rector. "Nashville Sees More Contemporary Influence as Country Music Aims to Broaden Scope in Next Decade," *Variety,* January 23, 1980, p. 78.

CHAPTER **17**

Pilots of the Airwaves

THE DISC JOCKEY'S POSITION of prominence was born of necessity. Television's pre-emption of bigtime variety, comedy and drama programs left even network radio stations with no choice but to fill most of the void with recorded popular music. To make matters worse, by the early 1950s, most medium to large markets already had several popular music (and news) stations. Astute managements of network affiliates and independents alike knew, however, their survival in the Age of Television would require more than a stack of records. Nor did it take a genius to realize, with the greatly improved quality of post-War phonographs, together with the newly-developed long-playing record, anyone could, if he chose, bypass the radio to get pop music into the home. It would take some clearly defined degrees of difference to stand out. The music itself, how it was sequenced (as the pioneer Top 40 stations clearly demonstrated) and what went on *between* the records would be the critical determinants. Attention to these elements obviously existed before the McLendon and Storz chivarees rolled onto the dial. But it took Top 40 Radio to raise the public consciousness about the aural medium, to declare from Main Street to Madison Avenue that radio would not play dead in the steady gaze of Cyclops' eye. A catalyst, however, would be needed to make it work.

Top 40 Radio did not discover the disc jockey; Top 40 merely outfitted him with a new persona. If we accept the basic definition (*one who plays records over the air interspersed with comment*) then disc jockeys were around as long as radio. The term itself, however, and its meaning in contemporary usage, sprang up in the mid-1940s.[1]

Who may take credit for being the first disc jockey is open to wide interpretation. Lee de Forest, whose experiments with the vacuum tube were noted earlier, regularly used phonograph records in his tests around 1906. A few years later Charles "Doc" Herrold opened a small college of electrical engineering in San Jose and began transmitting every Wednesday afternoon. (That station would eventually become KCBS). Herrold's assistant was his young bride. Years later, Mrs. Herrold in recalling those days, raised the possibility that the first disc jockey might have been a woman:

> In that time it was wireless. We never heard the name, radio. It was the wireless telephone, as they called it. First, as I recall, it was just the voice. He [Herrold] was trying to improve the reception of the voice . . . And finally, as it was improved we started to broadcast the music. And I really believe I was the first woman to broadcast a program.[2]

Frank Conrad might have come closer in spirit to being a pioneer disc jockey. Conrad had attracted a following of sorts while working on his experimental station 8XK in the garage at his Wilkinsburg, Pennsylvania home, starting prior to World War I. Conrad admitted his pioneer "disc jockeying" was more a diversion than anything else:

> It was a hobby I carried out at home. As I got deeper and deeper into it, people would ask me to transmit . . . said they had some friends in and wanted to hear something coming out of the air. I would transmit talk and phonograph music and finally, to take care of it, I arranged to send a program twice a week, every Wednesday and Saturday night.[3]

After Frank Conrad went on to pursue more seriously his interest in broadcasting and 8XK became KDKA, that station, like other pioneer operations of the early 1920s, would occasionally use phonograph records. Primitive technology required that the microphone be held as close as possible to the phonograph's speaker. Since this was still the acoustical era—electric recording began in 1925—the resultant sound-quality was one step down from that derived through live transmission. Aside from technological limitations, the new radio art was perceived as a *live* entertainment form by the early stations, their audiences and by the government.

And especially by the government. By 1922, The Department of Commerce was favoring station applicants who promised to transmit live programs, eschewing the use of phonograph records. However, with the rush to get federal authorization permits to operate stations—the number went from 30 in 1922 to 556 in 1923—many stations kept right on playing records. Their increased use through the 1920s, however, played an insignificant part in the story of popular music on radio.

When NBC introduced its network in 1926 and radio was seeping into all parts of the country, it heightened the prestige of live entertainment. Independent stations were usually the ones with lower power and generally less desirable frequencies; they had no other choice but to build their program content around phonograph records. Network executives, their popular music stars and their affiliates sniffed contempuously at this practice. Often these programs used the artists' recordings, their theme songs and other trappings, hoping to pawn off the finished product as live offerings. So upset at this pettifoggery were some of the band leaders, they refused to record their theme songs. In the early 1930s, Fred Waring became incensed enough to discontinue making records because small stations around the country were using his material to devise shows and peddling them locally, often in competition with his network sponsor. The leader would not take his Pennsylvanians into a recording studio for the next ten years.[4]

While Waring and some of his contemporaries were fuming at such minor league skullduggery-cum-show-biz ingenuity—it must also be kept in mind stations of all size were subscribing to the newly-developed transcription services to supplement their record collections—there emerged in the two major cities on the East and West Coasts a phenomenon that would revolutionize the presentation of recorded popular music on the radio.

In 1933, when Al Jarvis developed his "make believe ballroom" concept on KFWB, Los Angeles, he attempted to create the illusion that he was actually in a dance palace with the big bands. In so doing, he elevated the stature of the announcer introducing the records, from one of nondescript anonynmity to one with an identifiable personality. Jarvis performed just as though he were doing big band remotes; the major difference was Al Jarvis injected more of himself into the proceedings. Whereas announcers assigned to dance or orchestra remote duties usually were required to limit themselves to brief song introductions and occasional banter with the maestros, Jarvis made a self-conscious effort to present a *show* of which he was an integral part, rather than just an obligatory appendage.

Two years later, after a Californian named Martin Block had landed in New York at WNEW, he took Jarvis's idea and established his own mythical ballroom. He thus became the cornerstone of what eventually ended up as the fulltime popular music station—with *respectability*. Martin Block's major contribution to popular music radio was his unique performing style surrounding the records. (After all, only General Manager Bernice Judis could decide *what* went on WNEW.) Block's uniqueness lay in *how* it was done. Like the bandleaders whose records he played, and like the announcers on live network shows, Martin Block fashioned an air style, one that would be instantly recognized, and one that was pleasing to the ear. Martin Block projected an intimacy foreign to the run-of-the-mill announcers who appeared between records on stations across America in the mid-1930s. And there were a lot of them at this time. For in spite of the Depression, as of January 1, 1936, there were 616 licensed operations on the air.

In a sense, Martin Block was following in the path of two seminal radio personalities who had skillfully mastered a distinctive microphone technique—Bing Crosby and Franklin D. Roosevelt. Several years earlier, Crosby and President Roosevelt had both carefully cultivated the art of voice projection, and thanks to network radio, altered the course of politics and crooning. What Block, Bing and FDR had in common was an intuitive grasp of the dynamics of broadcast technology (i.e. how to "play" a microphone) and communicate with the listener in a one-on-one basis. To all three, there was no "vast audience out there in radioland." There was only a collection of individual listeners, each one being talked to or sung for personally. Program directors would later call Martin Block's mode of communication *empathy* and write thousands of memos on "Relating to the Listener."

To modern ears, much of Block's patter would sound phony. Instead of coming right out and announcing a record, Block perpetrated the fabrication that he was there in person with the artist. To circumvent the Federal Communications Commission (whose regulations by now required a phonograph record to be identified as such) Block came up with an introduction that went something like this: "And now, just for the record, here's Benny Goodman and the band swinging out for all *Ballroom* patrons with 'The One O'Clock Jump.' Take it, Benny." After the record ended: "Thanks, Benny. That was great. I never heard the band sound better. And I really mean that, fellah." He had numerous variations of this hokum. Block's standard sign-off ("for you, and you, and especially for you") left listeners with a cozy afterglow. They *knew* he really meant it.

The key to Martin Block's success was that he, first and foremost, established rapport with listeners. Believability followed. For even though most of his audience knew his "Ballroom" was a contrivance, there was a willing supension of disbelief. There was no contradiction between the downright flim-flam of the way Block handled the entertainment content and the credibility he enjoyed as an on-air pitchman.* He became radio's first super salesman-disc jockey by following the cardinal rule of selling: he sold himself. John V.B. Sullivan points out the first tangible evidence of his pulling power occurred early in Block's career at WNEW. The station sales manager suggested offering a one-dollar box of Fathers' Day cigars only on the Block program. Next day 150 one-dollar bills landed on the executive's desk.[5] Once during a winter snow storm, a Block sponsor offered refrigerators at a special discount if shoppers would go immediately to his store. After Block's spiel, 109 listeners had trudged through the snow to take advantage of the bargain.[6]

---

* For air personalities, past and present, the most formidable weapons in the disc jockey's quiver, whether going after a raise or a better job, are high ratings and sales success stories.

Block went on to become one of the top on-air salesmen in broadcasting history. This commercial salesmanship and his ability to weave the fantasy of the ballroom were of the same piece of cloth. Jack Sullivan recalls when WNEW moved its operations to Fifth Avenue in 1946, the station designed a "make believe ballroom" studio. "It had a crystal chandalier. It had ballroom chairs around the edge painted with red velvet seats . . . All the people I would show through there—whether Tony Bennett, a sales rep, a contest winner or an ad agency man—99.9% of them would say, 'You know, it doesn't look exactly as I thought.' The point is everybody had his own idea of what the *Make Believe Ballroom* looked like."[7]

Block's audience extended beyond the New York Metropolitan Area. For although WNEW's power was only 10,000 watts at the time, it had a good frequency (1130), and it benefited from the fact that the less crowded spectrum of the 1930s did not require existing stations to perfect elaborate antenna arrays for protecting other stations as is the case with today's squeezed frequencies. History will never record how many teenage boys were inspired to become disc jockeys because of Martin Block. In addition, he exerted a powerful influence on American pop music in another way. Based in New York with its entertainment field centrality, and broadcasting from the country's premier station for recorded music, Block knew most of the band leaders and vocalists personally. If Martin Block liked a recording, the artist who made it had climbed a few inches further up the slippery show biz pole.

George Simon, a reporter for *Metronome,* one of the popular music periodicals of the day, and later chonicler of the big band era, considered Block's influential program a major factor in many artists' success—Glenn Miller's, for example:

> Block's *Make Believe Ballroom* served as a barometer of a band's [Miller's] popularity. Block liked the sound and he liked Glenn and so the new records began to get some important air time . . . [The Make Believe Ballroom] on WNEW was then far and away the most important spot for big bands.[8]

By the late 1930s and early 1940s, Block's imposing voice had become a familiar one on the American airwaves. Recognizing his potency, several sponsors selected him as their announcer for top network popular music programs, including *Your Hit Parade* and the *Chesterfield Supper Club,* as well as the soap opera, *Pepper Young's Family.* But the *Make Believe Ballroom* remained his *tour de force.*

As the country more noticeably began to shake off the effects of the Depression and started tooling up its defense arsenal, the number of licensed stations had grown considerably. During the stagnant period from 1931 to January, 1936, only 13 new licenses were issued. But between 1936 and January 1, 1940, licensee ranks swelled by 149 to 765. New station owners were aware that hooking up with a network during this period was a virtual impossibility. It has been said more than once by those recalling the so-called "Golden Age of Radio," that a network affiliation was "a license to steal." Going into the radio business, sans network, for these newcomers meant relying mainly on recorded popular music. Thus, the late 1930s and early 1940s found the disc jockey trade growing by leaps and bounds.

Some of those who cut their show business eye teeth with a turntable, a microphone and a stack of 78 records, would become familiar American household names. The rest, a much larger group, would find fame (of sorts), but be limited to a local following; in some cases, their celebrity spread beyond their station's coverage area to a knowledgeable cognoscenti that included other disc jockeys, broadcasting professionals, record company types, pop artists, as well as assorted middlemen and hangers-on who have always lurked on the fringes of the popular music world. If a listener, tired of live popular music on the networks in the 1940s, had a powerful receiver capable of picking up every station in America, he would have wanted to sample the leading platter spinners of the day. Those whom he would have frequently tuned in were an assortment of personalities who demonstrated that good showmanship could carry a popular music program—no matter if it did consist of "just records."

In Washington, Arthur Godfrey was doing the wake-up show on WJSV ("Willingly Jesus Suffered Victory") whose on-air location was not given as Washington, but Mt. Vernon Hills, Virginia. The station's call letters were subsequently changed to WTOP. Earlier, Godfrey had been at WFBR, Baltimore and WMAL, Washington, the latter sacking him for his irreverent and unorthodox comments, particularly about sponsors. One of Godfrey's initial assignments, in addition to his *Sundial* show on WJSV, was his reconstruction of Washington Senators baseball games. He and his co-announcer, Arch McDonald, originated the program from various Peoples' Drug Stores in Washington, using record "fills" if their Western Union ticker failed, or if rain delays occurred. But it was his morning show capers a decade later around which Godfrey built a reputation that would eventually lead to network stardom on radio and television.

When the CBS brass installed Arthur Godfrey in the key morning slot on its New York flagship station, WCBS, it was undoubtedly with the intention of dethroning the host of WOR's early-riser goings-on, John B. Gambling. Already an institution by this time, having begun on WOR in the mid-1920s, Gambling consistently featured more talk than music.

Gambling's initial foray into morning radio provides another one of the more interesting examples of how casual events often influenced the early careers of radio's pioneer performers. A former wireless operator in the British Navy, Gambling stayed in New York after his discharge and joined WOR as a studio engineer. One morning in March, 1925, the regular announcer for Bernarr MacFadden's exercise program failed to show

up. Gambling quickly grabbed the microphone, a chore that he performed so well he was appointed the program's chief announcer. When
the physical culture "buff" left the show some months later, Gambling
took over. His popularity subsequently led WOR to drop the calisthenics
and install *Gambling's Musical Clock*. The show was later tagged with a
more appropriate title, *Rambling with Gambling*. Recordings ultimately
replaced studio musicians, and when Gambling retired in 1959, John A.
Gambling replaced his father. A Gambling dynasty may be in the works
at WOR. For in 1978, John R. Gambling had joined his father on the air
as part of the grooming process in the line of secession.

If John B. Gambling, the elder, relied more on chatter than on music,
station personalities elsewhere in the early 1940s were re-inforcing the
original role of the voice between the records: to comment *about* the records. Jack Lescoulie was a morning man on WNEW, while Stan Shaw
became the station's initial host of the *Milkman's Matinee*—one of the
nation's first midnight-to-dawn recorded music sources. Freddy Robbins,
a glib knowledgeable man-about-pop who had come from WITH, Baltimore and Alan Courtney were favorites on WOV, New York. (There were
reports of Robbins' *1280 Club* being heard as far away as Virginia.) Far-
ther uptown, Harlem listeners were digging a hip white record spinner on
WHOM. He had come to WHOM from WBNX, a small New York station, where he featured mostly records by black swing bands. His real
name was Sid Torin, but to his coterie of black admirers, he was Symphony Sid. Torin's use of a pseudonym was a practice that would gain
wide usage in the disc jockey profession, as will be noted later. Symphony
Sid's late night bill of fare consisted of "sepia" and "race" records at first
and then bop-cum-mainstream jazz. He remained at WHOM through most
of the decade. New York contemporaries of Symphony Sid included Gene
King, whose *Midnight Jamboree* on WEVD (Eugene V. Debs) featured
current bands and vocalists, and WOR's Henry Morgan, whose notoriety
derived more from spoofing sponsors' commercials than from his musical
expertise.

As would be expected, the biggest volume of recorded music was being
pumped out into the airwaves of America's show business hub. But far
removed from Manhattan, across the land in the larger cities, certain announcers were developing a following, thanks to a shrewd blend of chitchat and popular music. Steve Allen began his broadcasting career as a
disc jockey on KOY, Phoenix in 1942. Baltimore turntables helped launch
the careers of Gene Klavan and Win Elliot (WBAL), as well as Eddie Hubbard and Gene Rayburn (WITH). In Philadelphia, two important names
stood out when you mentioned popular music on radio: Doug Arthur, of
WIBG's *Danceland;* and Bob Horn whose *C'Mon and Dance* on WIP provided college students in the Delaware Valley with musical therapy to ease
their late night studies. Jack Paar's last job before being inducted into

military service was as head greeter on the *Sun Greeter Club,* WBEN, Buffalo.

World War II saw the budding disc jockey phenomenon become suspended in limbo. The federal government's strict regulations on what could and what couldn't be said over the air; the drafting of many record spinners and their youthful followers; the ASCAP flap with broadcasters in 1941; Petrillo's ban against recording, begun in 1942 and not totally resolved until 1944—all contributed to the anemic condition of what had been another growing and fascinating development during radio's first two decades.

The unprecedented wartime profits reaped by network affiliates and independents alike continued into 1946. In those closing days of pre-television euphoria, network stations were offering their standard fare of soap operas, comedy, drama, news and a generous amount of live popluar music. On many of these stations, the "platter spinner," if he existed at all— live local programs were still preferred to plug network gaps—occupied a position of importance in the business of entertaining the listening public roughly akin to that of a sexton ringing a church bell. Station management had little confidence in him; he was usually low man in the staff announcer pecking order. Top announcers got to do the news, the live shows, the remotes. In many cases, the pre-War image of a non-network radio station that had to rely on phonograph records was one of second-rate radio. Conventional wisdom at this time, shared by many broadcasters and listeners alike, could be stated quite simply: if these announcers that play records were any good, they'd be working at a network station.

There were obviously some countervening opinions because as of January 1, 1947, the FCC had issued authorizations for 1517 stations, and the vast majority of that number were network affiliates. By January 1, 1948, the number on the air leaped to 1621. With only so many network affiliations to go around, and with television just over the horizon, program content would have to come from somewhere. Unless some genius had a secret program weapon up his sleeve, or an unidentified show biz angel was ready to launch a fifth major radio network, there could be only one answer: recorded popular music. To fill so much airtime, however, required more than someone who had a gift of gab and/or a knowledge of popular music. It called for a mysterious alchemy in which the gab and the music would blend into one. Not every disc jockey who landed behind a microphone in those post-War days became such an alchemist, but the profession grew in numbers and influence.

If our super-powerful receiver could have been plugged in during the second half of the 1940s, a listener could have pulled out of the air an assortment of delivery styles and approaches. For without undue alarums and excursions, he had arrived—the full blown, gen-u-ine, no-more-identity-crisis, an American original, THE DISC JOCKEY. Across the dial the new pied pipers plied their trade: in Chicago, Wally Phillips (WGN), Howard Miller (WIND) and (WCFL), Dave Garroway (WMAQ), succeeded by Mike Wallace and his then-wife, Buff Cobb, Hugh Downs (WMAQ); in New York, Rayburn and Finch and Al "Jazzbo" Collins (WNEW); in Los Angeles, Dick Haymes, Alex Cooper, Bob McLaughlin, Gene Norman, and Peter Potter (KLAC's "Big 5"); in Pittsburgh, Bill Cullen (KDKA); in Philadelphia, Joe McCauley (WIP); in Cleveland, Soupy Sales (WJW). In the air everywhere there were disc jockeys.

By late 1946 and early 1947, all sorts of radio personalities were abandoning their accustomed roles and becoming disc jockeys. Ted Husing, the highly respected former sports director of CBS turned up on WHN, New York as emcee of a daily record show. Paul Whiteman was launched with appropriate ruffles and flourishes by the ABC Network to do a five-a-week spin. Tommy Dorsey, who had discarded his orchestra, signed up to do a syndicated disc jockey stint, carried via transcription on 450 stations. Andre Baruch, one of network radio's top announcers, joined his wife Bea Wain, ex-big band vocalist, on WMCA, New York for a Mr. and Mrs. Deejay showcase.

So important had the disc jockey become in a relatively short time that *Time* in mid-summer, 1947 officially certified the legitimacy of the profession by featuring a survey showing the astronomical salaries some disc jockeys were pulling down:

Paul Whiteman (ABC)	—$208,000
Martin Block (MBS & WNEW, N.Y. & KFWB, L.A.)	—$512,000
Tommy Dorsey (Syndication)	—$300,000
Ted Husing (WHN, N.Y.)	—$256,000
Andre Baruch & Beau Wain (WMCA, N.Y.)	—$150,000
Al Jarvis (KLAC, L.A.)	—$190,000
Arthur Godfrey (WCBS, N.Y. & WTOP, Wash.)	—$150,000
Ray Perkins (KFEL, Denver)	—$Unav.
Jack Eigen (WINS, N.Y.)	—$200,000[9]

There were other signs in 1947 that the disc jockey was changing not only the nature of popular music, but the way it "happened." Early that year, Kurt Webster, who conducted the *Midnight Dancing Party* on WBT, Charlotte, North Carolina (and dubbed himself, "The Midnight Mayor of Charlotte"), resurrected a recording Ted Weems had made in 1932. The tune was "Heartaches," which Webster quickly adopted as his theme. It went into fourth place its first week on *Your Hit Parade,* became the number one song on April 19th and 26th, and placed in the top seven through June 21st, for a total 13-week run. So popular was Webster's *Midnight Dancing Party,* that WBT on occasion moved the show to remote locations. One such remote originated in York, Pennsylvania, 450 miles from Charlotte. With WBT's 50,000 watt clear channel facility, York listeners had no trouble receiving the program. Webster's following was verified when he came to York's Valencia Ballroom for a "live" broadcast in the spring of 1947. Valencia manager Steve Tassia remembers Webster's show filling the ballroom and creating an aura of excitement akin to that of the big bands a decade earlier.[10]

No sooner had the "Heartaches" craze subsided than Eddie Hubbard, a disc jockey on WIND, Chicago began playing a contemporary recording (by The Harmonicats) of a maudlin, 1913 barroom ballad, "Peg 'O My Heart." The tune went into first place on *Your Hit Parade* in its initial appearance on the show. Before it dropped off the nation's "official" song rating index, "Peg 'O My Heart" had held first place for ten weeks. Only eight songs did as well or better in the entire history of *Your Hit Parade*. When the year ended "Peg 'O My Heart" was the top song of 1947. "Heartaches" finished in ninth place.

As radio entered the 1950s, the hot glare of the tube was becoming more intense. Rudy Vallee, one of network radio's super-star casualties, undoubtedly spoke for others in his shoes. In turning disc jockey (WOR), he delivered his version of an obituary for the medium: "Radio as I knew it, is alack-a-day, no more, no more."[11] Rudy Vallee was right, of course: radio as *he* knew it was no more. And in broadcasting circles, it didn't take long to realize that the disc jockey was a *local* creature. Veteran Al Jarvis pointed out one of the many problems of a national disc jockey: "Look at what happens with varying weather conditions. I'm out driving in a real California downpour and I have the radio on to a deejay show. As a listener I'm not paying any attention to the fact that the guy is broadcasting from New York. All of a sudden he says, 'Isn't this a beautiful day?' Boom—that program is shot for me. I can't believe anything he says."[12] In addition, to Jarvis's fundamental concept of localism, there was another drawback. The listener encountered an uneven program flow when the traditional network fare was inter-mixed with a record show, no matter how big the host's name. Such juxtapositioning violated the block principle of programming so important to an all-music station.

One's former status as a national radio personality did not necessarily make him a card-carrying member of the disc jockey fraternity. The Vallee's and Dorsey's didn't last very long. Paul Whiteman may have been Mr. Popular Music in the 1920s, but as a network disc jockey he laid an egg. Although ABC racked up $5,000,000 in advertising, the show was dropped after one year. During these waning years of network radio, as television continued to take its toll, stations of all sizes, including network affiliates were turning to their turntables. They had no place else to go. The average station, according to a 1953 *Billboard* poll, was devoting nearly half of its air time to disc jockey and other recorded music shows, with stations 5000 watts and over filling 41.6% of their airtime in that matter, and lower power outlets, with 49.8%. Fifty-seven percent indicated they were airing more record shows than a year ago, and 59% said they had more sponsors.[13]

As more of their number rode the kilocycles, there was another sign of the growing importance of disc jockeys: their paychecks. "THE RICHEST GUYS IN RADIO," trumpeted a *Variety* headline late in 1954. "Go into big city or small town around the country and it's the disc jockey with the local following who has established himself as the solid citizen with the high-bracketed income tax return . . . These are the boys with the local chunks of time and percentage arrangements, and they're having a field day . . ." *Variety* cited some examples:

Los Angeles

Peter Potter, Al Jarvis and Larry Finley (KFWB)	—$ 60,000
Bill Leyden, Red Rowe, Zeke Manners, Frank Bull and Bob McLaughlin (KFWB)	—$ 25,000
Dick Haymes, Alex Cooper, Jim Ameche, and Gene Norman (KLAC)	—$ 25,000
Ira Cook, Johnny Grant, and Dick Whittinghill (KMPC)	—$ 25,000

New York

John B. Gambling (WOR)	—$150,000
Martin Block (WABC alone)	—$100,000
Jerry Marshall (WNEW)	—$ 75,000
Jack Sterling (WCBS)	—$ 60,000
Allyn Edwards (WRCA)	—$ 50,000
Art Ford (WNEW)	—$ 40,000
Jim McCoy (WRCA)	—$ 35,000
Al (Jazzbo) Collins (WRCA)	—$ 30,000

Chicago

Howard Miller (WIND)	—$ 70,000

Washington

Eddie Gallagher (WTOP)	—$ 50,000

Pittsburgh

Rege Cordic (KDKA)	—$ 50,000 [14]

If stations in Toledo and Tuscon and Tacoma couldn't match those figures, disc jockey pay in most medium to large markets was relatively good—and, the job did not call for any heavy lifting.

What exactly did these guys, these disc jockeys, do to rate such good salaries? Why did more and more of them keep turning up on the dial? What kind of aural charisma did they project to make people go out and buy their sponsors' products? What was the big deal anyway? The big deal was that the disc jockey had become the new pied piper of American popular music. Saxie Dowell, former sideman-singer with Hal Kemp, and later a bandleader himself, assessed their role at the close of the big band era: "The deejay today is a replacement—a replacement for the traveling bands and artists, the publishers' contact men and the singers, who used to cover their assigned territories in person to spread the plug songs of the day. In other words, the disc jockey today is the showcase for talents and tunes and a showcase for the public." [15]

No less a popular music titan than Bing Crosby was aware the old order was passing. The Old Groaner noted that "the whole music business has shaken out and changed a lot, but not all for the better, by any fair means of foul . . . the way the game is played now, it's the disc jockey— as much as, or more than the singers—who produce the hits. A young singer starting out now has to woo them because they run the business . . . Some of them bother me. I really believe that if a disc jockey is going to set himself up as a judge, he should have some real knowledge of what he's about. It's apparent that many who speak in the accents of authority are all accent and no authority. By playing and replaying a song which has nothing but nuisance value, a large nuisance and a lot of sales can be brought about. But in the long run, that practice will give this business a short haul and a bad shake." He further despaired of the "tuneless trend that seems to be the coming vogue." [16] Then Crosby took off on the content of some of the things the disc jockeys were playing. Songs of another day (e.g. "Sweet and Lovely" and "Love Thy Neighbor") "survived my assult on them. No screams. No honks . . ." [17] Perhaps in referring to "honks" and "screams," Der Bingle had heard the primal cry of rock and roll rising in the land.*

In any event, the response to Crosby's evaluation was immediate. From large and small markets came the reactions, pro and con; they provided a microcosmic view of how deejays viewed their role in popular music at the time:

FOR CROSBY

Gordie Baker (WSPR, Springfield, Mass.): "Certainly Bing is right; Mike Woloson (WNOR, Norfolk, Va.): "A lot of d.j.'s . . . have no knowledge of music, of the artists, or their backgrounds, or of what the word, variety, means." Rex Dales (WCKY, Cincinnati, Ohio): "Bing's really right. We have become the medium of exposure for new songs and new artists. Many of us have become so occupied with trying to come up with something 'different,' we've lost sight of everything save 'self-promotion' "; Dick Whittinghill (KMPC, Los Angeles, Calif.): "When a disc jockey starts to feel that he is more important than the talent on records he plays, look out"; Ray Perkins (KIMN, Denver, Col.): "Bing's analysis is fair." [18]

---

* Bill Haley's recording of "Shake Rattle and Roll" had gone as high as seventh place on "Billboard's Hot 100" in August, 1954. "Dim, Dim the Lights" by Haley reached the eleventh spot about the same time as Crosby's polemic in November of 1954. It should be kept in mind, *Your Hit Parade* was still on television at this time. The "Hot 100" was *Billboard's* weekly tabulation of the nation's best selling records. The two were not always in agreement. For what it's worth, the week Crosby made his comments, the #1 song in America, according to both listings was "Mr. Sandman."

AGAINST CROSBY

Rudy Ertis (WTOL, Toledo, Ohio): "It seems absurd to assume the d.j.'s as a group are so well knit together that they will act in the same manner for the sheer joy of it, go out promoting a 'tuneless trend' "; Al Radka (KFRE, Fresno, Calif.): "The public, not the d.j.'s, makes the hits"; Dick Gilbert (KTYL, Phoenix, Arizona): "Crosby's falling for a fallacy when he states that jockeys are predominantly responsible for producing the hits"; Nick Nickson (WBBF, Rochester, NY): "Things are changing. Bing came along at a time the nation needed comfort and solace. The ballad was the ideal form of popular music. It does seem in looking back, songs always seem better." [19]

If some deejays at this time were experiencing identity crises, others knew exactly who they were—or more accurately who they were *supposed* to be. In New Orleans, and Dallas, and Omaha, the vanguard of the talking heads followed their leaders, Storz and McLendon, to become the first wave of shock troops of Top 40 Radio. Adhering to the carefully crafted policy books of a format formula, Top 40 *energized* popular music. The jock was told where the music, the contest promos, the commercials were to go. The clock hour spelled it all out. From the inception of Top 40, the disc jockey was drilled on one word—*relate:* "Relate to the audience in everything you say between records, your records, your jokes, your weather forecasts." And there were always those call letters. The listener must never forget the call letters. It was WDGY time, WDGY temperature, WDGY-land. Because of these and other imperatives, critics often accused Top 40 of dehumanizing the disc jockey. In most cases, this was far from the case; format radio *was* personality radio.

As the Top 40 parade rumbled across American radio dials, there were deejays who could be exciting, or abrasive, or funny, or cocky, or fast-talking. They could illuminate, or infuriate, or cogitate; some could even desecrate. In Top 40 Radio, doctrinaire McLendon and Storz variety—the dj act was one of the most carefully produced acts in American show business history. The disc jockey was vital to the aural ambiance of Top 40.

Minute attention was paid to details. The studio and transmitting equipment was the latest and best—always. The SOUND of the station had to be right. The disc jockey was required to stand *up* to the microphone to do his shows, not sit down *with* the mike. He was at the controls with his turntables and console board. He set the levels of loudness and softness and spun the records. He *was* the pilot of the airwaves. There were no directors in a control room, pointing fingers, throwing cues and calling the shots through the studio window. The Top 40 dj was his own producer-director. No phone calls from wife or girl friend were permitted; the phone was for contest call-ins only. He was critiqued constantly, on the air, and off; he never knew when he was being taped by management.

If he talked too little or too much, or blew an element of his show, he heard about it quickly, from the program director or from the hard-driving general manager Himself. The disc jockey's name was the name of the show. It was the *Ed Jock Show;* no more *Record Room* or *Wax Works.* If a holdover personality from old time radio couldn't make the transition, he was dismissed.

But popular music was always the centerpiece of the Top 40 format. No disc jockey therein was allowed to comment unfavorably on the music. The word, "record" on the air was a no-no. Introductions to tunes were embellished with a minimum of words ("Here's the buckskin guy himself with #5 in WDGYland this week—Pat Boone and 'Love Letters in the Sand' "). The deejay talked over a record in announcing it, only if it had an instrumental introduction, the length of which he knew to the split second. His timing was so precise that the last record right before the news had to end without being cut. A piece of popular music was more than record—it was a *performance* on a Top 40 station, and the jock was every bit as important as the night club emcee bringing on the next act. Top 40 Radio was so much more than 30 or 40 recordings played over and over with yak between them—it was a carefully constructed mosaic of show-manship held together by the disc jockey. And when rock and roll became the *sine qua non* of Top 40 Radio, the musical acts he introduced on record, challenged him to new heights.

The program fragmentation that had been set off by the demise of the networks found unique expression in select parts of radioland during the late 1940s and early 1950s. Scattered throughout the South, rhythm and blues (r. & b.) deejay shows followed no prescribed format. In fact, the growing acceptance of this relatively new (to white ears, anyway) black music posed the problem of how to handle it on the air:

> The most telling point raised by the exponents of the exclusively r & b type program is that these discs can be heard only on the r & b shows, and that is why such shows have an audience in the first place . . . How-ever deejays who favor a somewhat mixed program claim there is no dividing line between an r & b and a jazz record (and occasionally even a pop record) and that many jazz and pop discs fit brightly into the pro-gram and give it a wider appeal.[20]

Before its wider progagation by the r & b jocks, recorded black music on radio was a scarce commodity. In the early 1940s there were few places on the dial where the music content was aimed at black audiences. (WJLD, Birmingham and WHAT, Philadelphia, were notable exceptions). Jack L. Cooper, radio's first important black disc jockey, had built a reputation on WSBC, Chicago. Cooper was considered a top air salesman-entertainer of his time. It was not until 1948, however, that WDIA, Memphis featured black deejays, playing mostly blues, rhythm and blues, and gospel. Memphis, with its high concentration of blacks, was a logical place to launch such a program approach. B.B. (for Blues Boy) King, Howling Wolf, Sonny Boy Williamson and Rufus Thomas were blues artists who doubled as jocks on WDIA. A handful of other blacks on smaller stations in the South helped spread the r & b message. But it was the white disc jockeys on stations owned by Whites in the South who were spinning an ever-increasing line-up of records by black artists such as Dinah Washington, Amos Milburn, Wyonie Harris, Charles Brown, The Ravens, The Orioles, et al. Nevertheless, it was in the populous Northeast that a disc jockey gave rhythm and blues its greatest boost, later claiming he renamed it rock and roll, and finally earn for the fraternity its greatest notoriety.

Alan Freed, who was born in Johnstown, Pa., December 15, 1921, and grew up in Salem, Ohio, began his radio career in 1943 on WKST, New Castle, Pa., playing classical records. He moved to WAKR, Akron, Ohio where he did *Request Review* for O'Neil's Department Store for four years starting in 1946. After a contract dispute* prevented him from signing with WADC, Akron, he moved to Cleveland where he planned to do a TV version of *Request Review*. The show failed, and in 1951 he became a dj on WJW. Lee Mintz, the proprietor of the record store that sponsored Freed's show, noticing increase sales of r & b records, prevailed upon Freed to play more of them on his show. Freed demurred at first. Possibly reflecting his training as a classical trombonist, he felt rhythm and blues had a limited appeal.

After watching white teenagers buy the records at Mintz's, he convinced the station's general manager that the music belonged on the air. Thus was born the *Moon Dog Show*, billed later as the *Moon Dog House Rock and Roll Party*. The program title was inspired by the theme song Freed had chosen, "Blues for Moon Dog," by Todd Rhodes. The Moon Dog sobriquet was dropped when he invaded New York radio later, where an eccentric street musician, "The King of The Moon Doggers," enjoined Freed from using the name. But on WJW, Freed was The Moon Dog. He howled over the music, and between plays, he kept time with the beat by pounding on a telephone book. The nasality of his voice and the way he projected it, along with its gravelish quality (derived by having a polyp removed) made him "sound black." Featuring recordings by black artists such as Ivory Joe Hunter, Bo Diddley, Chuck Berry (with whom Freed is listed as co-author of "Maybelline") and Joe Turner, the *Moon Dog Show*, riding WJW's 50,000 watts, went beyond Cleveland's environs, as he indicated on an introduction to one of his WJW shows:

> Hello everybody. How are you tonight? This is Alan Freed, your old King of the Moon-doggers. It's time again for another of your favorite rock 'n'

---

* Many radio stations include in their employment contracts a clause prohibiting key personnel from going to a competitive station for a specified period of time, usually six months.

roll specials, blues and rhythm records by all the gang in the Moondog Kingdom, from the Midwest to the East Coast. We're going to be sendin' hello's to a lot of folks who have written to us from all over The Moondog Kingdom, all around the Cleveland area, Newark, New Jersey, New York City, Long Island—wherever you are.[21]

Later, the program was picked up for re-broadcast by several other stations. Freed called the dances, which he promoted on his show and which he emceed, "Moon Dog Coronation Balls," and found receptive crowds in Ohio and Western Pennsylvania.

Freed left Cleveland for New York in December, 1954 where his show was heard for over four years, first on WINS, and later on WABC, both 50,000 watters. Scheduled in the best teen-age time slot, 6:30 or 7:00 p.m. to 11:00 p.m., Alan Freed proved his Cleveland success was no fluke. When he left the studio for broadcast-record hops from such places as St. Nicholas Arena, requests had to be limited to telegrams—telephone lines couldn't handle the traffic. Freed produced stage shows that drew record crowds at the Brooklyn and Broadway Paramount Theaters. His $300,000 box office from the 1958 Christmas Week Show at the Broadway Paramount evoked shades of Benny Goodman and Frank Sinatra.

After being accused of inciting a riot of sorts at a Boston concert, Freed resigned from WINS in May, 1959 and moved to WABC. He was fired later that year for refusing to sign a statement that he had not accepted bribes for playing specific records. In May, 1960 he was arrested on the bribery charge in Los Angeles, where he had taken his act to KDAY. The indictment alleged Freed had received over $30,200 from certain record companies for pushing their records. Not long after, he was accused of evading $47,920 in income taxes. In 1962, he turned up at WQAM, Miami where his punishment was announced: $300 and six months suspended sentence. The Moon Dog's howls were last heard on KNOB, Los Angeles. Alan Freed, 47, died a broken man on January 19, 1965, Lyndon Johnson's inauguration day.

Alan Freed's tragedy was obviously one of greed. He and the disc jockeys who where guilty of accepting payola, it turned out, were a small minority. But the publicity given the payola scandals of 1959–60 was so pervasive that, two decades later, payola would still be perceived as a phenomenon limited to disc jockeys.

Payola of one form or another, of course, is as old as commerce. Political payola in the 1970s had become so commonplace that newspapers often relegated stories of influence-peddling and pay-offs to inside pages. In the pop music business, it was a refined art by the 1980s. *Variety* focused attention on the practice in 1916 when the entertainment weekly's business manager, John J. O'Connor, was instrumental in forming the Music Publishers Protective Association, a group of 35 song publishers who banded together for one purpose: to end the bidding against each other in offering vaudeville performers money for singing their songs. The middleman who took care of paying the artists was the song plugger.

When sheet music was popular music's chief medium, and before mechanical reproduction, the song plugger was the key figure in the hit-making process. Isaac Goldberg, Tin Pan Alley's first chronicler, called him "the liaison-officer between Publisher and Public. He is the publisher's lobbyist wherever music is played. He it is, who by all arts of persuasion, intrigue, bribery, mayhem, malfeasance, cajolery, entreaty, threat, insinuation, persistence and whatever else he has, sees to it that his employer's music shall be heard . . ." [22] Al Jolson, who enjoyed the sport of kings, was reported to have received a horse from a song plugger for favoring a certain song.

Rumors of "pay for play" flourished during the dance band era. The maestros, it was said, got their part of the action through performance fees and royalty payments. George Simon a reporter for *Metronome*, a popular music magazine of the period, recalled a comment by Tommy Dorsey that reflected the feelings of many orchestra leaders: "They [the song-pluggers] come in and instead of a direct, 'Here's a tune I think will be good for the band, please look it over,' they try hard as hell to be subtle, put their arms around me, shake my one hand with two of theirs— all in an attempt to have me believe that they love me, and that I'm one helluva wonderful guy. But through it all, I know exactly what they're driving at, and that any minute they're going to drive in for the kill with the usual stuff about the 'most terrific tune of the year.' " [23]

If payola was part of the popular music tradition, there was little talk about it publicly during the big band era. (The most prominent surfacing of the subject involved *Your Hit Parade*.) When the disc jockey replaced the orchestra leader as the chief honcho in the music delivery system, however, payola was to become a household term. The first flush of rhythm and blues that helped usher in the "new" popular music of the early 1950s brought with it the suggestion that payola was involved. As the number of disc jockeys playing r & b records increased, so did the accusations.

In 1954, *Variety*, in its continuing anti-payola crusade (begun in the magazine's early days), ran a hard-hitting series of editorials in August. Written by Editor Abel Green, the commentaries covered payola from several angles. In discussing disc jockeys, Green deferred to Mitch Miller, Artists and Repertory Director, Columbia Records. The central theme of Miller's rambling discourse on payola was his assertion that payola was caused by "the abdication of the stations to the disc jockeys." [24]

The tempo of the 1950s payola flap increased in proportion to the fast-rising influence of the disc jockey and rock and roll. In a move to air mutual concerns about the emerging "modern radio," and to elevate the status of the disc jockey (who had been taking more and more payola lumps), the Storz Stations organized the first Annual Pop Music Disc

Jockey Convention. The conclave held in Kansas City, March, 1958, was attended by representatives of the broadcasting and recording industries. On hand to continue on-going his crusade against Top 40 Radio was Mitch Miller. Titled "The Great Abdication," the bearded a & r director of Columbia Records took the conventioneers to task for what he claimed was their wooing of the teen and sub-teen audience. (Many industry observers at the time wondered what Miller would have said, had his own Columbia label been producing hit records.) In spite of Miller's self-serving speech which caused no small reaction in the trade, the Storz organization went ahead and planned Pop Music—DJ Convention II. It was this convention, more than any single event, that would be used to hang the payola mill-stone around the neck of Top 40 Radio.

The Storz-sponsored gathering at the Miami Beach Americana Hotel, over the 1959 Memorial Day week-end, was no different from any of that uniquely American genre, The Convention. As anyone who ever attended one knows, all the events and resources of a professional or trade parley are not listed on the printed agenda. But because of enormous publicity, the Storz Miami convention was perceived to be worthy of an x-rated film plot. The sensationalism it generated helped indirectly to lead to Congressional hearings. Bill Stewart, a Storz program executive at the time, later recalled one reason the second (and last) Storz Disc Jockey Convention came to get its bad reviews:

> . . . Down there in Miami the press was really out to get us.* This guy came in and wrote a story on the convention for a national magazine. He also wrote a story for the local newspaper and the final day of the convention which was headlined, "Booze, Broads, and Bribes" across the front of the paper. Alliterative, but not actually true. It sure did cause quite a lot of consternation for me, because my wife came down. We were going to go to the Bahamas when I picked her up at the airport, she had already bought a copy of the paper . . . I still hear more wild stories about what was supposed to have happened there that are so far from the truth.[25]

For a clearer understanding of the disc jockey payola scandals, it is necessary to appreciate an investigation epidemic that swept America beginning in the early 1950s. Wrong doing, alleged or otherwise, is the red meat of the news, and the press found plenty of it to report: The McCarthy

---

* There was a great deal of truth in what Stewart said. A highly respected broadcaster, he was no thin-skinned, blame-it-on-the-press apologist for the industry. Segments of the press at the time were giving the payola issue a big play. Some newspapers which owned old-line stations that were smarting under the competition of the upstart Top 40 stations were in that vanguard. Many a broadcaster was amused at such Uriah Heep hypocrisy, knowing first hand of another kind of payola practiced at various newspapers around the country. This version of payola known as "double-billing" involves the local advertiser receiving two invoices for the same ad—one listing the actual local rate; the second at a higher (usually double) amount for submission to a national manufacturer, in order to collect the co-operative advertising allowance.

circus; The Kefauver Committee's hearings on organized crime; The Dodd
Committee inquiring into TV sex and violence; the McClellan Committee's
probing of Jimmy Hoffa for shady union practices; Presidential Assistant
Sherman Adams's forced resignation for acceptance of a vicuna coat from
a business man; Adam Clayton Powell's indictment by a federal grand jury
for alleged income tax evasion. But these paled alongside the revelation
that television's first folk hero, Charles Van Doren, had been fed the answers during his long stay on the television quiz program, *Twenty-One*,
and that his agonizing performances in the isolation booth were those of
a skilled actor. Van Doren was summoned to appear before the Oren Harris Committee, where he admitted the deception.

Responding to the climate of the time, the FCC required sworn statements from all licensees, covering detailed reports for all program material
involving undisclosed payment. Until now, the payola-in-broadcasting furor had been a sort of formless morality play. But in early 1960, it became
a certified media event. And besides, it was an election year. Hearings were
held in Washington before a committee whose official designation was The
Sub-Committee of the Committee on Interstate and Foreign Commerce,
House of Representatives, 86th Congress, Second Session on Payola and
Other Deceptive Practices. The committee was headed by Congressman
Oren Harris whose group had also, several years earlier, investigated the
manner in which television licenses were granted. During those proceed-
ings it was revealed that the Chairman became a 25% owner in KRBB-
TV, El Dorado, Arkansas with a promissory note that went unpaid. KRBB-
TV's request for a power increase, earlier denied, was promptly approved.
Harris, who subsequently sold his stock, nevertheless stayed on to head
the next instance of "legislative oversight." [26]

Throughout the winter and into late spring a select group of disc jockeys paraded before the Harris Committee. Except for Alan Freed, the radio
jocks' names were familiar only to the trade and in cities where their shows
were heard. For some, their testimony resembled confessions at an old-
fashioned mourner's bench; for others, the hearings provided a nationwide
forum for stern denials. Only one national "name" personality testified
before the Harris Committee. He was an authentic celebrity who had gotten that way as a *television*, not a radio, disc jockey.

Dick Clark's *Bandstand* dj show had started out on WFIL Radio, and
was subsequently shifted to WFIL-TV. Clark's co-host, Bob Horn, was
fired in 1956 for drunken driving, alleged income tax evasion and other
personal problems, leaving Clark as the sole emcee. ABC, seeking to buck
the strong afternoon competition on CBS and NBC, installed Clark as
headman of *American Bandstand*. Essentially, the program was a daily
record hop with a camera turned on it. In addition to the canned music,
there were guest artists who lip-synched the words to their records. By
April, 1960 when Clark was appearing before the Harris Committee,
American Bandstand was attracting $12 million in advertising, while his

earnings in salary and ownership in record and allied music companies were reported to be around $500,000.[27] Dick Clark maintained composure throughout his turn in the barrel. His all-American Boy image stayed intact as he gave neatly polished answers. Clark's opening statement telegraphed to the Committee what kind of witness he would be:

> I have no doubts but that some of my copyrights received by my publishing firms and some of the records, owned, distributed or pressed by the companies in which I had an interest were given to my firms, at least in part because of the fact that I was a network television performer. However, the conflict between my position as a performer and my record interests never clearly presented itself to me until this Committee raised the questions of payola and conflicts of interest.[28]

Oren Harris seemed to enjoy sharing the spotlight with a television celebrity. "Mr. Clark," the Chairman said near the end of one day's questioning, "I do not intend to detain you any further, except that I have one question I wanted to ask you. What do you do, or how do you bring about the situation that causes all these fine young people to squeal so loud at a particular time? Do you have some kind of cue that you give them to do it? Or is that one of your trade secrets you don't want to give away?" Clark found the "twinkle in the Chairman's eye" as a signal "we were coming down the homestretch."[29]

Clark's appearance lasted several days. His inside show biz revelations apparently fascinated the Committee even if they didn't "buy" his whole story. But as for zeroing in on him as they did on Alan Freed and the radio disc jockeys, it never happened. When Chairman Harris adjourned the hearings, 207 persons (not all disc jockeys) in 42 cities were accused of accepting $263,245 in payola. Using the standard formula (6 dj's per station average), this meant, with 4068 stations on the air at the time, the vast majority of the nation's disc jockeys were clean.

As a result of the Harris hearings, The Federal Communications Act was amended in September, 1960 to make the acceptance of payola punishable by a $10,000 fine and a prison term. Because of licensee responsibility under the new law, most stations thereafter instituted a Payola Affadavit as a condition of hire. One is also required to be signed semi-annually by all regular radio & television station employees:

> I, _____, do hereby swear or
> affirm that I have never received while in the
> employment of   (Company Name)   , or any of its
> subsidiaries, nor will I receive or accept any
> favor, gift, service, money or other valuable
> consideration directly or indirectly paid or
> promised from any person or entity for the purpose

of influencing me to give preference to particular music, records, program material or advertisers, or to broadcast commercial advertising with the intention that I, rather than my employer, will receive some form of favor or valuable consideration for said advertising.

I do hereby swear or affirm that my employment with   (Company Name)   is my full-time occupation, and that I have not and will not invest or speculate in or sell my services as advisor or consultant to any enterprise using the advertising services of   (Company Name)   without prior express and written consent of   (Company Name)

                                                    _____
                                                              (Signature)

                                                    _____
                                                              (Position)

Date: _____   _____
                                                              (Station)

The disc jockey who rode in on the swelling tide of musical radio in the 1950s was merely an up-dated version of the radio announcer, that unseen presenter who had always held such a fascination for the listening public. In the modern era, the disc jockey, ostensibly hired to be a presenter of recorded pop music, often became as important as the music he presented. The arrival of Top 40 brought with it the accusation that the disc jockey was a chattering robot, subordinated to the format, and deprived of creating an on-the-air persona. While this was true at certain poorly-run operations, the well-managed Top 40 station encouraged the development of unique air personalities. Many of America's leading jocks not only thrived in that seminal format, but continued to do so after they changed to different venues.

Except in a few instances—notably the major city personality featured on a nationally syndicated music show—the disc jockey has been a local phenomenon. His name may be highly regarded in the trade, but his listening public is limited by the strength of his station's signal. After Martin Block and Alan Freed, it is difficult to come up with any universal household names. Yet, since the mid-1950s, a clutch of disc jockeys can be singled out for recognition. In one way or another, they put their stamp on their profession, and in many cases, helped shape the perceptions of musical radio for millions. Although many of the nominees in the round-up that follows might well be seconded by a scrupulously objective industry panel, the list is highly arbitrary. Some were still imposing presences on the air going into the 1980s, while others are long gone and remembered only by their one-time fans:

DISC JOCKEY	STATION WHERE MOST RECOGNITION OCCURRED
Dick Biondi	WKBW, Buffalo
Arnie "Woo Woo" Ginsburg	WMEX, Boston
Hunter Hancock	KGFJ, Los Angeles
Johnny Holliday	WHK, Cleveland
Jumpin' George Oxford	KSAN, San Francisco
Robin Seymour	WKMH, Detroit
Steve Dahl	WLUP-FM, Chicago
Larry Lujack	WLS, Chicago
Robert W. Morgan	KHJ, Los Angeles
Murphy in The Morning	WAYS, Charlotte
Pat O'Day	KJR, Seattle
Gary Owens	KMPC, Los Angeles
Dr. Don Rose	KFRC, San Francisco
Charley Tuna	KHJ, Los Angeles
Dick Whittinghill	KMPC, Los Angeles
Wolfman Jack	WNBC, New York
Dan Daniels	WMCA, New York
Don Imus	WNBC, New York
Dan Ingram	WABC, New York
Murray the K	WINS, New York
Bruce Morrow	WINS, New York
B. Mitchell Reed	WMCA, New York
Bob and Ray	WHDH, Boston
Charlie and Harrigan	KLIF, Dallas
Harden and Weaver	WMAL, Washington
Dick Purtan	WXYZ, Detroit
Gary McKee	WQXI, Atlanta
Bill Tanner	WHYI-FM, Ft. Lauderdale

When the disc jockey swarmed over post-television radio dials, there was no doubt that the performer should be male. Deep-voiced masculinity, it was assumed, was what you had better bring with you to an audition. This was an obvious hold-over from early radio. On the major networks where women were perfectly acceptable as producers, actresses and writers, there were no women announcers. At the station level, a few women who filled announcing jobs were heard from time to time during radio's first three decades. But for all practical purposes, that part of radioland was an all-male preserve.

One of the few women to invade those ranks in the waning days of mass entertainment radio used the *nom d'air, Lonesome Gal.* Heard first on WING, Dayton, in 1947, *Lonesome Gal* was a contrived sliver of show biz hokey in which a sometime actress, Jean King, delivered her patter in a painfully obvious, come-hither voice. In 1949, the show was syndicated and her late night purrings ("Hiiieee, baaaayyyyybeeee") were heard in select markets coast to coast. Photographed in a half-mask (and also worn on personal appearances), *Lonesome Gal* was the subject of an early 1950s minor media hype in which she was profiled in several general circulation magazines.

It was not until the late 1960s, that female disc jockeys began to be heard with any regularity—i.e. took on a dj identity, as contrasted with homemaker-hostesses or news readers. Album rock stations broke first ground. At Tom Donahue's experimental KMPX, San Francisco, Dusty Street started as station engineer and was subsequently given an airshift. Later, when that cradle of underground rock changed call letters to KSAN, Bonnie Simmons became one of the better-known West Coast djs. In Los Angeles, KMET was the home of Mary Turner in the early 1970s. Boston's ruling album rock station, WBCN, introduced two female jocks who went on to successful careers, Debbie Ullman and Maxanne Satort. However, the name most often mentioned in connection with pioneer women record spinners is Allison Steele. Originally Steele was part of a gimmick format, "Girl Power" which fielded an all-female air staff. After the novelty wore off, and WNEW-FM management returned to a more conventional style operation, Steele was retained in an otherwise male jock line-up. Liz Kiley who eventually went into management was on the air at WABC, New York, WIFI, Philadelphia and WPGC, Washington.

Program consultant Donna L. Halper says, "Women growing up in the 1960s had a hard time breaking in, even at the college radio level. And because most announcers they heard were male, they had no female role models to draw from, nor any standards by which to judge their abilities. Thus, the first women announcers often had problems finding a natural sound. Some did develop a pseudo-sexy style, while others sounded 'cute' or girlish. Ten years later, as more women got on the air, we can see that a variety of styles are being used, and the trend is toward a straightforward natural presentation."[30]

That female disc jockeys—and male ones too—have come a long way, there can be no doubt. From a sort of aberrational makeshift program entity that was originally grafted on to radio, the disc jockey has become inseparable from the popular music tree. Through the years, no performer has been as vulnerable to a fickle public as the disc jockey. Dangers of over-exposure loom larger to the disc jockey than to any other entertainer.

Yet, as musical radio kept growing, listener perceptions, by and large, have been favorable.

How the disc jockey will fare in radio's future is perhaps, a matter best left to programming seminars. But for present purposes, it is appropriate to note that no matter what new technologies may hold in store, a place will probably always be found for the disc jockey who can demonstrate irresistible showmanship. Bob Eastman, Top 40 salesman extraordinaire, had a response for those who said, "Top 40 Radio was too imitative and after a while, all stations sound alike." Eastman loved nothing more than to answer such charges with one of his "position papers." All stations, said Bob Eastman, could be playing the same music, yet a few would always stand out because of what went on *between* the records. That particular Eastman Encyclical he called, "Definable Degrees of Difference in Radio." Who could create a more "definable degree of difference" in radio than the disc jockey?

There is no push-button control of the human spirit. Until radio communicates robot to robot, rather than person to person, the quicksilver versatility and adaptability of man's art and intelligence will remain unchallenged by any electronic substitute for the amusing and amazing disc jockey.

NOTES

1. Etymologist William Morris claims he can "attest the term, disc jockey appeared in a dictionary I edited (*Words: The New Dictionary*) in early 1947. Taking into account the time involved in getting a dictionary ready for publication, this means it must have been current in the early 1940's." Morris, William and Mary, *Dictionary of Words and Phrase Origins,* Harper and Row, (New York), 1962, p. 199).
2. Sybil Herrold. Reminisces. *The First Fifty Years of Radio,* 6-LP Documentary, produced by Westinghouse Broadcasting Company, 1970.
3. Frank Conrad. Reminisces. *Ibid.*
4. Kiefer, Peter T. Liner Notes, *Waring's Pennsylvanians,* RCA-Victor, LPV-554.
5. John V. B. Sullivan interview.
6. "Radio's Little David Doesn't Fear TV," *Fortune,* October, 1952, p. 132.
7. Sullivan interview.
8. Simon, George. *Glenn Miller and His Orchestra,* Crowell, (New York), 1974, pp. 155 and 201.
9. ———. "The Jockeys," *Time,* June 9, 1947, p. 59.
10. Interview with Stephen Tassia, October 2, 1980.
11. ———. "High-Ho Everybody," *Time,* March 6, 1950, p. 61.
12. ———. "Al Jarvis, Original Disc Jockey Says Music Biz Overrates Deejays," *Variety,* March 24, 1954, p. 47.
13. Gehman, Nev. "National Poll Pinpoints Radio's Disc Show Growth," *Billboard,* February 28, 1953, p. 1+.
14. ———. "The Richest Guys in Radio," *Variety,* December 29, 1954, p. 21.
15. Dowell, Saxie. "In the Music Business," *Variety,* October 20, 1954, p. 56.
16. Crosby, Bing. "I Never Had to Scream," *Look,* November 2, 1954, pp. 76 & 77.
17. *Ibid.*
18. ———. "Bing Sure Started Something," *Variety,* November 17, 1954, pp. 53 and 56.
19. *Ibid.*
20. ———. "The R & B Deejay: A Growing Factor," *Billboard,* February 23, 1953, p. 57.

21. "Radio Retrospect—The Ole Moondog," *Ultimate Radio Bootleg,* Hook City Records, Vol. 5.
22. Goldberg, Isaac. *Tin Pan Alley.* Frederick Ungar, (New York), 1961, p. 203.
23. Simon, George. *The Big Bands.* MacMillan, (New York), 1967, pp. 60–61.
24. Green, Abel. "Payola—Continued," *Variety,* August 18, 1954, p. 47.
25. Hall, Claude. Bill Stewart Interview, *This Business of Radio Programming,* Billboard Publishing Co., (New York), 1977, p. 165.
26. Barnouw, Eric. *The Image Empire,* Oxford, (New York), 1970, p. 68.
27. Chapple, Steve and Garofalo, Reebee. *Rock and Roll Is Here to Pay,* Nelson Hall, (Chicago), 1977, p. 63.
28. Clark, Dick and Robinson, Richard. *Rock, Roll and Remember,* Crowell, (New York), 1976, 209 & 210.
29. *Ibid.* p. 222.
30. Letter to author, December 11, 1980.

CHAPTER **18**

The Book of Numbers

AMERICA, AS WE ALL KNOW, is a land of numbers freaks. It is therefore astonishing that broadcasting did not develop a program rating system earlier in its first decade. When researcher Archibald Crossley was asked to develop the Cooperative Analysis of Broadcasting (C.A.B.) at the behest of advertisers and agencies in 1929 (replacing mail-pull and newspaper-sponsored popularity contests), it was the industry's first foray into scientific audience studies. They began with the 1930–31 season.

In 1935, C. E. Hooper introduced a competitive service that like Crossley's C.A.B., was based on a national scientifically selected telephone sample. The introduction of methods to measure program popularity established Crossley and Hooper as industry demigods, with network performers now confronted by ratings "report cards" issued regularly. For those having anything to do with a show, their "C.A.B." and/or "Hooperating" was their ultimate test for survival.* Hooper, because of superior methodology, eventually dominated the field until 1943. That year A. C. Nielsen, an established marketing researcher, entered the radio scene. Nielsen introduced the Audimeter, a small electronic device that registered, in code, continuous minute-by-minute program tuning. Audimeters placed in a scientifically selected national home sample were created to eliminate the capriciousness of listener memory. When television took over radio's function in mass entertainment, Nielsen dropped the older medium.

---

* The story is told that Fred Allen, after a visit to Crossley's offices, quipped: "How can a man be so big in radio and have holes in his carpet?"

Radio research around this time, like the programming itself, went "local," and Hooperatings were modified to measure audience on a market-by-market basis. Hooper's major competition in the post-television era came from The Pulse, Inc., a firm whose methodology was based on face-to-face interviews with listeners chosen by scientific sampling. In the mid-1960s, the arrival of Arbitron signalled the beginning of the end for Pulse and Hooper, leaving the newcomer with the field virtually to itself.

Arbitron methodology is based on listener "diaries" placed in a scientifically selected home sample in a given area. Whatever its strengths or weaknesses, Arbitron has been, since the early 1970s, the overwhelmingly accepted research service by buyers of advertising. Since Arbitron's inception, a number of competitive radio audience measures have come and gone. Two that have survived into the 1980s and seemed determined to give Arbitron a run for their numbers are Media Statistics, Inc. (Mediastat) and Radio Marketing Research, Inc. (The Birch Report); both are based on telephone sampling.*

Thus, ratings have historically been radio's most dominant leitmotif. Since the very first C.A.B. rating, controversy has accompanied the endless tattoo of numbers down through the years. Those who would march to a different drummer find there is ultimately no escape from the need for some kind of numerical ranking of what is presented on the air. The loudest uproar over ratings, of course, is reserved for the sample, its size, and its selection. "How," the question is asked, "can 400 diaries or phone calls possibly be representative of 200,000 persons, or 1200 meter tapes be an accurate gauge of the nation-at-large?" "Trust us," say the professional researchers. "A good sample is representative of the whole—just like a blood specimen from the human body, or as a thimbleful of vinegar and oil taken from a barrel in which the two products have been carefully mixed."

The growth of FM and the proliferation of formats have added new fuel to the controversy. The rising cost of radio stations in the 1970s, high overhead, and inflation have evoked an understandable craving on the part of owners and managers to achieve good ratings. Highly motivated program personnel consider a rating book their report card, and a "good book" is highly favorable to the advancement of their careers. Salesmen want high numbers because of their value in the marketplace. Most trade papers devote column after column of type to the subject—sometimes reaching the ludicrous levels of medieval scholastics who counted angels on the head of a pin. Many newspapers, although primarily concerned with publishing television ratings regularly, print the newest radio Arbitrons with the same solemn pronouncement as the latest Consumer Price Index.

Knowledgeable hands in the research field, as well as those at the

---

* Birch subsequently bought out Mediastat and absorbed it into his parent organization.

station and advertiser/agency levels, know ratings are only *estimates,* approximations that carry with them certain limitations; they stress that ratings are a quantitative and not a qualitative, measure. Yet despite these caveats, ratings continue to be radio's Holy Grail. There are some in the business who become prisoners of the numbers. Their obsession with numbers often undercuts the strength of the medium itself. Enlightened radio professionals, on the other hand, know the limitations of ratings and proceed accordingly. They know there are many things ratings do *not* do:

Ratings do *not* measure facilities.
Ratings do *not* measure the total sphere of station influence.
Ratings do *not* measure the attitudes of listeners toward stations or personalities.
Ratings do *not* measure agency/advertiser acceptance.
Ratings do *not* measure a station's responsibility.
Ratings do *not* measure believability.
Ratings do *not* measure prestige.
Ratings do *not* measure impact.
Ratings do *not* measure results.
Ratings do *not* necessarily measure audience.

It cannot be stressed too strongly that the relationship between sales/programming and ratings is not just one of numbers. It affects the whole life and thought of the industry, and to consider all the ramifications of this would be to go outside the limited, and therefore more manageable, scope of this chapter. Radio will always need a quantitative measure supplied by credible professional researchers—the more, the better. Still, the medium also needs to know more than *how many*. Recognizing this soon after the great format explosion began, enlightened managements started generating special qualitative research. Conducted in behalf of, and paid for by, a single local station, such research is sometimes administered by station personnel, sometimes by professionals. In the main, qualitative studies are done so that the station may learn more about how the listening public perceives its programming. There follows a listing of several widely used qualitative research techniques. Descriptions of methodological applications will be limited to popular music:

FOCUS GROUPS

Focus groups have been around as long as marketing research. Package goods companies, in particular, have been consistent users of the focus group forum. A group of people are brought together to discuss certain topics, usually for a period of two to two-and-a-half-hours. The moderator, or interviewer, or leader raises various subjects, *focusing* the discussion on items of interest and concern to the researcher and his client, in accordance with an outline or general guide. The focus group, relatively new to radio research, can be a valuable tool for management in assessing attitudes and reactions toward the station's programming.

A research specialist is needed to set a focus group in motion. Large stations are usually members of a group operation and have access to such a person on staff; otherwise, one must be hired from the outside. The specialist supervises the recruiting which is done generally by hiring a marketing firm or, if it meets proper standards, by a college sociology or psychology department. Ample time is allowed to recruit from eight to ten persons who are selected according to pre-determined criteria. These may include: amount of radio listened to; number of stations listened to (at least two different stations several days a week for at least an hour a day minimum); consumer behavior patterns; socio-economic circumstances; and age and sex. A focus group is not lined up using statistical methodology; rather by putting together a solid interfusion of white- and blue-collar workers, a few skilled technicians, some professionals, housewives and students. It is up to the professional researcher to select a skilled moderator—one who can extract responses from all participants, make the group feel comfortable, keep things moving, be aware of media "experts" who seek to dominate the discussion to show their knowledge—in general, one who understands group dynamics. The researcher must prepare a guide/outline in conjunction with station management, make certain the moderator understands it thoroughly, and arrange a suitable meeting place. At no time are participants aware of the station conducting the research. (If a videotape of the focus group is desired, the physical layout of the room becomes a major factor.) Audio taping of the proceedings is manditory. Once the focus group is assembled, it is apparent why a skilled moderator is needed: a group covering radio programming takes on different dimensions from a group dealing with bath soap or toothpaste; hence, a person able to deal with subtle, and sometimes ambiguous, impressions is necessary for maximum results. The following question sequence is illustrative of how the moderator may pursue a topic:

> What do you like about the music on WXXX? Dislike?
>
> Do you listen to WXXX to hear *new* music?
>
> When you think of pop music, do you generally think of WXXX, WYYY, or WZZZ?
>
> If you like the music, but dislike the disc jockeys, would you still listen to a station?
>
> Which is more important for you to get your day started "right"—a funny disc jockey, or the music you like?
>
> Which of these stations provides the best disc jockey-music mix— WXXX, WYYY, or WZZZ?
>
> If WXXX were a car, what kind of car would it be?

The moderator is not interested in obtaining a consensus of any kind; the moderator's job is to get feedback from participants. In the week or so following the session, moderator and researcher provide a summary of what was learned from the group, together with the audio cassette.

What purpose does the focus group serve? If it is well run, it should provide station management with new insights. Perhaps a recurring point kept coming up, e.g. that the station plays too much unfamiliar music, or too many oldies. The station may then want to have a quantitative study made to see if those perceptions are re-inforced by further scientific sampling.

CALL OUT RESEARCH

The call out system involves sampling a group of persons as to their evaluations of records. Results may then serve as one of the factors in constructing the weekly playlist. A weekly sample of 75 to 100 persons are selected by some standard means of randomness according to age and sex. Short excerpts of 10 to 15 seconds for each of 30 to 60 records are played on the telephone and respondents are asked to rate the tune on a simple numerical scale: 1 = dislike, 2 = no strong feelings one way or another, 3 = like it a great deal.

MODIFIED FOCUS

This research is handled along focus group lines, except that is conducted more often, since its purpose is limited to obtaining reactions to new records. The music focus group is impanelled usually every three or four weeks. Ideal group sizes should range from 10 to 15 persons. The age range must match the demographic appeal of the stations. A screening of pop/adult records, for example, by 14-year olds would be meaningless. Unlike the general focus groups that must be differently constituted on each occasion, the modified version for music can include the same persons from time to time. Respondents are asked to fill out a questionnaire similar to the one listed below after each record is played—usually 10 per session:

MUSIC QUESTIONNAIRE

RECORD 1
Have you heard *this record* before?

Yes	____
No	____
Not Sure	____

If *"yes"*, please check one of the following statements:

I'm *tired* of it	____
I'm *neutral* on how much I've heard it	____
I'd like to hear it *more*	____

Do you like or dislike this record?

     I *dislike* it / / / / / / / I *like* it

Any other comments?

_____

_____

_____

OTHER POPULAR MUSIC RESEARCH

Some older, less sophisticated means of obtaining audience music preferences are considered less reliable by professional program people, but they must nevertheless be considered in the interest of thoroughness: *Local record store sales*—Unless a representative sample of stores is chosen, results could be misleading. Stores can sometimes hype a record or album and not give a true sales picture. *The trade press*—This has become a leading indicator of national or regional popularity. Music directors like to keep an eye on what's happening in the rest of the country. However, this information must always be balanced with local record store sales. *Billboard* and *Variety* have pioneered in covering national sales action for records. (*Variety's* record and sheet music charts were two of the few indicators of music popularity during pre-*Hit Parade* days.) *Record World* and *Cash Box* also offer regular national sales information. Airplay data— a *Variety* feature since the 1930s—became increasingly important in the 1970s. *Billboard*, *Radio and Records* and *Variety* were all publishing weekly charts showing what records were being played on selected stations around the country. *Radio and Records* and *Billboard* further refined their charts by indicating airplay according to format, e.g. pop/adult, contemporary, etc. Radio's increasing dependence on popular music saw the rise in the 1970s of another publication, the weekly "tip sheet." Those enjoying the widest circulation are The *Friday Morning Quarterback* published by Kal Rutman in Cherry Hill, N.J. and The *Gavin Report*, (See Appendix, page 379) published by Bill Gavin in San Francisco. Rutman and Gavin are two of popular music's most informed practitioners; every week they manage to crank out a gallimaufry of record sales information, airplay reports, predictions about new releases, trade gossip and reprints of articles appearing in other segments of the trade press.

A half century spanned the period between Archibald Crossley's uncomplicated C.A.B. methodology and the sophisticated trappings of modern radio research. Yet, controversy continued to swirl around the subject. In a stinging indictment delivered at the 1980 convention of The National Association of Broadcasters, Ernie Martin, Director of Research, Cox

Broadcasting Company, admonished the industry for its floundering. Re-working the Lewis Carroll classic, he titled his speech "Alice in Media-land," likening broadcasters to the lost Alice who asked the Cheshire Cat "where to go from here." Since Alice said she didn't care, the Cat observed that it really didn't matter then which way Alice went.

"We're looking at radio research much like naive Alice," Martin claimed. "We're seeking directions . . . without really caring which way we go . . . we learn to lie with statistics, to confuse and obscure logic under clouds of numbers."

Whether they agreed entirely with Ernie Martin or not, most broad-casters freely admitted that research was their number-one concern. And so it would probably remain. History, alas, records only one perfect piece of research: when the Lord commanded Moses in the wilderness of Sinai to "take a census of all the congregation of the people of Israel by families, by fathers' houses, according to the number of names, every male, head by head" (Numbers 1:2), it is noted simply that Moses "numbered them in the wilderness of Sinai." (Numbers 1:19).

CHAPTER 19

Program Doctors and Syndicators

In the "business," the arrival of the Arbitron Book at a radio station is an awe-inspiring event. Key personnel (also known as the station brain trust), anxiously pace back and forth in the front office. Solemnly, the white-covered, red-lettered Books are brought in. Alarums and excursions follow. Imagine the following scenario at WXXX, a station whose ratings have been sliding in the last two Books. Now, in this, the latest Arbitron, WXXX's average share of "total persons 12+, Mon.–Sun., 6AM–12M" has slipped another two points. Quietly, the key personnel take their Books and repair to their individual offices, where they can separately pore through 156 pages of refined data, searching for some balm of Gilead to soothe their troubled spirits. This done, the owner-manager is left alone, as he drifts into the lowest and most unenvied state of melancholia to which the radio profession can descend.

The owner-manager had a gut feeling he was in for another bad Book; frankly, he thought it would be a lot worse. He was getting concerned. Not that he wanted to hit the panic button; he just didn't like the way things were going at WXXX. Sales were holding their own, but with inflation and all, profits were skidding—not drastically, but enough to indicate a trend. The owner-manager has a number of options: he can do nothing and hope things get better; he can make a few heads roll; or he can change formats. Or he can make a phone call.

Which is precisely what the owner-manager in his current state of importunity does. Yes, says the voice at the other end, he understands the problem. And, yes, he has a few thoughts about this "mildly ailing" station he would like to share with the owner-manager—face-to-face. But, gosh, he is awfully busy right now, and can't come to the station for at least another month. (Persons in his line of work must never appear to be immediately available.) Meanwhile, would the owner-manager send him some tapes of the mildly ailing station?

So it comes to pass on the appointed day, the Very Important Visitor arrives at WXXX. He is promptly ushered into the front office, there to hold court for the assembled key station personnel. Taking charge, the Very Important Visitor straightway launches into his monolog. There are indeed things wrong with WXXX's air product—he spotted them instantly on the tapes. Nothing, however, that couldn't be remedied. Now philosophical, now anecdotal, now pontifical, all the while stroking his ample beard, the Very Important Visitor lays out his battle plan for improving the mildly ailing WXXX. Regaling the WXXX braintrust with one success story after another, his message is clear, although he never comes right out and says the words, "I'll turn this damn station around." Apprehensive key station personnel listen intently. But as key personnel are sometimes wont to do when their considerable imaginations take flight, they envision him as something other than the expert who is in their midst. "Put a sari on him," goes one line of thought, "and he becomes an Eastern mystic." "No, put him in a pair of jeans," goes another's, "and he's Alan Ginsberg." Some members of a station's high command have even been known to demonstrate their displeasure on these occasions by infelicitous behavior—a happenstance often encountered by the Very Important Visitor, and one with which he is fully prepared to cope. He is used to cool receptions from the staffs at radio stations. But then he wasn't brought here to conduct a charm school.

The Consultant. He is a presence, with or without a beard. Consider him one of a growing group of middlemen who have pitched their tents in the suburbs of an ever-expanding radioland. *Inside Radio's* "Consultant Directory" for March, 1981 listed 97* sales and program management consultants—most of whom specialized in programming, that area where angels have often feared to tread. Program consultants have been around as long as radio. However, their rise to exalted status was a phenomenon of the 1970s. The first of the breed to attract industry attention and define the role of modern consultancy was Bill Drake, Thomas O'Neill's program guru at KHJ, Los Angeles. Drake, a quasi-employee of RKO-General at the time, was really a consultant and proved it when he decided to go the free-lance route after his Boss job was finished.

The cornucopia of popular music that poured out of the radio music box since 1960 to be fashioned into one format or another made the consultant inevitable. By February, 1981, there were 4599 commercial AM

---

* In addition, there were probably another couple of dozen who were not listed.

and 3312 commercial FM stations on the air, along with 1096 FM educational and PBS outlets—to put it bluntly, far too many stations for all to thrive. Enter the consultant who is supposed to offer objective views to the management of a floundering station, or to one that recently changed hands, or to one newly signed-on.

Consultants generally fall into two classifications: firms that offer consultancy as part of a syndicated music service; and the non-affiliated specialist. In the former group, Bonneville Broadcast Consultants, operating out of Tenafly, New Jersey, is part of Bonneville International, a broadcast conglomerate (headquartered in Salt Lake City and owned by the Church of the Latter Day Saints) that includes AM, FM and TV stations, a radio spot sales rep firm, and a syndicated music service. Bonneville was one of the early members of the expanding consultation family, entering the field in 1971, a year after the introduction of the company's beautiful music syndication package. The firm offers complete management, program, promotion and engineering counsel. Bonneville consultation is tilted heavily toward beautiful music, middle-of-the-road and adult-contemporary formats that appeal to over-25 demographic groups.

In defining the consultant's role, Frank Murphy, Bonneville vice president, points out it is not merely a matter of coming to a client station, listening in a hotel room and then recommending sweeping changes to justify the fee: "First of all we do a thorough market analysis, including listening to all competitive stations, and we study all quantitative data such as Arbitron and any other ratings information, as well as any qualitative research the client may have done or that we might have conducted in behalf of the station. After we look at the research and do our listening, we only recommend and suggest. These recommendations must be tailored from market to market, of course. We try to affiliate with blue chip broadcasters in the first place—those who are interested in making a solid commitment to success, part of which is the consultancy agreement." [1]

The consultant sometimes becomes entangled in the extremely sensitive area of station politics. Murphy recalls a case where "we recommended some changes at the upper and middle management levels, and in a matter of 18 months the station turned around and came from virtually nowhere to number two or three in the market." [2] The program consultant usually gets involved in all phases of the on-air sound: format execution, selection of talent, placement of commercials and other non-musical elements, and engineering. Especially engineering.

Marlin Taylor, president of Bonneville Broadcast Consultants, cites an experience in this regard. It began with a telephone call from the manager of a client station. An out-of-town associate, reported the manager, had found his station hard to listen to because of an irritating quality in the technical sound: "Now this is a good station. It has pretty good facilities, a concerned staff, a chief engineer who cares and sincerely works at maintaining his station. He believed that everything was right, all equipment set up according to manufacturer specifications and Bonneville Broadcast Consultants' recommendations. Yet . . . the manager knew his station didn't sound good . . . We dispatched our Electronic Wizard to the scene to go through the entire broadcast system with the station's engineers, find the problems and make corrections. As in the case in most stations, no one deficiency was found, just a lot of little things . . . Today our manager is extremely happy with the new beauty to be found in his station's sound." [3] In addition to Taylor and Murphy, both of whom enjoyed successful careers in programming at the station level, Bonneville's senior consultant staff consists of three other persons (including an engineer), all with local station experience. Some station managements take more kindly to consultants "who served in the trenches," as they like to put it.

At the other end of the spectrum, with consultation skewing toward younger-appeal formatted stations, is the firm of Burkhart/ Abrams,/Michaels/Douglas, located in Atlanta. Consultant Kent Burkhart likes to be known as a "radio doctor," because "we make sick stations well." A Todd Storz alumnus (program director at WQAM Miami), he served as a program executive for several companies after leaving the Top 40 inventor. Striking out on his own in the early 1970s and off to a good start with eight station clients at $20,000 per year each, Burkhart encountered one Lee Abrams around this time. Abrams, then only 22, was already a program "wunderkind," having gotten credit for sharpening Detroit's illustrious rocker, WRIF. Not content to stay in one place, the precocious programmer declared himself a consultant, choosing as his first project the honing of a rock format that zoomed in on young adults, 18–34. Abrams sold the idea to WQDR, Raleigh, North Carolina. With perhaps some sort of musical pre-destination at work, Burkhart and Abrams teamed up, and just like two physicians who paint their names on the same shingle, the program doctors were ready to offer ailing stations their expertise. Dr. Burkhart specializes in consulting Top 40, Adult Contemporary and dance music formats, while Dr. Abrams concentrates on the "superstar" format for Album Oriented Rock outlets. At the heart of the Burkhart/Abrams operation is their research which Lee Abrams described in an interview with the editors of *Broadcasting,* as "amazingly" valuable.

"At about 700 or 800 record stores every week, you distribute these little cards, and whenever anybody buys a record, they fill out their name, age, phone number, the record they bought and put it in the box. At the end of the week, the music director in that market would select a box filled with cards and send them back to us. We would then have a record of thousands of people who bought any given album. Let's say a Fleetwood Mac album comes out on January 1; by January 7, we have called back thousands of people who bought the album to find out the demographic spectrum of the record, the favorite song, what they don't like about it . . . We find exactly which cuts sold the album, exactly the right two songs to play." [4] Burkhart/Abrams also does a major yearly study in the form of a questionnaire mailed to over a million persons. It contains simple questions such as, "Who are your favorite artists?," "what are your favorite songs?" Graphs are then constructed for songs and artists and Dr. Abrams gets a reading: "Take the group, Chicago. We look back at the graph and we see that in 1970 they had 85,000 responses as the favorite group. By 1974, it went down to about 30,000. By 1978, to 6,000 and now it's 2000 and so forth . . . That information continues to multiply. We find which artists are trending up, which are trending down, so we can get a good handle on exactly what music styles are happening." [5]

Given the fickleness peculiar to their demographic specialization, the program doctors keep their ears open for subtle changes in slang popular with youth, and then share that intelligence with their client stations. "It's all part of the package," Burkhart told the *New York Times*. "Right now, [September, 1979] the hottest word in the country is 'hot.' Everything is 'hot.' About six months ago, 'get down' went out, and 'bad'—meaning good—went out about a year ago. The key words don't change that often, maybe four or five times a year, but if you're not on top of the changes you lose. A dj on a rock station who says 'far out' right now would sound awfully stupid." [6]

Burkhart/Abrams/Michaels/Douglas, Bonneville and other consultant organizations of their ilk (such as Drake Chenault, Century 21, Fox and Fox, Radio Programming/Management), along with some of the better-known specialists who operate as one-man shows (John Sebastian, Jeff Pollack, Dave Moorhead, Mike Joseph, Bob Henaberry, Todd Wallace)—all perform, more or less, the traditional consultant's role. Although they rely on one form of research or other from which to draw their conclusions, the majority of consultants are in the "classic" mold, and base their judgments—whether they admit to it or not—on what Kent Burkhart calls a "blend of science and emotion." This is understandable since they come mostly from programming backgrounds and hence see things through program prisms.

By the late 1970s, another kind of consultant had emerged, and although fewer in number, this new breed had a different purview of radio station counseling. Using marketing principles, their procedures are firmly rooted in research. In the vanguard of advocates using this approach is The Research Group (based in San Luis Obispo, California) a subsidiary of Sunbelt Communications, Ltd., and owner of radio stations in medium-sized markets. The Group—as it likes to be known—is essentially concerned with providing varied research tools to aid stations in improving their programming, their promotion and sales efforts.

Headed by Bill Moyes, The Group's professional staff consists of five persons, each with intense marketing and research concentrations in their academic disciplines and work experience. Moyes draws sharp distinctions between the standard services of the conventional consultant and those of The Group's: "When we go into a market, we develop a relationship with a station client—an on-going relationship. If the station is not doing well and wants to consider possibilities for complete re-programming, that is, re-positioning the product so as to occupy a meaningful and long-lasting niche in the market from which it can build a lot of revenue and profit, then we would examine a wide range of possibilities. This is done through some fairly sophisticated positioning market research."[7]

When this research is completed and the station has carefully defined its position and mobilizes its resources to strengthen that position, The Group's "real" work begins: "the effort to help it stay on top and gain strength." Such post-positioning efforts The Group calls *diagnostic* and *therapeutic*. Moyes defines the former as "an approach where we look for ways to stay in touch with the particular target 'life groups'* . . . to look at their changing images of us as a station and each of our competitors, so that we understand the changing complexion of the marketplace . . . Our second kind of study is therapeutic, that is, [research] to keep the product that we have well in line. The most common type of therapeutic research that we use is music-oriented . . . One of the most important things [a station] can do is choose the music properly. So we have developed systems—rather sophisticated and expensive systems—which help a station target much more effectively than anything that's been done in the past . . . Therapeutic research insures [the station] that they have enough information so they can stay on the right track . . . We do what-ever it takes to build the station strongly in [its] target . . . But we are not babysitters. We are not trying to substitute for good management."[8]

The concomitant growth of consultancies that accompanied station proliferation in the 1960s and 1970s also saw the burgeoning of another associated business—syndicated music. Syndication, which arrived via 16-inch transcriptions in 1929 and thrived for the next two decades, returned in a new form to play an even greater part in radio's attunement to the television era. Ironically, the denigrating term, "canned music," that attended those primitive ET's found a counterpart in modern syndication. For when post-television syndicated music came to radio, the tag hung on it was "automation"—the implication being that since pre-recorded reels were set up for continuous play on special equipment, (replacing the record-by-record-on-a-turntable method) the music was somewhat inferior. Also, it was said, automation eliminated much of the announcer's "human" part of the act, and was thus lower-class musical radio. A residue of these stigmata will always remain, but as long as there's a radio music box to pull in a signal, there will be a syndicator.

Pre-recording music on tape and delivering it as a format entity to radio stations began as a sort of sideline. Roger Jones, a developer of early

---

* Moyes says this is not a demographic group (25 to 44, or 18 to 35, etc.) but a "cohesive unit of persons having similar tastes in music and lifestyle, regardless of where their ages start and end . . . and obviously we're after those life groups which are more in the adult range, because that's where the disposable income is today."

radio automation systems, decided around 1960 that station customers who bought his equipment might also be prospects for music to go with it. He guessed correctly. Jones called his taped music package IGM (International Good Music). Eventually Jones spun off the music side of the enterprise to a group who organized under the name, BPI (Broadcast Programming International); the hardware part remained IGM, and both continued to thrive. Surprisingly, by 1968, IGM was still the only music-format syndicator of consequence serving the industry. However, not long afterward, that situation changed, and by 1980, over two dozen major firms were cranking out automated popular music formats.

Providing a complete format of pre-recorded music was an obvious by-product of three pivotal technological advances: magnetic tape, FM and stereo. With improvements in transmission, reception and station expansion—there were only two FM stereo operations in 1960—the syndicator came into his own. One estimate in late 1979 placed the number of stations using packaged music at 1500.[9] Long gone, of course, are the days of "bicycling" tapes from station to station. Gone too is the era of minimum quality control. The modern syndicator is very much alert to the need for staying current in state-of-the-art technology. Format syndication with all its refinements became, in the 1970s, a boon primarily to stations in small-to-medium-sized markets. Stressing this point, Tom McIntyre, vice president for Marketing, Century 21 Productions, told *Television/Radio Age,* "New automated equipment is more flexible and allows station management to have better control over programming, rather than leaving it to the whim of the deejay. In the smaller markets, they can't pay deejays very well, so they're not getting good talent. If they do, they won't hold it for long, because the smaller markets are just feeder markets for the larger ones."[10]

A syndicated smorgasbord makes it possible for a station to select virtually any popular music format that exists. That the creation of syndicated formats is big business in musical radio can be seen in the competitive offerings available. Taking just three formats as examples, the NAB 1980 *Syndicated Radio Programming* Directory lists a seemingly endless variety of modern canned music: Beautiful Music (15 competitive versions); Country (18 competitive versions); Adult Contemporary/MOR (26 competitive versions).

Modern syndication is a highly specialized industry—every bit as thoughtfully crafted and intricately engineered as any product produced in a sophisticated manufacturing plant. The *modus operandi* of one such syndicator is indicative of how an automated popular music system works. Century 21 offers six basic formats to subscribers: *Simply Beautiful, Super Country, The E-Z Format* (middle-of-the-road), *The A–C Format* (adult contemporary), *Album Oriented Z* (album rock), *The Z Format* (contemporary). When a station signs with Century 21, it is guaranteed an initial library, plus a given number of updates throughout the year:

FORMAT	HOURS IN INITIAL LIBRARY	TAPE UPDATE PER YEAR
Simply Beautiful	225	75
Super Country (traditional)	94	106
Super Country (modern)	70	106
The E–Z Format	65	88
The A–C Format	70	88
Album Oriented Z	76	102
The Z Format	82	140

—Source: Century 21

"Customized Sound Hours" are provided according to daypart in tempo, style, music mix, announcing, promos, news, weather and commercial load. The following figure depicts how a clock-hour can be tailored to a station's requirements:

•   •   •

One of the controversies surrounding the syndicated format since its inception has been, that in its purest form, it lacks the spontaneity of "live," local announcers. Wrong, say the proponents of automation, the polish of professional announcers on the tapes more than makes up for that deficiency. At least one piece of evidence seemed to point to insufficient localism as the syndicated music service's greatest drawback. In a 1979 survey conducted by *Broadcast Management/Engineering,* one of the questions asked of non-subscribers in a detailed questionnaire sent to 2000 radio stations was, "What do you dislike about syndicated programming services?" In a returned sample of 755, non-subscribers listed "not localized, no local indentity" as their greatest turn-off. Listed in second place was the closely related reason, "canned, repetitious, monotonous." [11] These concerns may also have been shared by other subscribers as well, because by the late 1970s, more and more syndicators were implementing a combination of live and automated called "live-assist radio." As far as listeners are concerned, it apparently didn't matter much. In a study for *Inside Radio* conducted by consultant Todd Wallace, respondents overwhelmingly answered, "it didn't matter." [12]

A second product created in radio syndication factories* is the pop music special. This may take the shape of a once-a-week program, a three-or-twelve-hour one-time spectacular, a year-end round-up of the year's top tunes, or any of a number of other configurations.

Syndication, from *Freddie Rich and The Friendly Five Footnotes on the Air* to *The E-Z Format,* embodies a continuity in musical radio that

---

* Syndication firms also produce many non-musical features such as talk shows, how-to series, sports items, commentaries and drama, as well as station I.D. and commercial jingles.

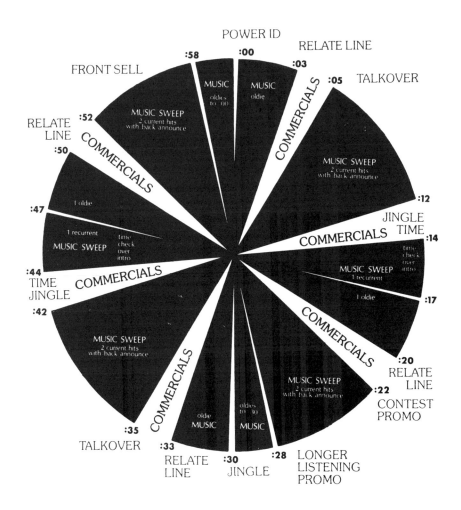

transcends artistic and technological considerations. An expression of the entrepreneur's desire to fill a need (and make a buck), the syndicator's product will always have a place in the pop music mix. Like the rest of the radio industry that looked toward the year 2000, syndicators were talking satellites—getting their wares on the "birds." Some of the talk was obviously pie in the sky and good old show biz hype. But whether the delivery system to the radio music box is terrestrial or celestial, one thing is certain: The American listener will continue to enjoy a musical fare so varied, there's no telling what's coming up next.

NOTES

1. Interview with Frank Murphy, May 26, 1981.
2. *Ibid.*
3. "The Taylor Report," Volume V, Issue II, July 14, 1978 (Newsletter published for Bonneville clients).
4. ———. "Staying in Tune with the Times," *Broadcasting*, August 24, 1980, p. 54.
5. *Ibid.*, p. 56.
6. Tony Schwartz. " 'Doctors' Who Prescribe for Ailing Radio Stations," *New York Times*, Section 2, September 9, 1979, p. 32.
7. Interview with Bill Moyes, May 6, 1981.
8. *Ibid.*
9. Edmond M. Rosenthal. "Radio Music Packagers Aim at Demographic Shift," *Television/Radio Age*, October 8, 1979, p. 35.
10. *Ibid.*, pp. 35–36.
11. ———. "What Managements Like and Dislike About Syndicated Programs: Findings of the BM/E Study," *Broadcast Management/Engineering*, June, 1979, p. 25.
12. Re-printed in John Leader, "Automation: Reel Two," *Radio and Records*, September 21, 1979, p. 18.

The transistor, which revolutionized the entire field of communications in the mid-1950s, played a particularly important role in radio receivers. The unmistakable sound of Top 40 made stations employing that format easy to identify on small portable radios. This model sold for $29.95 in 1963.

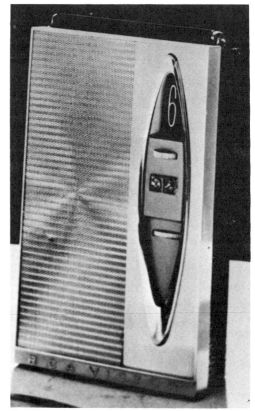

(Courtesy RCA)

Below: As late as 1963, many sets were equipped with only an AM band. This "Almanac RFA 30" model carried a suggested retail price of $39.95.

(Courtesy RCA)

The Storz Stations' brain trust in the mid-1950s. (l. to r.) Kent Burkhart, John Barrett, Todd Storz, Eddie Clarke and Bill Stewart.

Before starting a group of successful Top 40 stations in the mid-1950s, Texas entrepreneur Gordon McLendon had organized The Liberty Broadcasting System, a sports network. McLendon himself did many of the re-created and live play-by-play broadcasts.

Bill Drake, controversial developer of "Boss Radio," was the first of the modern consultants.

Supersalesman Bob Eastman's jaunty stride was a familiar sight on Madison Avenue in Top 40's heyday, as he and his "young tigers" implored reluctant advertising agencies to buy time on the stations he represented.

The advent of rock and roll and the parallel development of the 45 rpm recording created a big spurt in record collecting as a hobby in the mid-1950s—just as swing had done two decades earlier. The ease with which 45s could be handled and shelved was a special bonus to radio stations.

Two views of the Philadelphia Story in the late 1950s—musically speaking. At left Dick Clark (l.), guest Sonny James (c.), and producer Tony Mamarella on the WFIL-TV-originated *American Bandstand,* ABC's answer to late afternoon soap operas on CBS and NBC. Clark was a star witness in the U.S. Senate's 1960 payola hearings, and although he came through unscathed, he left a number of skeptical observers. Around the same time, WRCV hoped a "bring-back-the-big-bands" movement would help diffuse the rock phobia. In photo below, Bruce Davidson (l.) Capitol Records executive and Glen Gray (r.) of Casa Loma fame visited dee-jay Jack Pyle, (c.) leader of the bands' drive. The campaign failed in less than two years, and WRCV became all-news KYW.

(Courtesy Bruce Davidson)

(Author's collection)

Elvis Presley

(Author's collection)

Buddy Holly

(Courtesy Capitol Records)

Rick Nelson

Author's collection)

Bob Dylan

(Courtesy Capitol Records)

Minnie Ripperton

(Courtesy Capitol Records)

Bob Seger

(Courtesy Capitol Records)

Steve Miller

(Courtesy Capitol Records)

Natalie Cole

(Courtesy Capitol Records)

Sammy Hagar

(Courtesy Warner Bros. Records)

Carly Simon

(Courtesy Capitol Records)

Carole King

The arrival of rock and roll and its eventual splintering enabled stations which wanted to be "contemporary" to present an endless array of colorful pop music performers. Record companies often fashioned their finished product with radio in mind, concentrating as much on the "total sound" as on the artistry. On this page and the two following are some individuals and groups who became rock stars.

(courtesy Capitol Records)

The Beatles

(author's collection)

The Beach Boys

(author's collection)

The Who

(author's collection)

Fleetwood Mac

The Eagles

Bee Gees

Led Zeppelin

Roy Acuff and The Crazy Tennesseans, c. 1938. (l. ro r.) Cousin Jody, Jess Easterday, Tiny, Roy Acuff, Red Jones.

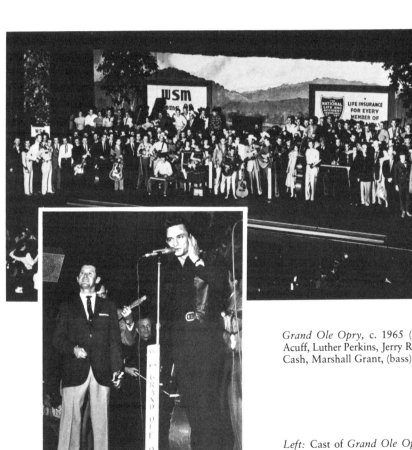

Grand Ole Opry, c. 1965 (l. ro r.) Roy Acuff, Luther Perkins, Jerry Rivers, Johnny Cash, Marshall Grant, (bass).

Left: Cast of *Grand Ole Opry,* c. 1953. Ryman Auditorium.

(Courtesy Country Music Foundation Library and Media Center, Nashville, Tenn.)

Many stations continued to feature live c. & w. groups long after other live performers were discarded in favor of recorded music. On WMT, Cedar Rapids, Tom Owens and His Cowboys were still going strong in 1949.

Before her *Breakfast Club* and *Kukla, Fran and Ollie* fame, Fran Allison was on the WMT staff. Here she livens up proceedings with Les Hartman's Cornhuskers broadcasting from the International Harvest Exhibit of the Dairy Cattle Congress in the mid-1940s.

(Courtesy Capitol Records)

Glen Campbell

(Courtesy MCA Records)

Oak Ridge Boys

(Courtesy Capitol Records)

Merle Haggard

(Courtesy Capitol Records

Anne Murray

(Courtesy Jim Shea/1980)

Jerry Lee Lewis

Country had become part of the popular music mainstream by the late 1960s. At one time or another, Glen Campbell, The Oak Ridge Boys, Merle Haggard, Anne Murray and Jerry Lee Lewis had paraded under the country banner and "crossed over" to the general pop charts.

Kurt Webster
WBT, Charlotte

Gary Owens
KMPC, Los Angeles

Robert W. Morgan
KMPC, Los Angeles

Wink Martindale
KMPC, Los Angeles

Dick Whittinghill
KMPC, Los Angeles

Dr. Don Rose
KFRC, San Francisco

Dick Purtan
CKLW, Detroit

Larry Lujack
WLS, Chicago

Dan Ingram
WABC, New York

Don Imus
WNBC, New York

Allison Steele
WNEW-FM, New York

Wolfman Jack

Gary McKee
WQXI, Atlanta

Bill Tanner
WHYI-FM-
Fort Lauderdale/Miami

Murphy-in-the-
Morning
WAYS, Charlotte

After 1948, disc jockeys became the new stars of radio. Although they are considered "local" phenomena, those shown above gained national recognition in the trade because of some unique approach.

(Photos courtesy stations listed. Wolfman Jack photo courtesy, Agee, Stevens and Acree.)

Pop artists' "visits" to disc jockey shows are part of pop music promotion. In photo above Stevie Wonder (c.) "stopped by" to visit Jay Clarke (r.), WABC, New York. Record company promotion men such as Kelly West, Motown, arrange the itineraries. In photo on right Peter Criss (r.) of the group KISS visits deejay Danny Wright (l.), KJR, Seattle. Below Harry Chapin (r.) (looking over console) on a visit to WKIX, Raleigh, N.C.

(Courtesy *Radio and Records*)

After "The Chicken," KGB, San Diego, mascot became popular, many stations followed suit. In photos shown, mascots of KRLY, Houston and WBBG, Cleveland perform typical promotional chores.

Computers and other sophisticated hardware are used by syndicators such as Century 21 to supply station subscribers with the modern version of "canned music."

(Courtesy KMPS & WQOK)

Stations in all sizes of markets were taking advantage of the industry's advanced technology through the 1970s. Music could now be aired via cassette, cartridge, disk, and reel-to-reel in modern studios of such stations as KMPS, Seattle, and WQOK, Greenville, S.C. Commercials, news, and other elements could be easily blended in.

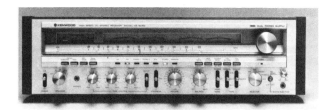

(Courtesy Kenwood)

The radio music box had come a long way since its crystal set days. By 1980, manufacturers were marketing elaborate receivers as components of elaborate home "sound systems." Other makers were capitalizing on Americans' yen for the unusual with novelty radios shown on the following two pages.

(Courtesy Harmon/Kardon)

(Courtesy Radio Shack)

(All Courtesy Chris Huber)

(author's collection)

(Courtesy Chris Huber)

(author's collection)   (Courtesy Chris Huber)

(Courtesy Christ Huber)   (author's collection)   (Courtesy Chris Huber)

Part Five
(1981 –   )

TUNE IN TOMORROW

Time present and time past
Are both present in time future,
And time future contained in time past.

—T.S. Eliot

CHAPTER **20**

Formats for The Future

HISTORY HAS RECORDED many forecasts that years later look awfully silly. One such golden oldie will suffice. President Harry Truman, in his memoirs, recalls being told the atom bomb secret soon after succeeding Franklin D. Roosevelt in office. Later when Vannevar Bush, head of the Office of Scientific Research and Development, came to the White House, Mr. Truman describes in his memoirs how he received "a scientist's version" of the powerful new weapon: "Admiral Leahy was with me when Dr. Bush told me this astonishing fact, 'This is the biggest fool thing we have ever done,' he observed in his sturdy, salty manner. 'The bomb will never go off, and I speak as an expert in explosives.' "[1]

Dr. Bush's bungled prediction notwithstanding, few fields of endeavor offer more tantalizing prospects for crystal ball gazing than communications. *Satellites* and *cable* were fashionable buzz words inside as well as outside the business by the late 1970s. Both obviously will impact broadcasting; forecasting how much and in what way have already filled volumes, even before much of the hardware had been built. As for musical radio—it is not an island. There will be many changes and adjustments in the sending and receiving of American popular music. It should not seem presumptuous, therefore, that these matters are fitting subjects with which to conclude this study. However, with the invitation to "tune in tomorrow" must also go the caveat stated in this chapter's opening sentence.

Looking toward the 1980s, more than one broadcaster was wringing his hands and echoing the industry's common *cri de coeur:* there were simply too many stations on the air, and not only that—there was always a good chance there might be more.[2] Nowhere was this better illustrated than in Los Angeles, a broadcasting microcosm of the United States. If nothing else, the following table might give the potential investor pause to consider alternatives before going into the radio business in Los Angeles:

AM Stations	Dial Location	FM Stations	Dial Location
KABC	790	KACE	103.9
KALI	1430	KBIG	104.3
KBRT	740	KBOB	98.3
KDAY	1580	KCRW	89.9
KEZY	1190	KCSN	88.5
KFAC	1330	KDUO	97.5
KFI	640	KEZY	95.9
KFRN	1280	KFAC	92.3
KFWB	980	KFOX	93.5
KGER	1390	KFSG	96.3
KGIL	1260	KGIL	94.3
KGOE	850	KHOF	99.5
KGRB	900	KHTZ	97.1
KHJ	930	KIIS	102.7
KIEV	870	KIQQ	100.3
KIIS	1150	KJLH	102.3
KKTT	1230	KJOI	98.7
KLAC	570	KKGO	105.1
KLIT	1220	KLON	88.1
KMPC	710	KLOS	95.5
KNSE	1510	KLVE	107.5
KNX	1070	KMAX	107.1
KPOL	1540	KMET	94.7
KPPC	1240	KNAC	105.5
KRLA	1110	KNJO	92.7
KTNQ	1020	KNOB	97.9
KTYM	1460	KNTF	93.5
KWIZ	1480	KNX	93.1
KWKW	1300	KOCM	103.1
KWOW	1600	KORJ	94.3
KWRM	1370	KOST	103.5
XEGM	950	KPCS	89.3
XPRS	1090	KPFK	90.7
XTRA	690	KQLH	95.1
		KRQQ	106.7
		KRTH	101.1
		KSAK	90.1
		KSPC	88.7

FM Stations	Dial Location
KSRF	103.1
KSUL	90.1
KUSC	91.5
KUTE	101.9
KWIZ	96.7
KWST	105.9
KWVE	107.9
KXLU	88.9
KYMS	106.3
KZLA	93.9 [3]

The scrambling for something "different" and the continuing audience fractionalization could mean only one thing: any popular music format to survive, whether existing or new, would always need to be honed with delicate precision, since its success depended on so many factors—positioning, competition, product available, personnel to execute it and equipment. The enumeration of several potentially thriving formats for the future, therefore, eschews Kent Burkhart's blending process, and relies more on emotion than on science.

THE "BACK TRACKS" FORMAT

"Nostalgia" is a dreadful way to describe a format, but nostalgia is perceived as the internal combustion engine that propels this one. In the classical music realm, Beethoven, Bach, Mozart and Haydn are not branded "nostalgia," nor are the orchestras (many of them long out of existence) which recorded these giants' works. Neither then should Rodgers and Hart, Fats Waller, Cole Porter, Duke Ellington, Harold Arlen, George Gershwin and lesser pop composers be considered "nostalgia." A vast body of native popular music, composed at an earlier time and performed by artists, many of whom are out of current favor, deserve to be heard. Broadcasters historically (and understandably) have followed the primary principle of musical radio: pop music is essentially a pursuit of the young. However, by the late 1970s, a growing number of stations, prompted mostly by competitive pressures, were looking at some startling figures: during that decade, they discovered, the under-18 population had decreased by 8 million; projections for the 1980s, indicated that the group aged 18–24—the primary years for forming new households—will experience a drop of some 4 million; and further reflecting the U.S. age structure, the median age of Americans will rise some five years in the final two decades of the century. But perhaps the projection that was most interesting indicated that by the year 2000, *half* the population will be over 35. If these projections are correct, then plainly, the sweet bird of youth has flown:

PROFILE OF THE POPULATION BY AGE GROUPS
(In percentages)

Age Group	1950	1960	1970	1980	1990	2000
Under 5	10.8	11.3	8.4	8.0	9.7	8.4
5–13	14.7	18.2	17.9	13.5	15.2	15.8
14–17	5.5	6.2	7.8	7.0	5.0	7.0
18–24	10.6	8.9	12.0	13.1	9.9	9.9
25–34	15.8	12.7	12.3	16.1	16.1	12.2
35–44	14.2	13.4	11.3	11.5	14.4	14.6
45–54	11.5	11.4	11.4	10.1	9.9	12.7
55–64	8.8	8.6	9.1	9.5	8.2	8.2
65 and over	8.1	9.2	9.8	11.1	11.7	11.3

—Source: Bureau of the Census, 1980.

Two leading national radio sales representatives, Eastman Radio and McGavern-Guild, both reported approximately one-quarter of the availability requests for their stations by early 1980 were zeroing in on the 25–54 demographic group; as recent as 1977 there were none.[4]

The "graying of America." It had already begun. And if more broadcasters were looking at demographic projections than ever before, they were also examining targeted formats being fashioned in syndication factories, hoping to capitalize on this expanding market. A few stations were even creating their own versions, but mainly it was the syndicated route that seemed the most practical one to follow. The accompanying table indicates how four syndicators were going about it with *Big Bands and More, Music of Your Life, Return Radio* and *Unforgettable.*

FORMAT/PRODUCER	DESCRIPTION	REPRESENTATIVE SELECTIONS IN A SAMPLE HOUR
Big Bands and More/ Drake-Chenault	What the name implies. Big bands mainly in their original 1930s and 1940s versions, plus vocalists, leaning toward late 1940s and 1950s.	"April in Paris" (Count Basie); "Learnin' The Blues" (Frank Sinatra); "Lover" (Peggy Lee); "Sunny Side of the Street" (Tommy Dorsey); "Day by Day" (Four Freshmen); "Satin Doll" (Ella Fitzgerald); "Artistry in Rhythm" (Stan Kenton); "String of Pearls" (Glenn Miller); "Little White Lies" (Dick Haymes); "Lady Be Good" (Artie Shaw); "And the Angels Sing" (Benny Goodman); "Love Letters in the Sand" (Pat Boone); "Young Man with a Horn" (Harry James); "On the

FORMAT/PRODUCER	DESCRIPTION	REPRESENTATIVE SELECTIONS IN A SAMPLE HOUR
		Street Where You Live" (Vic Damone); "Wood-choppers Ball" (Woody Herman).
Music of Your Life/ Al Ham Productions	Flavored with pre-rock vocalists of the late 1940s and early 1950s. Also stresses "classic pop hits of the 1940s, 1950s, 1960s and 1970s." Original and re-created big band tracks of 1930s and 1940s perfor-mances are included. Pro-ducer says format is "fore-ground" music and unlike "background" music "de-mands the listeners emo-tional involvement . . . An amalgam of the romantic and melodic mainstream tradition of American pop songs, as recorded by the artists who made them hits in the first place."	"Maybe" (Ink Spots); "It's Been a Long, Long Time" (Bing Crosby & Les Paul Trio); "Thinking of You" (Eddie Fisher); "Cherry Pink & Apple Blossom White" (Prez Prado); "Hello Dolly" (Louis Armstrong); "Frenesi" (Artie Shaw); "Sentimental Journey" (Les Brown/Doris Day); "Mona Lisa" (Nat King Cole); "How Important Can It Be" (Sarah Vaughn); "Blue Vel-vet" (Bobby Vinton); "Only Forever" (Bing Crosby); "Chopin's Polonaise" (Car-men Cavallaro); "Dear Hearts and Gentle People" (Dinah Shore); "Love Is A Many Splendored Thing" (Four Aces); "Theme From 'A Summer Place' " (Percy Faith); "I'll Never Smile Again" (Tommy Dorsey); "Symphony" (Freddy Mar-tin); "Jezebel" (Frankie Laine); "I Need You Now" (Eddie Fisher); "Lonesome Town" (Rick Nelson)
Return Radio/ William O'Shaughnessy	Launched at WRTN, New Rochelle by station owner and placed in syndication in 1980. An eclectic mix of established vocalists and big bands, past and present. Also incorporates artists "seldom heard on radio any-more." Cuts wide swath thru "society and country club" music, jazz, swing and show tunes. Producer stresses this is not a nostal-gia format. Says "old ain't necessarily good." Insists he uses music—old and new—that expresses "style and good taste."	Producer hesitates to sup-ply representative hour. Says, however, a "typical" hour will contain the fol-lowing: An obscure Rodg-ers & Hart song; "a musi-cian's" song which never became a hit; a group vocal by the Hi-Lo's or Anita Kerr or Jackie & Roy; a society orchestra (Ernie Hecksher, Lester Lanin, Michael Carney, or Peter Duchin); some Nat Cole (instead of "Crazy, Hazy Lazy Days of Summer," we'll play "Dinner for One, Please James"); Matt Den-nis; a song from a "saloon" singer recorded live (Hugh Shannon, Ronny Whyte,

FORMAT/PRODUCER	DESCRIPTION	REPRESENTATIVE SELECTIONS IN A SAMPLE HOUR
		Steve Ross); Frank Sinatra; Mabel Mercer; Caroll O'Connor; Fred Astaire; Rex Harrison; "The Tune New York, N.Y."; a Jerome Kern tune by David Allyn.
Unforgettable/ Toby Arnold	Tilted toward conventional M-O-R, with tinges of big band. A broad base of American popular songs "from Glenn Miller to Carly Simon." Eschewing material "too lush or too contemporary," stresses ballads and the "romantic" approach.	"That's Life" (Frank Sinatra); "Put Your Head on My Shoulders" (Lettermen); "Moonlight Serenade" (Glenn Miller); "Allegheny Moon" (Patti Page); "I Left My Heart in San Francisco" (Tony Bennett); "We've Only Just Begun" (Carpenters); "Love Is A Many Splendored Thing" (Four Aces); "It's Impossible" (Perry Como); "You Light Up My Life" (Debbie Boone); "Let's Dance" (Benny Goodman); "Boogie-Woogie Bugle Boy" (Andrews Sisters); "You're Nobody Till Somebody Loves You" (Dean Martin); "I'm in Love With You" (Ames Brothers); "Unforgettable" (Nat King Cole).

—Sources: Drake-Chenault, Al Ham Productions, Toby Arnold and William O'Shaughnessy

THE "SOUND TRACKS" FORMAT

An entirely separate cosmos is a format based on music from Hollywood and Broadway productions. Selections from original cast albums may well be a part of this format, but extreme care would have to be taken to program for aural, rather than visual, values. Cover versions, of course, would also be necessary. In the case of Broadway shows, not only could selections from cast albums be considered; versions of the material by other artists would be acceptable too. For example: *Ain't Misbehavin'*—In addition to Fats Waller's own prolific output of recordings (all re-issued and available, even if by overseas scrounging), there are numerous updated versions of his songs lurking in record bins across the country; *Sophisticated Ladies*—The Ellington songbook is so rich and deep, the point needs no belaboring. Judging by the abundance of *film* track albums issued since 1979 alone, the "SOUND TRACKS" format could have a healthy future in the 1980s:

American Gigolo	*Hard Country*
American Graffiti	*Honeysuckle Rose*
American Pop	*The Idolmaker*
Blues Brothers	*The Long Riders*
Bronco Billy	*Nine to Five*
Carny	*One Trick Pony*
Coal Miner's Daughter	*Popeye*
Cruising	*Ragtime*
Electric Horseman	*Roadie*
Empire Strikes Back	*Roam*
Every Which Way But Loose	*The Rose*
Exodus	*The Saturday Night Fever*
Fame	*Star Wars*
Flash Gordon	*Urban Cowboy*
Foxes	*The Way We Were*
FM	*Where the Buffalo Roam*
Grease	*Xanadu*

Sometimes the process works in reverse: first will come the top hit, then the film, as in *Harper Valley PTA, Middle Age Crazy, The Night the Lights Went Out in Georgia, The Cowgirl and the Dandy, The Gambler, Desperado* and *Goodbye Yellow Brick.*

THE "POSITIVE POP" FORMAT

This one will need fine tuning. But given the right positioning situation, it might fly. There is definitely an audience for contemporary Christian music. Putting a few facts in perspective leads to the conclusion there is an untapped market for "positive pop": a 1980 Gallup Poll reported 41 million Americans considered themselves born-again Christians; the Christian record industry is growing by leaps and bounds ($100 million dollars in 1980); Arbitron estimates there are 30 million listeners to some form of religious programming sometime during the week; in an indirect way, the "electric pulpit" (*700 Club, PTL Club, Rev. Jerry Falwell,* et al.) is helping energize the evangelical movement; and a trend toward political conservatism, expressed in the 1980 election, seemed to fit the growing conservative theological mood. Christian stations in the late 1970s were continuing to move away from sermonizing toward harmonizing. A trade paper, *Contemporary Christian Music,* every bit as professionally edited as *Rolling Stone* or *Billboard,* reviews new product, lists top selling records, profiles artists and reports on the Christian radio station scene. *Record World,* a standard publication in the pop field, runs charts for "Contemporary and Inspirational Gospel." The amply-headlined conversions of Bob Dylan, Al Green, Donna Summer and B.J. Thomas have done the cause no harm. Much of the contemporary Christian product is recorded and processed in the same manner as secular music; only the message is different. Obeying the Biblical injunction to "make a joyful noise," many Christian stations, as part of their repertory of contemporary gospel selections, also program the more traditional sounds of Mahalia Jackson, The Clara Ward Singers, Rev. James Cleveland and The Dixie Hummingbirds.

THE "NO FORMAT" FORMAT

Why not? When all else has failed, there may be merit in considering a place in the format spectrum for this unconventional wrinkle. Blocking out abrupt format changes by daypart is always a possibility, but the approach KARM, Fresno introduced in 1980 was singularly daring in an industry not always noted for bold innovations. KARM rotated nine formats: *Big Band; Fabulous 50s* (1949–54); *Golden Oldies* (1955–1964); *Solid Gold* (1965–1970); *Superstars of the 70s* (1970–1977); *Current Hits* (1978–1980), *Country, Million Sellers* and the *Best of Requests*. Station management was betting the boredom factor was strong enough across the Fresno dial that listeners would welcome something different every day.[5]

As musical radio headed into the 1980s, conventional program wisdom seemed as fixed as it was in the hidebound traditions of the early 1950s. It took a Todd Storz and a Gordon McLendon to shake things up and send the medium on its way rejoicing, even as Cyclops bestrode radioland. The rich American popular music lode assures there will always be bountiful material from which to fashion some new format. And while much of the industry could get caught up in the glamorous realm of space and talk of satellites and cable, somewhere there could also be an earthbound program whiz dreaming up a format that would attract listeners. Regardless of how that format got to the music box.

NOTES

1. Harry S. Truman. *Year of Decisions*, Doubleday, (Garden City), 1955, p. 11.
2. The question of how many stations can occupy the AM and FM bands is ultimately decided by the FCC. Indeed, the establishment of that agency to "protect" dial locations from interference was the primary reason for its creation in the first place. Because radio broadcasting is international in scope, technical matters such as frequencies must be coordinated with foreign nations. In some countries, the separation on the AM band is 9 kHz, while in the U.S. that separation is 10 kHz. Late in 1979, in preparation for the World Administrative Radio Conference (held every twenty years), the FCC, as then constituted under the Carter administration, instructed the U.S. delegation to the WARC to

agree to 9 kHz separations for U.S. stations. Using the 910 to 940 dial locations as examples, the AM band would appear as follows under the proposed plan:

EXISTING DIAL SETTING	SETTING UNDER 9 kHz SHIFT PLAN
910	909
920	918
930	927
940	936

—Source: National Radio Broadcasters Association

Most U.S. broadcasters opposed the changes. With the election of a Republican president in 1980 and a re-constitution of the FCC to favor the party in power, the push for the 9 kHz plan was slowed considerably. Under President Carter, the FCC's pro-9 kHz rationale was that the narrowing of the AM band would permit hundreds of new stations to go on the air under the ownership of minorities and women. Most industry insiders felt the 9 kHz proposal would not come to pass. They guessed right, it did not.

3. "AM/FM Radio Highlights." *Los Angeles Times* (Calendar), January 18, 1981, p. 50.
4. Eastman Radio. "Marketing Services Report," April 27, 1981, and McGavern-Guild. "Client Service Bulletin," June, 1981.
5. Tom Murphy. "What's on KARM? Radio Station Changes Programming Every Day, Keeps Listeners Confused," *Sunday Patriot-News* (Keystoner), December 14, 1980, p. 5.

CHAPTER 21

Notes from Outer Space: The Music Box Celestial

WORLD WAR II slowed down by perhaps a half-dozen years the technological revolution that resulted in television, FM, magnetic tape, the transistor, the long-play record and stereo. Since then, the most cheerful Pollyanna would concede international events have cast a more ominous shadow over the affairs of nations. The indomitability of the human spirit, however, decrees optimism—even if it is necessarily guarded. Advances in communications technology should come in quantum leaps as we move toward 2000 A.D. Predicting how this will impact on the conventional system of American commercial broadcasting has already filled volumes.

Alvin Toffler, whose earlier *Future Shock* made him *hors concours* against the rest of the crystal ball field, let go with an even more startling futures agenda to start the 1980s. In *The Third Wave*, Toffler claims, "What appears on the surface to be a set of unrelated events turns out to be a wave of closely interrelated changes sweeping across the media horizon from newspapers and radio at one end to magazines and television at the other. The mass media are under attack. New, demassified media are proliferating, challenging . . . The Third Wave thus begins a truly new era—the age of the de-massified media. A new info-sphere is emerging alongside the new techno-sphere . . . Taken together, these changes revolutionize our images of the world and our ability to make sense of it." [1]

Broadcasting has always been pre-occupied with technology. It has to be. The introduction, for example, of the electrical recording process, eliminating the tinny, unnatural sound of music reproduced acoustically,

342

changed the entire direction of musical radio. But radio is also affected by the marketplace. Radio is a competitive member of the media community, and unless it serves a purpose there, technology is of no consequence. The unique relationship of American media is fundamental and therefore needs to be examined briefly before proceeding to more escoteric matters.

That the great mass of Americans were spending more time with electronic media than print media has been known for decades. How great this disparity has become can be seen in the following table. It reveals the average time spent with major media in hours per day:

MEDIUM	ADULTS 18+	ADULTS 18–49
Radio	3:27	3:44
Television	3:57	3:28
Newspapers	0:34	0:34
Magazines	0:27	0:27

—Sources: RAB; RADAR, Fall, 1980 Report; Nielsen Audience Demographics Report, av. of March-May-July-Nov, 1980 from TvB; Ted Bates Instant Media Facts, 1978–79.

Even more revealing are the trends since 1970. The following table, excerpted from the annual Ted Bates/New York Media Trends Study (using the index form with 1970 as a base year) shows clearly that print media, in spite of sharply declining audiences, have taken their rates in the opposite direction. (Advertisers and their agencies soon take note of such imbalances.)

Another significant development of the 1970s that will influence the direction of broadcasting's future was the renaissance of network radio. Many who subscribed to Bert Parks' 1956 requiem for network radio had, a quarter-century later, to eat their words as they observed how the networks were back in the popular music business again. The radio networks weren't waiting for satellite delivery either; all (except CBS which sticks to news, sports, information and drama) were feeding popular music in some form.* Most presentations were week-end specials—a trend that appeared so well entrenched that the return to daily pop music "strip programming" (a la the *Chesterfield Supper Club* and *Club 15*) seemed remote. The following synopsis, by network, lists some of the typical pop music shows planned for 1980–81:

---

* CBS announced in mid-1981, it was putting together another network that would feature pop music aimed at young demographics.

TRENDS 1970–1981

	DAY NET TV	EVE NET TV	SPOT TV	MAGA-ZINES	NEWS-PAPERS	SUPPLE-MENTS	SPOT RADIO	NET RADIO	OUT-DOOR
Unit Cost Trends									
1970	100	100	100	100	100	100	100	100	100
1971	94	96	102	100	104	99	106	111	108
1972	98	109	95	97	107	102	112	117	119
1973	113	124	95	97	114	109	119	119	123
1974	121	137	100	102	130	121	124	117	134
1975	140	147	102	107	144	131	132	123	144
1976	163	160	130	110	159	135	151	129	156
1977	204	203	137	119	173	156	166	148	172
1978	227	228	140	130	190	168	179	159	191
1979	247	256	160	140	205	183	193	171	212
1980	279	300	179	156	226	201	213	195	237
1981 (est.)	296	324	192	173	248	221	231	207	263
Audience Trends									
1970	100	100	100	100	100	100	100	100	100
1971	107	103	104	99	100	98	104	112	104
1972	116	110	103	97	101	99	104	132	107
1973	119	111	105	98	102	102	111	134	108
1974	115	112	108	99	100	104	113	132	108
1975	127	120	110	97	98	108	114	136	110
1976	119	120	112	97	98	108	117	130	111
1977	116	121	112	96	99	106	119	136	112
1978	119	125	115	96	100	112	121	138	113
1979	123	125	121	96	100	112	124	139	113
1980	126	128	125	96	101	113	128	151	115
1981 (est.)	128	130	127	96	102	114	130	153	116

—Source: Ted Bates/New York

ABC

In addition to its two regularly scheduled weekly shows (*The King Biscuit Flower Hour,* Sundays on the FM Network and the *Silver Eagle,* alternating Saturdays on the Entertainment Network, ABC's special music programming included these features:

1981 Special Music Programming

Program	Dates	Type Programming	Network
King Biscuit Flower Hour	Start 1/4	Live Concerts	FM
Silver Eagle	Start 1/31	Live Country Concerts	Ent.
Super 70's +1	1/1	Omnibus, 11 years of music	Cont.
With Love: Rock 'n Roll Valentine	2/14	Omnibus, 12 hours of rock	FM
Rock Awards	3/7	Rock 'n Roll Awards	FM
Super Groups in Concert	3/28, 9/26, 10/31	"Police" concert (3/28)	FM
Rock Live	2/28	Hall & Oates concert	Cont.
Mello Yello Concerts	5/1–3, 10/9–11	Charlie Daniels, Christopher Cross, etc.	Cont./Ent./ FM
Neil Diamond	5/10	Concert	Cont.
"Here Comes Summer"	5/25	Omnibus Concerts	FM
"A Night on the Road"	4/25 plus various dates	Concerts (Kansas, Pat Benatar, etc.)	FM

MUTUAL

The rejuvenated Mutual Network which promotes news and sports as the "back bone" of its programming, nevertheless, jumped into the pop music waters in 1978 when it began feeding a weekly country clam-bake, *Jamboree, USA.* Since then, it aired specials from time to time, including: *Johnny Cash,* the *Beach Boys; Triple,* starring Barbara Mandrell, Larry Gatlin and the Charlie Daniels Band. *The Dick Clark National Music Survey* was blueprinted to review the nations top 30 hits each week, plus flashbacks, previews and interviews.

NBC

The pioneer which split its operation in two by forming "The Source," a network aimed at young adults and retaining its conventional operation, had obviously returned to popular music in no uncertain terms. "The Source," given its target audience, was resolutely committed to concerts or specials with such outfits as Styx, Stevie Nicks, Ted Nugent and Marshall Tucker. Daily 90-second vignettes such as *Rock Report, Today in*

Rock History and *Rock Comedy* helped keep the pop music flavor going. Meanwhile, over at the "regular" NBC, a *Music Plus* series highlighted artists like John Denver, Kris Kristofferson/Rita Coolidge, Carly Simon, Olivia Newton-John and Anne Murray, while *Country Session* showcased the likes of Jerry Lee Lewis, Willie Nelson, Charlie Pride, Mel Tillis, Brenda Lee and Tom T. Hall.

—Sources: ABC, Mutual and NBC

The following table reveals how the four major radio networks have re-gained grass roots affiliate strength since 1970, which in turn, has contributed to their growing economic vitality:

IN THE 1970s NETWORK RADIO ROSE FROM THE ASHES

| | ABC | | CBS | | Mutual | | NBC | |
| | | Percentage Sales Increase over | | Percentage Sales Increase over | | Percentage Sales Increase over | | Percentage Sales Increase over |
	Affil-iates	Previous Year	Affil-iates	Previous Year	Affil-iates	Previous Year	Affil-iates	Previous Year
1970	971	NA	245	NA	562	NA	242	− 2.9
1971	1130	NA	249	NA	563	−11.2	248	10.7
1972	1212	39	242	NA	582	−19.0	241	11.8
1973	1294	− 8	243	NA	630	13.6	234	−11.4
1974	1349	3	249	NA	651	13.3	232	− .9
1975	1372	18	247	NA	673	17.8	227	7.6
1976	1401	24	262	NA	730	36.4	244	22.0
1977	1439	29	266	NA	775	46.5	246	37.8
1978	1565	11	270	NA	915	23.9	267	6.4
1979	1584	13	276	NA	934	2.0	282	6.7
1980	1591	17	321	NA	898	9.2	289	11.0

—Sources: ABC, CBS, Mutual & NBC

While commercial television interests were growing increasingly concerned with how much satellites and cable would fractionalize home video, many industry seers were re-assessing the sound medium's role in the face of technological change. "Space birds" which have been standard equipment for the three major television networks* for a number of years have an obvious application to radio. Earth-orbiting satellites, 23,000 miles above the Equator, circle the earth once a day and thus remain in the same po-

---

* The most self-styled user outside the charmed circle of the three major networks was Ted Turner, celebrated maverick and owner of sports franchises, yachts and sundry other baubles. Turner was using satellites to feed programs from his Atlantic-based UHF station to cable systems in 45 states. His Cable News Network (CNN) was the first to challenge the commercial networks in the news field.

sition in relation to the earth's surface at all times. Earth stations (also called "terminals," or "parabolic bowls," or "dishes") aimed at satellites are capable of sending transmissions and receiving signals from anywhere in the United States and Canada.

The key section of a satellite, the transponder, acts as a repeater and bounces a signal back to earth, ready to be received by any number of earth stations. Television's requirements for satellite use are extremely complex compared to radio's. Twenty to twenty-four radio signals can fit into the transponder space that accommodates a single television signal. For radio networking, satellite transmission is an incredible advance. Technically, the sound is pristine clear, compared to static-potential existing in sound carried by land-leased telephone lines. Using computer-based digital technology, a network can customize its service for every affiliate. The major distinction between the conventional concept of a network, feeding the same programs to everyone, and satellite delivery, according to Robert Benson, ABC vice president, is that now stations will be able to pick and choose only the program they want. Affiliates would be delivered only the shows they want at the time they want them for "live" broadcast, with whatever breaks they want for local news, commercials and public service.[2] All four "old-line" networks were looking ahead to the satellite age. Their familiarity with the networking concept at least found them with an affiliate family already together. ABC,[*] CBS and NBC with their television tie-ins were not as free to move as Mutual. Unencumbered by such considerations, Mutual had already jumped aboard the "bird" and was transmitting programs via satellite by spring, 1981. (See Appendix, page 381)

By now the discerning reader must have figured out, given the resources and desire, that almost anyone could get into the network business. Which is why the four traditional radio networks can expect some stiff competition—particularly where popular music is concerned. Hardly a week went by in 1980 and early 1981 that the trade did not learn of plans for satellite program transmission. The *New York Times* forecast 19 national radio networks in operation by the end of 1981.[3] The following table lists those specially-customized national radio networks, either in operation, or ready to go into operation, during 1981:

NETWORK	ORGANIZED BY	PROGRAMMING
APR	Associated Press	News and information features
NPR	National Public Radio	Regular features
RKO I	RKO General	Aimed at 18–49, with emphasis on "18–34 call" news, sports, special events

[*] In June, 1981 ABC announced a 24-hour-a-day, seven-day-a-week satellite-delivered "live" music programming service, in addition to its existing four networks.

NETWORK	ORGANIZED BY	PROGRAMMING
RKO II	RKO General	Aimed at 25–54, with emphasis on "35–44 call" news, sports, special events
RKO III	RKO General	"Long and short-form programming blocks," Concerts, Countdown shows, & midnight–6am talk show planned 24-hour
Satellite Music Network	Burkhart/Abrams Org., in association with Midwest Radio-TV, John Tyler & Assoc. & United Video	"Modern" Country, Pop/Adult, news, weather and features 24 hours
Starfleet	John Blair Co.	Rock Concerts & Boston Pops
Transtar Radio Network	Sunbelt Communications	Music aimed at 25–34 year-olds 24 hours
Wall Street Journal	Dow-Jones	Business Reports

—Sources: *Broadcasting, Broadcast Communications, Radio and Records, Television/ Radio Age* and *Variety.*

The volume of programming delivered celestially will depend on the availability of satellites and transponders. Nine satellites were aloft in 1980, with construction cleared for 25, and 20 were launched-approved by the FCC. The cost—between $65 and $70 million per satellite—will obviously have a bearing on how much and how fast music is transmitted via the "bird." Satellite earth stations were selling for approximately $10,000, plus installation. Earth stations in an owner's backyard are capable of picking up more than 60 signals from orbiting satellites.

Cable can also be expected to affect the way we tune in tomorrow. Many cable television systems were offering all-band FM service for an additional monthly fee (usually around two dollars). The subscriber receives whatever FM stations the cable operator receives at the head-end. A second option offered by some cable systems is "processed FM service," also at approximately two dollars a month. This is available only to subscribers, because while the cable connects into the subscriber's FM receiver and the subscriber selects the stations received on his FM dial (just like all-band FM service) the cable operator may insert within the service any signal he desires. The third means that cable systems employ for the carriage of audio services is the carriage of a single service as background audio for a channel carrying automated services, such as weather, news, or program guides.[4]

Warner-Amex, based in Los Angeles, was planning a 24-hour music channel (MTV) for upward of two million homes around the country. The Music Channel, as local cable companies will refer to it, plans to run videotapes of pop music groups in action. Warner-Amex expects to have the videotapes supplied by record producers in the manner they now provide records to radio disc jockeys. The sound will come through stereo speakers and offer continuous programming—"more like an FM station with pictures than a 30- or 60-minute show."[5] In 1977, the same firm began testing Qube, a two-way cable system in Cincinnati. Warner-Amex supplies subscribers with a console box equipped with five response buttons. By "touching in" they can participate in studio programs such as amateur contests, game shows and public affairs talk programs. In expanding the system, Warner-Amex had already proven its capability for such subscriber services as banking, shopping at home and home security.[6]

Everywhere, it seemed, there were crystal balls revealing what the coming communications revolution would be like. Aristotle may have started it 2000 years ago when he wrote of "music of the spheres." (Edward Bellamy, the Victorian novelist, was so smitten by the notion of music carried by telephone lines into homes, he predicted a society eventually free of struggles.) "A Mob Scene of Competing Attractions" was a headline *TV Guide* used over one of its "Television in Transition" series.[7] In a 1977 study conducted by the National Association of Broadcasters, the portents for the future were bright. In spite of more competition, the study concluded, Radio will hold its own in the scramble for listeners and advertiser dollars; every U.S. household will have six radios in working order; the largest portion of the population will be at peak spending stage; average family income will increase dramatically.[8] In addressing a broadcasters convention late in 1980, Dr. Richard Rosenbloom, David Sarnoff Professor of Business Administration, Harvard University, was less sanguine: "As formats fragment, the audience profile is etched in even sharper outlines. The audience is there because radio has succeeded in delivering a service which they value and can't obtain elsewhere at comparable cost or convenience. New products and services becoming available to the providers and users of information services will create alternatives to radio as a means of meeting certain audience needs." Dr. Rosenbloom's crystal ball, however, also told him, "radio itself will be affected only in limited ways in the next ten years."[9]

"We should all be concerned about the future," Charles F. Kettering, inventor and General Motors executive, once said, "because we will have to spend the rest of our lives there." If the first 60 years of fascinating rhythm on the air was any indication, the future of musical radio is secure. For the listener, the broadcaster and the music maker, another Golden Age has only just begun. Stay tuned.

NOTES

1. Alvin Toffler. *The Third Wave,* Bantam edition, (New York), 1980, pp. 164–165.
2. Steve Knoll. "Satellites Bringing Sound to Radio Industry Revival," *Variety,* October 15, 1980, p. 305.
3. Andrew Feinberg. "The Return of the Radio Network," *New York Times,* April 12, 1981, p. F-7.
4. Howard M. Liberman. "Cable Carriage of Radio," *Counsel from the Legal Department,* National Association of Broadcasters Legal Advisory, Washington, D.C., September, 1980.
5. Robert Hilburn. "TV Goes FM: Rock Around the Clock," *Los Angeles Times* (Calendar), May 17, 1981, p. 6.
6. Tony Schwartz. "Cincinnati Getting Sophisticated 2-Way Cable TV," *New York Times,* May 7, 1981, p. C-18.
7. Neil Hickey. "A Mob Scene of Competing Attractions," *TV Guide,* May 16, 1981, p. 7.
8. *Radio in 1985.* National Association of Broadcasters, Washington, D.C., 1977.
9. Dr. Richard Rosenbloom. In speech, "The Coming Revolution in Broadcasting," delivered at National Radio Broadcasters "1980 Radio Expo," Los Angeles, October 5, 1980.

(Courtesy Cheryl Shelton-Hendricks, KAAY/KQ94)

New technologies afforded countless possibilities as radio headed toward the year 2000. In Little Rock, "trimulcasting" was introduced, offering cable viewers a chance to see what "morning drive" tuners-in were hearing on radio stations KAAY(AM) and KQ94(FM).

Nancy Wilson   Nat King Cole   Peggy Lee

Helen Reddy   Neil Diamond

(all photos courtesy of Capitol Records)

By the end of the 1970s, the "graying of America" had become apparent, and artists such as Nat King Cole, Nancy Wilson, Peggy Lee, Helen Reddy and Neil Diamond were being heard more frequently. Popular music aimed at older demographics looked like a good bet for a format of the future.

351

(Courtesy California Microwave)

(Courtesy Associated Press)

1980 was the year of the "dish." Nearly everyone in broadcasting was talking about these new pieces of hardware, also known as "earth stations." These devices serve as special antennae for picking up programs transmitted by satellites. In the top photo, an AM and an FM station use their dish to receive satellite transmissions for live or taped airing. In the bottom photo a 10-foot ground-mounted earth station can receive news reports fed via satellite for further delivery to subscriber stations by conventional telephone lines.

The "four old-line" networks which had deserted live popular music in the mid-1950s were certain to return to that form. Their decision was made easier by the formation of new competitive satellite networks. In 1980, Mutual offered its affiliates several holiday specials, including *Dick Clark Presents Barry Manilow* on Labor Day and *Triple,* on Easter weekend, starring Barbara Mandrell (shown in top photo with producer Ed Salamon). Larry Gatlin and Charlie Daniels rounded out the threesome.

Selected Bibliography

Books

Allen, Allen S. ed. *Harlem on My Mind.* New York: Random House, 1968.

Allen, Fred. *Treadmill to Oblivion.* Boston: Little, Brown and Co., 1954.

Allen, Walter C. *Hendersonia.* Highland Park, N.J.: Jazz Monographs, 1973.

Archer, Gleason. *Big Business and Radio.* New York: American Historical Company, 1939.

Archer, Gleason. *History of Radio to 1926.* New York: Arno, 1971.

Bannister, Harry. *The Education of a Broadcaster.* New York: Simon and Schuster, 1965.

Barnouw, Eric. *A Tower in Babel: A History of Broadcasting to 1933.* New York: Oxford, 1966.

Barnouw, Eric. *The Golden Web: A History of Broadcasting, 1933–1953.* New York: Oxford, 1968.

Barnouw, Eric. *The Image Empire: A History of Broadcasting from 1953.* New York: Oxford, 1970.

Belz, Carl. *The Story of Rock.* New York: Oxford, 1972.

Biow, Milton. *Butting In.* New York: Doubleday, 1964.

Blanford, Edmund L. *A Bio-Discography of Artie Shaw.* Sussex: Castle Books, 1973.

Boeckman, Charles. *And the Beat Goes On.* Washington: B. Luce, 1972.

Burns, George. *The Third Time Around.* New York: Putnam, 1980.

Calloway, Cab (w/Robbins, Bryant). *Of Minnie the Moocher and Me.* New York: Crowell, 1976.

Campbell, Robert. *The Golden Years of Broadcasting.* New York: Scribner's, 1976.

Carr, Patrick. ed. *The Illustrated History of Country Music.* Garden City, NY: Doubleday/Dolphin, 1980.

Chapple, Steve and Reebee Garofalo. *Rock and Roll Is Here to Pay.* Chicago: Nelson Hall, 1977.

Chase, Gilbert. *America's Music.* New York: McGraw-Hill, 1966.

Clark, Dick (w/Robinson, Richard). *Rock, Roll, and Remember.* New York: Crowell, 1976.

Condon, Eddie and O'Neal, Hank. *Eddie Condon's Scrapbook*. New York: St. Martin's, 1973.

Connor, D. Russell and Hicks, Warren. *B G on the Record*. New Rochelle: Arlington House, 1969.

Csida, Joseph and Csida, June B. *American Entertainment*. New York: Billboard Publications, 1978.

Dance, Stanley. *The World of Earl Hines*. New York: Scribner's, 1977.

de Lerma, Dominique-Rene. (ed.) *Black Music in our Culture*. Kent, Ohio: Kent State University Press, 1970.

Denisoff, R. Serge. *Sing A Song of Social Significance*. Bowling Green, Ohio: Bowling Green University Popular Press, 1972.

Dietz, Laurence. *Soda Pop*. New York: Simon and Schuster, 1973.

Dreher, Carl. *Sarnoff: An American Success*. New York: Quadrangle, 1977.

Eisen, Johnathan. (ed.) *The Age of Rock*. New York: Vintage, 1969.

Ellington, Duke. *Music Is My Mistress*. New York: Doubleday, 1973.

Elliott, Bob and Goulding, Ray. *Write if You Get Work*. New York: Random House, 1975.

Ewen, David. *The Life and Death of Tin Pan Alley*. New York: Funk and Wagnall's, 1964.

Fass, Paula S. *The Damned and the Beautiful: American Youth in the 1920's*. New York: Oxford, 1977.

Firestone, Ross. ed. *The Big Radio Comedy Program*. Chicago: Contemporary Books, 1978.

Flower, John. *Moonlight Serenade*. New Rochelle: Arlington House, 1972.

Fong-Torres, Ben. (ed.) *The Rolling Stone Rock 'N Roll Reader*. New York: Bantam Books, 1974.

Furnas, J. C. *Stormy Weather*. New York: G. P. Putnams, 1977.

Gillespie, Dizzy. *To Be or Not to Bop*. New York: Doubleday, 1979.

Gillett, Charlie. *Making Tracks*. New York: Dutton, 1974.

Gleason, Ralph. (ed.) *Jam Session: An Anthology of Jazz*. New York: Putnam, 1958.

Goldberg, Isaac. *Tin Pan Alley*. New York: Frederick Ungar, 1961.

Goldman, Eric F. *The Crucial Decade and After: America, 1945–1960*. New York: Vintage Books, 1960.

Goodman, Benny (w/Kolodin, Irving). *The Kingdom of Swing*. New York: Frederick Ungar, 1961.

Goulden, Joseph C. *The Best Years, 1945–1950*. New York: Athenum, 1976.

Gross, Ben. *I Looked and I Listened*. New York: Random House, 1954.

Gunther, John. *Taken at the Flood*. New York: Harper & Bros., 1960.

Hall, Claude and Hall, Barbara. *This Business of Radio Programming*. New York: Billboard Publications, 1977.

Hammond, John (w/Townsend, Irving). *John Hammond on the Record*. New York: Summit Books, 1977.

Haskins, Jim. *The Cotton Club*. New York: Random House, 1977.

Hopkins, Jerry. *The Rock Story*. New York: New American Library, 1970.

Hurst, Jack. *Grand Ole Opry*. New York: Abrams, 1975.

Karshner, Roger. *The Music Machine*. Los Angeles: Nash, 1971.

Lessing, Lawrence. *Man of High Fidelity: Edwin Howard Armstrong*. Philadelphia: J. B. Lippincott, 1969.

Lichty, Lawrence & Tapping, Malachi C. (ed.) *American Broadcasting: A Source Book on the History of Radio and Television*. New York: Hastings House, 1975.

Lombardo, Guy (w/Alshul, Jack). *Auld Acquaintance*. Garden City: Doubleday, 1975.

Lonstein, Albert I. and Marino, Vito. *The Compleat Sinatra*. Ellenville, New York: Cameron Publishing, 1970.

Lujack, Larry (w/Daniel A. Jedlicka). *Super Jock*. Chicago: Henry Regnery, 1975.

McCarthy, Albert. *The Dance Band Era*. Philadelphia: Chilton, 1971.

Mattfield, Julius. *Variety Musical Cavalcade*. Englewood-Cliffs, New Jersey: Prentice-Hall, 1962.

Merken, Alan. (ed.) *1927 Edition of The Sears Catalogue.* New York: Crown Publishers, 1970.

Miller, Jim. *The Rolling Stone Illustrated History of Rock and Roll.* New York: Rolling Stone Press, 1976.

Mitchell, Curtis. *Cavalcade of Broadcasting.* Chicago: Follett, 1970.

Nanry, Charles. *American Music: From Storyville to Woodstock.* New Brunswick, N. J.: Transaction, Inc., 1972.

Nelson, Ozzie. *Ozzie.* Englewood-Cliffs, New Jersey: Prentice-Hall, 1973.

Okum, Milton. *Great Songs of the Sixties.* New York: Quadrangle, 1970.

Paley, William. *As It Happened.* New York: Doubleday, 1979.

Passman, Arnold. *The Deejays.* New York: MacMillan, 1972.

Perry, Dick. *Not Just A Sound: The Story of WLW.* Englewood-Cliffs, New Jersey: Prentice-Hall, 1971.

Phillips, Cabell. *Decade of Triumph and Trouble, The 1940's.* New York: Macmillan, 1975.

Phillips, Cabell. *From the Crash to the Blitz, 1929–1939.* New York: Macmillan, 1969.

Pichaske, David. *A Generation in Motion.* New York: Schirmer Books, 1979.

Poindexter, Ray. *Golden Throats and Silver Tongues.* Conway, Arkansas: River Road Press, 1978.

Quinlan, Sterling. *Inside ABC.* New York: Hastings House, 1979.

Routt, Edd and others. *The Radio Format Conundrum.* New York: Hastings House, 1978.

Rust, Brian. *The Dance Bands.* London: Ian Allan, 1972.

Sanford, Herb. *Tommy and Jimmy: The Dorsey Years.* New Rochelle: Arlington House, 1972.

Schiedt, Duncan. *The Jazz State of Indiana.* (Published privately in Pittsboro, Indiana), 1972.

Settel, Irving. *A Pictorial History of Radio.* New York: Citadel, 1960.

Shapiro, Nat and Hentoff, Nat. (eds.) *The Jazz Makers.* New York: Grove Press, 1957.

Shaw, Arnold. *Honkers and Shouters.* New York: Macmillan, 1978.

Shaw, Arnold. *The Rockin' 50's.* New York: Hawthrone, 1974.

Shaw, Artie. *The Trouble with Cinderella.* New York: Collier Books, 1963.

Simon, George. *Glenn Miller and His Orchestra,* New York: Crowell, 1974.

Simon, George. *The Big Bands.* New York: MacMillan, 1967.

Simon, George. *Simon Says.* New Rochelle: Arlington House, 1971.

Slate, Sam and Cook, Joe. *It Sounds Impossible.* New York: MacMillan, 1963.

Sobel, Robert. *They Satisfy.* New York: Anchor Press/Doubleday, 1978.

Stearns, Marshall. *The Story of Jazz.* New York: New America Library, 1958.

Sudhalter, Richard M. and Evans, Philip R. *Bix: Man and Legend.* New Rochelle: Arlington House, 1974.

Summers, Harrison B. (ed.). *A Thirty-Year History of Radio Programs, 1926–1956.* New York: Arno, 1971.

Thompson, Charles. *Bing.* New York: McKay, 1975.

Toffler, Alvin. *The Third Wave.* New York: Bantam Books, 1981.

Treadwell, Bill. *Big Book of Swing.* New York: Cambridge House, 1946.

Truman, Harry S. *Year of Decisions.* Garden City: Doubleday, 1955.

Vallee, Rudy (w/McKean, Gil). *My Time Is Your Time.* Oblensky, 1962.

Walker, Leo. *Great Dance Bands.* Berkeley: Howell-North, 1964.

Waters, Howard J. *Jack Teagarden's Music.* Stanhope, N.J.: Walter C. Allen, 1960.

Wertheim, Arthur. *Radio Comedy.* New York: Oxford, 1979.

Whitcomb, Ian. *After the Ball.* London: Penquin Press, 1972.

Whittinghill, Dick. *Did You Whittinghill This Morning?* Chicago: Regnery, 1976.

Wilder, Alec. *American Popular Song.* New York: Oxford, 1972.

Williams, John R. *This Was Your Hit Parade.* Rockford, Maine: Courier-Gazette, 1973.

———. *Sold American: The First Fifty Years.* Published by the American Tobacco Company, 1954.

———. *The Sixties.* New York: Random House/Rolling Stone Press, 1977.

Newspapers & Periodicals

Baltimore Sun
Buffalo Evening News
Chicago Daily News
Harrisburg Sunday Patriot News
Lancaster Intelligencer Journal
Lancaster Sunday News
Los Angeles Times
New York Times
Philadelphia Daily News
Philadelphia Inquirer
Washington Post
Washington Star
York Dispatch

Ad Media
Advertising Age
Advertising and Communications Times
American Magazine
Billboard
Broadcast Communications
Broadcast Engineering
Broadcast Management/Engineering
Broadcast Programming and Production
Broadcasting
Business Week
Down Beat
Etude
Fortune
Forum
High Fidelity

International Musician
Journal of Broadcasting
Journal of Popular Culture
Journal of Research in Music Education
Life
Literary Digest
Look
Mississippi Rag
Musician
The Nation
Nation's Business
New York
New Yorker
Newsweek
Radio and Records
Radio Broadcast
Radio Guide
Radio Report
The Reporter
Saturday Evening Post
Saturday Review
Scribner's
Sponsor
Standard Rates and Data
Stereo Review
TV Guide
Television/Radio Age
Time
U. S. Radio
Variety

Encyclopedias & Dictionaries

Buxton, Frank and Owen, Bill. *The Big Broadcast, 1920–1950.* New York: Viking Press, 1972.

Dunning, John. *Tune in Yesterday: The Ultimate Encyclopedia of Old Time Radio, 1925–1976.* Englewood-Cliffs, N.J., Prentice-Hall, 1976.

Feather, Leonard. *The Encyclopedia of Jazz.* New York: Horizon Press, 1960.

Feather, Leonard. *The Encyclopedia of Jazz* (Rev.). New York: Horizon Press, 1966.

Gammond, Peter and Clayton, Peter. *Dictionary of Popular Music,* New York: Philosophical Library, 1961.

Gold, Robert S. *Jazz Talk.* New York: Bobbs-Merrill, 1975.

Kinkle, Roger. *The Complete Encyclopedia of Popular Music and Jazz, 1900–1950.* (4 vols.), New Rochelle: Arlington House, 1974.

Morris, William and Morris, Mary. *Dictionary of Word and Phrase Origins.* New York: Harper and Row, 1962.

Nugent, Stephen and Gillett, Charlie. *Rock Almanac.* New York: Anchor Press, 1978.

Roxon, Lillian. *Rock Encyclopedia.* New York: Grosset and Dunlap, 1971.

Shapiro, Nat. *Popular Music, 1950–1959* (vol. 1, 2nd ed.). New York: Adrian Press, 1967.

Shapiro, Nat. *Popular Music, 1940–1949* (vol. 2). New York: Adrian Press, 1965.

Shapiro, Nat. *Popular Music, 1960–1964* (vol. 3). New York: Adrian Press, 1967.

Shapiro, Nat. *Popular Music, 1930–1939* (vol. 4). New York: Adrian Press, 1968.

Shapiro, Nat. *Popular Music, 1920–1929* (vol. 5). New York: Adrian Press, 1969.
Shapiro, Nat. *Popular Music, 1965–1969* (vol. 6). New York: Adrian Press, 1973.
Shestack, Melvin. *The Country Music Encyclopedia.* New York: Crowell, 1974.
Walker, Leo. *The Big Band Almanac.* Pasadena: Ward Ritchie Press, 1978.
———. *ASCAP Biographical Dictionary.* New York: Cattell/Bowker, 1980.

Interviews

Bob Eastman
Ken Greenwood
Larry Grogan
Harold Miller
Bill Moyes

Frank Murphy
Bill Stewart
Steve Tassia
John V. B. Sullivan

(Gordon McLendon interview by KLIF staff)

Letters to Author

Tom Birch—Radio Marketing Research
Robert M. Chambers—ABC Radio Network
Norman Ginsburg—CBS Radio
Donna L. Halper
Al Ham—Al Ham Productions
Ted Hepburn—Ted Hepburn Co.
John Hickman—Veterans Administration
Agnes Law
John J. O'Neill—NBC Radio
Catherine Preston—Tobacco Merchants Association of the U.S.
Martin Rubenstein—Mutual Broadcasting System
Bill O'Shaughnessy—Return Radio
Norma Soffer—Statistical Research, Inc.

News Letters

Beyond the Ratings
Hall's Radio Report
Inside Radio
NAB Highlights

Airchecks

Aircheck Factory, 52.
Aircheck Records, 14 and 17.
Fanfare Records, LP 20–120.
Hindsight Records, 143 and 146.
Hook City Records, Vol. 5.
Increase Records, 2001, 2002, 2005, 2010, and 2012.
Jazz Panorama, 16.
Joyce Music Studio Tape, 249.
KLIF Library.
McCoy Recordings, Reels 382, 643, 1664, 1721, 2424, 2643, and 3502.
Mark 56 Records, 755.

Mercury Records, MK 98.
Museum of Broadcasting, Tapes R76:070, R76:0018, R77:0385, and R77:0450.
Nostalgia Lane Records, PBO 261.
O'Liners Greatest Shows on Earth, Vols. 1&2, 1978.
Radiola Records, MR1060.
Radio Yesteryear, Programs 358, 617, 769, 1004, 3641, and 5528.
Sandy Hook Records, 2002.
Spokane Records, 11.
Sunbeam Records, HB 308 and MFC 14.
WABC Library.
WMAL Aircheck.

Discographies

Hall, George (ed.). *Charlie Barnett and His Orchestra*. Laurel Md.: Jazz Discographies Unlimited, 1970.
Hall, George (ed.). *Harry James and His Orchestra* (vol. 1). Laurel, Md.: Jazz Discographies Unlimited, 1971.
Leadbetter, Mike and Slavel, Neil. *Blues Records, 1943–1966*. Amersham, Bucks (Eng.): Halstan, 1968.
Propes, Steve. *Those Oldies But Goodies: A Guide to 50's Record Collecting*. New York: Chilton, 1973.
Propes, Steve. *Golden Oldies: A Guide to 60's Record Collecting*. Radnor: Chilton, 1974.
Rust, Brian. *The Compleat Entertainment Discography*. New Rochelle: Arlington House, 1973.
Rust, Brian. *American Dance Band Discography, 1917–1942* (2 vols.). New Rochelle: Arlington House, 1975.
Rust, Brian. *Jazz Records, 1897–1942* (2 vols.). New Rochelle: Arlington House, 1978.

Miscellaneous

Toby Arnold. *Unforgettable*. (Presentation Tape).
Century 21. Various Brochures.
Crosby, Bing. Liner notes to *Early Rare Recordings,* Biograph BLP-C13.
Drake-Chenault. *Big Bands and More*. (Presentation Tape).
Driggs, Frank. Brochure accompanying *The Fletcher Henderson Story: A Study in Frustration,* Columbia Thesaurus of Classic Jazz, C4L 19.
Joyce Music Studios, Catalog (1970).
KGIR Program Schedule (1929).
Kiefer, Peter T. Liner notes to *Waring's Pennsylvanians,* Victor (Vintage) 554.
Kines, Larry F. Bing Crosby, 'Cremo Singer.' Kirkland, Washington: Larry F. Kiner, 1973.
Martin, Ernie. Speech before National Association of Broadcasters, April 15, 1980.
Radio Specialty Co., Catalog (1926).
Rating data. Arbitron, Burch, Hooper, Mediastat, Pulse, RADAR, Simmons.
RCA Thesaurus Cue Sheets, December, 1955–January, 1956.
Rosenbloom, Richard. Speech before National Radio Broadcasters Association Expo, October 5, 1980.
Sears Roebuck, Catalog (1927).
Spot Radio Stations. Standard Rate and Data Service, (Various issues).
WSBA Program Guide (1957).
WSM Souvenir Pamphlet (undated).

Whitburn, Joel. *Pop Annual, 1955–1977.* Menomonee Falls, Wisconsin: Record Research, Inc., 1978 (with supplements).

———. Brochure accompanying *The Ellington Era,* Vol. 2, Columbia Records C3L39.

———. *Cab Calloway Quizicale* script, Broadcast Pioneers Library.

———. *CBS: Documenting 38 Years of Exciting History.* Published by *Sponsor* Magazine. September, 1965.

———. *Commercial Radio Programming.* (Report of Fall, 1979 Radio Conference, Center for Public Resources). Published by Center for Public Resources, 1980.

———. *Encyclomedia, 1980 Radio Edition.* Published by Decisions Publications, 1980.

———. "Format Tracking Study." McGavern-Guild, June, 1981.

———. *Forty-Year Album of Pioneer Stations.* Published by *Sponsor* Magazine, 1962.

———. "Marketing Service Report—Client Service Bulletin," Eastman Radio, June, 1981.

———. *NBC: A Documentary.* Published by *Sponsor* Magazine, 1966.

———. *Radio Annual/Television Yearbook,* (1951 edition). Published by *Radio-Television Daily,* 1951.

———. *Radio Facts.* Published by Radio Advertising Bureau, 1980 and 1981.

———. *Radio in 1985.* Published by National Association of Broadcasters, 1977.

———. *Today's Radio Audience.* Published by The Arbitron Company, 1979.

———. *Twenty-Fifth Anniversary Edition.* Published by *Radio-Television Daily,* December, 1962.

———. *Broadcasting/Television Yearbooks.* (1975, 1976, 1977, 1978, 1979, 1980, 1981), Published by *Broadcasting* Magazine.

Radio & Television Documentaries

CBS 50th Anniversary Program—9/18/77.

NBC 50th Anniversary Program—10/16, 10/23, 10/30, 11/6, 11/13, 11/20—1976.

The First Fifty Years of Radio, Produced by Westinghouse Broadcasting Company, 1970.

The Rock & Roll Years, Produced by ABC-TV, 9/27/73.

The History of Rock, Produced by CBS-TV, 8/11/74.

The History of Rock and Roll, Produced by Drake-Chenault Enterprises, 1977.

Your Number One Song, Produced by the Canadian Broadcasting System, 1978.

Appendix

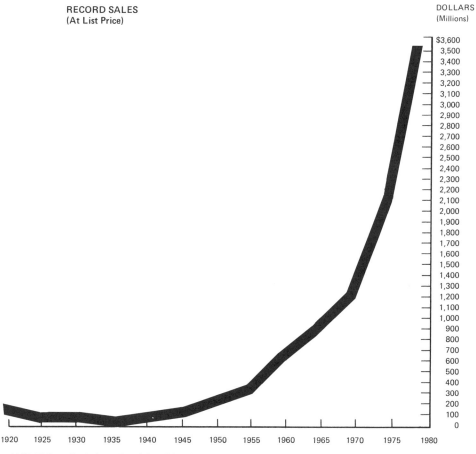

RECORD SALES
(At List Price)

DOLLARS
(Millions)

SOURCE: Recording Industry Association of America.

Graph showing phonograph record sales, 1920–1980

Table showing performance record of network musical shows, 1930-1939

PERFORMANCE RECORD OF
MAJOR PRIME TIME
NETWORK MUSICAL PROGRAMS
1930-1939

SEASON	NUMBER OF WEEKLY NAME BAND SHOWS DURING SEASON	NUMBER OF WEEKLY CONCERT MUSIC SHOWS DURING SEASON	NUMBER OF WEEKLY LIGHT MUSIC SHOWS DURING SEASON	BEST RATING* ACHIEVED IN ITS CATEGORY — NAME BAND	CLASSICAL	LIGHT
29/30	15	22	19		No Rating Taken	
30/31	14	26	24		No Rating Taken	
31/32	19	27	24	Lucky Strike Dance Orch. (27.8)	Atwater Kent Hr. (31.0)	Enna Jettick Melodies (18.0)
32/33	18	22	29	Paul Whiteman Orch. (19.1)	Sunday at Seth Parker's (23.4)	Kate Smith (14.3)
33/34	25	20	23	Paul Whiteman Orch. (29.9)	Cities Service Concert (21.3)	Baby Rose Marie (5.5)
34/35	26	22	27	Guy Lombardo Orch. (23.5)	Mme Schumann-Heink (23.5)	Jackie Heller (4.0)
35/36	24	27	23	Fred Waring Orch. (14.0)	Rubinoff Concert (14.6)	Kate Smith (11.1)
36/37	22	22	21	Wayne King Orch. (10.6)	Nelson Eddy (14.6)	Singin' Sam (7.9)
37/38	20	25	13	Guy Lombardo Orch. (12.6)	Voice of Firestone (12.9)	Jack Fulton (2.4)
38/39	16	16	9	Guy Lombardo Orch. (13.5)	Voice of Firestone (11.4)	Vocal Varieties (6.3)

*The rating represents the percentage of homes in America tuned to a given program during a selected week.

Source: A Thirty Year History of Programs Carried on National Radio Network 1926-1956, Harrison Summers, ed. Arno, 1971

Table showing hotel and ballroom big band locations for remote broadcasts

FEATURED ROOMS AND HOTELS	BALLROOMS	MISCELLANEOUS (Restaurants, Night Spots, etc)
Joseph Urban Room/Congress, Chicago	Aragon, Chicago	Glen Island Casino, Westchester, N.Y.
College Inn(Later The Panther Room)/Sherman, Chicago	Trianon, Chicago	Meadowbrook, Cedar Grove, N.J.
The Grill/Roosevelt, N.Y.	Palladium, Hollywood	Rustic Cabin, Armonk, N.Y.
Cocoanut Grove/Ambassador, L.A.	Jenkins Pavilion, Point Pleasant, N.J.	Southland, Boston
Biltmore Bowl/Biltmore, N.Y.	Steel Pier, Atlantic City	Rainbow Room, N.Y.
Green Room/Edison, N.Y.	Elitch's Gardens, Denver	Victor Hugo's, Hollywood
Blue Room/Lincoln, N.Y.	Starlight, Hershey, Pa.	Casino, Santa Catalina, California
Madhattan Room(Later Cafe Rouge)/Pennsylvania, N.Y.	Raymor, Boston	400 Restaurant, N.Y.
Ice Terrace/New Yorker, N.Y.	Playland, Rye, N.Y.	Paradise Restaurant, N.Y.
Astor Roof/Astor, N.Y.	Savoy, N.Y.	Surf Beach Club, Virginia Beach
Grill Room/Taft, N.Y.	Roseland, N.Y.	Playland, Rye, N.Y.
Casino-on-the-Park/Essex House, N.Y.	Palomar, L.A.	
Ritz Roof/Ritz-Carlton, Boston		
Peacock Court/Mark Hopkins, S.F.		
Century Room/Commodore, N.Y.		
Starlight Roof/Waldorf-Astoria, N.Y.		
Blue Room/Roosevelt, New Orleans		
Empire Room/Palmer House, Chicago		

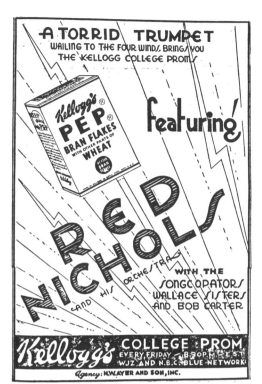

Display tune-in ad appearing in *Variety*, October 23, 1935 for *Kellogg's College Prom* show.

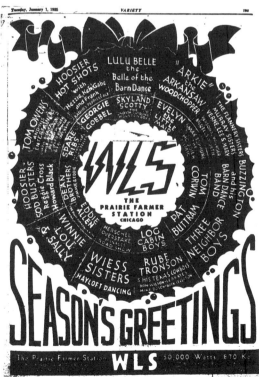

WLS, Chicago Seasons Greeting ad in *Variety*, January 1, 1935.

Spot Survey
Late Night Big Band
Broadcasts on Representative
Stations, 1935-1940

	11:00p.m. or 11:15p.m.	11:30p.m.	12:00m.	12:30a.m.
1935				
WEAF	Dick Fidler Orch		Jack Russell Orch.	Earl Hines Orch.
WABC	Frank Dailey Orch.		Herbie Kay Orch.	Freddy Bergin Orch.
WBNX	El Torreador Orch.			
WJZ		Bill Scotti Orch.		Joe Rines Orch.
WHN		Roof Dance Orch.		
WMCA		Red Gresch Orch.		Barney Zeeman Orch.
WEVD			Dance Orch.	
WLW			Tommy Tucker Orch.	Tommy Tucker Orch.
WOR				Horace Heidt Orch.
1936				
WEAF		Xavier Cugat Orch.	Stan Norris Orch.	
WABC	Willard Robinson Orch.	George Olson Orch.	Tommy Dorsey Orch.	Dick Stabile Orch.
WMCA	Dixon's Ambassadors			Marty Kellam Orch.
WJZ		Riley & Farley Orch.	Johnny Hamp Orch.	Jimmy Dorsey Orch.
WOR		Guy Lombardo Orch.	Shep Fields Orch.	Clyde McCoy Orch.
WIP		Jack Delmar Orch.		
KOA		Leo Reisman Orch.		
KHJ			Fred Waring Orch.	
WLW				Horace Heidt Orch.
1937				
WABC	Tommy Dorsey Orch.	George Olsen Orch.	Frank Dailey Orch.	
WEAF	Lou Breese Orch.	Al Donahue Orch.	Jerry Blaine Orch.	
WJZ		Eddie Orch.	Rudy Vallee Orch.	
WLW	Arlie Simmonds Orch.		Johnny Hamp's Orch.	
WOR	Billy Swanson's Orch.	Isham Jones Orch.	Horace Heidt Orch.	
WIP		Milton Kellam's Orch.	Benny's Troubadours	
WHN			Rhythm Ambassadors	
1938				
WEAF	Eddie LeBaron Orch.	Abe Lyman Orch.	Richard Himber Orch.	
WJZ	Dance Orch.	Frank Novak Orch.	Dance Orch.	
WOR	Artie Shaw Orch.	Mitchell Ayres Orch.	Dick Barrie Orch.	
WABC		Glenn Miller Orch.	Court Basie Orch.	
WHN		Don Bestor Orch.		
1939				
WJZ	Dance Orch.	Abe Lyman Orch.	Jan Savitt Orch.	
WOR	Bob Chester Orch.	Jimmy Dorsey	Jack Jenny Orch.	
WEAF		Emory Deutsch Orch.	Freddy Martin Orch.	
WABC		Shep Fields Orch.	Dance Orch.	
WHN		Xavier Cugat Orch.		
1940				
WABC	Blue Barron Orch.	Less Brown Orch.	Alvino Rey Orch.	
WJZ	Henry King Orch.	Ray Heatherton Orch.	Buddy Franklin Orch.	
WICC	Bernie Cummins Orch.			
WNEW	Dance Orch.	Bob Crosby Orch.	Horace Heidt Orch.	
WOR			Freddy Nagel Orch.	

Source: Radio Guide,
10/15/35, p. 18; 10/20/36, p. 39; 10/19/37, p. 36;
10/18/38, p. 26; 10/17/39, p. 35; 10/20/40, p. 24.

Table showing spot survey, big band late night broadcasts on representative radio stations,
1935 through 1940.

SEPTEMBER MUSIC SURVEY

THIS TABLE SHOWS THE LEADING SIX SELLERS IN SHEET MUSIC AND PHONOGRAPH RECORDS GATHERED FROM THE REPORTS OF SALES MADE DURING SEPTEMBER BY THE LEADING MUSIC JOBBERS AND DISK DISTRIBUTORS IN THE TERRITORIES

6 Best Sellers in Sheet Music

Reported by Leading Jobbers

	NEW YORK	CHICAGO	LOS ANGELES
SONG—No. 1	'We Just Couldn't Say Good-bye'	'We Just Couldn't Say Good-bye'	'We Just Couldn't Say Good-bye'
SONG—No. 2	'Shanty in Old Shantytown'	'Shanty in Old Shantytown'	'Masquerade'
SONG—No. 3	'Say It Isn't So'	'Masquerade'	'Shanty in Old Shantytown'
SONG—No. 4	'Masquerade'	'Three's a Crowd'	'Say It Isn't So'
SONG—No. 5	'Three's a Crowd'	'Goofus'	'Strange Interlude'
SONG—No. 6	'Love Me Tonight' (Robbins)	'Say It Isn't So'	'Love Me Tonight' (Robbins)

3 Leading Phonograph Companies Report 6 Best Sellers

Side responsible for the major sales only are reported. Where it is impossible to determine the side responsible for the sales, both sides are mentioned:

	NEW YORK	CHICAGO	LOS ANGELES
BRUNSWICK—No. 1	'I'll Never Be the Same,' 'Couldn't Say Good-bye' (Guy Lombardo Orch.)	'We Couldn't Say Good-bye' (Guy Lombardo Orch.)	'We Couldn't Say Good-bye' (Guy Lombardo Orch.)
BRUNSWICK—No. 2	'Say It Isn't So,' 'Got You Where I Want You' (Ozzie Nelson Orch.)	'I'll Never Be the Same' (Guy Lombardo Orch.)	'Love Me Tonight' (Robbins) (Bing Crosby)
BRUNSWICK—No. 3	'It Don't Mean a Thing,' 'Coney Island Washboard' (Mills Brothers)	'Say It Isn't So' (Ozzie Nelson Orch.)	'Bugle Call Rag' (Mills Brothers)
BRUNSWICK—No. 4	'I Guess I'll Have to Change My Plan,' 'As Long as Lives On' (Guy Lombardo Orch.)	'Bugle Call Rag' (Mills Brothers)	'Have to Change My Plan' (Guy Lombardo Orch.)
BRUNSWICK—No. 5	'Love Me Tonight,' 'Isn't It Romantic' (Jacques Renard Orch.)	'Three's a Crowd' (Tom Gerun's Orch.)	'Three's a Crowd' (Tom Gerun's Orch.)
BRUNSWICK—No. 6	'Bugle Call Rag,' 'The Old Man of the Mountain' (Mills Brothers)	'Coney Island Washboard' (Mills Brothers)	'Tea for Two' (Don Redmond Orch.)
COLUMBIA—No. 1	'Guess I'll Have to Change My Plans,' 'Maori' (Rudy Vallee)	'Sweethearts on Parade' (Louis Armstrong Orch.)	'Shantytown' (Ted Lewis Orch.)
COLUMBIA—No. 2	'Strange Interlude,' 'Same Old Moon' (Rudy Vallee)	'Maori' (Rudy Vallee Orch.)	'Have to Change My Plan' (Rudy Vallee Orch.)
COLUMBIA—No. 3	'We Just Couldn't Say Good-bye,' 'Good-bye to Love' (Fred Martin Orch.)	'Hell's Bells' (Art Kassel Orch.)	'Something in the Night' (Lee Morse)
COLUMBIA—No. 4	'Sheltered by the Stars,' 'Another Night Alone' (Roger Wolfe Kahn Orch.)	'Old Shantytown' (Ted Lewis Orch.)	'It Was So Beautiful' (Harry Richman)
COLUMBIA—No. 5	'Let's Have a Party,' 'Old Man of the Mountain' (Joe Haymes Orch.)	'It Was So Beautiful' (Harry Richman)	'Shine' (Louis Armstrong Orch.)
COLUMBIA—No. 6	'It Was So Beautiful,' 'I Love a Parade' (Harry Richman)	'Strange Interlude' (Rudy Vallee Orch.)	'Cat and Fiddle' Gems (Savoy Hotel Orch.)
VICTOR—No. 1	'I'll Never Be the Same,' 'Couldn't Say Good-bye' (Paul Whiteman Orch.)	'Sweethearts Forever' (Wayne King Orch.)	'Say It Isn't So' (George Olsen Orch.)
VICTOR—No. 2	'Three on a Match,' 'Here's Hoping' (Paul Whiteman Orch.)	'Everybody Sez I Love You' (Isham Jones Orch.)	'We Couldn't Say Good-bye' (Paul Whiteman Orch.)
VICTOR—No. 3	'So Ashamed,' 'My Heart's at Ease' (Ruby Newman Orch.)	'All-American Girl' (George Olsen Orch.)	'Three on a Match' (Paul Whiteman Orch.)
VICTOR—No. 4	'As You Desire Me,' 'The Lady I Love' (Russ Columbo)	'I'll Never Be the Same' (Paul Whiteman Orch.)	'As You Desire Me' (Russ Columbo)
VICTOR—No. 5	'Music Everywhere,' 'And Still I Care' (Isham Jones Orch.)	'Say It Isn't So' (George Olsen Orch.)	'Good Night Vienna' (London Mayfair Orch.)
VICTOR—No. 6	'Say It Isn't So,' 'Love Me Tonight' (George Olsen Orch.)	'Three on a Match' (Paul Whiteman Orch.)	'So Didn't Say Yes' (Leo Reisman Orch.)

'Your Hit Parade'	VARIETY COMPILATION OF AIRPLAY ON 3 MAJOR NETWORKS	VARIETY COMPILATION OF SHEET MUSIC SALES	VARIETY COMPILATION OF RECORD SALES
Broadcast of Apr. 3, 1937	Compiled Mar. 28-Apr. 3 & Published in Issue of Apr. 7, 1937	(None published in issue of Apr. 7, 1937)	Listed only as "last week" & Published in Issue of Apr. 7, 1937
Boo Hoo	I've Got My Love to Keep Me Warm		Little Old Lady
Little Old Lady	Too Marvelous for Words		Boo Hoo
I've Got My Love to Keep Me Warm	Boo Hoo		Moonlight & Shadows
What Will I Tell My Heart?	Trust in Me		When My Dreamboat Comes Home
When The Poppies Bloom Again	Little Old Lady		What Will I Tell My Heart?
Moonlight and Shadows	Where Are You?		This Year's Kisses
Trust in Me	Sweet Is The Word for You		On a Little Bamboo Bridge
	On a Little Bamboo Bridge		When The Poppies Bloom Again
	Moonlight and Shadows		Trust in Me
			I've Got My Love to Keep Me Warm
Broadcast of Apr. 23, 1938	Compiled Apr. 11-17 & Published in Issue of Apr. 20, 1938	(None published in issue of Apr. 20, 1938)	(None published in Issue of Apr. 20, 1938)
Ti Pi Tin	Ti Pi Tin		
Goodnight Angel	How'd Ya Like to Love Me?		
Please Be Kind	Please Be Kind		
Whistle While You Work	On the Sentimental Side		
On The Sentimental Side	It's Wonderful		
How'd Ya Like to Love Me?	You're an Education		
Love Walked In	Sunday in the Park		
Heigh Ho	Love Walked In		
At a Perfume Counter	Goodnight Angel		
You're an Education	Cry, Baby, Cry		
Broadcast of Mar. 4, 1939	Compiled Feb. 27-Mar. 5 & Published in Issue of Mar. 8, 1939	For week ending Mar. 4, & Published in Issue of Mar. 8, 1939	(None published in Issue of Mar. 8, 1939)
Deep Purple	Gotta Get Some Shuteye	Deep Purple	
Umbrella Man	Penny Serenade	Penny Serenade	
Penny Serenade	Could Be	Umbrella Man	
Jeepers Creepers	You're a Sweet Little Headache	Funny Old Hills	
I Have Eyes	Deep Purple	I Cried for You	
Could Be	Heaven Can Wait	Little Sir Echo	
You're a Sweet Little Headache	This Is It	I Have Eyes	
I Get Along Without You Very Well	This Night	You're A Sweet Little Headache	
Deep in a Dream	I Have Eyes	I Promise You	
I Cried for You	I Cried for You	God Bless America	

SOURCE: *Variety:* "Most Played on Air," April 7, 1937, p. 49 and "Last Week's 15 Best Sellers," Ibid. p. 51; "Breakdown of Network Plugs," April 20, 1938, p. 40; "Network Plugs, 8AM to 1AM," March 8, 1939, p. 49 and "15 Best Sheet Music Sellers," Ibid., p. 49.

Table showing comparisons of song rankings by *Variety's* Airplay, Sheet Music & Record Sales with "Hit Parade" rankings, for random weeks in 1937, 1938 and 1939

Radio and Television
Set Sales
1946 - 1955

	Radio		Television	
	Units	Retail Value	Units	Retail Value
1946	14,000,000	$700,000,000	6,000	$1,000,000
1947	17,000,000	$800,000,000	179,000	$50,000,000
1948	14,000,000	$600,000,000	970,000	$226,000,000
1949	10,000,000	$500,000,000	2,970.000	$574,000,000
1950	13,958,000	unav.	7,355,000	$1,397,000,000
1951	10,989,000	unav.	5,312.000	$944,000,000
1952	10,475,000	unav.	6,194,000	$1,064,000,000
1953	12,466,000	unav.	6,870,000	$1,170,000,000
1954	10,243,000	unav.	7,410,000	$1,042,000,000
1955	14,190,000	unav.	7,758,000	$1,078,000,000

Source: Broadcasting·Cable Yearbook, 1980, and Electronic Industries Association 1980 Market Data
Book.

Total Advertising Billings
Radio v. TV
1946 - 1955

	Radio	Television
1946	$334,078,914	unav.
1947	$374,086,686	unav.
1948	$416,720,279	$8,700,000
1949	$425,357,133	$27,530,000
1950	$453,564,930	$90,629,000
1951	$456,543,000	$208,595,000
1952	$473,151,000	$283,070,000
1953	$477,206,000	$384,692,000
1954	$451,330,000	$538,122,000
1955	$456,481,000	$681,100,000

Source: Broadcasting·Cable Yearbook, 1980.

Table showing radio and television set sales and advertising billings, 1946–1955

SHARE OF RADIO AUDIENCE

SCRANTON-WILKES, PA

TIME	WARM	STATION A	STATION B	STATION C	STATION D	STATION E	STATION F	STATION G	STATION H	STATION I	STATION J	OTHER
OCTOBER THROUGH DECEMBER, 1958												
Monday through Friday 7:00AM-12Noon	31.3	5.3	6.9	0.3	8.9	8.7	10.5	*	0.3	0.4	5.1	0.2
Monday through Friday 12Noon-6:00PM	29.0	12.4	9.1	0.4	8.3	11.1	10.0	*	1.1	0.5	3.7	0.1
MARCH THROUGH MAY, 1960												
Monday through Friday 7:00AM-12Noon	37.3	7.0	5.7	--	8.5	11.3	4.1	19.7	3.5	1.1	1.0	0.8
Monday through Friday 12Noon-6:00PM	42.3	5.2	7.6	--	13.7	8.2	6.2	8.1	3.9	3.1	1.5	0.3

*De-listed for conducting hypo contest during rating period

SOURCE: CE Hooper Inc., Hooperatings Scranton-Wilkes Barre, Pa., October-December, 1958 & March-May, 1960.

Table, Hooperatings for WARM, Scranton—Wilkes-Barre for October through December, 1958 and March through May, 1960. Table is laid out to simulate an actual page from the Hooper Audience Surveys.

TOP TWENTY

THE OFFICIAL TOP TWENTY SURVEY OF THE PEORIA
AREA ACCORDING TO RECORD AND SHEET MUSIC
SALES, COIN MACHINE OPERATORS AND D. J.
REQUESTS AS TABULATED BY PEORIA'S
MUSIC AND NEWS STATION
WPEO

NOVEMBER 1, 1957

TITLE	ARTIST	THIS WEEK	LAST WEEK
JAILHOUSE ROCK	ELVIS PRESLEY	1	2
WAKE UP LITTLE SUZIE	EVERLY BROS.	2	1
MY SPECIAL ANGEL	BOBBY HELMS	3	4
SILHOUETTES	RAYS	4	7
CHANCES ARE	JOHNNY MATHIS	5	5
YOU SEND ME	SAM COOKE	6	—
LOTTA LOVIN'	GENE VINCENT	7	3
LOT OF SHAKIN' GOIN' ON	JERRY LEE LEWIS	8	6
REET PETITE	JACKIE WILSON	9	9
HONEYCOMB	JIMMIE RODGERS	10	8
I'M AVAILABLE	MARGIE RAYBURN	11	10
PLAYTHING	NICK TODD	12	11
HAVE I TOLD YOU LATELY	RICKY NELSON	13	14
HAPPY HAPPY BIRTHDAY, BABY	TUNE WEAVERS	14	17
MELODIE D'AMOUR	AMES BROS.	15	18
HULA LOVE	BUDDY KNOX	16	13
JUST BETWEEN YOU AND ME	CHORDETTES	17	12
TILL	ROGER WILLIAMS	18	20
ALONE	SHEPHERD SISTERS	19	19
I'LL REMEMBER TODAY	PATTI PAGE	20	15

THIS WEEK'S PICK HITS

"Ping Pong" — Glow Tones

"Love Me Forever" — Eydie Gorme

"Goodbye, She's Gone" — The Sprouts

THIS WEEK'S PICK ALBUM

THE HELEN MORGAN STORY —

Gogi Grant—RCA Victor

THE NEW WPEO - THE STATION WHERE YOU ENJOY MUSIC MORE AND ENJOY MORE MUSIC

WPEO, Peoria, Ill. Top Twenty Tune Sheet from 1957.
Would Top 40 play in Peoria? It would and did.

The New WSBA "Hi-Fi Radio" 910 • HITS of the WEEK

This Week	APRIL 28, 1962		Last Week
1	SOLDIER BOY★	The Shirelles	1
2	WISH WE WERE MARRIED	Ronnie & The Hi-Lites	9
3	MASHED POTATO TIME	Dee Dee Sharp	2
4	STRANGER ON THE SHORE	Mr. Acker Bilk	7
5	DEAR ONE	Larry Finnegan	4
6	LOVER PLEASE	Clyde McPhatter	6
7	TWISTIN' MATILDA	Jimmy Soul	13
8	SLOW TWISTIN'	Chubby Checker	3
9	GOOD LUCK CHARM	Elvis Presley	5
10	JOHNNY ANGEL	Shelley Fabares	8
11	LOVE LETTERS	Kathy Lester	10
12	P.T. 109	Jimmy Dean	12
13	SHE CRIED	Jay And The Americans	11
14	YOU BETTER MOVE ON	Arthur Alexander	17
15	SHE CAN'T FIND HER KEYS	Paul Peterson	14
16	SHOUT! SHOUT!	Ernie Maresca	38
17	FUNNY WAY OF LAUGHIN'	Burl Ives	15
18	ONE WHO REALLY LOVES YOU	Mary Wells	29
19	OLD RIVERS	Walter Brennan	23
20	SO THIS IS LOVE	The Costells	26
21	EVERYBODY LOVES ME★	Brenda Lee	24
22	YOUNG WORLD★	Ricky Nelson	16
23	UPTOWN	Crystals	22
24	KING OF CLOWNS	Neil Sedaka	32
25	JAM (PART 1)	Bobby Gregg	21
26	TELL ME	Dick & Deedee	33
27	JOHNNY JINGO★	Hayley Mills	34
28	DON'T PLAY THAT SONG	Ben E. King	36
29	CONSCIENCE	James Darren	20
30	YOU ARE MINE	Frankie Avalon	37
31	ADIOS AMIGO★	Jim Reeves	30
32	CATERINA	Perry Como	39
33	RUNAWAY	Lawrence Welk	40
34	JOHNNY	Roy Adams	
35	WHAT'D I SAY (PART 1)	Bobby Darin	
36	DEEP IN THE HEART OF TEXAS	Duane Eddy	
37	I'LL TAKE YOU HOME	The Corsairs	
38	MOST PEOPLE GET MARRIED	Patti Page	
39	NO NOT AGAIN	Jive Five	
40	LOVERS WHO WANDER	Dion	

PICK HIT OF THE WEEK
HOW IS JULIE—The Lettermen
★ WSBA Former Pick Hit

THE NEW WSBA — 910 ON YOUR RADIO
HARRISBURG — YORK — LANCASTER

The New WSBA "Hi-Fi Radio" 910 • TOP TUNES of the WEEK

This Week	APRIL 21, 1962		Last Week
1	SOLDIER BOY★	The Shirelles	1
2	MASHED POTATO TIME	Dee Dee Sharp	2
3	SLOW TWISTIN'	Chubby Checker	4
4	DEAR ONE	Larry Finnegan	3
5	GOOD LUCK CHARM	Elvis Presley	5
6	LOVER PLEASE	Clyde McPhatter	7
7	STRANGER ON THE SHORE	Mr. Acker Bilk	9
8	JOHNNY ANGEL	Shelley Fabares	6
9	WISH WE WERE MARRIED	Ronnie & The Hi-Lites	13
10	LOVE LETTERS	Kathy Lester	8
11	SHE CRIED	Jay And The Americans	11
12	P.T. 109	Jimmy Dean	18
13	TWISTIN' MATILDA	Jimmy Soul	10
14	SHE CAN'T FIND HER KEYS	Paul Peterson	15
15	FUNNY WAY OF LAUGHIN'	Burl Ives	35
16	YOUNG WORLD	Ricky Nelson	12
17	YOU BETTER MOVE ON	Arthur Alexander	23
18	NUT ROCKER	Jack Ross	14
19	TWO OF A KIND★	Frankie Avalon	21
20	YOU ARE MINE	Bobby Gregg	24
21	JAM (PART 1)	Crystals	
22	UPTOWN	Walter Brennan	39
23	OLD RIVERS	Brenda Lee	34
24	EVERYBODY LOVES ME★	The Drifters	29
25	LITTLE GIRL IS SMILING	The Costells	37
26	SO THIS IS LOVE	Sue Thompson	19
27	TWO OF A KIND★	Connie Francis	17
28	DON'T BREAK THE HEART★	Mary Wells	
29	ONE WHO REALLY LOVES YOU	Perry Como	33
30	CATERINA	Red Foley	30
31	THE HAPPY SONG★	Lawrence Welk	38
32	RUNAWAY	Dick & Deedee	31
33	CINDERELLA	Hayley Mills	32
34	JOHNNY JINGO★	Neil Sedaka	40
35	KING OF CLOWNS	Ben E. King	
36	ADIOS AMIGO★	Jim Reeves	
37	SHOUT! SHOUT!	Ernie Maresca	
38	VIOLETTA	Ray Adams	36
39		Bobby Darin	
40	WHAT'D I SAY (PART 1)	Bobby Darin	

PICK HIT OF THE WEEK
FORTUNE TELLER—BOBBY CURTOLA
★ WSBA Former Pick Hit

THE NEW WSBA — 910 ON YOUR RADIO
HARRISBURG — YORK — LANCASTER

The New WSBA "Hi-Fi Radio" 910 • HITS of the WEEK

This Week	APRIL 14, 1962		Last Week
1	SOLDIER BOY★	The Shirelles	1
2	MASHED POTATO TIME	Dee Dee Sharp	3
3	GOOD LUCK CHARM	Elvis Presley	3
4	SLOW TWISTIN'	Chubby Checker	5
5	DEAR ONE	Larry Finnegan	4
6	JOHNNY ANGEL	Shelley Fabares	6
7	LOVER PLEASE	Clyde McPhatter	7
8	LOVE LETTERS	Kathy Lester	13
9	STRANGER ON THE SHORE	Mr. Acker Bilk	8
10	TWISTIN' MATILDA	Jimmy Soul	17
11	SHE CRIED	Jay And The Americans	12
12	YOUNG WORLD	Ricky Nelson	12
13	WISH WE WERE MARRIED	Ronnie & The Hi-Lites	19
14	NUT ROCKER	B. Bumble & The Stingers	11
15	SHE CAN'T FIND HER KEYS	Paul Peterson	16
16	LET ME IN	The Sensations	9
17	TWO OF A KIND★	Connie Francis	10
18	P.T. 109	Jimmy Dean	29
19	T...	Sue Thompson	18
20	BONNIE	Bobby Rydell	28
21	YOU ARE MINE	Frankie Avalon	27
22	DREAM BABY★	Roy Orbison	26
23	YOU BETTER MOVE ON	Arthur Alexander	31
24	JAM (PART 1)	Bobby Gregg	32
25	LOVE ME WARM AND TENDER	Paul Anka	20
26	ANYTHING THAT'S PART OF YOU★	Elvis Presley	34
27	THE TWIST	David Seville & Chipmunks	23
28	CINDERELLA	Jack Ross	24
29	LITTLE GIRL IS SMILING	The Drifters	30
30	THE HAPPY SONG★	Red Foley	35
31	JOHNNY JINGO★	Hayley Mills	40
32	KING OF CLOWNS	Neil Sedaka	39
33	CATERINA	Perry Como	33
34	EVERYBODY LOVES ME★	Brenda Lee	
35	FUNNY WAY OF LAUGHIN'	Burl Ives	29
36	WHAT'D I SAY (PART 1)	Bobby Darin	
37	SO THIS IS LOVE	The Castells	37
38	TELL ME	Dick & Deedee	
39	OLD RIVERS	Walter Brennan	38
40	I WILL	Vic Dana	

PICK HIT OF THE WEEK
ADIOS AMIGO — Jim Reeves
★ WSBA Former Pick Hit

THE NEW WSBA — 910 ON YOUR RADIO
HARRISBURG — YORK — LANCASTER

3-Top Tune Sheets of WSBA, York, Pa. for consecutive weeks, April 14, 21, and 28, 1962

The Genealogy of Rock Radio

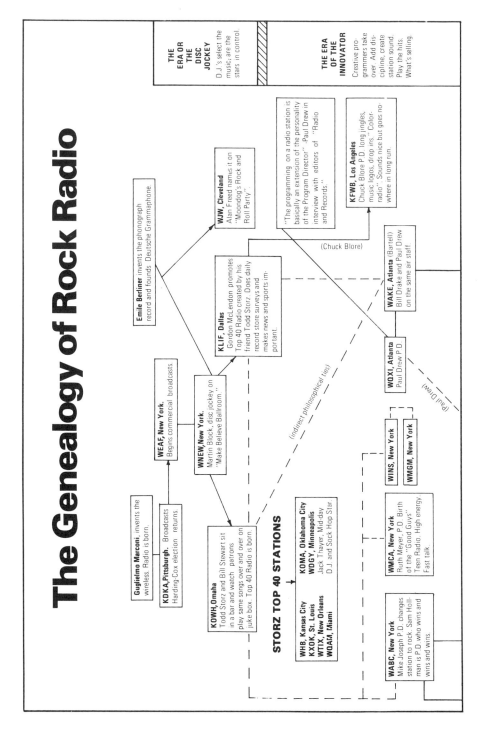

THE ERA OR THE DISC JOCKEY
D.J.'s select the music, are the stars in control.

THE ERA OF THE INNOVATOR
Creative programmers take over. Add discipline, create station sound. Play the hits. What's selling.

Emile Berliner invents the phonograph record and founds Deutsche Grammaphone.

WEAF, New York. Begins commercial broadcasts.

WNEW, New York. Martin Block, disc jockey on "Make Believe Ballroom."

Guglielmo Marconi, invents the wireless. Radio is born.

KDKA,Pittsburgh. Broadcasts Harding-Cox election returns.

KOWH,Omaha
Todd Storz and Bill Stewart sit in a bar and watch patrons play same songs over and over on juke box. Top 40 Radio is born.

WJW, Cleveland
Alan Freed names it on "Moondog's Rock and Roll Party."

KLIF, Dallas
Gordon McLendon promotes Top 40 Radio created by his friend Todd Storz. Does daily record store surveys and makes news and sports important.

"The programming on a radio station is basically an extension of the personality of the Program Director"- Paul Drew in interview with editors of "Radio and Records."

KFWB, Los Angeles
Chuck Blore P.D. long jingles, music logos, drop ins." Color-radio". Sounds nice but goes nowhere in long run.

(Chuck Blore)

WAKE, Atlanta (Bartell)
Bill Drake and Paul Drew on the same air staff.

WQXI, Atlanta
Paul Drew P.D.

(Paul Drew)

(indirect philosophical ties)

WINS, New York

WMGM, New York

STORZ TOP 40 STATIONS

WHB, Kansas City
KXOK, St. Louis
WTIX, New Orleans
WQAM, Miami

KOMA, Oklahoma City
WDGY, Minneapolis
Jack Thayer, Mid-day D.J and Sock Hop Star

WMCA, New York
Ruth Meyer, P.D. Birth of the "Good Guys" Teen Radio. High energy. Fast talk.

WABC, New York
Mike Joseph P.D. changes station to rock. Sam Holl-man is P.D. who wins and wins and wins.

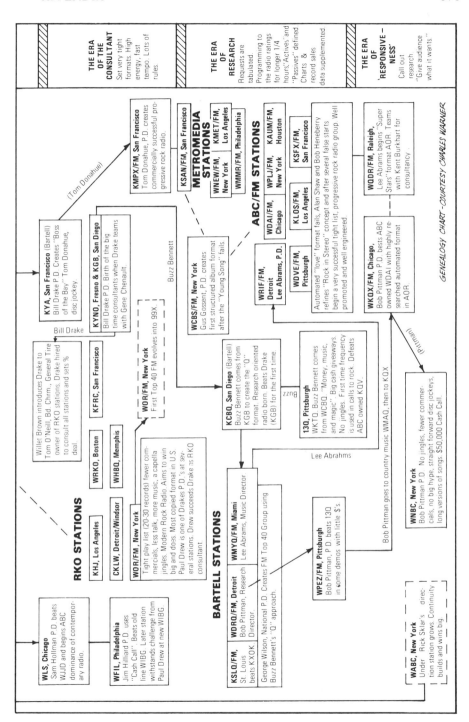

GENEALOGY CHART—COURTESY CHARLES WARNER

TYPICAL STATION LOGOS whose designs denote musical radio.

Station call letters, whether chosen originally for their "soundability" or not, when reproduced as logos, are often shown to depict a musical motif. With the format explosion came increased emphasis on "outside" promotion (billboards, newspapers, TV), and the need for arresting graphics. Examples are shown on this page.

374

BROADCAST MUSIC TERMS

	PERFORMANCE MEDIUM																	
	VOCAL								INSTRUMENTAL									
	Ensemble				Solo				Ensemble									Solo
TYPE OF MUSIC	Small group	Chorus	With instrumental combo	With orchestra	With piano, organ, etc.	With chorus	With inst. ensemble	With vocal and inst. ensemble	With instrumental ensemble	With piano, organ, etc.	Combo	Dance band	"Big" band	Military or symphonic band	Symphony orch.	Chamber (small) orchestra	String orchestra	Chamber ensemble	Inst. w/orchestra	Instrument w/piano	Other (guitar, harp, etc.)	Organ	Piano	Electronic

POPULAR MUSIC
Not necessarily limited to a specific historical or compositional type, not to any particular medium

- Current hits
- Trend music
- General popular music
  - Film music
  - Show tunes
  - Standards
  - Jazz-oriented
  - Country rock
  - "Middle-of-the-road"
- Jazz
  - Dixieland
  - Swing
  - Modern
  - Popular
- Folk Music
- Rock
  - Progressive Rock
- Rhythm and Blues
- Country and Western

SERIOUS MUSIC

by stylistic (historical) type
- Light classic
- Pre-baroque
- Baroque
- Classic
- Romantic
- Modern

by type of composition
- Solo or chamber forms
- Concerto
- Orchestra music (Symphony, ballet, symphonic, poem, etc.)
- Opera, operetta
- Oratorio, cantata
- Motet, madrigal, etc.
- Songs, arias

Ethnic

Religious
- (Sacred)
- Gospel
- Spiritual

Novelty

Spot Radio Stations

1969 Standard Rate and Data Service Chart

Descriptive Terms/ Music and Format

Shown below in alpha order are terms employed to describe either a station's music or its format.

The terms are in use in the industry. They appear in industry periodicals, broadcast industry reports, record industry reports, etc. Knowledgeable people within the industry state these terms are meaningful and understandable by SRDS users.

The list is not represented as all inclusive. Additional terms will be added as they are brought to SRDS' attention.

A

Adult Contemporary
Adult Contemporary and Gold
Adult Rock
Album Oriented Country
Album Oriented Rock
Album Rock
All American Country
AOR

B

Beautiful Music
Big Band
Black
Bluegrass
Bolero

C

Caribbean
Classical
Classic Gold
Concert
Contemporary
Contemporary/AOR
Contemporary Black
Contemporary Country/Western
Contemporary Disco
Contemporary Gold
Contemporary Good Music
Contemporary Instrumentals
Contemporary Oldies
Contemporary Popular
Contemporary Rock
Contemporary Soul
Contemporary/Talk
Contemporary Top 30
Cosmopolitan
Country
Country Gospel
Countrypolitan
Country Pop
Country Rock
Country & Western
Country & Western (Nashville)
Current Hits

D

Dinner
Disco
Disco Rock
Disco/Soul
Dixieland

E

Easy Listening
Easy MOR
Easy-Rock

F

Farm
Fine Music
Folk
Folk Rock

G

General Popular
Gentle Country
Gold
Golden Oldies
Good Country Music
Good Listening
Good Music
Gospel
Great Country

H

Hard Jazz
Hard Rock
Hawaiian
Heavy Rock
Hit Parade

I

Inspirational
Instrumental

J

Jazz
Jazz/Blues/Rhythm
Jive

L

Latin
Light Classical
Light Rock

M

Mainstream Jazz
Mariachi
Mellow Adult Contemporary
Mellow Rock
Metropolitan Country
Mex-Tex
Modern Country
Modern Jazz
Modern Nashville
Mood
MOR (Background)
MOR/Beautiful Music
MOR Contemporary
MOR (Personality)
MOR Popular
MOR/Progressive Rock
MOR/Talk/News
MOR (Uptempo)

N

News
News/Beautiful Music

P

Personality Contemporary
Personality Top 40
Popular
Pop Disco
Pop Rock
Pop Western
Progressive
Progressive Black
Progressive Country
Progressive Rock

R

Religious

Religious/black
Rhythm and Blues
Rock

S

Sacred Music
Salsa
Semi-Classical
Show Tunes
Soft MOR
Soft Rock
Solid Gold
Sophisticated Swing
Soul
Soul Disco
Spanish
Spiritual
Sports
Standard Popular
Standards
Super Soul
Swing
Symphonic

T

Talk
Talk/News
Top 20
Top 40
Top 40 Rock
Top Pops
Town & Country
Traditional Country
True Progressive

U

Uptempo Gospel

W

Western

Y

Young Adult Contemporary
Young & Beautiful

1980 Standard Rate and Data Service—Descriptive Terms for Music Formats

The radio station you grew up with grew up.

93 KHJ is the radio station we all grew up with. In Los Angeles or New York, Chicago or Dallas, Milwaukee, Philadelphia or Detroit you listened to your rock 'n roll radio station because it was playing your music and it talked to you.

We all grew up listening to The Beatles, The Rolling Stones, Elvis Presley, Bob Dylan. We shared a common language in their music. And it was the music that brought us together in the good times and kept us together through the bad.

But we've been changing. And the music's been changing, too. New artists can't quite replace the anticipation we used to feel when an album came out in 1964, 1969, or 1972. Until a whole new kind of song started to be heard everywhere around the country.

The songs were coming from a long tradition; and the names were not really new. Kenny Rogers, Dolly Parton, Willie Nelson, Waylon Jennings, and many, many more. What was new, and wonderful, was that we heard them and we recognized music we liked again.

This is why KHJ is playing their songs. Because they're your songs now.

The new 93 KHJ will be giving you your music. We'll be giving you special features: concerts and events headlining the artists you want to hear. We'll give you radio the way you want it; with news and weather and all the information you need every day. We'll give you a chance to hear yourself and your neighbors on the air winning good things — the things you need to make it easier to make it, every day.

We want you to call us and tell us, "What makes a cowboy a cowboy." We want to hear all the good things you believe in that cowboys stand for. Because we believe everyone can be a cowboy in their heart. And we believe...

We all grew up to be cowboys.

The new 93KHJ

K H J ad that appeared in Los Angeles Times Calendar ad when station switched to Country Music. ("The Radio Station You Grew Up With")

(Courtesy *Radio Active*)

The bumper sticker became one of the most copied Top 40 gimmicks. Accepted eventually by stations of all musical persuasions, "spotting" cars bearing call letter stickers as the basis for contests developed into standard radio promotion. Bumper sticker copy is often inter-changeable with that used on billboards.

378

The Top Forty

(Editor, Dave Sholin)

(Underlined sides show the strongest potential for continued growth.)

2W	LW	TW	
5.	3.	1.	Starting Over-John Lennon (Geffen)
2.	1.	2.	Hungry Heart-Bruce Springsteen (Columbia)
8.	5.	3.	THE TIDE IS HIGH-Blondie (Chrysalis)
7.	6.	4.	EVERY WOMAN IN THE WORLD-Air Supply (Arista)
12.	10.	5.	PASSION-Rod Stewart (Warner Brothers)
1.	2.	6.	More Than I Can Say-Leo Sayer (Warner Brothers)
11.	8.	7.	TELL IT LIKE IT IS-Heart (Epic)
14.	11.	8.	HEY NINETEEN-Steely Dan (MCA)
4.	4.	9.	Guilty-Barbra Streisand & Barry Gibb (Columbia)
6.	7.	10.	Love On The Rocks-Neil Diamond (Capitol)
13.	12.	11.	One Step Closer-Doobie Brothers (Warner Brothers)
13.	14.	12.	I MADE IT THROUGH THE RAIN-Barry Manilow (Arista)
24.	17.	13.	I LOVE A RAINY NIGHT-Eddie Rabbitt (Elektra)
16.	15.	14.	DE DO DO DO DE DA DA-Police (A&M)
--.	27.	15.	SAME OLD LANG SYNE-Dan Fogelberg (Full Moon/Epic)
20.	18.	16.	TIME IS TIME-Andy Gibb (RSO)
21.	20.	17.	CELEBRATION-Kool & The Gang (De-Lite)
29.	22.	18.	MISS SUN-Boz Scaggs (Columbia)
3.	9.	19.	Lady-Kenny Rogers (Liberty)
36.	25.	20.	KEEP ON LOVIN' YOU-REO Speedwagon (Epic)
15.	19.	21.	Suddenly-Olivia Newton-John & Cliff Richard (MCA)
26.	23.	22.	Together-Tierra (Boardwalk)
30.	28.	23.	GAMES PEOPLE PLAY-Alan Parsons Project (Arista)
33.	29.	24.	SEVEN BRIDGES ROAD-Eagles (Asylum)
--.	34.	25.	GIVIN' IT UP FOR YOUR LOVE-Delbert McClinton (Capitol)
10.	16.	26.	Hit Me With Your Best Shot-Pat Benatar (Chrysalis)
9.	13.	27.	Never Be The Same-Christopher Cross (Warner Brothers)
--.	36.	28.	NINE TO FIVE-Dolly Parton (RCA)
37.	32.	29.	COLD LOVE-Donna Summer (Geffen)
32.	30.	30.	Gotta Have More Love-Climax Blues Band (Warner Brothers)
17.	21.	31.	Everybody's Got To Learn-Korgis (Elektra)
40.	37.	32.	WINNER TAKES IT ALL-Abba (Atlantic)
--.	--.	33.	WHO'S MAKING LOVE-Blues Brothers (Atlantic)
25.	24.	34.	Girls Can Get It-Dr. Hook (Casablanca)
--.	--.	35.	A LITTLE IN LOVE-Cliff Richard (EMI)
--.	39.	36.	MY MOTHER'S EYES-Bette Midler (Atlantic)
22.	26.	37.	I Believe In You-Don Williams (MCA)
--.	--.	38.	AIN'T GONNA STAND FOR IT-Stevie Wonder (Tamla)
--.	--.	39.	HEARTBREAK HOTEL-Jacksons (Epic)
--.	--.	40.	HE CAN'T LOVE YOU-Michael Stanley Band (EMI)

The Top Contenders

WOMAN-John Lennon (Geffen) (LP cut)
LOVE TKO-Teddy Pendergrass (Philadelphia International)
SKATEAWAY-Dire Straits (Warner Brothers)
SMOKEY MOUNTAIN RAIN-Ronnie Milsap (RCA)
RAPTURE-Blondie (Chrysalis) (LP cut)

Comment

The last chart of 1980 is dominated by softer sounds, the biggest of which is Fogelberg's SAME OLD LANG SYNE. Virtually every station reported huge requests on this timely love song.
Reports of listeners demanding more music from "Double Fantasy", especially "WOMAN", "WATCHING THE WHEELS", and "BEAUTIFUL BOY".
Instant response to Blondie's "RAPTURE" at every station that plays this track.
Have a beautiful holiday.

THE GAVIN REPORT, One Embarcadero Center, Suite 1816, San Francisco, CA 94111 (415) 392-7750

The *Gavin* Top 40 List for December 19, 1980

Tape 418

Image Standards

Intro	Time	End	Segment	Title	Artist(s)	Composer(s)
:22	2:55	C	418E01	The Shadow Of Your Smile	Ray Charles	P. F. Webster, Mandel
:16	3:35	F	418E02	When Love Touches Your Life	Johnny Mathis	R. Ortolani
:19	2:57	F	418E03	Constant Rain	Sergio Mendes	J. Ben, N. Gimbel
:14	2:55	F	418E04	This Town	Frank Sinatra	L. Hazlewood
:12	2:34	C	418E05	You Don't Have To Say You Love Me	Midnight Voices	P. Donaggio, V. Pallavicini, V. Wickham, S. Napier-Bell
:11	3:37	C	418E06	What I Did For Love	Shirley Bassey	Klegan, Hamlisch
:14	2:20	C	418E07	Baby Won't You Please Come Home	Dean Martin	Warfield, Williams
:13	2:40	C	418E08	What A Wonderful World	Engelbert Humperdinck	Weiss, Douglas
:13	2:35	C	418E09	Please Love Me Forever	Lettermen	Malone, Blanchard
:09	3:08	C	418E10	Something So Right	Barbra Streisand	P. Simon
:20	2:27	C	418E11	I Love You So Much It Hurts	Andy Williams	F. Tillman
:13	2:34	C	418E12	The Sweetest Sounds	Ray Conniff	R. Rodgers
:29	3:18	F	418E13	Misty Roses	Sandpipers	T. Hardin
:17	4:37	F	418E14	The Warmth Of The Sun	Melissa Manchester	Wilson, Love

CENTURY 21 PROGRAMMING - QUALITY CONTROL OK

Music Research __gc__ __Kraft & Howard__ Mastering Engineer __KRAFT/LINKER__
Music Matrix __Kraft & Howard__ Checking Engineer _____
Announcers __None__ Duplicating Engineer _____

PROGRAMMING, INC.
4340 Beltwood Parkway, Dallas, TX 75234
(214) 934-2121 or toll-free (800) 527-5959

(Courtesy Century 21)

A music sheet playlist for one hour of music programming taken from a syndicated format—Century 21's "E-Z" format.

MUTUAL BROADCASTING SYSTEM
Westar Satellite Distribution

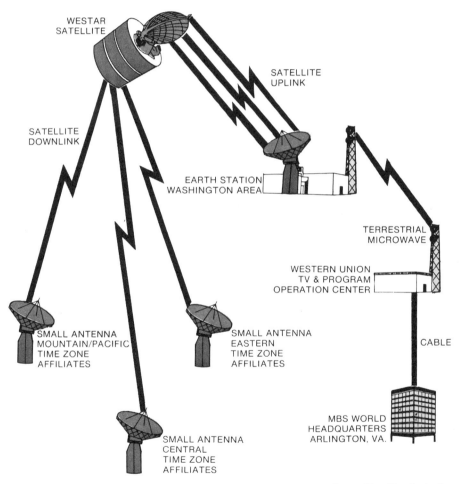

WESTAR
SATELLITE

SATELLITE
UPLINK

SATELLITE
DOWNLINK

EARTH STATION
WASHINGTON AREA

TERRESTRIAL
MICROWAVE

WESTERN UNION
TV & PROGRAM
OPERATION CENTER

SMALL ANTENNA
MOUNTAIN/PACIFIC
TIME ZONE
AFFILIATES

SMALL ANTENNA
EASTERN
TIME ZONE
AFFILIATES

CABLE

SMALL ANTENNA
CENTRAL
TIME ZONE
AFFILIATES

MBS WORLD
HEADQUARTERS
ARLINGTON, VA.

Mutual Network Satellite Delivery System Diagram. (Shows how programs are beamed via satellite to affiliates)

AMERICA'S FAVORITE POPULAR MUSIC, 1920–1980 *

1920

Avalon
Daddy, You've Been a Mother
  to Me
Hold Me
I'll Be with You in Apple
  Blossom Time
The Japanese Sandman
Look for the Silver Lining
San
When My Baby Smiles at Me
Whispering
Whose Baby Are You

1921

Ain't We Got Fun
All By Myself
April Showers
I'm Just Wild About Harry
Ma, He's Making Eyes at Me
My Man
Say it with Music
The Sheik of Araby
Three O'Clock in the Morning
Wang-Wang Blues

1922

L'Amour Toujours L'Amour
Carolina in the Morning
Chicago, That Toddling Town
China Boy
I'll Build a Stairway to
  Paradise
My Buddy
Runnin' Wild
Toot Toot Tootsie
Trees
Wonderful One

1923

Barney Google
Beside a Babbling Brook
Bugle Call Rag
Charleston
I Cried for You
It Ain't Gonna Rain No Mo'
Linger Awhile
Swingin' Down the Lane
Who's Sorry Now
Yes! We Have no Bananas

1924

All Alone
Everybody Loves My Baby, but
  My Baby Don't Love Nobody
  but Me
Fascinating Rhythm
I'll See You in My Dreams
June Night
Nobody's Sweetheart
The Prisoner's Song
Rose Marie
Somebody Loves Me
Tea for Two

1925

Always
Dinah
Don't Bring Lulu
Five Feet Two, Eyes of Blue
If You Knew Susie, Like I
  Know Susie
Just a Cottage Small—By a
  Waterfall
Moonlight and Roses
Only a Rose
Sweet Georgia Brown
Valencia

1926

Baby Face
Black Bottom
Breezin' Along with the Breeze
Bye Bye Blackbird
I Know That You Know
It All Depends on You
One Alone
Someone to Watch over Me
When Day is Done
When the Red, Red Robin Comes
  Bob, Bob, Bobbin' Along

1927

Ain't She Sweet
Among My Souvenirs
At Sundown
The Best Things in Life Are
  Free
Girl of My Dreams
Me and My Shadow
Rain
Side by Side
Sometimes I'm Happy
The Song is Ended but
  the Melody Lingers On

1928

Button Up Your Overcoat
Carolina Moon
Doin' the Raccoon
I'll Get By
Jeannine, I Dream of Lilac
  Time
Makin' Whoopee!
My Lucky Star
That's My Weakness Now
Together
You're the Cream in My Coffee

---

* Selections for the years 1920–1934 are highly arbitrary; they are listed alphabetically. Virtually all pop tunes during this period were licensed by The American Society of Authors, Composers, and Publishers (ASCAP). These songs represent a distillation of slightly longer compilations for each year listed in ASCAP's register which states, "objective criteria were used. Various lists and surveys were correlated with ASCAP's own records of performances of the works of its members." (*35 Years of Hit Tunes,* [1917–1952] American Society of Composers, Authors, and Publishers, undated.)

The years 1935–1954 represent the songs that were ranked by *Your Hit Parade.* Although that show lasted through 1959, beginning in 1955, *records* rather than *songs,* became the accepted standard for judging popularity. Thus, 1955–1980 listings are based on the "charts." For these years, the listings represent each year's "Number One Records," based on *Billboard* rankings and published in Joel Whitburn's *Pop Annual, 1955–1977* and supplements for 1978, 1979 and 1980. Whitburn's publications are accepted as the industry's standard reference works.

1929

Deep Night
Happy Days Are Here Again
If I Had a Talking Picture
    of You
I'm a Dreamer, Aren't We All
More Than You Know
Stardust
When it's Springtime in the
    Rockies
When the Organ Played at
    Twilight, the Song That
    Reached My Heart
Without a Song
You Do Something to Me

1930

Beyond the Blue Horizon
Body and Soul
Cheerful Little Earful
Dancing with Tears in My Eyes
Exactly Like You
On the Sunny Side of the Street
Something to Remember You By
Stein Song
Time on My Hands
When Your Hair Has Turned to
    Silver (I Will Love You
    Just the Same)

1931

As Time Goes By
Between the Devil and the Deep
    Blue Sea
Goodnight Sweetheart
I Don't Know Why
I Love a Parade
Life is Just a Bowl of Cherries
Out of Nowhere
Sweet and Lovely
When the Moon Comes Over the
    Mountain
You're My Everything

1932

Brother, Can You Spare a Dime
How Deep is the Ocean?
In a Shanty in Old Shanty Town
Just an Echo in the Valley
Let's All Sing Like the Birdies
    Sing
Let's Put Out the Lights
Little Street Where Old Friends
    Meet
Night and Day
Shuffle Off to Buffalo
Somebody Loves You

1933

Boulevard of Broken Dreams
Did You Ever See a Dream Walking?
Easter Parade
Have You Ever Been Lonely, Have
    You Ever Been Blue?
It's Only a Paper Moon
It's the Talk of the Town
Lazy Bones
Love is the Sweetest Thing
Smoke Gets in Your Eyes
Who's Afraid of the Big Bad Wolf

1934

All I Do is Dream of You
Blue Moon
I Only Have Eyes for You
Moonglow
The Object of My Affection
P. S. I Love You
Santa Claus is Coming to Town
Stay as Sweet as You Are
Tumbling Tumbleweeds
Winter Wonderland

1935

1. In a Little Gypsy Tea Room
2. Red-Sails in the Sunset
3. Cheek to Cheek
4. On Treasure Island
5. I'm in the Mood for Love
6. Chasing Shadows
7. In the Middle of a Kiss
8. Lullaby of Broadway
9. East of the Sun
10. You Are My Lucky Star

1936

1. Did I Remember?
2. The Way You Look Tonight
3. In the Chapel in the
    Moonlight
4. Is It True What They Say
    About Dixie?
5. These Foolish Things
6. Lost
7. Alone
8. Goody Goody
9. When Did You Leave Heaven?
10. Lights Out

1937

1. September in the Rain
2. It Looks Like Rain in
    Cherry Blossom Lane
3. That Old Feeling
4. Pennies from Heaven
5. Boo Hoo
6. Sailboat in the Moonlight
7. Once in a While
8. Whispers in the Dark
9. It's De-lovely
10. Vieni, Vieni

1938

1. My Reverie
2. I've Got a Pocketful of
    Dreams
3. Music, Maestro, Please
4. A-Tisket A-Tasket
5. Says My Heart
6. Ti-Pi-Tin
7. Please Be Kind
8. Love Walked In
9. I Let a Song Go Out of my
    Heart
10. Thanks for the Memory

1939

1. South of the Border
2. Deep Purple
3. Scatterbrain
4. Over the Rainbow
5. Wishing
6. And the Angels Sing
7. Moon Love
8. Stairway to the Stars
9. The Beer Barrel Polka
10. Jeepers Creepers

1940

1. The Woodpecker Song
2. I'll Never Smile Again
3. There I Go
4. Careless
5. When You Wish Upon a Star
6. Imagination
7. Only Forever
8. Practice Makes Perfect
9. All the Things You Are
10. Indian Summer

1941

1. I Hear a Rhapsody
2. Intermezzo
3. Frenesi
4. Amapola
5. Maria Elena
6. Tonight We Love
7. I Don't Want to Set the
   World on Fire
8. My Sister and I
9. You and I
10. Yours

1942

1. White Christmas
2. The White Cliffs of Dover
3. Sleepy Lagoon
4. Elmer's Tune
5. My Devotion
6. He Wears a Pair of Silver
   Wings
7. Jingle, Jangle, Jingle
8. One Dozen Roses
9. Don't Sit Under the Apple
   Tree
10. Blues in the Night

1943

1. People Will Say We're in
   Love
2. You'll Never Know
3. Paper Doll
4. As Times Goes By
5. There Are Such Things
6. Sunday, Monday or Always
7. Comin' in on a Wing and
   a Prayer
8. In the Blue of Evening
9. I've Heard That Song Before
10. Don't Get Around Much Any
    More

1944

1. I'll Be Seeing You
2. My Heart Tells Me
3. Long Ago and Far Away
4. I'll Get By
5. I'll Walk Alone
6. Amor
7. Swinging on a Star
8. I Love You
9. Shoo-Shoo Baby
10. The Trolley Song

1945

1. Till the End of Time
2. Dream
3. If I Loved You
4. Don't Fence Me In
5. Sentimental Journey
6. It's Been a Long, Long Time
7. My Dreams Are Getting Better
   All the Time
8. On the Atchison, Topeka,
   and the Santa Fe
9. Laura
10. Accentuate the Positive

1946

1. They Say It's Wonderful
2. The Gypsy
3. Symphony
4. To Each His Own
5. Oh, What it Seemed to Be
6. Ole Buttermilk Sky
7. Five Minutes More
8. All Through the Day
9. I Can't Begin to Tell You
10. It Might As Well Be Spring

1947

1. Peg o' My Heart
2. The Anniversary Song
3. Near You
4. Linda
5. For Sentimental Reasons
6. I Wish I Didn't Love You So
7. Mam'selle
8. That's My Desire
9. Heartaches
10. How Soon

1948

1. A Tree in the Meadow
2. Now is the Hour
3. Buttons and Bows
4. It's Magic
5. Ballerina
6. On a Slow Boat to China
7. You Can't Be True, Dear
8. Serenade of the Bells
9. My Happiness
10. I'm Looking Over a Four
    Leaf Clover

1949

1. Some Enchanted Evening
2. Again
3. Far Away Places
4. Cruising Down the River
5. You're Breaking My Heart
6. I Can Dream, Can't I?
7. Bali H'ai
8. Forever and Ever
9. Riders in the Sky
10. Don't Cry, Joe

1950

1. My Foolish Heart
2. Mona Lisa
3. Bewitched, Bothered and
   Bewildered
4. Goodnight, Irene
5. Dear Hearts and Gentle
   People
6. All My Love
7. Harbor Lights
8. The Third Man Theme
9. La Vie en Rose
10. If I Knew You Were Comin'
    I'd've Baked a Cake

1951

1. Too Young
2. Because of You
3. How High the Moon
4. Come On-a My House
5. Be My Love
6. On Top of Old Smokey
7. Cold, Cold Heart
8. If
9. Loveliest Night of the Year
10. Tennessee Waltz

1952

1. Blue Tango
2. Wheel of Fortune
3. Cry
4. You Belong to Me
5. Auf Wiedersehen Sweetheart
6. I Went to Your Wedding
7. Half as Much
8. Wish You Were Here
9. Here in My Heart
10. Delicado

1953

1. Song from Moulin Rouge
2. Vaya Con Dios
3. Doggie in the Window
4. I'm Walking Beside You
5. You, You, You
6. Till I Waltz Again with You
7. April in Portugal
8. No Other Love
9. Don't Let the Stars Get
   in Your Eyes
10. I Believe

1954

1. Little Things Mean A Lot
2. Wanted
3. Hey There
4. Sh-Boom
5. Make Love to Me
6. Oh, My Papa
7. I Get So Lonely
8. Three Coins in the Fountain
9. Secret Love
10. Hernando's Hideaway

1955

1. Let Me Go Lover - Joan Weber
2. Hearts of Stone - Fontane Sisters
3. Sincerely - McGuire Sisters
4. The Ballad of Davy Crockett - Bill Hayes
5. Cherry Pink and Apple Blossom White - Perez Prado
6. Rock Around the Clock - Bill Haley & His Comets
7. The Yellow Rose of Texas - Mitch Miller
8. Love Is a Many-Splendored Thing - Four Aces
9. Autumn Leaves - Roger Williams
10. Sixteen Tons - Tennessee Ernie Ford
11. Memories Are Made of This - Dean Martin

1956

1. The Great Pretender - Platters
2. Rock and Roll Waltz - Kay Starr
3. The Poor People of Paris - Les Baxter
4. Heartbreak Hotel - Elvis Presley
5. The Wayward Wind - Gogi Grant
6. I Almost Lost My Mind - Pat Boone
7. My Prayer - Platters
8. Don't Be Cruel - Elvis Presley
9. The Green Door - Jim Lowe
10. Love Me Tender - Elvis Presley
11. Singing the Blues - Guy Mitchell

1957

1. Don't Forbid Me - Pat Boone
2. Young Love - Tab Hunter
3. Butterfly - Andy Williams
4. Round and Round - Perry Como
5. All Shook Up - Elvis Presley
6. Love Letters in the Sand - Pat Boone
7. Let Me Be Your Teddy Bear - Elvis Presley
8. Tammy - Debbie Reynolds
9. Honeycomb - Jimmie Rodgers
10. Wake Up Little Susie - Everly Brothers
11. Jailhouse Rock - Elvis Presley
12. You Send Me - Sam Cooke
13. April Love - Pat Boone
14. At the Hop - Danny & The Juniors

1958

1. Get A Job - Silhouettes
2. Don't - Elvis Presley
3. Tequila - Champs
4. Twilight Time - Platters
5. Witch Doctor - David Seville
6. All I Have To Do Is Dream - Everly
   Brothers
7. The Purple People Eater - Sheb Wooley
8. Yakety Yak - Coasters
9. Patricia - Perez Prado
10. Poor Little Fool - Ricky Nelson
11. Nel Blu Dipinto Di Blu (Volare) -
    Domenico Modugno
12. Little Star - Elegants
13. It's All in the Game - Tommy Edwards
14. It's Only Make Believe - Conway Twitty
15. Tom Dooley - Kingston Trio
16. To Know Him Is to Love Him - Teddy Bears
17. The Chipmunk Song - Chipmunks

1959

1. Smoke Gets in Your Eyes - Platters
2. Stagger Lee - Lloyd Price
3. Venus - Frankie Avalon
4. Come Softly to Me - Fleetwoods
5. The Happy Organ - Dave "Baby" Cortez
6. Kansas City - Wilbert Harrison
7. The Battle of New Orleans - Johnny
   Horton
8. Lonely Boy - Paul Anka
9. A Big Hunk O' Love - Elvis Presley
10. The Three Bells - Browns
11. Sleep Walk - Santo & Johnny
12. Mack the Knife - Bobby Darin
13. Mr. Blue - Fleetwoods
14. Heartaches by the Number - Guy
    Mitchell

1960

1. Why - Frankie Avalon
2. El Paso - Marty Robbins
3. Running Bear - Johnny Preston
4. Teen Angel - Mark Dinning
5. The Theme from "A Summer Place" - Percy
   Faith
6. Stuck on You - Elvis Presley
7. Cathy's Clown - Everly Brothers
8. Everybody's Somebody's Fool - Connie
   Francis
9. Alley-Oop - Hollywood Argyles
10. I'm Sorry - Brenda Lee
11. Itsy Bitsy Teenie Weenie Yellow Polkadot
    Bikini - Brian Hyland
12. It's Now or Never - Elvis Presley
13. The Twist - Chubby Checker
14. My Heart Has a Mind of Its Own - Connie
    Francis
15. Mr. Custer - Larry Verne
16. Save the Last Dance for Me - Drifters
17. I Want to be Wanted - Brenda Lee
18. Georgia on My Mind - Ray Charles
19. Stay - Maurice Williams & The Zodiacs
20. Are You Lonesome To-Night? - Elvis Presley

1961

1. Wonderland by Night - Bert Kaempfert
2. Will You Love Me Tomorrow - Shirelles
3. Calcutta - Lawrence Welk
4. Pony Time - Chubby Checker
5. Surrender - Elvis Presley
6. Blue Moon - Marcels
7. Runaway - Del Shannon
8. Mother-in-Law - Ernie K-Doe
9. Travelin' Man - Ricky Nelson
10. Running Scared - Roy Orbison
11. Moody River - Pat Boone
12. Quarter to Three - U. S. Bonds
13. Tossin' and Turnin' - Bobby Lewis
14. Wooden Heart - Joe Dowell
15. Michael - Highwaymen
16. Take Good Care of My Baby - Bobby Vee
17. Hit the Road Jack - Ray Charles
18. Runaround Sue - Dion
19. Big Bad John - Jimmy Dean
20. Please Mr. Postman - Marvelettes
21. The Lion Sleeps Tonight - Tokens

1962

1. The Twist - Chubby Checker
2. Peppermint Twist - Joey Dee & The Starliters
3. Duke of Earl - Gene Chandler
4. Hey! Baby - Bruce Channel
5. Don't Break the Heart that Loves You - Connie Francis
6. Johnny Angel - Shelly Fabares
7. Good Luck Charm - Elvis Presley
8. Soldier Boy - Shirelles
9. Stranger on the Shore - Mr. Acker Bilk
10. I Can't Stop Loving You - Ray Charles
11. The Stripper - David Rose
12. Roses Are Red - Bobby Vinton
13. Breaking Up is Hard to Do - Neil Sedaka
14. The Loco-Motion - Little Eva
15. Sheila - Tommy Roe
16. Sherry - 4 Seasons
17. Monster Mash - Bobby "Boris" Pickett & The Crypt-Kickers
18. He's A Rebel - Crystals
19. Big Girls Don't Cry - 4 Seasons
20. Telstar - Tornadoes

1963

1. Go Away Little Girl - Steve Lawrence
2. Walk Right In - Rooftop Singers
3. Hey Paula - Paul & Paula
4. Walk Like A Man - 4 Seasons
5. Our Day Will Come - Ruby & The Romantics
6. He's So Fine - Chiffons
7. I Will Follow Him - Little Peggy March
8. If You Wanna Be Happy - Jimmy Soul
9. It's My Party - Lesley Gore
10. Sukiyaki - Kyu Sakamoto
11. Easier Said Than Done - Essex
12. Surf City - Jan & Dean
13. So Much In Love - Tymes
14. Fingertips - PT. 2 - Little Stevie Wonder
15. My Boyfriend's Back - Angels
16. Blue Velvet - Bobby Vinton
17. Sugar Shack - Jimmy Gilmer & The Fireballs
18. Deep Purple - Nino Tempo & April Stevens
19. I'm Leaving It Up To You - Dale & Grace
20. Dominique - Singing Nun

1964

1. There! I've Said It Again - Bobby Vinton
2. I Want to Hold Your Hand - Beatles
3. She Loves You - Beatles
4. Can't Buy Me Love - Beatles
5. Hello, Dolly! - Louis Armstrong
6. My Guy - Mary Wells
7. Love Me Do - Beatles
8. Chapel of Love - Dixie Cups
9. A World Without Love - Peter & Gordon
10. I Get Around - Beach Boys
11. Rag Doll - 4 Seasons
12. A Hard Day's Night - Beatles
13. Everybody Loves Somebody - Dean Martin
14. Where Did Our Love Go - Supremes
15. The House of the Rising Sun - Animals
16. Oh, Pretty Woman - Roy Orbison
17. Do Wah Diddy Diddy - Manfred Mann
18. Baby Love - Supremes
19. Leader of the Pack - Shangri-Las
20. Ringo - Lorne Greene
21. Mr. Lonely - Bobby Vinton
22. Come See About Me - Supremes
23. I Feel Fine - Beatles

1965

1. Downtown - Petula Clark
2. You've Lost that Lovin' Feelin' - Righteous Brothers
3. This Diamond Ring - Gary Lewis & The Playboys
4. My Girl - Temptations
5. Eight Days a Week - Beatles
6. Stop! In the Name of Love - Supremes
7. I'm Telling You Now - Freddie & The Dreamers
8. Game of Love - Wayne Fontana & The Mindbenders
9. Mrs. Brown You've Got a Lovely Daughter - Herman's Hermits
10. Ticket to Ride - Beatles
11. Help Me, Rhonda - Beach Boys
12. Back in My Arms Again - Supremes
13. I Can't Help Myself - Four Tops
14. Mr. Tambourine Man - Byrds
15. (I Can't Get No) Satisfaction - Rolling Stones
16. I'm Henry, VIII, I Am - Herman's Hermits
17. I Got You Babe - Sonny & Cher
18. Help! - Beatles
19. Eve of Destruction - Barry McGuire
20. Hang on Sloopy - McCoys
21. Yesterday - Beatles
22. Get Off of my Cloud - Rolling Stones
23. I Hear a Symphony - Supremes
24. Turn! Turn! Turn! - Byrds
25. Over and Over - Dave Clark Five

1966

. The Sounds of Silence - Simon & Garfunkel
. We Can Work It Out - Beatles
. My Love - Petula Clark
. Lightnin' Strikes - Lou Christie
. These Boots Are Made for Walkin' - Nancy
  Sinatra
. The Ballad of the Green Berets - Ssgt.
  Barry Sadler
. (You're My) Soul and Inspiration -
  Righteous Brothers
. Good Lovin' - Young Rascals
. Monday, Monday - Mama's & The Papa's
. When A Man Loves A Woman - Percy Sledge
. Paint It, Black - Rolling Stones
. Paperback Writer - Beatles
. Strangers in the Night - Frank Sinatra
. Hanky Panky - Tommy James & The Shondells
. Wild Thing - Troggs
. Summer in the City - Lovin'Spoonful
. Sunshine Superman - Donovan
. You Can't Hurry Love - Supremes
. Cherish - Association
. Reach Out I'll Be There - Four Tops
. 96 Tears - ? (Question Mark) & The
  Mysterians
. Last Train to Clarksville - Monkees
. Poor Side of Town - Johnny Rivers
. You Keep Me Hangin' On - Supremes
. Winchester Cathedral - New Vaudeville
  Band
. Good Vibrations - Beach Boys
. I'm A Beliver - Monkees

1967

Kind of a Drag - Buckinghams
Ruby Tuesday - Rolling Stones
Love is Here and Now You're Gone - Supremes
Penny Lane - Beatles
Happy Together - Turtles
Somethin' Stupid - Nancy Sinatra & Frank
  Sinatra
The Happening - Supremes
Groovin' - Young Rascals
Respect - Aretha Franklin
Windy - Association
Light My Fire - Doors
All You Need is Love - Beatles
Ode to Billie Joe - Bobbie Gentry
The Letter - Box Tops
To Sir with Love - Lulu
Incense and Peppermints - Strawberry
  Alarm Clock
Daydream Believer - Monkees
Hello Goodbye - Beatles

1968

1. Judy in Disguise (With Glasses) - John Fred
   & His Playboy Band
2. Green Tambourine - Lemon Pipers
3. Love is Blue - Paul Mauriat
4. (Sittin' On) The Dock of the Bay - Otis
   Redding
5. Honey - Bobby Goldsboro
6. Tighten Up - Archie Bell & The Drells
7. Mrs. Robinson - Simon & Garfunkel
8. This Guy's in Love with You - Herb Alpert
9. Grazing in the Grass - Hugh Masekela
10. Hello, I Love You - Doors
11. People Got to be Free - Rascals
12. Harper Valley P.T.A. - Jeannie C. Riley
13. Hey Jude - Beatles
14. Love Child - Diana Ross & The Supremes
15. I Heard it Through the Grapevine - Marvin
    Gaye

1969

1. Crimson and Clover - Tommy James & The
   Shondells
2. Everyday People - Sly & The Family Stone
3. Dizzy - Tommy Roe
4. Aquarius/Let the Sunshine In - 5th Dimension
5. Get Back - Beatles
6. Love Theme from Romeo & Juliet - Henry Mancin
7. In the Year 2525 - Zager & Evans
8. Honky Tonk Woman - Rolling Stones
9. Sugar, Sugar - Archies
10. I Can't Get Next to You - Temptations
11. Suspicious Minds - Elvis Presley
12. Wedding Bell Blues - 5th Dimension
13. Come Together/Something - Beatles
14. Na Na Hey Hey Kiss Him Goodbye - Steam
15. Leaving on a Jet Plane - Peter, Paul & Mary
16. Someday We'll Be Together - Diana Ross &
    The Supremes

1970

1. Raindrops Keep Fallin' on my Head - B. J. Thomas
2. I Want You Back - Jackson 5
3. Venus - Shocking Blue
4. Thank You Falettinme Be Mice Elf Again - Sly & The Family Stone
5. Bridge Over Troubled Water - Simon & Garfunkel
6. Let It Be - Beatles
7. ABC - Jackson 5
8. American Woman - Guess Who
9. Everything is Beautiful - Ray Stevens
10. The Long and Winding Road - Beatles
11. The Love You Save - Jackson 5
12. Mama Told Me (Not to Come) - Three Dog Night
13. (They Long to Be) Close to You - Carpenters
14. Make it with You - Bread
15. War - Edwin Starr
16. Ain't No Mountain High Enough - Diana Ross
17. Cracklin' Rosie - Neil Diamond
18. I'll Be There - Jackson 5
19. I Think I Love You - Patridge Family
20. The Tears of a Clown - Smokey Robinson & The Miracles
21. My Sweet Lord - George Harrison

1971

1. Knock Three Times - Dawn
2. One Bad Apple - Osmonds
3. Me and Bobby McGee - Janis Joplin
4. Just My Imagination (Running Away With Me) - Temptations
5. Joy to the World - Three Dog Night
6. Brown Sugar - Rolling Stones
7. Want Ads - Honey Cone
8. It's Too Late - Carole King
9. Indian Reservation - Raiders
10. You've Got a Friend - James Taylor
11. How Can You Mend a Broken Heart - Bee Gees
12. Uncle Albert/Admiral Halsey - Paul & Linda McCartney
13. Go Away Little Girl - Donny Osmond
14. Maggie May - Rod Stewart
15. Gypsys, Tramps & Thieves - Cher
16. Theme from Shaft - Isaac Hayes
17. Family Affair - Sly & The Family Stone
18. Brand New Key - Melanie

1972

1. American Pie - Don McLean
2. Let's Stay Together - Al Green
3. Without You - Nilsson
4. Heart of Gold - Neil Young
5. A Horse with No Name - America
6. The First Time Ever I Saw Your Face - Roberta Flack
7. Oh Girl - Chi-Lites
8. I'll Take You There - Staple Singers
9. The Candy Man - Sammy Davis, Jr.
10. Song Sung Blue - Neil Diamond
11. Lean on Me - Bill Withers
12. Alone Again (Naturally) - Gilbert O'Sullivan
13. Brandy (You're A Fine Girl) - Looking Glass
14. Black & White - Three Dog Night
15. Baby Don't Get Hooked on Me - Mac Davis
16. Ben - Michael Jackson
17. My Ding-A-Ling - Chuck Berry
18. I Can See Clearly Now - Johnny Nash
19. Papa Was A Rollin' Stone - Temptations
20. I Am Woman - Helen Reddy
21. Me and Mrs. Jones - Billy Paul

1973

1. You're So Vain - Carly Simon
2. Superstition - Stevie Wonder
3. Crocodile Rock - Elton John
4. Killing Me Softly With His Song - Roberta Flack
5. Love Train - O'Jays
6. The Night the Lights Went Out in Georgia - Vicki Lawrence
7. Tie a Yellow Ribbon Round the Old Oak Tree Dawn
8. You Are the Sunshine of My Life - Stevie Wonder
9. Frankenstein - Edgar Winter Group
10. My Love - Paul McCartney & Wings
11. Give Me Love (Give Me Peace on Earth) - George Harrison
12. Will it go Round in Circles - Billy Preston
13. Bad, Bad Leroy Brown - Jim Croce
14. The Morning After (Song from The Poseidon Adventure) - Maureen McGovern
15. Touch Me in the Morning - Diana Ross
16. Brother Louie - Stories
17. Let's Get It On - Marvin Gaye
18. Delta Dawn - Helen Reddy
19. We're an American Band - Grand Funk
20. Half-Breed - Cher
21. Angie - Rolling Stones
22. Midnight Train to Georgia - Gladys Knight & The Pips
23. Keep on Truckin' - Eddie Kendricks
24. Photograph - Ringo Starr
25. Top of the World - Carpenters
26. The Most Beautiful Girl - Charlie Rich
27. Time in a Bottle - Jim Croce

<u>1974</u>

1. The Joker - Steve Miller Band
2. Show and Tell - Al Wilson
3. You're Sixteen - Ringo Starr
4. The Way We Were - Barbra Streisand
5. Love's Theme - Love Unlimited
   Orchestra
6. Seasons in the Sun - Terry Jacks
7. Dark Lady - Cher
8. Sunshine on My Shoulders - John
   Denver
9. Hooked on a Feeling - Blue Swede
10. Bennie and the Jets - Elton John
11. TSOP (The Sound of Philadelphia) -
    MFSB featuring The Three Degrees
12. The Loco-Motion - Grand Funk
13. The Streak - Ray Stevens
14. Band on the Run - Paul McCartney & Wings
15. Billy, Don't Be a Hero - Bo Donaldson &
    The Heywoods
16. Sundown - Gordon Lightfoot
17. Rock the Boat - Hues Corporation
18. Rock Your Baby - George McCraw
19. Annie's Song - John Denver
20. Feel Like Makin' Love - Roberta Flack
21. The Night Chicago Died - Paper Lace
22. (You're) Having My Baby - Paul Anka
23. I Shot the Sheriff - Eric Clapton
24. Can't Get Enough of Your Love, Babe -
    Barry White
25. Rock Me Gently - Andy Kim
26. I Honestly Love You - Olivia Newton-John
27. Nothing from Nothing - Billy Preston
28. Then Came You - Dionne Warwicke & Spinners
29. You Haven't Done Nothin - Stevie Wonder
30. You Ain't Seen Nothing Yet - Bachman-
    Turner Overdrive
31. Whatever Gets You Thru the Night - John
    Lennon and the Plastic Ono Nuclear
    Band
32. I Can Help - Billy Swan
33. Kung Fu Fighting - Carl Douglas
34. Cat's in the Cradle - Harry Chapin
35. Angie Baby - Helen Reddy

<u>1975</u>

1. Lucy in the Sky with Diamonds - Elton John
2. Mandy - Barry Manilow
3. Please Mr. Postman - Carpenters
4. Laughter in the Rain - Neil Sedaka
5. Fire - Ohio Players
6. You're No Good - Linda Ronstadt
7. Pick up the Pieces - AWB
8. Best of My Love - Eagles
9. Have You Never Been Mellow - Olivia Newton-
   John
10. Black Water - Doobie Brothers
11. My Eyes Adored You - Frankie Valli
12. Lady Marmalade - Labelle
13. Lovin' You - Minnie Riperton
14. Philadelphia Freedom - Elton John Band
15. (Hey Won't You Play) Another Somebody Done
    Somebody Wrong Song - B. J. Thomas
16. He Don't Love You (Like I Love You) - Tony
    Orlando & Dawn
17. Shining Star - Earth, Wind & Fire
18. Before the Next Teardrop Falls - Freddy
    Fender
19. Thank God I'm A Country Boy - John Denver
20. Sister Golden Hair - America
21. Love Will Keep Us Together - Captain &
    Tennille
22. Listen to What the Man Said - Wings
23. The Hustle - Van McCoy & The Soul City
    Symphony
24. One of These Nights - Eagles
25. Jive Talkin' - Bee Gees
26. Fallin' in Love - Hamilton, Joe Frank &
    Reynolds
27. Get Down Tonight - K. C. & The Sunshine
    Band
28. Rhinestone Cowboy - Glen Campbell
29. Fame - David Bowie
30. I'm Sorry - John Denver
31. Bad Blood - Neil Sedaka
32. Island Girl - Elton John
33. That's The Way (I Like It) - K. C. & The
    Sunshine Band
34. Fly, Robin, Fly - Silver Convention
35. Let's Do It Again - Staple Singers

1976

1. Saturday Night - Bay City Rollers
2. Convoy - C. W. McCall
3. I Write the Songs - Barry Manilow
4. Theme from Mahogany (Do You Know Where You're Going To) - Diana Ross
5. Love Rollercoaster - Ohio Players
6. 50 Ways to Leave Your Lover - Paul Simon
7. Theme from S.W.A.T. - Rhythm Heritage
8. Love Machine (Part 1) - Miracles
9. December, 1963 (Oh, What A Night) - Four Seasons
10. Disco Lady - Johnnie Taylor
11. Let Your Love Flow - Bellamy Brothers
12. Welcome Back - John Sebastian
13. Boogie Fever - Sylvers
14. Silly Love Songs - Wings
15. Love Hangover - Diana Ross
16. Afternoon Delight - Starland Vocal Band
17. Kiss and Say Goodbye - Manhattans
18. Don't Go Breaking My Heart - Elton John & Kiki Dee
19. You Should Be Dancing - Bee Gees
20. (Shake, Shake, Shake) Shake Your Booty - K. C. & The Sunshine Band
21. Play That Funky Music - Wild Cherry
22. A Fifth of Beethoven - Walter Murphy & The Big Apple Band
23. Disco Duck (Part 1) - Rick Dees & His Cast of Idiots
24. If You Leave Me Now - Chicago
25. Rock'n Me - Steve Miller
26. Tonight's the Night (Gonna Be Alright) - Rod Stewart

1977

1. You Don't Have to be a Star (To Be in By Show) - Marilyn McCoo & Billy Davis, Jr.
2. You Make Me Feel Like Dancing - Leo Sayer
3. I Wish - Stevie Wonder
4. Car Wash - Rose Royce
5. Torn Between Two Lovers - Mary MacGregor
6. Blinded by the Light - Manfred Mann's Earth Band
7. New Kid in Town - Eagles
8. Love Theme from "A Star is Born" (Evergreen) - Barbra Streisand
9. Rich Girl - Dary Hall & John Oates
10. Dancing Queen - Abba
11. Don't Give Up On Us - David Soul
12. Don't Leave Me This Way - Thelma Houston
13. Southern Nights - Glen Campbell
14. Hotel California - Eagles
15. When I Need You - Leo Sayer
16. Sir Duke - Stevie Wonder
17. I'm Your Boogie Man - K. C. & The Sunshine Band
18. Dreams - Fleetwood Mac
19. Got to Give it Up - Marvin Gaye
20. Gonna Fly Now (Theme from "Rocky") - Bill Conti
21. Undercover Angel - Alan O'Day
22. Da Doo Ron Ron - Shaun Cassidy
23. Looks Like We Made It - Barry Manilow
24. I Just Want to be Your Everything - Andy Gibb
25. Best of my Love - Emotions
26. Star Wars Theme/Cantina Band - Meco
27. You Light Up My Life - Debby Boone
28. How Deep Is Your Love - Bee Gees

1978

1. Baby Come Back - Player
2. Stayin' Alive - Bee Gees
3. (Love Is) Thicker Than Water -
   Andy Gibb
4. Night Fever - Bee Gees
5. If I Can't Have You - Yvonne Elliman
6. With a Little Luck - Wings
7. Too Much, Too Little, Too Late -
   Johnny Mathis/Deniece Williams
8. You're the One That I Want - John
   Travolta & Olivia Newton-John
9. Shadow Dancing - Andy Gibb
10. Miss You - Rolling Stones
11. Three Times a Lady - Commodores
12. Grease - Frankie Valli
13. Boogie Oogie Oogie - Taste of Honey
14. Hot Child in the City - Nick Gilder
15. You Needed Me - Anne Murray
16. MacArthur Park - Donna Summer
18. You Don't Bring Me Flowers - Barbra
    Streisand & Neil Diamond
19. Le Freak - Chic

1979

1. Too Much Heaven - Bee Gees
2. Da Ya Think I'm Sexy? - Rod Stewart
3. I Will Survive - Gloria Gaynor
4. Tragedy - Bee Gees
5. What a Fool Believes - Doobie Brothers
6. Knock on Wood - Amii Stewart
7. Heart of Glass - Blondie
8. Reunited - Peaches & Herb
9. Hot Stuff - Donna Summer
10. Love You Inside Out - Bee Gees
11. Ring My Bell - Anita Ward
12. Bad Girls - Donna Summer
13. Good Times - Chic
14. My Sharona - The Knack
15. Sad Eyes - Robert John
16. Don't Stop 'Til You Get Enough -
    Michael Jackson
17. Rise - Herb Alpert
18. Pop Muzik - M
19. Heartache Tonight - Eagles
20. Still - Commodores
21. No More Tears (Enough is Enough) -
    Barbara Streisand/Donna Summer
22. Babe - Styx
23. Escape (The Pina Colada Song) -
    Rupert Holmes

1980

1. Please Don't Go - KC & The Sunshine Band
2. Rock With You - Michael Jackson
3. Do That to Me One More Time - Captain &
   Tennille
4. Crazy Little Thing Called Love - Queen
5. Another Brick in the Wall (Part II) -
   Pink Floyd
6. Call Me - Blondie
7. Funkytown - Lipps, Inc.
8. Coming Up (Live at Glasgow) - Paul McCartney
   & Wings
9. It's Still Rock and Roll to Me - Billy Joel
10. Magic - Olivia Newton-John
11. Sailing - Christopher Cross
12. Upside Down - Diana Ross
13. Another One Bites the Dust - Queen
14. Woman in Love - Barbra Streisand
15. Lady - Kenny Rogers
16. (Just Like) Starting Over - John Lennon

TOP ALBUM SELLERS FOR 1950S, 1960S AND 1970S

1950's

With A Song In My Heart	Jane Froman
Calypso	Harry Belafonte
South Pacific	Soundtrack
An American In Paris	Soundtrack
My Fair Lady	Original Cast
Young Man With A Horn	Harry James & Doris Day
The Kingston Trio At Large	Kingston Trio
Gigi	Soundtrack
Elvis Presley	Elvis Presley
The Great Caruso	Mario Lanza

1960's

West Side Story	Soundtrack
Days Of Wine & Roses	Andy Williams
A Hard Days Night	Beatles
Mary Poppins	Soundtrack
The Monkees	Monkees
More Of The Monkees	Monkees
Hair	Original Cast
Abbey Road	Beatles
The Singing Nun	The Singing Nun
Sgt. Pepper's Lonely Hearts Club Band	Beatles

1970's

The Stranger	Billy Joel
Bridge Over Troubled Water	Simon & Garfunkel
Tapestry	Carole King
Rumours	Fleetwood Mac
Songs In The Key Of Life	Stevie Wonder
Frampton Comes Alive	Peter Frampton
Elton John's Greatest Hits	Elton John
Grease	Soundtrack
Saturday Night Fever	Soundtrack
Some Girls	Rolling Stones

Selected Discography[*]

Part I

Ben Bernie and His Orchestra—Sunbeam HB310
Coon/Sanders Nighthawks: Radio Aces—RCA Victor (Vintage) LPV511
Duke Ellington: Rockin' in Rhythm—1929–1931—MCA2077 or The Complete Duke Ellington, Vol. 1—CBS 67264
Fletcher Henderson and Don Redman: Developing an American Orchestra—Smithsonian Collection R006
George Olsen—RCA Victor (Vintage) LPV549
Rudy Vallee: The Young Rudy Vallee—RCA Victor LPM 2507
Fred Waring: Waring's Pennsylvanians—RCA Victor (Vintage) LPV554
Paul Whiteman, Vol. 1—RCA Victor (Vintage) LPV555
1927—RCA Victor (Vintage) LPV545
The Twenties—Columbia C3L35

Part II

Bing Crosby: The Bing Crosby Story—Epic E2E201; or Rare Early Recordings, 1929–1934—Biograph BLP-C13; or Wrap Your Troubles in Dreams—RCA Victor (Vintage) LPV584; or A Legendary Performer—RCA Victor CPL1-2086
Tommy Dorsey: The Incomparable Tommy Dorsey—Readers Digest RDA-92A
Benny Goodman: 1938 Carnegie Hall Concert—Columbia OSL160

---

*To deal with the sixty-year cavalcade of musical radio in narrative alone is to miss an important part of the story. Obviously, to understand better the twists and turns of American popular music requires listening to the music itself. The polyglot profusion of recorded

394

Glen Gray: And the Casa Loma Orch.—Swingfan 1024
Guy Lombardo: A Legendary Performer—RCA Victor CPL1-2047
Glenn Miller: A Memorial, 1944–1969—RCA Victor VPM6019; or A Legendary Performer—RCA Victor CPM 2-0693
Artie Shaw: The Complete Artie Shaw, Vol. 1—Bluebird AXM2-5517
The Great Band Era—Readers Digest RD25K
Sweet Bands, 1932–1934–Nostalgia Book Club P514843
Count Basie: Good Morning Blues—MCA2-4108

Part III

Teresa Brewer: Music, Music, Music—Coral CRL57027
Rosemary Clooney: Greatest Hits—Columbia CL 1230
Nat King Cole: Story—Capitol SWCL 1613
Perry Como: Till the End of Time—RCA Victor LPC109
Doris Day: Greatest Hits—Columbia CL1210
Eddie Fisher: The Best of—RCA Victor LPM3375
Connie Francis: Greatest Hits—MGM E-3793
Eddy Howard: The Uncollected—Hindsight HSR119
Stan Kenton: Greatest Hits—Capitol SM 2327
Frankie Laine: Greatest Hits—Columbia CL1231
Guy Mitchell: Greatest Hits—Columbia CL1226
Patti Page: Golden Hits—Mercury MG 20495
Dinah Shore: Buttons and Bows—Harmony HL 7188
Frank Sinatra: In Hollywood—Columbia CL2913 and this is Sinatra!-Capitol W768
Jo Stafford: Greatest Hits—Columbia CL1228

Part IV

The 1950s

Chuck Berry: Golden Decade—Chess LPS 1514
Bo Diddley: 16 All Time Great Hits—Checker LP2989
Pat Boone: Pat's Greatest Hits—Dot DLP 3071
Fats Domino: The Very Best of—United Artists 233
Everly Brothers: Greatest Hits—Barnaby 6006 (Re-package of Cadence tracks)
Bill Haley and the Comets: Greatest Hits—Springboard SPB 4066
Buddy Holly: A Rock and Roll Collection—Decca DXSE7-207
Jerry Lee Lewis: Original Golden Hits—Sun 102
Rick Nelson: Million Sellers—Imperial LP9232
The Platters: Collection of Golden Hits—Mercury 20213
Elvis Presley: Worldwide 50 Gold Award Hits, Vol. 1—RCA Victor 6041

---

material provides an excellent means of sampling the popular music of the past six decades. But in choosing a discography of artists and performances, one also finds the pathway strewn with booby traps. Are the choices too arbitrary, thereby eliminating some important discs? Is it cricket to include some items that are out of print? Will the reader who happens to be an afficionado-collector of one period or other find some selections mundane? The above discography therefore is offered with the following disclaimer: it is only one listener's idea of the 12″ long play records that are illustrative of the *main* currents in American popular music.

The 1960s

Beach Boys: Best of B. B., Vol. 1—Capitol DT2545
Beatles: The White Album—Apply SWBO 101
Blood, Sweat, and Tears—Columbia CQ30994
Byrds: Greatest Hits—Columbia CS 9516
Ray Charles: Greatest Hits—ABC Paramount ABCS415
Chubby Checker: Biggest Hits—Parkway SP 7022
Creedence Clearwater Revival: Creedence Gold—Fantasy 9418
Lovin' Spoonful: The Best of—Kama Sutra 8056
Mamas and The Papas: 20 Golden Hits—Dunhill DSX 50145
Diana Ross & The Supremes: Greatest Hits—Motown 869
Simon and Garfunkel: Greatest Hits—Columbia KC31350
Three Dog Night: Joy to the World—Dunhill 50178
The Who: Tommy—Polydor PD 2-9502

The 1970s

Allman Brothers: Idlewild South—Atco SD 33-342
Bee Gees: Best of—Atco 33-292
David Bowie: Diamond Dogs— RCA Victor CPL1 0576
Jim Croce: Life and Times—ABC 769
Neil Diamond: Greatest Hits— Bang BLPS 219
Eagles: Their Greatest Hits—Asylum 7E1052
Fleetwood Mac: Bare Trees—Reprise MS 2080
Billy Joel: Piano Man—Columbia KC 32544
Gordon Lightfoot: Very Best of G. L., Vol. 1—United Artists LA381
Seals and Croft: Diamond Girl—Warner Brothers 2699
Carly Simon: Anticipation—Elektra 75016

Country and Western

Roy Acuff: Best of—Capitol ST1870
Chet Atkins—RCA Victor LSP2887
Glen Campbell: Greatest Hits—Capitol SW752
Johnny Cash: Greatest Hits, Vol. 2—Columbia 30887
Sonny James: The Biggest Hits—Capitol 629
Waylon Jennings: Wanted! The Outlaws—RCA Victor AFL1-1321
Loretta Lynn: Greatest Hits, Vol. 2—MCA460
Dolly Parton: Best of, Vol. 2—RCA Victor APL1-1117
Tex Ritter: An American Legend—Capitol SKC11241
Marty Robbins: Greatest Hits—Columbia CS8639
Hank Thompson: Best of—Capitol ST 1878
Conway Twitty: 20 Greatest Hits—MGM 25ES4884
Porter Wagoner: The Carroll County Accident—RCA Victor LSP 4116
Hank Williams: Greatest Hits—MGM E3918
Country and Western Radio—Radiola MR1069
Stars of the Grand Ole Opry, 1926–1974—RCA Victor CPL 2-046

Index